'This astute book masterfully explains how Erdoğan's plans to exploit the Syrian war for his own ends have perverted Turkish domestic politics, plunged his country further into authoritarianism, and changed the course of history. A fascinating, instructive and ultimately powerful cautionary tale.'

Fiona Hill, former Deputy Assistant to the U.S. President, and author of *There Is Nothing for You Here*

'Superbly narrates the tragic intersection of Syria's civil war and Turkey's ravenously ambitious president. Politicians clung to power in Damascus and Ankara, but "Erdoğan's War" helped shatter Syria and undermined what had been an aspiring Turkish democracy. A sad story, very ably told.'

David Ignatius, columnist, *The Washington Post*

'Early in Syria's peaceful uprising, Turkish officials were alarmed by Assad's brutal survival tactics, and perplexed by his turning from Turkey's friendly leader. But Syria and Syrians became props for Erdoğan's own political survival. This is a fascinating story, and no one tells it better than Tol.'

Frederic C. Hof, former U.S. Special Envoy to Syria

'A timely and insightful examination of Erdoğan's project and its geostrategic implications. Well-written, richly informed and powerfully argued, this is a must-read for anyone interested in Turkey today, or in how strongman politics and great power ambitions are changing countries and the world order.'

Vali Nasr, Majid Khadduri Professor of Middle East Studies and International Affairs, Johns Hopkins University

'A compelling, richly researched picture of Erdoğan as a populist, not an Islamist—a political chameleon with an uncanny sense for power. Tol's clear writing makes sense of Turkey's role in Syria's catastrophic war, its slide into authoritarianism, and where it might be going.'

Marc Lynch, Professor of Political Science and International Affairs, The George Washington University

'Expertly traces Turkish decisions and actions in the Syria conflict, providing unique context as we consider NATO's role post-Ukraine. Tol's dissection of Turkey under Erdoğan's unique leadership will help future generations of military and diplomatic leaders understand this critical, but frequently frustrating, NATO ally.'

Gen. Joseph L. Votel (Ret.), commander of U.S. Central Command 2016–19

'A compelling narrative that unveils Erdoğan's unique chameleon-like qualities through the lens of the Syrian war. By connecting Erdoğan's domestic strategy with his controversial foreign policy, Tol provides a treasure trove of knowledge, information and insight for future historians.'

Cengiz Çandar, award-winning journalist and former advisor to President Turgut Özal

'A sharp and penetrating analysis of Turkey's transformation under Recep Tayyip Erdoğan, and of foreign policy's role in that process. A very well-written and engaging book that covers everything you need to know to understand today's Turkey.'

Yaşar Yakış, former Turkish Minister of Foreign Affairs

ERDOĞAN'S WAR

GÖNÜL TOL

Erdoğan's War

A Strongman's Struggle at Home and in Syria

HURST & COMPANY, LONDON

First published in the United Kingdom in 2022 by
C. Hurst & Co. (Publishers) Ltd.,
New Wing, Somerset House, Strand, London, WC2R 1LA
© Gönül Tol, 2022
All rights reserved.

The right of Gönül Tol to be identified as the author of this publication is asserted by her in accordance with the Copyright, Designs and Patents Act, 1988.

A Cataloguing-in-Publication data record for this book is available from the British Library.

ISBN: 9781787387980

This book is printed using paper from registered sustainable and managed sources.

www.hurstpublishers.com

Printed in Great Britain by Bell and Bain Ltd, Glasgow

*To Alan Kurdi, the two-year-old Syrian Kurdish refugee boy
who drowned crossing the Mediterranean;*

*And to millions of children who have borne the brunt of a senseless war:
we all owe them an apology.*

CONTENTS

Acknowledgements	xi
List of Abbreviations	xiii
Introduction	1
1. Erdoğan's Strategy Towards Hegemony	15
2. Erdoğan Turns to Islam	75
3. The Syrian Gambit: Assad Must Go	123
4. From Religion to Nationalism	171
5. Attacking Kurds Trumps Toppling Assad	205
6. Erdoğan's Nationalist Gamble Backfires	241
7. Syrians Must Go	263
Conclusion	287
Notes	297
Index	335

ACKNOWLEDGEMENTS

Writing this book has been an exercise in juggling a career and motherhood under Covid-19. Like millions of working mothers, I often felt that I failed at both. I was lucky to have the support of my husband, Ömer Taşpınar, who convinced me otherwise. From reading the draft to giving me advice on the title to keeping our little son occupied so I could write, he was as important to finishing this book as I was. I thank him for that. I am also thankful to my son, Kerem, who has brought immense joy and happiness into my life. He inspired me to pay closer attention to the suffering of refugee children and how much a parent can sacrifice for their kids. Special thanks go to my parents and my siblings for putting up with me over the years it has taken to finish this book.

My heartfelt appreciation goes to Lisel Hintz, who contributed her time and expertise to this book when I most needed help. She is not only a brilliant Turkey scholar and a meticulous editor but also a wonderful friend. I will forever remain indebted. There is a long list of colleagues and friends to whom I owe a debt of gratitude. Foremost among them is Cengiz Çandar. I have not only relied on his work during the course of writing this book but was also inspired by the attention to detail in his writings. I am grateful to him for encouraging me when I had doubts, reading the draft and giving me valuable feedback. I would also like to thank John F. Stack Jr for being an incredible mentor and friend who has always supported my work.

My thanks are extended to Christopher Phillips, Meliha Altunışık, İlhan Uzgel, Brian Katulis and Bilal Saab who all read and

ACKNOWLEDGEMENTS

commented on the draft. I have greatly benefited from my interviews and conversations with Ali Yaycıoğlu, Ruşen Çakır, Menderes Çınar, Ali Balcı, General Joseph L. Votel (ret.), Yaşar Yakış, Ertuğrul Kürkçü and Samir Aita. I would like to express my gratitude to the President of the Middle East Institute, Paul Salem, who has shared my enthusiasm for this book and put up with my distractions during the course of writing it. Huge thanks to those who took the time, and at times the risk, to talk to me candidly about sensitive issues while I was researching for the book. I am forever grateful for the opportunities they afforded me to get a nuanced understanding of complicated matters. I am also indebted to the two anonymous reviewers for their feedback. Their suggestions have made the book stronger. Last but not least, I would like to extend my sincerest gratitude to our brilliant, hard-working interns at the Middle East Institute, Hannah Kim, Gülşen Doğan and Danielle Cohen, for their help with the references.

LIST OF ABBREVIATIONS

AFAD	Turkey's Disaster and Emergency Management Authority (Afet ve Acil Durum Yönetimi Başkanlığı)
AKP	Justice and Development Party (Adalet ve Kalkınma Partisi)
ANAP	Motherland Party (Anavatan Partisi)
AQI	al-Qaeda in Iraq
COI	Commission of Inquiry for Syria
COMCEC	Standing Committee for Economic and Commercial Cooperation
DP	Democrat Party
DTP	Democratic Society Party (Demokratik Toplum Partisi)
ECHR	European Court of Human Rights
ESZ	Euphrates Shield Zone
FJP	Freedom and Justice Party
FSA	Free Syrian Army
GAP	The Southeast Anatolia Development Project (Güneydoğu Anadolu Projesi)
GNA	Government of National Accord
HDP	Peoples' Democratic Party (Halkların Demokratik Partisi)
HRW	Human Rights Watch
HSYK	Supreme Board of Judges and Prosecutors (Hakimler ve Savcılar Yüksek Kurulu)
HTS	Hayat Tahrir al-Sham

LIST OF ABBREVIATIONS

İHO	Imam Hatip schools (İmam Hatip Okulları)
IRCICA	Research Centre for Islamic History, Art and Culture (İslam Tarih, Sanat ve Kültür Araştırma Merkezi)
ISI	Islamic State in Iraq
ISIS	Islamic State of Iraq and Syria
JCP	Justice and Construction Party
JFS	Jabhat Fateh al-Sham
KCK	Kurdistan Communities Union (Koma Civakên Kurdistanê)
MBZ	Mohammed bin Zayed
MHP	Nationalist Movement Party (Milliyetçi Hareket Partisi)
MİT	Turkish Intelligence Agency (Milli İstihbarat Teşkilatı)
MP	Motherland Party
MÜSİAD	Association of Independent Industrialists and Businessmen (Müstakil Sanayici ve İşadamları Derneği)
NSC	National Security Council
NSP	National Salvation Party
NSPD	National Security Policy Department
PYD	Democratic Union Party (Partiya Yekîtiya Demokrat)
RTÜK	Radio and Television Supreme Council (Radyo ve Televizyon Üst Kurulu)
SDF	Syrian Democratic Forces
SEEs	State economic enterprises
SESRIC	Statistical, Economic and Social Training Centre for Islamic Countries
SMEs	Small- and medium-sized enterprises
SNA	Syrian National Army
SNC	Syrian National Council
TİKA	Turkish Cooperation and Coordination Agency (Türk İşbirliği ve Koordinasyon İdaresi Başkanlığı)
TIS	Turkish-Islamic Synthesis
TMSF	Turkish Government's Savings Deposit Insurance Fund (Tasarruf Mevduatı Sigorta Fonu)

LIST OF ABBREVIATIONS

TOKİ	Turkey's Mass Housing Administration (Toplu Konut İdaresi Başkanlığı)
TPP	True Path Party
TSK	Turkish Armed Forces (Türk Silahlı Kuvvetleri)
TÜGVA	The Service for Youth and Education Foundation of Turkey (Türkiye Gençlik Vakfı)
TÜRGEV	Turkish Foundation to Serve the Youth and Education (Türkiye Gençlik ve Eğitime Hizmet Vakfı)
TÜSİAD	Association of Turkish Industrialists and Businessmen (Türk Sanayicileri ve İş Adamları Derneği)
TUSKON	Confederation of Turkish Businessmen and Industralists (Türkiye İşadamları ve Sanayiciler Konfederasyonu)
UNSC	United Nations Security Council
VP	Virtue Party (Fazilet Partisi)
WP	Welfare Party (Refah Partisi)
YÖK	The Council of Higher Education (Yüksek Öğretim Kurulu)

INTRODUCTION

"Once an Islamist, always an Islamist," said a Western diplomat of Turkey's then Prime Minister Recep Tayyip Erdoğan. We were sitting in a Washington café in the fall of 2012, a few days after Erdoğan unveiled what many called his "Islamist manifesto" at his party's congress. Islamists from the region were guests of honor at the event. Hamas leader Khaled Meshaal stood next to the Egyptian Muslim Brotherhood's newly elected President Mohammed Morsi who delivered a speech thanking Erdoğan for his support during the uprising that toppled the autocrat Hosni Mubarak.

The ruling party's congress took place against the background of a watershed moment in the history of the Arab world. A wave of popular uprisings was ousting long-time autocrats and paving the way for the rise of Islamists. Erdoğan had thrown his full support behind them. This was in stark contrast to his previous policies. After the Justice and Development Party (Adalet ve Kalkınma Partisi AKP) was founded in 2001, Erdoğan declared that he had broken with his Islamist past. In his first two terms in office, he refrained from interfering in the domestic affairs of regional countries and cultivated friendly ties with Arab autocrats—backing forces arrayed against autocratic regimes was a dramatic volte-face. The diplomat I was sitting with in that café did not think Erdoğan had changed at all. "I never believed Erdoğan when he said he was no longer an Islamist," he said. "Turkey's decision not to participate in the 2003 Iraq war proved me right. It was Erdoğan the Islamist's first step in crafting an Islamist foreign policy and turning Turkey away from the West."

ERDOĞAN'S WAR

I heard similar comments from Western officials and Turkish secularists who often worried about what they saw as Erdoğan's problematic foreign policy behavior or his authoritarian approach. To many of his critics, from the day he came to power until his twentieth year at the helm, the culprit behind everything wrong with Erdoğan's Turkey has always been the same: his Islamist ideology. There are two underpinning assumptions behind this thinking. The first is that ideology, Islamist ideology in particular, is an unchanging, constant force in the life of a politician. The second is that Erdoğan's Islamist ideology is the key driver of the country's authoritarian turn and his controversial foreign policy moves. I find these assumptions problematic. Thinking that a politician can have one and only one point of view throughout their entire political career would be assuming too much. Like any other politician, Erdoğan's number one goal is to stay in power and he is ready to employ whatever ideology serves that goal best. He is first and foremost a populist, a term that will be explained in the following pages. He pairs his populism with different ideologies and Islamism is only one of them. Therefore, I argue that Islamism is not the chief reason for the country's degeneration into autocracy or Turkey's troublesome foreign policy under Erdoğan. It is only one of many factors that have taken Turkey to where it is now, and foreign policy has played a more complicated part in that process than has been accounted for. I believe not enough attention has been given to the function of foreign policy in the country's authoritarian transformation. The aim of this book is to shed light on that role by expounding how the war in Syria helped Erdoğan defeat his opponents and build an authoritarian regime.

What is a populist?

Ideologies are often seen by political actors as an instrument to generate consent for their agenda. They might be shaped and transformed to fit politicians' survival strategies. What makes Erdoğan unique is his adeptness in adopting different, sometimes conflicting, ideologies with great ease. Throughout his many years in office, he has utilized a variety of ideological outlooks, from conservative democracy to Islamism and nationalism, to eliminate his

INTRODUCTION

rivals and consolidate power. The historical rifts between Turkey's ethnic and religious minorities and the Turkish-speaking Sunni Muslim majority, and between the secular and religious sectors of the country, allowed Erdoğan to leap from one ideology to another to mobilize support for his agenda.

While the ideologies Erdoğan employed changed, one thing has remained constant during the two decades he has been in power. Erdoğan has always been a populist. There is much confusion about what a populist is. The most widely accepted definition is that populists frame politics as a war between the virtuous, ordinary masses and a corrupt elite.[1] Populists define who the "real people" are and claim that they alone represent "the people." "The people" can take many forms including race, ethnicity and religion. Politicians may use populism as a political style to attack the establishment, polarize society and claim moral superiority. However, populism itself does not offer a holistic view of how society, politics and the economy should be ordered, therefore populists usually pair it with ideologies to provide substance to their populist style. The ideological flexibility that populism offers allows populists to exploit broad issues such as nationalism, religion or ethnicity and strategically change their ideological outlooks to fit their goals.[2]

Since he came to power, Erdoğan has utilized populism to ensure his political survival. Although the populist discourse was less pronounced in his early years in office, he used populist rhetoric to appeal to the country's marginalized segments including nonsecular practicing Muslims, Kurds, Alevis and other ethnic and religious minorities. These groups were alienated by the country's elitist founding ideology, Kemalism, which sought to establish a secular, modern, nation-state out of the multinational Ottoman Empire. Erdoğan sought to appeal to these marginalized groups by employing an anti-elitist narrative, presenting himself as "of the people" and a true democrat who speaks on behalf of the masses. His definition of "the people" changed depending on the ideological outlook he chose to attach to his populist style. During the AKP's first two terms in office, Erdoğan advocated democracy and human rights to sideline the secularist establishment, particularly the military. He disavowed his Islamist past and described his AKP as "conservative democratic." He presented curbing the secularist establishment's power as taking the state from the elites and handing it over to "the people," who were kept out of the corridors of power by the secularist elite.

After he reined in the secularist military, he employed Islamist populism to establish an executive presidency. Erdoğan defined "the people" as the "oppressed Muslims," the *ummah* (the community of believers), united against an "unjust, immoral West" and its domestic collaborators. When Islamist populism failed to secure enough support for a presidential system that would grant Erdoğan unchecked powers, he switched tactics and paired his populism with Turkish nationalism, which promotes ethnic Turkishness at the expense of other ethnic groups, primarily the Kurds. "The people" became those who subscribed to Turkish nationalism's claims and backed Erdoğan's autocratic vision. Kurds, who sought recognition of their ethnic identity, and everyone else who opposed granting Erdoğan unchecked powers were defined as "terrorists," "traitors" and an "enemy of the people."

Foreign policy has been key in substantiating these ideological outlooks. To Erdoğan, foreign policy has never been primarily about the international pushes and pulls. It has been first and foremost about his domestic strategy to keep his grip on the country. Foreign policy serves as the medium through which his chosen ideology is expressed and reproduced. In other words, foreign policy has helped Erdoğan tell the voters what he stands for and how he imagines the national identity.[3] Erdoğan has used foreign policy not only to construct his identity but also as a vehicle to divide and eliminate his rivals and consolidate his base.[4] Thus, foreign policy has been part and parcel of his war against his domestic opponents. In particular, Syria has played a unique role in Erdoğan's political survival strategy. This book is an attempt to shed light on that role.

What is the book about?

Recep Tayyip Erdoğan has become Turkey's longest-serving leader. On his way to the top, he has fought many battles. This

INTRODUCTION

book tells the story of those conflicts against his domestic enemies through the lens of the Syrian war, which became critical in his battle to remain in power. It traces Erdoğan's transformation from a "conservative democrat" into an Islamist and a Turkish nationalist and how this transformation has come to shape his policy on Syria. Highlighted is Erdoğan's constantly shifting strategy to consolidate his rule and how these shifts transformed Turkey's role in post-uprising Syria from an "advocate of democracy" to a country fanning the flames of civil war, to an "occupier." From the first days of Erdoğan's rule through to failed coup that attempted to topple him; the Kurdish peace process; Arab uprisings and the refugee crisis, this is the tale of how one man's quest to remain in power has tied together the fate of two countries and changed them forever.

One might ask: why focus on one man to tell the story of a country's transformation, especially if that country is Turkey, which was once considered to be a "beacon of democratic consolidation in a volatile neighborhood"? Why treat Erdoğan as a semi-God or a sultan whose choices single-handedly determined the fate of Turkey? Are there no other factors such as the country's institutions, its political culture, competing constituencies, even external actors such as the European Union, of which Turkey has been trying to become a member for decades, that need to be factored in? There are indeed actors other than Erdoğan who have played important roles in Turkey's transformation in the last two decades. This book tells the story of Erdoğan's war against those actors and how he managed to win many battles. It does not treat Erdoğan as a sultan who acted in an unrestrained political environment to single-handedly determine the fate of the country. On the contrary, the narrative tries to show how Erdoğan had to operate in a setting that constrained the means available to him to realize his goals. One of the tools he has used quite effectively has been foreign policy. The steps he has taken on that front have helped him undermine his opponents and centralize power.

The main argument of the book is that it is not Erdoğan's Islamist ideology that has been the main catalyst in Turkey's authoritarian turn. Erdoğan is not an ideologue. He is a political chameleon, constantly changing colors to survive. Multiple factors have contributed to the country's authoritarian turn. This book focuses on the significance of foreign policy in that transformation and argues that post-war Syria occupies a unique place in Erdoğan's efforts to consolidate his authoritarian grip on the country.

A synopsis

When Erdoğan's ruling AKP first came to power in 2002, his chief rival was the military. As the secularist Republic's self-appointed guardians, the military had often intervened in politics, forcing the country's first Islamist prime minister to resign and paving the way for the Islamist parties' closure. The fate of previous Islamist parties had taught Erdoğan a valuable lesson—that one had to avoid direct confrontation with the military to survive politically. Instead of pursuing a direct clash, Erdoğan sought to sideline the military by adopting a pro-European Union stance which called for a pro-reform agenda at home. The EU was a natural ally for Erdoğan in his search for protection against the secularist establishment. It had already set curbing the military's influence in politics as a precondition for Turkey's entry into the Union and further democratization that would come with EU membership would automatically address issues important to Erdoğan's conservative base, such as the headscarf ban.

To appeal to skeptical constituencies whose support was important to constraining the military's power, Erdoğan disavowed his Islamist past, recast the AKP as a pro-Western "conservative democratic party" that was committed to the secular principles of the constitution and pushed forward Turkey's objective of EU membership. He declared that winning EU membership for Turkey and implementing democratic reforms were his top policy priorities. By pursuing membership in an organization that was rejected as a "Christian club" by the country's Islamists, Erdoğan signaled to the liberal and secular segments of the country that he was no longer an Islamist. The pro-EU agenda helped Erdoğan construct his identity as a conservative democratic leader whose number one goal was to make Turkey a "true democracy."

INTRODUCTION

He cast himself as the voice of the masses neglected by the privileged elite and branded his secularist opponents in politics and bureaucracy, who were skeptical about his pro-EU agenda, as obstacles to Turkey's democratization.

In the Middle East, Erdoğan pursued a pragmatic, cautious, pro-status quo policy. Like the pro-EU agenda, Erdoğan's pre-Arab uprisings Middle East policy was part of his strategy to win the war against the military without engaging in a fierce fight that could destroy his political future. This policy, which was dubbed the "zero problems with neighbors" policy, sought to cultivate close ties with regional countries using trade and investment as the primary drivers, but avoiding interference in their domestic affairs. It was both an offensive and a defensive move against the military. It was defensive in that it tried to avoid a secularist backlash by pursuing a policy that was largely in line with the military's pro-status quo stance vis-à-vis the region, and tried not to cross the military's "identity redlines" as the fight against Islamism and Kurdish separatism.[5] It was offensive because by cultivating close ties to regional countries, Erdoğan hoped to diminish the military's role in politics. For decades, the narrative that Turkey was surrounded by hostile countries legitimized the military's oversized sway in politics. With a "zero problems with neighbors" policy, the Erdoğan government wanted to challenge that narrative and limit the military's role in political decision-making by desecuritizing Turkey's Middle East policy.

Pre-war Syria became the place where Erdoğan tested out this policy. He cozied up to an "infidel regime" that had carried out the Hama massacre against thousands of Muslim Brotherhood members in the 1980s to quell an Islamic uprising. The Hama massacre remained etched in the memories of Turkish Islamists, including Erdoğan, but he put that aside to make Syria the success case of his new foreign policy outlook.

The pro-EU stance Erdoğan embraced earlier in his tenure and his zero problems with neighbors policy facilitated his efforts to sideline the secularists. This foreign policy line helped him construct his image as a leader who had put Islamism behind him and solidify his alliance against the military's influence in domestic and foreign policies. Erdoğan's strategy worked brilliantly. It allowed him to wrap his power grab in a pro-reform, pro-EU language and a noble cause seeking zero problems with neighbors. By the time uprisings spread across much of the Arab world in 2011, Erdoğan had defeated the military and monopolized power in his own hands.

Erdoğan's next target was grabbing unrestrained power by replacing the country's parliamentary system with an all-powerful executive presidency. However, he would not be able to justify establishing what was practically a one-man rule with the conservative democratic brand. Nor would the pro-democracy coalition he mobilized early in his tenure rally behind such a project. Erdoğan decided to rely on the country's religiously conservative segments and the Kurds. To appeal to them, he embraced an Islamist populist agenda. One of the key pillars of that agenda was constructing a national identity that gave primacy to Sunni Muslimhood and the Ottoman legacy. This formulation gave Erdoğan room to appeal to the Kurds as well. Stressing common Islamic ties legitimized his efforts to find a peaceful resolution to the Kurdish problem. Despite the initial progress on the Kurdish front, Erdoğan's post-2011 strategy led to a majoritarian understanding of democracy in which the Sunni Muslim majority that backed Erdoğan was entitled to primacy and the rest were considered "the enemy of the people."

A clarification is warranted here. Erdoğan adopted a "thin" understanding of Islamism after he sidelined the secularist establishment. The steps he took after 2011 were not a systematic attempt to change the secular nature of the state. Rather, they were superficial displays of religiosity to legitimize his efforts to secure unprecedented powers. It is necessary to provide a precise definition of Islamism here—but it is equally difficult to offer one. There are many disparate groups considered to be Islamist. Their aims, objectives and interpretations of Islamic tradition and practice vary widely. But in the broadest sense, Islamists define Islam not just as a religion but also as a political ideology and think that Islam should play a key role in the way politics is conducted, law is applied and society is organized. Erdoğan took steps to increase the visibility of Islam in the public space. He assigned to Islam a central place in the country's national identity and took further measures such as

INTRODUCTION

Islamizing the national curriculum and filling Turkish bureaucracy with followers of religious orders. He thereby reversed some of the symbolic tenets of Turkey's historical practice of secularism. Yet those moves have not amounted to a radical transformation of the state's relationship with Islam. Erdoğan's goal was to generate support from conservative segments of the country for his power grab, not establish Islamic governance.

Erdoğan's Islamist populist domestic agenda translated into a foreign policy that advocated Muslim unity and alliance with other Islamists globally. Like his domestic, Islam-flavored agenda, his pro-Islamist foreign policy remained "thin" without a coherent plan. Erdoğan's shift from a populist with a self-identified conservative democratic brand to an Islamist populist radically changed his country's alliances. Ankara's support for Arab Islamists during the uprisings strained its relations with the regimes Erdoğan had cultivated close relations with, particularly in the Gulf. But Erdoğan's volte-face was not part of a well-thought out, coherent, broader project to establish a new regional order. The main aim of his regional policies was to consolidate his rule. He wanted to capitalize on the Arab uprisings to reinforce the boundaries he had drawn at home, between those who backed his plan to establish a one-man rule and those who did not. To Erdoğan, real democracy meant the rise of Islamic identity against the culturally alienated, Westernized elite. In his mind, Turkey under his watch was a shining example of this democratic awakening where the "true representatives" of the pious masses came to power through elections and ended the reign of "internal colonizers." Only those who shared his conservative Islamic values belonged to the nation. Those who were opposed to him were called domestic foes, allies of the West and the enemies of true democracy and the will of the people.

Erdoğan framed his support for the Arab Islamists seeking to topple autocratic regimes as support given to a similar transformation in the region. In his narrative, just like in Turkey, the "true Muslims" would bring down "illegitimate," Westernized, "Godless" regimes and establish real democracies. Turkey could spearhead that transformation and become the leader of the Muslim world. This is what he said to his followers. It was the perfect upbeat message at a time when Erdoğan sought more powers to complete his historical mission of leading Turkey to greatness. This ambitious narrative, however, was divorced from the policies he pursued. Despite his strong support of the Islamists trying to overthrow the regimes in Egypt and Syria, he did not uniformly back the anti-regime protests in the region. In Bahrain, for instance, in an effort not to alienate the Saudis, Turkey refrained from supporting the uprising. Nor did Erdoğan have a vision to help the transition to democracy of countries experiencing popular protests beyond supporting the Islamists.

Once again, Syria came in handy to bolster Erdoğan's efforts to realize his domestic goals. Shortly after the popular protests erupted in the neighboring country, Erdoğan, who assumed that the Islamist wave that had swept across Egypt and Tunisia would swiftly bring the Islamists in power in Syria too, threw his support behind the Islamist elements within the opposition to topple the man he once called "brother." Turkey became a base and supplier of arms to the rebels, including radical groups. Erdoğan's actions fanned the flames of civil war and bolstered the jihadis within opposition ranks. His actions in post-war Syria had devastating implications for that country, but they offered Erdoğan an opportunity to burnish his Islamist credentials to appeal to conservatives at home and delegitimize the secularist main opposition party. He often drew parallels between himself and those seeking to oust Assad and equated Turkey's secularist main opposition party to the Baathist Assad regime, which he said had oppressed pious Sunni masses for decades.

When Erdoğan's strategy of using Islam to secure the backing of pious Turks and Kurds for the executive presidency failed, largely due to the Kurds' reluctance to support it, Erdoğan changed his plans again. This time, he turned to Turkish nationalism. After the pro-Kurdish party's strong showing denied Erdoğan's party a parliamentary majority in the 2015 elections, he cultivated an alliance with nationalists who view the Kurds as the biggest threat to the country's territorial integrity. He fused anti-elite rhetoric with nationalist appeals to launch a war against the Kurds to consolidate his nationalist alliance. Erdoğan not only targeted the Kurdish mili-

INTRODUCTION

tants who have been waging an insurgency against the Turkish state for decades but also the democratically elected Kurdish politicians and Kurdish civil society. The war against the Kurds paid off. It secured the nationalists' backing for the executive presidency and helped Erdoğan establish his one-man rule.

Once again, Syria was crucial in advancing Erdoğan's domestic agenda. After his nationalist turn, Erdoğan recalibrated his Syria policy. Toppling the Assad regime took a back seat to curbing Kurdish gains in northern Syria. Ankara began working with Damascus to secure the regime's acquiescence for the military incursions it launched against the Syrian Kurds. Turkey's military incursions helped Erdoğan boost his nationalist credentials and consolidate his anti-Kurdish alliance at home. Syria was not only a battleground where Erdoğan fought his domestic enemies. The civil war there also provided him with ammunition for his domestic fight against the Kurds and everyone else who was opposed to his one-man rule. The de facto autonomy the Syrian Kurds gained and their rise as key players in the US-led fight against ISIS helped Erdoğan feed nationalist anxieties by framing the Kurds, and those who would stand by them, as the biggest existential threat to Turkish territorial integrity. It facilitated his efforts to criminalize legitimate Kurdish opposition and drive a wedge between his opponents.

Playing the nationalism card did wonders for Erdoğan. Thanks to his alliance with the nationalists, he was able to grab unprecedented powers. Erdoğan's anti-Kurdish alliance received its biggest boost from the war in Syria. But, there came a time when nationalism turned against Erdoğan and the war in Syria became a liability. In 2019, Erdoğan's party lost mayoral elections in almost all big cities in the country. The growing nationalist backlash against the millions of Syrian refugees was second only to economic problems in bringing about the AKP's poor performance. Election results showed that the nationalism Erdoğan had advanced for many years had come back to haunt him. It was his winning formula when nationalism targeted the Kurds; it became a liability, when the Syrian refugees became equally hated, if not more so, by large segments of the country. Many, including die-hard Erdoğan supporters, think that Syrian refugees are a problem that Erdoğan's shortsighted policies created. This anti-refugee mood is one of the reasons why there is a growing nationalist opposition to Erdoğan. The newly established nationalist party is the fastest growing party in the country and the one that mounts the most effective challenge to Erdoğan.

Erdoğan is at his most vulnerable. The chaos in the neighboring country offered him many opportunities to strengthen his grip at home. From the start of the Syrian uprising until 2015, the Syrian war helped Erdoğan's aspiration to cast himself as the protector of Islam and Muslims and his opponents as obstacles to "true democracy" and the "will of the people." It strengthened his narrative that Turkey was on a holy mission to help oppressed Muslims across the world rebel against their oppressors and that he needed unimpeded powers to lead Turkey on that mission. From 2015 onwards, Erdoğan capitalized on the developments in Syria to rally the nationalists behind his plan to establish an executive presidency by adopting a heavy-handed military approach to the Kurdish question.

The days when the conflict in Syria strengthened Erdoğan's hand in his war against domestic opponents are over. As public opinion toward the Syrian refugees began to sour, Turkey's involvement in the war has become more unpopular. As a result, Erdoğan recalibrated his priorities in the war-torn country again. Preventing the regime's takeover of the last rebel stronghold, which could unleash another flow of refugees towards Turkey's borders, has become his top goal in Syria. Erdoğan hopes that a safe zone inside Syria that can host the Syrian refugees living in Turkey will make the refugee issue go away. As the war there draws to a close, Erdoğan wants to make one final push to use the Syrian war to ensure his grip on power.

In sum, this book aims to tell the intertwined story of two wars: Erdoğan's war against his domestic rivals and the war in Syria. It hopes to articulate how the Syrian war has shaped and been shaped by Erdoğan's own struggle to monopolize power. The first chapter provides a window into Erdoğan's strategy toward hegemony from the day he came to power until the Arab uprisings started. It explores how Erdoğan slowly and cautiously eliminated his secularist rivals in the country's bureaucracy, military, judiciary, and

INTRODUCTION

media with the help of a pro-EU agenda and a regional policy advocating "zero problems with neighbors."

Chapter Two examines the next phase in Erdoğan's war, after he defeated the secularist establishment. It focuses on Erdoğan's turn to Islam to take the helm of an all-powerful executive presidency. An in-depth look will be taken at how Erdoğan utilized Islam to secure the backing of pious Turks and Kurds to seize unconstrained power. The chapter then moves on to detail the ways in which the Arab uprisings helped Erdoğan in his effort to cast himself as the protector of Islam and Muslims and those who were opposed to his autocratic vision as his new enemies. Chapter Three chronicles how Erdoğan's turn to Islam and his endeavors to construct a national identity along Sunni Muslim lines at home translated into a policy that sought to topple the Assad regime in Syria and replace it with an Islamist-run government. It articulates how the steps Erdoğan took in Syria contributed to the Syrian uprising's transformation into civil war and its radicalization.

Chapter Four discusses the failure of Erdoğan's efforts to use Islam to mobilize support for his presidential plans, largely due to Kurdish-led opposition to his autocratic vision. It details Erdoğan's turn to Turkish nationalism in response and how the Kurds became his new target. The change in Erdoğan's domestic plans held significant implications for his Syria policy, which is the subject of Chapter Five. The chapter zooms in on how Erdoğan's nationalist turn led to a shift in his priorities from ousting the regime to curbing Kurdish advances in northern Syria. It shows that Erdoğan ended up empowering the very regime he desperately sought to overthrow in order to obtain Assad's acquiescence to Turkey's military incursions that aimed to check Kurdish advances. It argues that after years of arming the anti-Assad opposition, Erdoğan dealt one of the biggest blows to that same opposition so that he could extend his newly launched war against Turkey's Kurds into Syria.

Chapter Six argues that after having served Erdoğan's goals for many years, Turkish nationalism finally came back to haunt him. The discussion delves into the growing nationalist reaction against the millions of Syrian refugees, which became one of the main reasons for Erdoğan's loss in the 2019 municipal elections. The

ERDOĞAN'S WAR

chapter takes stock of the growing challenges he faces and argues that Erdoğan is at his most vulnerable. The last chapter discusses the implications of Erdoğan's declining political fortune for Syria. Due to a growing protest from large segments of the country and the opposition parties' increasingly vocal criticism of his Syria policy, Erdoğan was forced to act. The chapter explores the military incursion Erdoğan launched into Syria, a few months after his party lost almost all major cities in municipal elections, to secure a zone that would host Turkey's Syrian refugees. It discusses Erdoğan's efforts to prevent a regime takeover of Idlib, the last opposition stronghold, which would unleash another tide of refugees towards Turkey's borders. The book ends with the tragic story of the human toll that Erdoğan's war to consolidate power has taken on the lives of many.

1

ERDOĞAN'S STRATEGY TOWARDS HEGEMONY

Given the rise and fall of political Islam in Turkey in the 1990s, what were Recep Tayyip Erdoğan's options for political survival? His newly established AKP had just swept into power but was it possible for an Islamist-rooted politician to govern a country where real power rested in the hands of the secularist military? To Erdoğan, winning the electoral battle was perhaps the easy part. Now he had to win the war.

The following section tells the story of Erdoğan's strategy against the military during his first decade in office, when he still feared being overthrown by the generals, and how he used foreign policy as an effective weapon to circumvent not just the military but the entire secularist establishment.

Erdoğan rises

"The mosques are our barracks, the domes our helmets, the minarets our bayonets and the faithful our soldiers..." Istanbul's Islamist Mayor Recep Tayyip Erdoğan was reciting a poem in a 1998 rally, four years after his party, the Islamist Welfare Party, shocked Turkey when it captured the mayoral seats in Istanbul and Ankara and made sweeping gains in the Kurdish southeast. Standing before an enthusiastic crowd, Erdoğan was fired up. His supporters interrupted his speech with chants of "God is great." The country's secular old guard—a powerful class that includes the military and judiciary—was on tenterhooks. To them, Erdoğan's speech sounded like a call for a holy war against the secular foundations of the Republic. A decision by a quasi-military court conveyed the secularists' unease. Erdoğan was sentenced to ten months in prison, of which he served four months, for "inciting religious hatred" and was banned from politics.[1]

Four years later, Erdoğan was standing before journalists as the leader of a newly established splinter party—the Justice and Development Party (AKP)—that had swept into power in the 2002 general elections. He was a different man, or so he said. "What good did Islamism do for us?" asked Erdoğan, to spell out his disillusionment. In his newly enlightened mind, "Byzantism and theocracy" were "a nuisance for both religion and state" and he belittled those who spoke of a "shariah state."[2] He disavowed his Islamist past and recast the AKP as a pro-Western, "conservative democratic party" that was reconciled to the secular principles of the constitution. The new party's program reflected Erdoğan's new-found moderation. It strongly emphasized democracy, individual freedom, human rights and the rule of law, while party leaders downplayed the social issues at the core of the Islamist agenda such as the headscarf ban for women in public office and universities. The party program stated that secularism is a sine qua non condition for democracy and the guarantee of freedom of religion.[3] After the party's election victory in November 2002, party leader Erdoğan attempted to allay secularist fears that the new government might impose an Islamic lifestyle. He promised that they would not interfere with people's everyday life and removing the headscarf ban was not on the party's agenda.[4] Instead, Erdoğan iterated, the government would focus on implementing democratization reforms to fulfill the country's decades-old quest to become a member of the European Union.[5]

Erdoğan's message of change and the AKP's promise of a more prosperous, democratic and stable Turkey struck a chord in a country shaken by a financial crisis, years of shaky coalitions, military interventions, terror attacks and backsliding on democracy

ERDOĞAN'S STRATEGY TOWARDS HEGEMONY

and human rights. The AKP appealed well beyond its predecessor's Islamist base, capturing votes from ultranationalists, liberals, center-right and even center-left voters.[6] But to the party's secularist critics, Erdoğan and the AKP leadership were Islamists in disguise. Many privately hoped that the AKP would face the same fate as its predecessors that were shut down either by military intervention or rulings by the constitutional court.

Erdoğan had no illusions about the difficult task that lay ahead. His party had just captured 34 percent of the total vote and garnered 363 of the Parliament's 550 seats, but his secularist opponents remained very powerful.[7] They had controlled the bureaucracy since 1923 when the Turkish Republic was founded on the rubble of the Ottoman Empire by a ruling elite consisting of military officers and civil servants led by the country's founder, Mustafa Kemal Atatürk. The dissolution of the multi-ethnic, multi-religious Ottoman Empire had taught the Republican elite two lessons: that ethnic heterogeneity posed a threat to the survival of states and Islam retarded progress.[8] Their vision, known as Kemalism, reflected those lessons. They imagined the new country as an ethnically homogenous nation and kept Islam under tight state control. The institutions of the new Republic became the guardian of this Kemalist vision.

Among these institutions, of particular concern to Erdoğan was the powerful military, which had the will and capacity to intervene in politics when it deemed necessary. In the first two weeks after the elections, the secularist establishment reminded the AKP several times that it would suffer the same fate as its predecessors if it "crossed the line."[9] Erdoğan got the message. The shutting down of former Islamist parties had taught him that directly confronting the secularist establishment was a dead-end. Instead, Erdoğan used Turkey's EU accession process to carry out reforms that would, among other things, curb the military's interference in politics. By committing himself to Turkey's EU membership bid, Erdoğan burnished his image as a "conservative democrat" and built a coalition including the secular right wing, liberals and social democrat groups that supported his democratization agenda.

After Turkey's EU drive lost momentum, the "zero problems with neighbors" policy aided Erdoğan's efforts to curb the mili-

17

tary's power. For decades, the military had argued that Turkey was surrounded by hostile countries that posed existential risks to the country's territorial integrity. This security-oriented approach to Turkey's neighborhood helped the military legitimize its oversized influence in politics. The "zero problems with neighbors" policy challenged this narrative, arguing that Turkey's neighborhood was full of opportunities and Turkey had to develop friendly ties with its neighbors to take advantage of them. Desecuritizing Turkey's regional policy helped Erdoğan limit the military's power in foreign policy making. Using a pro-reform, pro-EU agenda and a desecuritized Middle East policy to bring down his archrival was the culmination of years of learning from party closures, military coups and a decades-old bitter fight against the secularists.

Erdoğan complemented this strategy with a populist narrative. He split society into two camps: the privileged elite that controlled all levers of power and the masses deprived of the opportunities available to those elites. Whereas his predecessor Necmettin Erbakan, the founder of Turkish political Islam, was a German-educated engineer and a flashy dresser, Erdoğan branded himself as an outsider, a simple man from the tough Istanbul district of Kasımpaşa who was removed from the politics of corruption and a true democrat who reclaimed power for the oppressed masses. "In this country, there is a segregation of Black Turks and White Turks," Erdoğan said. "Your brother Tayyip belongs to the Black Turks."[10] The White Turk/Black Turk divide is common in Turkish politics, the former referring to privileged secular urban segments of the country working mainly in state bureaucracy, the army and business sector while the latter refers to the uneducated lower classes. Erdoğan argued that the Black Turks were denied the opportunities available to the White Turks by an elitist system that had been kept in place by the Kemalist establishment, particularly the military. For Turkey to become a true democracy, the argument went, the military's power had to be reined in. Spearheading a "silent revolution" to "bring the people's voice into politics" was Erdoğan's mission, a mission that was viewed as essentially moral by Erdoğan and his followers.[11] Couching his effort to sideline the secularists in the language of democracy,

ERDOĞAN'S STRATEGY TOWARDS HEGEMONY

wrapping it with a populist narrative and a pro-EU, desecuritized Middle East policy turned out to be a brilliant strategy.

2002–05: Years of reform and EU enthusiasm

On February 4, 1997, the Turkish army rolled its tanks onto the main street of Sincan, an outer suburb of the capital Ankara, during the morning rush hour. The Islamist Welfare Party (WP) mayor of Sincan was arrested in response to the "Jerusalem nights" he had organized where calls for jihad against Israel were issued. This marked the beginning of the army's open campaign against the country's first Islamist prime minister, Necmettin Erbakan. The events that followed paved the way for developments that would determine the country's fate in the next two decades.

The WP, the AKP's predecessor, rose to power when it came first in the 1995 elections with 21 percent of the vote. In an effort to stem what they thought was an Islamic tide against the secular nature of the Republic, the military and its secularist allies in the media and business community pressured the center-right parties, the True Path Party (TPP) and the Motherland Party (MP), that came second and third in the elections to form a coalition government. After the secular right coalition collapsed due to internal squabbling and corruption charges, Necmettin Erbakan, the longtime leader of political Islam in Turkey, formed a coalition with the TPP and became the country's first Islamist prime minister.

The Islamists' rise to power as a coalition partner in a country that had carried out the most radical secularization program in the Muslim world triggered a deep-seated fear within the secularist camp that the Islamists would introduce Islamic law as the basis of public life.[12] But despite the WP's growing appeal among the public, especially in low-income neighborhoods, the party had to operate in a political environment where civilian and military bureaucracy were controlled by the secularists. The WP was limited in its ability to pursue a domestic Islamist agenda.[13] Aside from a number of soft policy proposals such as lifting the ban on wearing headscarves in public buildings or more flexibility for those observing the religious requirements of fasting and praying during the month of Ramadan, the WP looked very much like any other center-right party in government.[14]

Squeezed by the secularist establishment at home, Erbakan turned to foreign policy to leave his ideological mark on the country's foreign affairs. He paid his first visit as prime minister to Iran, Libya and Sudan. His aim was to defy Turkey's image solely as a Western country and highlight its Muslim identity. The visits irritated the military. Particularly troubling was Erbakan's October 1996 visit to Libya where the Libyan leader Muammar el-Qaddafi condemned Turkey for turning its back on Islam and for its ties to NATO and Israel, and called for an independent Kurdistan while Erbakan listened silently. Qaddafi's remarks led to an uproar in Turkey. The mass-circulation newspaper *Sabah* ran a headline reading "Night of Shame" and argued "a barefoot Bedouin stood in front of Erbakan and the Turkish delegation and hurled insults at Turkey."[15] Turkey recalled its ambassador to Libya in protest and the opposition parties started floating rumors of a military coup after Erbakan returned from his Libya trip.

The last straw came when the WP mayor of Sincan hosted an event to protest against Israel's occupation of East Jerusalem on January 31, 1997. Among the guests was the Iranian ambassador to Turkey. Placards supporting Hezbollah and Hamas were accompanied by "Down with Israel" chants and denunciations of deepening Turkish-Israeli ties. Since the military had embarked on cultivating closer ties with Israel to demonstrate Turkey's secular credentials and counter Iran and Syria's support for Islamist groups and the PKK, criticism of the alliance had become common among Islamic circles in Turkey. But the Sincan rally was too close to Ankara, bastion of the state's secularist ideology, and it was happening in the presence of the Iranian ambassador, who delivered a speech with the permission of the Islamist prime minister condemning Turkey's secular system and calling for its replacement with Islamic sharia law.[16] For the military, democracy had to be restored, starting in Sincan.[17] A few days later, tanks rumbled through Sincan, which became the opening salvo in a showdown between the military and the civilian government led by Erbakan.

The military's fear of a growing Islamist threat to the secular foundation of the Republic under Erbakan led to what has been

ERDOĞAN'S STRATEGY TOWARDS HEGEMONY

dubbed a "post-modern coup," which was backed by the opposition parties, mainstream media and some civil associations. On February 28, members of the National Security Council, a group comprising military personnel and high-level politicians, pressured Erbakan to implement an eighteen-point plan aimed at reinforcing secularism. The NSC memorandum called for the extension of obligatory public schooling from five to eight years to force the closure of middle-level Imam Hatip schools, which were originally founded by the state to train young men to serve as imams and preachers, and to reduce the number of Quranic courses. It also demanded close surveillance of religious orders and their financial sources and the re-examination of relations with Iran. The Supreme Board of Higher Education enforced a strict dress code for university personnel and students. The headscarf was banned in all states as well as private universities while male students with beards cut in a "religious manner" were expelled from universities. Instead of using direct force, the military applied continued pressure on Islamic actors through a series of measures until Erbakan resigned a few months later and was replaced by another civilian government.

The February 28 meeting of the NSC marked the beginning of a long period of military pressure on Islamists. Throughout the "February 28 process," which also came to be known as a "soft coup" because intervention did not result in direct military control of the government, the military set up a "Western working group" to monitor the economic and political activities of the "fundamentalist groups," corporations suspected of financing Islamic movements came under investigation, and a national security strategy was developed to brand Islamism as the biggest threat to the Republic. Under pressure from the military, the Constitutional Court banned the WP on the grounds that it had become the center of anti-secularist activities and Erbakan was banned from politics for five years.[18] In response to pro-WP protests, the military threatened to use force against Islamic groups.[19] After the WP's closure, senior members established the Virtue Party (VP), but they could not escape their predecessors' fate either. In April 1999, a year after the WP was shut down, the public prosecutor filed a lawsuit for closure of the VP.

The European Union, which had long been rejected as a "Christian club" by Turkey's Islamists, sided with the Islamists against the authoritarian practices of the state. In the December 1997 Luxembourg Summit, the prime minister of Luxembourg said that Turkey was run by the military and thus was unfit to become an EU member.[20] The EU commissioner for enlargement and the European Parliament were equally blunt after the VP was shut down. They criticized the party's closure, arguing that it was an obstacle to achieving pluralist democracy and freedom of expression.[21]

The February 28 intervention and subsequent restrictions on Islamic actors sparked a process of self-reflection and critique, leading prominent Islamists to adopt changes in their views. In the 1980s, the Islamists had radical ideas about politics and society. They were critical of the West and Western concepts such as democracy, secularism and human rights. Prominent Islamists argued that these Western concepts had caused "turmoil" in their thought and spirit and had to be replaced by Islamic ones.[22] They were also critical of the westernizing Republican elite who, through abolishing the caliphate, closing down religious orders and banning religious education, swept Islam to the individual sphere and excluded it from public life. To them, the Kemalist project of reforming society and politics along secular lines had to be reversed through Islamizing society and politics.

The February 28 process upended all these views and led to the rise of what some called the "post-Islamists."[23] Mehmet Metiner, a prominent Islamist figure of the 1980s and '90s who served as a member of Parliament for the AKP, was one of the many self-critical figures who revised his ideas after the intervention. He criticized Islamism's authoritarian tendency to exclude non-Islamic actors after coming to power, its rejection of Western democracy and its quest to capture state institutions, and announced his support for democracy and secularism.[24] Another prominent figure within Islamist circles who became one of the founders of the AKP, Bülent Arınç, said "if we are to be realistic, we should not come up against and clash with the military."[25] Yalçın Akdoğan, who played a key role in articulating the AKP's ideology as "conservative democracy," laid out the new party's thinking on concepts that were vehemently rejected by the old Islamist schools such as secularism, liberalism and democracy.[26]

The AKP elite did not see themselves as challengers of modernity and modern political ideas and institutions. Instead, they demanded the formation of a liberal democratic regime and voiced their opposition to the Kemalist regime not in the name of Islam but that of democracy, human rights, rule of law and pluralism.[27] They supported an Anglo-Saxon type of secularism where the state does not interfere with religion and leaves space for religious groups in the social sphere. In a speech Prime Minister Erdoğan delivered at the Ambrosetti Forum in Italy, he rejected efforts to refer to the common Christian heritage of European countries in the draft EU constitution, arguing that religion should not have a place in the European constitution because the EU stands for secularism, human rights and the rule of law.[28]

The February 28 process prompted a reevaluation of the Turkish Islamists' view of the EU as well. A sea change had already been under way. Even Necmettin Erbakan, who had fiercely criticized the EU and Turkey's membership bid, had softened his approach.[29] But the February 28 process took that transformation to a whole new level.

The reformists split from the VP and led by Erdoğan, Abdullah Gül and Bülent Arınç found themselves demanding the same thing as the EU: democratization and guarantees for civil and political rights in Turkey. In their search for protection against the secularist establishment including the army and the judiciary, they found a natural ally in the EU. The EU had already put curbing the military's involvement in politics as a precondition for Turkey's entry into the EU, and the further democratization that would come with EU membership would automatically address issues that had haunted Islamist parties and their conservative base, such as party closures and the ban on the headscarf.

In a clear break from the Islamist tradition, which harbored deep suspicions about Western democracy and human rights and opposed Turkey's history of westernization, the Erdoğan-led AKP made Turkey's EU accession the central pillar of the government's agenda. Right after the AKP's election victory, party leader

Erdoğan went on a tour of major EU capitals to elicit a date from the EU for the commencement of accession negotiations in the upcoming EU summit in December 2002.[30] During its first three years in power, the ruling AKP adopted two constitutional amendments and eight legislative packages designed to align Turkey's laws and norms with the EU with the aim of securing a start date for Turkey's accession negotiations in the EU's December 2004 summit. Collectively, these reform measures liberalized the country's political system. They expanded freedom of expression, facilitated Kurdish broadcasting and education, abolished the death penalty and anti-terrorism provisions that authorized punishment for propaganda against the unity of the state and subjected Turkish courts to the European Court of Human Rights.

These measures also helped the Erdoğan government carry out the most radical reform of the military's political role in the history of the Republic. The Seventh EU Harmonization package introduced in 2003 changed the structure of the National Security Council (NSC), an institution that was the embodiment of the military's standing in politics and seen as the "shadow government."[31] The package repealed the NSC's executive powers and turned it into an "advisory body" exclusively in matters concerning national security. It increased the number of voting civilians in the NSC to a majority and allowed greater parliamentary scrutiny of the military budget. Previous provisions mandating the government to give "priority consideration" to the NSC's recommendations were abolished.[32] The constitutional package of eight amendments that was passed in 2004 increased civilian influence over the defense budget, and abolished the military's right to appoint one member on The Council of Higher Education (YÖK) and the Radio and Television Supreme Council (RTÜK). The amendments also abolished the State Security Courts, criminal courts founded after the 1980 military coup to try crimes against the state, and curbed the military courts' power to try civilians for offences related to criticizing the military.[33]

Erdoğan took other steps to weaken the military's power in politics. The military had seen the Cyprus question as a vital national security issue and rebuffed international attempts to reunify the island.[34] Cyprus has been divided since 1974 when Turkey militarily intervened in the north in response to a Greece-backed military coup on the island. The island was effectively partitioned, with a Turkish Cypriot government in the north and an internationally recognized Greek Cypriot government in the south.[35] The 1999 EU Helsinki Summit announced that the Greek Cypriots would join the EU as the representative of all Cypriots in 2004 but encouraged unification before that date.[36] The summit accepted Turkey as a candidate for EU membership but tied Turkey's membership to the settlement of the Cyprus issue.[37] However, the Turkish military exhorted the government to reject international attempts to reunify the island.[38] Erdoğan, however, adamant in his quest to make Turkey an EU member, was ready to support unification efforts. This would not only win European favor but also help his efforts to shift the epicenter of foreign policy making from the military to the civilian government.

In a radical departure from the official line that supported "two communities-two separate states," Erdoğan suggested a solution based on "two communities-single state."[39] Both Greek and Greek Cypriot politicians were positively surprised. Yorgos Papandreou, the Greek foreign minister, said it was the first time that he was hearing a Turkish politician backing such a solution and it could be a historic opportunity for Cyprus.[40] Facing a secularist backlash, including resistance from the Turkish Cypriot community leader Rauf Denktaş, Erdoğan backed down. But he continued to support UN-led reunification efforts. He backed the final plan presented by the UN Secretary General Kofi Annan in 2004, which proposed a bicommunal, bizonal federation of two states on Cyprus. The plan was approved in a referendum by the majority of Turkish Cypriots but rejected by the majority of Greek Cypriots. In 2004, Cyprus became a member of the EU as a divided island. The decision frustrated Erdoğan, who had taken a considerable political risk by backing the UN peace plan. However, Erdoğan's efforts to achieve a unified island were acknowledged by the European Council and Turkey was granted a date to begin formal accession negotiations with the EU.[41]

Erdoğan's stance on the Cyprus question was indicative of the two-pronged approach Erdoğan pursued early in his tenure vis-à-vis the secularist establishment. On the one hand, he actively tried to marginalize the establishment by adopting a Europeanist and desecuritized posture in foreign policy and a reformist domestic agenda prioritizing democracy over security. Indeed, the measures taken as part of the AKP's democratization agenda shifted the balance of power in civil-military relations in the former's favor. On the other hand, Erdoğan was careful not to confront the military directly and backed down when he faced resistance.

There were other instances of Erdoğan's pragmatism. In 2003, the country's secularist President Ahmet Necdet Sezer refused to invite lawmakers' wives who cover their heads to his annual Republic Day reception to celebrate the eightieth anniversary of the foundation of the Republic. Prime Minister Erdoğan's wife, Emine, was also kept off the list but Erdoğan ordered members of his cabinet to attend the reception in an effort to ease the tension.[42] In 2004, Erdoğan said his government had no intention of changing the Internal Service Act of the military, which allowed it to intervene in politics. Erdoğan deferred to the military on matters considered to be red lines for the generals such as the fight against Islamism and Kurdish separatism. He kept quiet when the chief of general staff, Hilmi Özkök, complained about the reservations of Abdullah Gül, who briefly served as the prime minister when Erdoğan was banned from office, concerning the dismissal of officers from the military on the grounds that they were involved in Islamist activities. Erdoğan toed the military's line and criticized AKP parliamentarians during a debate on whether amnesty should be granted to non-violent members of terrorist organizations.[43]

Erdoğan was pragmatic even on issues that were important to his conservative base. In 2003, his government started working on a draft law to remove the discrimination faced by graduates of the religious Imam Hatip schools (İHO), which were first established to train imams and preachers after the foundation of the Turkish Republic in 1923, in the university entrance examination. Over the years, an increasing number of İHO graduates chose not to become preachers but to continue their education in secular higher institutions. But they had to achieve higher scores than graduates of other schools in the university examination to be admitted, a measure aimed at preventing İHO graduates from attending secular institutions of higher learning and consequently their penetration into bureaucratic posts. After Chief of General Staff Özkök issued a warning, Erdoğan decided not to push the draft bill through parliament.[44]

Emboldened by the AKP's electoral success in the 2004 local elections, Erdoğan made another attempt to abolish the discrimination faced by İHO graduates. The government defied a warning from the General Staff and the parliament approved the reform package. After secularist President Sezer vetoed the bill on the grounds that it was incompatible with the constitutional principle of secularism, Erdoğan backed down saying "As a government we are not ready to pay a price."[45] He then took another controversial step. As part of a reform package for Turkey's penal code, the AKP proposed to criminalize adultery.[46] The move drew strong criticism from the EU. The EU Commissioner Gunter Verheugen said that the European Union countries could interpret the proposal as Islamic law entering Turkish law at a time when Turkey was engaged in a dialogue with the EU to become a member.[47] After a wave of protests from the EU and the secularist opposition, the government withdrew the clause.[48]

Erdoğan's strategy paid off. While his cautious approach vis-à-vis the military's red lines denied the military an excuse to bring down Erdoğan, his assertive reform agenda secured him the backing of unlikely constituencies and curbed the military's power. The reforms Erdoğan's government carried out during the early years of its tenure liberalized the country's political system. However, in retrospect, some of those reforms paved the way for Erdoğan's power grab in later years. Even during the reform years, there were troubling signs of what was to come.

Erdoğan used state institutions to stop the rise of his political opponents. In 2004, the Turkish government's Savings Deposit Insurance Fund (TMSF) seized control of 200 companies owned by Cem Uzan, a businessman whose newly established political party had risen to challenge the AKP. Uzan had launched the "Genç Parti" (the Young Party) in 2002 and to the surprise of many the party captured 7 percent of the vote in the 2002 elections. The party's popularity kept growing after the elections, prompting Erdoğan to state that "our only rival is the Young Party."[49]

Uzan was later accused of siphoning $5.8 billion from the company's flagship bank and the Uzan group's holdings, including Turkey's first private TV channel, Star TV, and Star newspaper, which were seized and sold to pay back his debts. The Doğan Media Group, which at the time had good relations with the Erdoğan government, purchased Star TV and the newspaper was sold to a pro-AKP business group.[50] It was one of the earliest dents in Erdoğan's carefully crafted image of a reformer.

2005–07: Years of Euro-fatigue and stalled reforms

In February 1998, a year after the military launched the "February 28 process," İstanbul University notified students and faculty that students with headscarves and long beards would not be permitted to enter lectures and exams. Leyla Şahin was in her fifth year of medical school at İstanbul University at the time. She was denied entrance into the university because of her headscarf. Şahin brought a suit against Turkey at the European Court of Human Rights (ECHR), claiming it had violated her right to education by denying her the right to religious expression.[51] In June 2004, in a near unanimous verdict handed down by the ECHR, Turkey was found not to have violated Şahin's right to education.

Leyla Şahin became a member of parliament for the AKP in 2015 but the decision of the ECHR, which is not part of the EU, dealt one of the first blows to the Euro-enthusiasm of Erdoğan and his ruling AKP. The ECHR's decision had come after another troubling development for Turkey-EU ties. In May 2004, less than a month after the Greek Cypriots rejected the UN peace plan, Cyprus became a member of the EU. The decision frustrated Erdoğan, who had taken a considerable political risk by backing the UN peace plan.

Mixed signals from the EU regarding Turkey's membership strengthened Erdoğan's view that he could no longer rely on the EU to confront the secularist establishment and break down the restrictions on religion in Turkey. After announcing in 2004 that accession talks with Turkey could formally begin in a few months, Europeans began to rethink the fact that Europe could expand to include a majority Muslim country and border a troubled Middle East.[52] Germany and Austria suggested that the EU consider a "privileged partnership" instead of full membership for Turkey.[53] French President Jacques Chirac said that Turkey would have to undergo a "major cultural revolution" to join the EU and that Ankara's membership talks could last up to fifteen years and might fail.[54] These statements convinced the Turkish public that the EU was treating Turkey's membership differently from other candidates because Turkey is a Muslim-majority country, and that Turkey's EU membership was not guaranteed. Turkish nationalists grew increasingly critical of the EU, arguing that EU-induced reforms granted the Kurds more rights while it weakened the military and thus the fight against the PKK. European demands for unilateral Turkish concessions to settle the Cyprus problem after the AKP had already given concessions by backing the Annan plan soured Turkish public opinion against the EU further.

After having ridden the pro-EU tide in the country and made Turkey's EU membership the focus of his domestic and foreign policy agenda, Erdoğan found himself under increasing pressure from a skeptical opposition and strong ultranationalist sentiment in the country. The Turkish public's support dropped significantly with 46.9 percent saying, "the EU is a Christian club."[55] The growing anti-EU sentiment strengthened the ultranationalist, Euro-skeptic Nationalist Movement Party (MHP) and threatened to erode the AKP's parliamentary majority in the next elections.

Erdoğan's instinct for political survival led him to put the brakes on the government's reform zeal. By 2005 when formal accession negotiations with the EU began, his interest in the EU had already cooled considerably. He gave assurances to the EU that his government remained committed to the reform track but he took troubling steps that suggested otherwise. In March 2005, Erdoğan defended the use of excessive force by the police to break up a peaceful demonstration marking International Women's Day. Erdoğan said the women provoked the violence. The penal code adopted in June 2005 hardened penalties for the expression of non-violent views deemed to insult the nation or harm national interests. Erdoğan similarly defended the military's use of excess force when riots broke out in the Kurdish city of Diyarbakır, leaving several hundred civilians injured. In 2006, the government adopted amendments to the antiterror law that expanded the security forces' authority to deal with terrorism and removed safeguards against torture.[56]

2007–11: Years of consolidation of power

Unbounded by the EU reform agenda and emboldened by electoral success, Erdoğan and his party spent their second term in power capturing key institutions of the state from the secularists. The first target was the presidency.

Before switching to a presidential system in 2017, Turkey had a parliamentary system of government and its presidency was often termed symbolic, although the 1982 constitution had granted considerable powers to the president including blocking laws and personnel appointments. During the AKP's first term in office, the presidency was held by an ardent secularist, Ahmet Necdet Sezer, who served as the head of the Constitutional Court before becoming the president in 2000. Sezer often vetoed AKP-proposed laws and appointments on the grounds that they conflicted with the secularist principles of the state. He became a key player in delaying the AKP's reform agenda and the party's efforts to capture more levers of state power.[57] Sezer's seven-year term was scheduled to expire in 2007 and the stakes were high both for Erdoğan and the opposition in the question of who came next.

The presidential election provided a glimpse into Erdoğan's strategy for the AKP's second term. He faced a choice. He could nominate one of the heavyweights of the party, such as himself, Foreign Minister Abdullah Gül or speaker of the parliament Bülent Arınç who had all come from a staunch Islamist background and whose wives wore the headscarf. But nominating one of these names would provoke a strong opposition from the secularists. In the secularists' minds, the AKP already held too much power through its control of parliament and the office of the prime minister. The presidency functioned as a bulwark against Erdoğan's

ERDOĞAN'S STRATEGY TOWARDS HEGEMONY

efforts to capture the state entirely. They thought a headscarf-wearing first lady would undermine the secular foundations of the Republic further. Erdoğan's potential candidacy had already caused much uproar within secularist sectors of society and Turkish bureaucracy, with hundreds of thousands of people marching in Ankara against Erdoğan's prospective candidacy chanting "we do not want an *imam* in Çankaya."[58] Chief of Staff General Yaşar Büyükanıt warned that the new president had to "adhere to basic principles of the Republic and the ideal of a secular, democratic state in deed as well as word."[59] Outgoing president Sezer joined the chorus issuing another warning to Erdoğan that the Turkish secular system "faced a threat unprecedented since the foundation of the Republic."[60]

These warnings significantly raised the stakes for Erdoğan. Instead of escalating tensions with the secularists, his party could nominate a "compromise candidate" within its ranks. Those who wanted to avoid a clash with the secularist camp pushed for Defense Minister Vecdi Gönül, whose wife did not wear a headscarf. The type of candidate the government would settle on proved to be an indication of Erdoğan's strategy towards the secularists in the years to come. In the party's first term, he had trod carefully. He avoided clashing with the secular establishment directly, pushed for his agenda on controversial matters but backed down when he faced opposition from the secularists. This time, Erdoğan decided to up the ante. Although he acquiesced to the military's demand not to stand for the presidency, he nominated an equally problematic candidate for the military after pressure from the party's hardliners: Abdullah Gül.[61]

Gül's candidacy provoked a strong response from the secularists. They held large-scale "Republican" demonstrations in Turkey's major cities. In Istanbul, the country's largest city, as many as one million people rallied, praising the army and accusing Erdoğan and Gül of trying to establish an Islamist state.[62] The main opposition CHP took steps to deny Gül the presidency. It boycotted the first round of voting in the parliament, which used to elect the president, to prevent a quorum and invalidate the vote. After boycotting the vote, it petitioned the Constitutional Court to nullify it. A few days later, the Constitutional Court, which was dominated by secularists, declared the election invalid.

The most critical development took place on April 27. In a veiled threat of a coup, the military issued a memorandum on its website declaring itself the "definite defender of secularism" and warning that it would act when necessary.[63] The memorandum had been hastily drafted by General Yaşar Büyükanıt, who was known to be more worried about Erdoğan's "secret Islamist agenda" than his predecessor Hilmi Özkök. The statement implicitly threatened a coup if the government pushed ahead with Gül's appointment. The military's move, which was famously called the "e-memorandum," sent shock waves across the country. Staunch secularists applauded it but many others were deeply disturbed. Thousands who attended the Republican rallies chanted "no shariah, no coup, (we want) a democratic Turkey."[64] Liberals argued that the e-memorandum took the country's democratic gains back a decade while others warned the move could jeopardize Turkey's EU membership.[65]

The constituency most disturbed by the e-memorandum was Erdoğan's conservative supporters. It reminded the country's pious sector of the military's intervention on February 28 that unleashed the years-long overt campaign against Islamic circles. As the prime minister of a coalition government at the time, Erbakan was not strong enough to stand up against the military. He stood by as the military took draconian measures in its fight against an alleged increase in "Islamic fundamentalism" and was finally forced to resign. As the leader of a party that ruled the country as a one-party government, Erdoğan was in a different position. The victims of the February 28 process demanded a tougher response from him. All eyes were on Erdoğan and the response from his government.

The AKP did not disappoint its pious base. In an unprecedented act of defiance, the government expressed "regret" over "inappropriate remarks" and cautioned the military to be "more careful."[66] Government spokesperson Cemil Çiçek said they flatly rejected the "e-memorandum" and that judiciary had to decide whether it should be the subject of a the judicial probe.[67] To capitalize on the polarized environment and the sense of victimhood among the country's conservative segments after the military memorandum, Prime Minister Erdoğan called early national elections in July, which had been scheduled to take place in November. The e-memorandum and the government's response proved to be a turning point in Erdoğan's efforts to consolidate power. What was designed to be a move by the military to undercut Erdoğan ended up strengthening him. It dealt another blow to the military's ability to exert its influence in politics.

The Erdoğan government's decision to stand up against the military was a bold move. Years later, Abdullah Gül said that Erdoğan was reluctant to confront the military at the time but he had pushed Erdoğan to give the military a strong response.[68] Others have argued that Erdoğan knew about the upcoming high-profile trials against military officers and was emboldened by what became the biggest blow to the military's involvement in politics.[69]

Erdoğan used the e-memorandum masterfully in his election campaign to galvanize his base and those who were critical of the military's intervention in politics. It worked. Coupled with the party's successful economic policies and the opposition's ineptitude, the e-memorandum helped the AKP capture 47 percent of the vote—up from 34 percent in the 2002 elections.[70] The Erdoğan government's landslide victory was not only a personal humiliation to Büyükanıt, who believed that the public shared his concerns about Erdoğan and the AKP and would punish them at the ballot box,[71] it was also a major setback to the image of the military and a boost to Erdoğan.

This book's focus is the role foreign policy has played in the country's descent into autocracy, but it is important to highlight the key part economic success has played in Erdoğan's consolidation of power. Erdoğan's AKP rose to power following the worst economic crisis in decades on the promise of political stability and economic prosperity. The economy was already rebounding from the 2001 crisis when the AKP took office thanks to the economic recovery program led by the previous government and overseen by the IMF.[72] But the voters did not think the recovery was fast enough and blamed the policies of the coalition governments of the 1990s for the country's economic woes, paving the way for the sweeping electoral victory of the newly established AKP and the first single-party government in over a decade. Erdoğan, desperate to join the EU, continued to follow the IMF's recommendations. He pushed through radical structural reforms imposed by the IMF and the World Bank, which freed the Central Bank from political control, rehabilitated the banking system and introduced transparency in government procurement procedures.[73] These measures, along with a confluence of other factors including warm ties between Erdoğan's government and the EU and the Muslim democrat image he enjoyed in Western capitals, brought inflation down from near 80 percent to 8 percent annually and led to an increase in direct foreign investment and rapid economic growth. Erdoğan complemented the neoliberal program, which worsened workers' economic conditions, with a populist touch to blunt the impact of liberalization and prevent an electoral backlash from the poorer segments of the country. His "neoliberal populist" strategy included providing clientelist aid, consumer credit and loan options.

The particular neoliberal economic policy Erdoğan followed helped him achieve several goals. Through privatization of state economic enterprises (SEEs), Erdoğan not only weakened the labor movement and politically neutralized the working class but also challenged the secularist establishment's hold over the economy through their control over the SEEs. All the while, Erdoğan secured the backing of the working class through the populist measures he introduced such as providing income support and easy credit to low-income groups.[74] These reforms, coupled with major institutional and political changes due to a renewed resolve to join the EU, led to the establishment of a rule-based framework which reined in the executive discretion and delegated decision-making to independent bodies.[75] The result was an increase in direct foreign investment and a growing economy that lifted millions of Turks into the middle class. Near continuous economic growth broadened Erdoğan's electoral base and provided more resources for his patronage network. Although economic growth slowed significantly from 2007 onwards, the vast patronage network Erdoğan established and the populist policies he pursued continued to exchange economic benefits for political support.

ERDOĞAN'S STRATEGY TOWARDS HEGEMONY

The AKP's 2007 electoral victory came against this background of what many called Erdoğan's "economic miracle." A month after the election, Abdullah Gül was sworn in as president. With Gül's presidency, for the first time in Turkey's history, a non-secularist was elected as president and an epic battle between Erdoğan's party and the secularist establishment began.

Taking on the military

The Turkish military, long the self-appointed guardian of secularism, historically played an outsized role in Turkish politics. While in liberal democracies civilian governments control the military, in Turkey the military has wielded considerable political autonomy from the democratically elected governments. It directly intervened in politics three times (1960, 1971 and 1980) and forced out a democratically elected government in 1997 without having to use force. After each intervention, the military took steps to institutionalize its participation in politics and entrench its veto power in political matters to the extent that made direct military intervention unnecessary.[76] No civilian government managed to change the military's privileged status. But things were about to change dramatically under Erdoğan.

In early June 2007, an anonymous telephone call to the local Gendarmerie Headquarters in the northeastern province of Trabzon paved the way for a process that would end almost half a century of military domination. The caller claimed that grenades and explosives were stored in the attic of a house in an Istanbul slum. The gendarmerie notified the Istanbul police, who raided the house and found dozens of grenades and fuses. The owner of the premises and his nephew who was renting the house were taken into custody for questioning. Based on their statements, a retired army major and a retired noncommissioned officer were arrested. Later in the month, during a second police raid, a cache of weapons and explosives was discovered in the house of another retired major.[77]

Waves of arrests continued. With each wave, the investigation targeted more prominent figures and cast its net wider. Not only retired military officers were among the hundreds of detainees; they included businessmen, NGO leaders, newspaper columnists, journalists, mafia leaders, political party heads, lawyers, academics, even the spokesperson of the Turkish Orthodox Patriarchate and a writer of erotic novels. Linking these individuals were their staunch secularist and ultranationalist views on politics. The first indictment prepared by the Istanbul Prosecutor's Office on July 14, 2008, charged the 86 suspects with "membership in an armed terrorist organization," "attempting to overthrow the government of the Turkish Republic by use of violence and coercion," "inciting people to armed rebellion against the government of the Turkish Republic," "encouraging the military to insubordination" and "inciting people to hatred and enmity."[78] The name of the alleged network being investigated was Ergenekon, named after a mythical Turkish valley. Public Prosecutor Zekeriya Öz led the investigation. In several massive indictments totaling thousands of pages, the Prosecutor charged people with membership of the "Ergenekon armed terrorist organization." Zekeriya Öz was widely believed to be a member of the Turkish Islamic Gülen movement that allied itself with the AKP. Although the two movements came from different Islamic traditions, the AKP's newfound position of influence after the 2002 elections brought Erdoğan and the Gülenists together in a tactical alliance against a common foe, the military.

The Ergenekon investigation led by Öz became the biggest and most controversial case in the history of the country. To its proponents, particularly supporters of the AKP, Kurdish nationalists, liberals and some leftists who had suffered most at the hands of the state, the investigation offered a historic opportunity to cleanse what the Turks referred to as *"derin devlet"* or "deep state," an alleged clandestine network of military officers and their civilian allies who intimidated and sometimes murdered dissidents thought to pose a threat to the state.[79] To them, the investigation could provide an opportunity for Turkey to finally become a fully democratic country. To its opponents, mostly secularists opposed to Erdoğan and the AKP, the investigation was a farce designed by the government and its sympathizers to discredit and silence secularist opposition.

Initially, the indictments had some credibility because of the well-known, decades-long collaboration of the state with organized crime. The fact that the AKP's coming to power in 2002 had caused considerable discomfort among the secularist ultranationalists, who feared an Islamic takeover of the state, together with Turkey's long history of military intervention, had made the investigation's claim that there was an Ergenekon network plotting to overthrow the Erdoğan government all the more plausible to many sectors of the country. After all, just a couple months earlier, the military had attempted to interfere in the political process, again. Therefore, initially, the investigation was widely welcomed within Turkey. Its link to the Gülen movement was not understood in the beginning, but as the rash of arrests started targeting opponents of the movement, this became clear, casting doubt on the real intention of the investigation. For example, Hanefi Avcı, a local police chief who had been sympathetic to the movement at one point but later published a book accusing the movement of manipulating judicial processes, was arrested. So were several journalists who were about to publish footage implicating police officers in planting evidence on Ergenekon suspects.[80]

As the investigation progressed, doubts grew concerning its conduct and intent. It started targeting an increasingly unlikely group of suspects whose only commonality appeared to be their opposition to the AKP, with little or no evidence. The investigation included deep inconsistencies, lacked proof that a network called Ergenekon existed or had ever existed and failed to live up to judicial standards, with long detention periods without a formal charge being made. Details of the investigation started leaking to the pro-government press, apparently to intimidate the opposition.[81] Raising further doubts about the real intent of the investigation was the timing of pre-dawn raids. When the Erdoğan government came under pressure, the investigation gathered steam.

The Ergenekon trials targeted journalists, businessmen, intellectuals and retired military officers. The Sledgehammer (*Balyoz*) indictment that followed was even bolder. It directly attacked the military, alleging that military leadership held a seminar in 2003 as part of a plan to overthrow the AKP government.[82] Like

Ergenekon, this case also began with an anonymous tip-off. Materials including a CD claiming to include classified military documents detailing a coup plan were delivered to the fiercely anti-military daily *Taraf*. However, computer forensics showed the documents to be forged, a fact ignored by the courts. The investigation pressed ahead. A total of 250 military officers received lengthy jail sentences.[83]

The Ergenekon investigation paved the way for a process which many thought would finally rid Turkey of shady connections, end the era of military coups and help Turkey's democratization process. But it turned out to be a missed opportunity. If the grenades found in an Istanbul slum had led to the formation of an independent commission, both secularists and Islamists would have had the opportunity to come to terms with the country's past.[84] Instead, it raised further doubts about the future of the country's democracy and rule of law.

But the trials served the goals of those who launched them. Through Ergenekon and Sledgehammer, the Erdoğan-Gülen alliance was able to subdue the military and demoralize secularist circles in the country. Erdoğan's involvement in the whole process remained a question mark. In response to the opposition's criticism over the political nature of the case, Erdoğan proudly declared himself to be the "prosecutor."[85] But some prominent analysts who followed the case closely argued that it was a purely Gülenist affair, claiming that Erdoğan supported the process but did not drive it.[86] At times, Erdoğan seemed uncomfortable with the progression of the case, thinking it had gone too far and tarnished the party's image. In 2011, the Supreme Board of Judges and Prosecutors, dominated by pro-government judges, removed Public Prosecutor Zekeriya Öz from the case.[87] Pro-AKP columnists argued that the decision to remove Öz from the investigation reflected growing concerns of Erdoğan and within his government about the conduct of the investigation and its widening scope, which they thought would undermine the government's legitimacy.[88]

Others argued that Erdoğan was heavily involved in the Ergenekon investigation. In a 2018 book, Ahmet Sever, a former aide to Turkey's previous president Abdullah Gül, argued that

ERDOĞAN'S STRATEGY TOWARDS HEGEMONY

Erdoğan worked closely with the Gülen movement to co-ordinate the trials.[89] No matter the nature of his role, Erdoğan became the biggest winner. The military was finally out of his way.

Next target is the judiciary

The Ergenekon investigation revealed the extent of the Gülen movement's reach into what had been considered one of the bastions of Turkish secularism: the judiciary. But the 2008 case against the AKP to shut down the party and ban its leading members from politics for allegedly plotting an Islamic state reminded Erdoğan that there was still work to be done. Despite his party's comfortable parliamentary majority, the government's ability to legislate had been limited by the judiciary during its eight years in power. Some of the constitutional and legislative changes proposed by the AKP, such as lifting the ban on wearing headscarves in universities and higher education reforms, had been knocked back by the Constitutional Court. The opposition parties, lacking the majority in parliament to prevent the passage of legislation they were opposed to, often looked to the judiciary to challenge the government's legislative agenda.

An investigation into the activities of Islamic networks, including the Gülen movement, led by a staunch secularist public prosecutor in the eastern town of Erzincan, İlhan Cihaner, made a comprehensive overhaul of the judiciary an even more urgent task for Erdoğan and his Gülenist allies. Cihaner's investigation claimed to have uncovered a number of criminal activities by people close to Erdoğan and the Gülen movement including fixing state contracts.[90] The Ministry of Justice asked Cihaner to drop the investigation, stripped him off his powers when he refused and appointed the case to another prosecutor.[91] Cihaner was charged with membership of the alleged "Ergenekon terrorist organization" and sent to prison.

In response to Cihaner's dismissal, the Supreme Board of Judges and Prosecutors (HSYK), the sole body overseeing the appointment of judges and prosecutors, stripped the new prosecutor and three others considered to be AKP loyalists of their powers. The

HSYK and Erdoğan accused each other of politicizing the rule of law. Both were right.

The Turkish judiciary has always been highly politicized. The courts have served as the guardian of the founding Kemalist ideology and functioned for decades as a mechanism by which secularist elites "threatened by democratic transition guard and distort political process."[92] Turkey transitioned to democracy in 1950 when it first held free and fair elections, but democracy was often stalled by military interventions and a politically motivated *juristocracy*. Turkey's Constitutional Court, often hailed as the country's commitment to the rule of law, retarded the country's democratic consolidation through shutting down political parties that were considered to pose a threat to the state due to their alleged commitment to political Islam or Kurdish nationalism. The Constitutional Court limited the scope of political participation and held at bay demands from the country's religiously conservative and Kurdish communities for political inclusion.[93]

In the absence of an effective political opposition, the judiciary was often seen by the secularists as the last bulwark against what they thought were Erdoğan's efforts to dismantle the Kemalist ideology and establish an Islamic form of government. The Constitutional Court's unsuccessful attempt to shut down the AKP and efforts to prevent Abdullah Gül's accession to the presidency on procedural grounds were clearly politically motivated and based on unsubstantiated evidence.

In response, Erdoğan embarked on a project that promised to create an independent judiciary but turned out to be a move to staff it with AKP loyalists. On March 22, 2010, the Erdoğan government announced a package of proposed changes to the country's 1982 constitution, drafted under military rule with deeply illiberal and anti-democratic provisions. The amendment package included provisions to establish an Ombudsman, permit collective bargaining for public sector workers and affirmative action measures for women, make serving military personnel liable to prosecution in civilian courts and make outlawing political parties difficult.[94] But the most controversial changes in the proposed package were the ones concerning restructuring the Constitutional Court and the

HSYK. Seven of the eleven-member Constitutional Court were drawn primarily from among the five next highest courts in the country, with the remaining four drawn from among senior administrative officers and lawyers and the Council of Higher Education (YÖK).[95] The seven-member HSYK, which comprised judges from the same courts and personnel from the Ministry of Justice, coordinated the promotions to appellate courts and the higher judiciary. The narrow composition of the HSYK helped the imposition of an ideological litmus test on judicial promotions, ensuring that the members of the high judiciary were strong supporters of the Kemalist ideology.

The government's package proposed increasing the number of members of the Constitutional Court, a great majority of whom would be appointed by the president and the rest by the parliament. The package kept in place the existing practice of selecting some members from candidates proposed by the higher courts, but by increasing the number of the court's members, it ensured they lost their majority status and would become a numerical minority.[96] The Erdoğan government proposed to dramatically increase the number of HSYK members, which was broadly in line with EU recommendations. But contrary to those recommendations, the government's package kept the minister of justice and the undersecretary on the Board but reduced their authority, expressing concerns of undue executive influence.[97] The EU and the Venice Commission (the Council of Europe's advisory body, composed of independent experts, on issues of constitutional law and politics) supported the changes but its opponents argued they would significantly increase the government's control over the judiciary.

AKP sympathizers had already started working their way up through the judiciary after the party's 2007 election victory. They were mostly Gülenists. Unlike the followers of the AKP's Islamist tradition, who had not widely been able to enter law schools due to the limitations imposed by the secularist education system, the Gülenists had managed to increase their influence within the judiciary.

President Abdullah Gül decided to put the amendments to a referendum. The secularist main opposition CHP and the ultranationalist MHP led the "no" bloc. The Islamist Felicity Party and the Great Union Party (*Büyük Birlik Partisi*) joined the AKP in the "yes" camp while the pro-Kurdish Peace and Democracy Party (*Barış ve Demokrasi Partisi*) boycotted the vote. Prime Minister Erdoğan campaigned tirelessly. "To prevent future military coups, to make sure this country's democracy is not interrupted again, vote yes. Yes to freedom, yes to a strong Turkey", Erdoğan told the cheering crowds. He defended the reforms arguing that they would bring the charter into line with the EU, an argument he had used previously in curbing the generals' power.

Fethullah Gülen and his movement threw their full support behind Erdoğan. Gülen said even the dead would rise from their graves to vote yes in favor of the amendments[98] while his supporters went from door to door campaigning on the government's behalf.[99] Supporters of Erdoğan, the majority of liberals and some leftists hailed the amendments as an important step towards full democratization and harmonization of Turkish legislation with EU requirements. Opponents, on the other hand, saw the changes as Erdoğan's attempt to seize complete control of the judiciary. On September 12, 2010, on the thirtieth anniversary of the 1980 coup, Turkish voters approved the package of constitutional reforms by a wide margin.

The US and the EU welcomed the result. EU Enlargement Commissioner Stefan Fuele said in a statement, "As we consistently said in the past months, these reforms are a step in the right direction as they address a number of long-standing priorities in Turkey's efforts towards fully complying with the accession criteria."[100] German Foreign Minister Guido Westerwelle said the vote was critical for Turkey's bid to join the European Union while President Barack Obama "acknowledged the vibrancy of Turkey's democracy."[101]

To the dismay of those who supported the amendments thinking they would depoliticize the judiciary, the constitutional reform package merely changed its ideological hue. Subsequent steps taken by Erdoğan revealed the true color of his reform efforts. Secularists in the judiciary were replaced with AKP loyalists. After bringing the powerful military to heel, Erdoğan and his allies had overhauled the secularist judiciary.

ERDOĞAN'S STRATEGY TOWARDS HEGEMONY

Muzzling the press

"We are not going to bow to media terror. We are not going to surrender to the dictatorship of the media." Prime Minister Erdoğan, speaking at his party's congress in Istanbul in September 2008, was furious with Aydın Doğan, who owned Turkey's largest media company and had supported the February 28 process against the Islamist government in 1997. Erdoğan's remarks came after Doğan's newspapers and TV stations ran stories about a multi-million euro embezzlement scandal involving Deniz Feneri, a Turkish charity with links to Erdoğan. Doğan's media group's reporting came after a court in Frankfurt jailed three Turkish-born men convicted of embezzling millions of euros that the charity's German sister organization collected as aid for needy Muslims in Turkey, Pakistan and Palestine.[102] The men pleaded guilty and detailed how the money was transferred to people in Turkey and Germany who had close ties to Erdoğan. Zahid Akman, a senior government official in Turkey, was one of them. He was implicated as a mastermind behind the scam in the Frankfurt court ruling. The story made headlines in Doğan's newspapers in the days that followed.

Doğan's response to Erdoğan's statements was equally harsh. He said that his media group would continue to cover corruption allegations and that attacks against the media by the prime minister of a democratic country were not acceptable.[103] Doğan ended up having to accept a lot more. His media group was hit with a record $2.5bn tax fine, sending its shares down 20 percent. Bankers at the time thought the fine was large enough to threaten the group's survival.[104] The companies in the Doğan group were banned from bidding for state tenders for a year and one of Doğan's executives was detained on suspicion of links to Ergenekon.[105]

The first signs of Erdoğan's quest to bring the media under his control came in 2004 when the Turkish state's Savings Deposit Insurance Fund (TMSF), empowered to move in when private firms default on debts, seized control of 200 companies owned by Erdoğan's political opponent Cem Uzan and sold them to a pro-Erdoğan business group and Doğan, who at the time had good relations with the Erdoğan government. But Erdoğan's efforts to muzzle the press became more systematic after his party's election victory in 2007. Until then, the mainstream media, with the exception of the staunch secularist *Cumhuriyet* newspaper, held positive views of Erdoğan. That started to change after 2007 as secularist media became increasingly critical of corruption allegations and Erdoğan's efforts to lift the ban on headscarves. As a result, Erdoğan's outbursts against the media grew stronger.

Tuncay Özkan was the founder of the country's most fiercely anti-government national television channel, KanalTürk, and a principal organizer of the Republican rallies that swept through the country in 2007 protesting against the government's attempts to appoint Abdullah Gül to the presidency. In 2008, KanalTürk was sold to an associate of Erdoğan and Tuncay Özkan was arrested on charges of involvement in the Ergenekon plot. The Sabah group, which controlled a major share of media outlets, most notably the country's largest circulating *Sabah* newspaper and the ATV television channel, was taken over by TMSF in 2007 for alleged irregularities. A year later, the group was sold to Çalık Holding which had close ties to Erdoğan. Çalık's CEO was Erdoğan's son-in-law, Berat Albayrak, and Berat's brother ran the media wing of the company. The sale was controversial for other reasons as well. Although the Çalık group was the only bidder, the auction was not annulled and two state-owned banks provided $350 million to finance the deal, the largest credit ever provided by either bank.[106]

Erdoğan's efforts did not end an era of press freedom in the country. Turkish media was never free. The military often intervened in newsrooms, journalists were jailed for "supporting terror" or "insulting Turkishness" and editors and staff members were often fired for their views. Newspaper bosses trod carefully so as not to cross the military's red lines, such as the war with the PKK or Islamists. In 1997, Aydın Doğan and his media group wholeheartedly supported the military's intervention that forced Islamist Prime Minister Erbakan to resign and introduced draconian measures targeting the country's Islamic sectors. Yet, the media landscape was still competitive. The military did not micromanage content other than the two issues that were important to the generals. Journalists went after politicians, posed difficult questions in front of the camera and held them to account.

Things got better after the AKP's victory in 2002. Turkey revamped its press law, replaced prison sentences for certain violations with fines and made it more difficult to confiscate newspapers.[107] A Turkish press council was created to keep the press in check, replacing state oversight.[108] The steps taken under Erdoğan after 2007 not only reversed the initial reformist trend but paved the way for the opening of the darkest chapter in the history of Turkish media. TMSF played a major part in this strategy. By securing an unprecedented monopoly over the media, Erdoğan had removed one of the last barriers to consolidating his rule.

Erdoğan takes politics beyond the water's edge

Foreign policy has ben instrumental in Erdoğan's consolidation of power.[109] It legitimized his efforts to take on his chief opponent, the military, in the eyes of secular, liberal and conservative sectors of the country. For decades, generals used the considerable influence they held in domestic politics to dominate foreign policy making. At the same time, they utilized crises on the foreign policy front to expand their influence at home. As the domestic and regional security situation worsened, the generals advanced the narrative that Turkey faced existential threats that were fed by outside actors. This narrative secured public backing for the generals' grip on the country's domestic and foreign policies. Erdoğan recognized a militarized, securitized foreign policy's function for the military, and saw that his reigning in of the generals' power had to include a foreign policy strategy.

Until the Arab uprisings started, Erdoğan's strategy of using foreign policy to sideline his opponents rested on two foreign policy positions: the pro-EU agenda and the "zero problems with neighbors" policy. These policies helped Erdoğan's domestic efforts to weaken the military in several ways. They both burnished Erdoğan's "post-Islamist," "centrist," "conservative democrat" image and helped him secure the backing of pro-reform, pro-market, globalist, and secularist constituencies who were otherwise unlikely to support an Islamist-rooted politician like Erdoğan. Erdoğan relied on this wide-ranging liberal-conservative coalition to carry out EU reforms that subdued the military. In other words, Turkey's EU predisposition and the steps Erdoğan took to secure membership of this elite club of European democracies was the glue that held his eclectic coalition together. The pro-EU credentials afforded Erdoğan the legitimacy in the eyes of critical constituencies to establish civilian control of the military. The "zero problems with neighbors" policy further weakened the military's grip. By forging close economic ties with regional countries, Erdoğan challenged the military's narrative that Turkey was surrounded by hostile actors. Desecuritizing Turkey's regional policy denied the military a significant role in foreign policy, which in turn helped Erdoğan undercut the military's role in domestic politics.

These two foreign policy positions were instrumental not just in emasculating the military and the rest of the secularist establishment but also in weakening the CHP, the secularist main opposition party. The CHP had an ambiguous stance vis-à-vis Turkey's EU membership bid. It backed Turkey's EU membership in principle but also feared that EU reforms would deal a blow to the secularists' hold on the country's bureaucracy. The party was also critical of Erdoğan's efforts to cultivate friendly ties with the country's neighbors, arguing this would jeopardize Turkey's security interests.[110] Erdoğan used his secularist rivals' criticism of his foreign policy to strengthen his populist narrative that he was the "real democrat," the "voice of the oppressed" and the CHP was the party of the elite standing in the way of the country's democratization for fear of losing its privileges.

Erdoğan used foreign policy masterfully. His two-pronged policy helped him purge his domestic opponents in the name of democracy with the backing of the West and large segments of Turkish society. The following pages will delve into the details of how Erdoğan managed to subdue his chief opponent by pursuing a cautious policy that did not stray too far from Turkey's traditional foreign policy, and how Syria became a window onto that strategy.

ERDOĞAN'S STRATEGY TOWARDS HEGEMONY

Erdoğan steals the Kemalist dream

Turkey's membership of the EU was an issue that divided Kemalists and Islamists in the 1990s. The Kemalists, who were firmly committed to Turkey's modernist, Western and secular identity, supported Turkey's membership while the Islamists saw the EU as a "Christian club" and took on the task of protecting Turkey's indigenous values against the EU.[111] There were, however, exceptions to the pro-EU stance within the Kemalist camp. Those who identified themselves with the left saw the EU's economic integration as an extension of its imperialist project and were opposed to the European common market, arguing "They're partners, we're the market" (*Onlar ortak, biz pazar*).

Nevertheless, by 2002, there emerged a wide pro-EU bloc cross-cutting the secular-Islamist divide. The "soft coup" and the EU's stance criticizing the coup led to a surge of support for Turkey's EU membership among the country's Islamists and liberal secularists who were concerned about the military's intervention in politics. Economic stagnation, rampant corruption and the government's postponement of badly needed structural reforms in the financial sector brought the secularist Istanbul-based big business community, the Association of Turkish Industrialists and Businessmen (TÜSİAD) and the pro-Islamic Association of Independent Industrialists and Businessmen (MÜSİAD) together in support of EU membership. Erdoğan and the newly established AKP rode this growing pro-EU wave, made the EU the anchor of the party's political survival strategy and became the "new carrier of the Kemalist dream of European integration."[112]

During its first three years in power, Erdoğan's AKP adopted two constitutional amendments and eight legislative packages to align Turkey's laws and norms with the EU.

These reforms helped the Erdoğan government carry out the most radical reforms on the military's political status in the history of the Republic. Erdoğan used Turkey's EU membership process to justify purging the Kemalists from the judiciary as well. He defended the reforms to restructure the judiciary, which ended up being staffed by Erdoğan loyalists, arguing that they would bring the charter into line with the EU, an argument he had previously in staunching the generals' power.

But from 2005 on, Turkey's commitment to EU membership started to waver. Secularist critics of Erdoğan saw that he was using the EU as a tool to weaken the Kemalist establishment. European pressure to settle the Cyprus problem, extend cultural rights to the Kurdish minority and recognize the deaths of Ottoman Armenians during World War I as genocide angered the nationalists. Caricatures published by a Danish daily in 2005 that included portrayals of the Prophet concealing a bomb inside a turban and as a knife-wielding nomad flanked by shrouded women reinforced the Turkish public's view that the EU was a Christian club. The Dutch and French referendums on the EU constitution in 2005, which were turned into a plebiscite against Turkish membership by Islamophobe politicians, further soured the Turkish public on EU membership.

Erdoğan had his own reasons to put the brakes on the EU membership bid. The European Court of Human Rights' decision that Turkey had not violated Leyla Şahin's right to education by banning the headscarf in university campuses, as well as EU criticism of the AKP's proposal to criminalize adultery, led him to conclude that the EU was not a reliable ally in his efforts to confront the secularist establishment and break down the restrictions on religion in Turkey. Erdoğan was also concerned about electoral dynamics. The ultranationalist Euro-skeptic Nationalist Movement Party (MHP) had been benefiting from the rising anti-EU sentiment at home. The MHP leader Devlet Bahçeli rebounded from his 2002 election defeat by accusing Erdoğan of being a lackey of the EU. Worried about losing the AKP's single-party majority in the parliament should the MHP surpass the 10 percent electoral threshold in the next elections, Erdoğan made an about-face in his commitment to EU membership.

Problems on the Turkey-EU front paved the way for another foreign policy move that served Erdoğan's efforts to emasculate the military.

ERDOĞAN'S STRATEGY TOWARDS HEGEMONY

Zero problems with neighbors

Ahmet Davutoğlu, who served as Erdoğan's chief foreign policy advisor for seven years before becoming foreign minister in 2009, was the ideologue of Erdoğan's foreign policy and the architect of Turkey's engagement with the Middle East; he coined the "zero problems with neighbors" policy. Before entering politics, Davutoğlu was an academic who sought to theorize a Middle East policy that was different from what he saw as the Kemalists' defensive and passive outlook on the region. His years of academic work provided an intellectual framework for Erdoğan's power grab. His foreign policy doctrine gave Erdoğan the ideas and metaphors to employ in domestic politics against his rivals. The "zero problems with neighbors" policy, which sought to develop close ties with Turkey's neighbors, primarily the ones in the Middle East, served that function until the Arab uprisings started. It was the foreign policy extension of Erdoğan's two-pronged approach towards the military, which advocated taking bold enough steps to marginalize the generals but not so bold as to provoke a response that would threaten Erdoğan's rule.

As a young academic and a prominent Islamist intellectual, Davutoğlu's writings in the 1990s had theorized a much more audacious foreign policy, one that sought to go beyond the Islamist populism of the past generation of Turkish Islamists. Turkish Islamists had long argued that the nation-states in the Middle East were artificially created by Western states to divide the Muslim community (*ummah*) and keep it weak. They promoted the unification of the *ummah* under the leadership of Turkey. The first Islamist prime minister, Necmettin Erbakan, was a strong believer in Islamic solidarity and advocated the idea that Muslims across the world could be unified into one *ummah*. He called for the establishment of a Muslim customs union, an Islamic NATO, an Islamic United Nations and a single Islamic currency—but he failed to implement any of those ideas during his short tenure as prime minister. Davutoğlu wanted to go beyond the rhetoric and provide a realistic roadmap to unite the *ummah*.

In his academic work, Davutoğlu held deeply skeptical views about the West. He argued that the West backed undemocratic regimes in the Muslim world, including in Turkey, because it was afraid that democracy would bring to power Islamic actors who hold anti-Western views. To Davutoğlu, the Kemalists, just like the Arab regimes, were the culturally alienated "illegitimate" elites who did not represent the will of the pious masses and imposed a top-down secularization on society. They were kept in power by a West that saw these undemocratic regimes as a safety valve against the rise of Islamic actors.[113] Davutoğlu often emphasized the unbridgeable gap between Islam and the West. He argued that Western civilization was suffering from consumerism and immorality and it was in a state of civilizational crisis because the Enlightenment rejected divine revelation as a source of knowledge. He argued that Islamic civilization was superior to Western civilization and that the Muslim world must resist Western hegemony.[114]

In Davutoğlu's view, Turkey had a critical role to play in this resistance. He thought that the collapse of the Ottoman Empire had left a political vacuum and paved the way for two tragic developments in the region: colonialism and the Cold War, which he saw as an "unnatural aberration, an abnormality in the history of the region."[115] Colonialism had led to carving up the region into nation-states and the Cold War kept this "abnormality" in place. According to Davutoğlu, political borders, including those of Turkey, were artifacts that split the *ummah*. Only through reunification, he argued, could the region realize its full potential. Turkey, as the heir to the Ottoman Empire that brought peace and stability to the Muslim lands, his argument went, had to take on this historic mission to once again unify the Muslims. Turkey had to use its Islamic identity and the Ottoman past to cultivate close economic, political and cultural ties with its fellow Muslim countries in the neighborhood. Davutoğlu saw this as the most natural way for Turkey to expand its sphere of influence.

To Davutoğlu, the Kemalists' rejection of Turkey's Islamic and Ottoman past made the country turn its back on the Middle East. Their prejudices against Islam and Arabs put Turkey on the fringe of regional developments and prevented it from playing a dominant role in the region.[116] For Turkey to claim leadership in transforming the Western-imposed regional order, Davutoğlu argued, it first had to go through a democratic transformation itself. His party's rise to power was a significant step towards that goal but for true democratic transformation to follow, the AKP had to capture control of all the levers of power from the secularist establishment. The "zero problems with neighbors" policy served that goal. It complemented Erdoğan's other endeavors to strip the military of its power by denying the generals the outsized influence they exerted on foreign policy making.

The brilliance of the "zero problems with neighbors" policy was its dual character. It was both an offensive and a defensive strategy that sought to subdue the military without risking a major clash with the generals. Davutoğlu, who in contrast to Erdoğan is an ideologically oriented figure, might have harbored a grand vision for the region when he theorized about and implemented the "zero problems with neighbors" policy. For Erdoğan, however, the policy was the foreign policy extension of his pragmatic approach to cautiously weaken the secularist military. It entailed cultivating friendly ties with regional countries, mostly based on trade and investment, without disregarding secularist sensitivities. The next section will explain what those secularist sensitivities are. It will argue that the "zero problems with neighbors" policy was radical enough to challenge the main premise of the Kemalists with respect to the Middle East but was not provocative enough to invite a strong secularist reaction. It was mostly in line with previous governments' efforts to establish friendly relations with regional countries.

The Kemalist view on the Middle East

For most of its history, Turkey has had a poor relationship with the Middle East, the roots of which go back to the years of Ottoman decline in the nineteenth century. To save the Ottoman state, which was being challenged by European interventions, territorial losses and the rise of nationalist sentiments among the imperial subjects, the Young Turk Movement, which was founded in 1889, advocated an Ottomanist ideology. This ideology was meant to save the multi-ethnic, multi-religious Empire by generating political loyalty to the fatherland (*vatan*) among the different ethnic groups through granting constitutional equality to all subjects under a modernized Ottoman state. The Young Turks themselves reflected that ethnic mosaic. They were Turks, Kurds, Arabs, Circassians and Albanians who shared a similar urban, educated middle class identity with close ties to the Ottoman military and the state. But the Ottomanist ideology had to be discarded because the non-Muslims of the Empire such as the Greeks, Bulgars and Armenians did not denounce their nationalist claims in exchange for equality before the constitution. After significant territorial losses and resulting demographic changes, this cosmopolitan ideology gave way to a Turkish nationalist ideology.

This shift in the Young Turks' ideology from Ottomanism to Turkish nationalism led to a rift between "Arab federalists and Turkish centralists."[117] The Arab nationalists' collaboration with the British against the Ottoman Empire in the hopes of establishing an independent Arab state created an official narrative in the Turkish psyche that characterized Arabs as "back-stabbers." The carving out of Arab states from Ottoman territories further severed ties between the Turks and Arabs.

This deep sense of suspicion and "betrayal" by Arabs colored the views of the Turkish elite who led the national independence struggle against Western powers under Mustafa Kemal and founded the modern Turkish Republic in 1923. The 1923 Treaty of Lausanne, which established the borders of the new Republic, granted Turkey full sovereignty in return for renouncement of all territorial rights to the Ottoman Arab provinces. The new Turkish Republic was created as an antithesis to the Arab world.[118]

This was most apparent in the new Republic's identification as a secular state engaged in a project of Westernization. Although the new state was unmistakably Muslim with an unprecedented Muslim majority, made possible through Turkish-Greek population exchanges and non-Muslim migration from the country due to discriminatory policies, the Kemalist state embarked on a project of building a secular national culture. The radical steps to eliminate Islam from the public sphere and control its public manifestations amounted to a cultural revolution meant to completely destroy the symbols and institutions of the Ottoman Empire.

ERDOĞAN'S STRATEGY TOWARDS HEGEMONY

The domestic reforms undertaken during the nation-building process set the stage for the country's Middle East policy. In the eyes of the Kemalist elite, Islam became the other of the new national culture and the Middle East was seen as an unstable, conflict-ridden, backward region. In the Kemalist imagination, the "Middle East represented what Turkey was, and not what Turkey wanted to be."[119] The modern Republic had to turn its face towards the West and pursue a cautious and non-interventionist policy towards its Arab neighbors. As a result, Turkey showed little interest in the Middle East. When Turkey became involved in regional affairs during the Cold War years, it was not due to a cultural identification with the region or valuing relations with the countries which were once part of the Ottoman Empire. Turkish involvement was a function of its Western alliance. Turkey's brief activism in the region in the 1950s was due to Ankara's desire to become a member of NATO and forge closer ties to the West. Once it secured NATO membership in 1952, it saw the region through the lens of Western security priorities. The quest to contain Soviet influence and Arab nationalism became the main prism through which Turkey engaged with regional countries.[120] In the 1950s when the center-right Democrat Party (DP) was in power, Turkey took part in Western-backed regional arrangements such as the British-led Middle East Command in 1951, the Middle East Defense Organization in 1952, and eventually the Baghdad Pact in 1955 to prevent Soviet incursion. The DP elite saw Turkey's engagement in the Middle East as a way to forge closer ties with the West.

Despite its engagement in regional affairs, little changed in Turkey's view of the Middle East. Even the DP, which split from the secularist CHP and laid claim to pious masses, held similar prejudices against Arabs and the Middle East as its predecessor. The Middle East was still considered to be a problematic, backward region that would only import problems to Turkey. Turkey continued to identify itself with the West, not with the Muslim Middle East. Many within the party were worried about the spillover of Islamist movements if Turkey got too involved in the region. In a reflection of that fear, the DP government banned the entry of Muslim Brotherhood brochures into Turkey in 1955.[121]

From the mid-1960s on, Turkey reverted to its passive Middle East policy. Until the end of the Cold War, Ankara tried not to become entangled in regional conflicts and supported the status quo. Maintaining borders and non-involvement in the domestic affairs of regional neighbors became the cornerstone of Ankara's policy.[122]

After the Cold War, developments in Turkey and the region made the Kemalists' policy of ignoring the region impossible. Center-right Prime Minister Turgut Özal's neoliberal reforms in the 1980s led to a resurgence of Islamic revivalism and Kurdish nationalism in Turkey. The rise of Islamic-oriented media, educational institutions and business associations provided grounds for the rise of an Islamic political identity. A similar transformation occurred on the Kurdish front. Economic expansion and political liberalization strengthened Kurdish demands for cultural rights. The Turkish state's rebuff of these claims led to an insurgency led by the PKK. These developments posed a challenge to the Kemalist monopoly in these spheres and heightened secularists' perception of threat.

Regional developments exacerbated the Kemalists' fears. The 1991 Gulf War paved the way for a stronger PKK presence in northern Iraq and a de facto Iraqi Kurdish state. The Kemalist establishment came to an unsettling conclusion that the Middle East could no longer be ignored. But as in the Cold War years, the Kemalists' engagement in the region lacked any cultural identification with the Middle East or references to the Ottoman past, which was deemed a threat to the secular nature of Turkey. Instead, they solely focused on advancing Turkey's national security interests through military alliances and the possible use of force. Countering the "Kurdish and the Islamist" threat was the main goal of their Middle East policy. Iran, Syria and Iraq fed the military's perception of threat. Post-Islamic revolution Iran was seen as a country that could try to export its Islamist ideology. The Turkish military feared that Iran's Kurdish minority, who had supported the uprising against the Shah, could establish an autonomous region. Fears of Kurdish separatism colored the military's view of Syria and Iraq. The Kurdish minorities in those countries and the PKK presence in both Iraq and Syria made them an existential threat.

ERDOĞAN'S STRATEGY TOWARDS HEGEMONY

The military advanced the narrative that Turkey was surrounded by hostile neighbors that were bent on destroying its secular character and carving out an independent Kurdish state. This alarmist, security-oriented approach depoliticized the country's foreign policy. Foreign, particularly Middle East, policy, was framed as the battle for survival of the Turkish Republic and thus beyond daily political debate. This narrative justified the military's involvement not just in foreign policy but also in domestic politics.

In the 1990s, several approaches that criticized this view emerged. Turgut Özal, who first served as prime minister of the center-right Motherland Party (MP) governments in the 1980s and president in the 1990s, was the first to break with the Kemalists' cautious Middle East policy. He argued that Turkey's traditional Middle East policy was too defensive. In the post-Cold War era, he thought, Turkey had to redefine its place in the region, desecuritize its approach to its neighbors and use its Islamic identity and Ottoman past as instruments to advance its interests. Despite his reference to Turkey's Islamic identity and Ottoman past, Özal saw the Middle East on utilitarian terms, not ideological. Unlike the Kemalists who viewed the region as a source of insecurity, Özal thought that the Middle East could offer Turkey many political and economic opportunities.

As the most critical figure in Turkey's transition to a neoliberal development model in the 1980s, Özal sought economic opportunities in Turkey's immediate neighborhood and made advancing economic relations with the region a cornerstone of his policy. He also thought that by cultivating close ties to its Arab neighbors, Turkey could cement its place in the Western alliance. Fearing a decline in Turkey's strategic importance to the West after the collapse of the Soviet Union, Özal pushed for policies that were in line with US goals in the region. Turkey threw its support behind the US during the 1990/91 Gulf crisis. It closed oil pipelines from Iraq and opened up its bases to coalition use for operations against Iraq. Özal pushed for further involvement in the conflict to demonstrate Turkey's value to the Western alliance. His activist policy and willingness to drag Turkey into regional conflicts drew the ire of the Kemalist establishment, leading to the resignation of General Necip Torumtay, the chief of Turkey's armed forces, in protest.[123]

Özal challenged Kemalist views on the Kurds as well. While the Kemalists saw the Kurdish question both at home and in the region through a security lens, Özal reached out to the Kurdish leaders in Northern Iraq, allowed the two Kurdish parties, Kurdistan Democratic Party and the Patriotic Union of Kurdistan, to open offices in Ankara and granted their leaders diplomatic passports.[124]

Ismail Cem, the foreign minister of the social democratic, DSP-led coalition government from 1997 to 2002, was another important figure who questioned the Kemalist Middle East policy. Cem was an interesting figure. Although he was a leading Kemalist-leftist intellectual, he criticized certain aspects of the Kemalist ideology. His most prominent critique was directed at the Kemalist Middle East policy, which he characterized as being "bereft of a historical dimension" and lacking the necessary cultural touch.[125] According to Cem, the Kemalist obsession with seeing everything through an Islam versus secularism divide had led to a belief that Turkey's involvement in the Middle East would jeopardize the country's secular order. Cem argued that distancing itself from a region with which it shared a common culture and history had prevented Turkey from taking center stage on the world scene.[126]

Like Özal, Cem wanted to use Turkey's Islamic identity and Ottoman past to enhance Turkey's interests and saw economic cooperation as an effective way to solve political problems with regional countries.[127] He pushed for an assertive Middle East policy and closer ties with the neighbors that were considered the most problematic by the Kemalist military. One such country was Syria, which hosted the PKK leader Abdullah Öcalan. Cem sent envoys to Damascus to solve the problems through dialogue and met with his Syrian counterpart to push for economic cooperation. His initial efforts failed. In 1998, the two countries came to the brink of war after Syria defied Turkey's repeated warnings to stop supporting the PKK and providing a haven for its leader Öcalan. But relations improved dramatically shortly after that. The same year, Turkey and Syria signed the Adana Agreement. Syria pledged to cease its support to the PKK and the two countries agreed to cooperate against terrorism.

ERDOĞAN'S STRATEGY TOWARDS HEGEMONY

Cem sought closer ties with Iran as well, another problematic country for the Kemalists who were critical of Iran's relations with Islamist groups in Turkey and its policy of turning a blind eye to PKK attacks from Iranian territory. The two countries had withdrawn ambassadors in February 1997 after Ankara accused the Iranian ambassador of fomenting Islamic radicalism in Turkey in response to Iranian ambassador's statements promoting the introduction of sharia law in Turkey. After a meeting between Cem and his Iranian counterpart Kamal Kharazi, the two foreign ministers decided to appoint new ambassadors. The Kemalist military criticized Cem's efforts to cultivate closer ties with Syria and Iran, the two countries considered to be supporting terrorism against Turkey. But Cem continued his efforts. He sought the cooperation of regional countries to ease the tension emanating from Iraq, tried to mediate in the Israeli-Palestinian conflict and pushed for a more active Turkish role in regional organizations.

In many ways, Davutoğlu's "zero problems with neighbors" policy was in line with Özal and Cem's endeavors to forge closer relations with regional countries using Turkey's Islamic and Ottoman past. They all viewed the region as a source of opportunity. Some call this foreign policy line "neo-Ottomanist." Many followers of the AKP's foreign policy treat the term as a new concept that was invented to refer to Erdoğan's regional policy. But in fact, the term was first coined by Cengiz Çandar decades ago to refer to Turgut Özal's foreign policy when he served as Özal's foreign policy advisor.

Özal and Davutoğlu's neo-Ottomanism was not only similar in the way they saw Turkey's past as an asset in its relations with regional countries, it was similar in how they approached the Kurdish question as well. The Empire had united diverse ethnic and religious groups. Özal saw neo-Ottomanism as a means of resurrecting the cosmopolitan spirit of the Empire that opened up space for different ethnic and religious groups. Davutoğlu similarly thought that the Kurds and the Turks could unite under the banner of Islam. A prominent Erdoğan advisor who was put in charge of the government's Kurdish policy, Yalçın Akdoğan, summarized this point well. In response to a question about the meaning of neo-Ottomanism, he said:

> It was a response to the desire and search of the conservative Muslims to feel proud of the Ottoman past, and an attempt to separate Turkey's understanding of Islam as Ottoman. In other words, Ottomanism represents our vernacularized understanding of Islam. This Islam is Sufi and state centric. The discourse of Ottomanism also seeks to address the Kurdish question that we do not need to be a nation-state in order to exist. We will address a number of issues if we integrate Turkish and Kurdish identities into Islam and then, this Islam will be filtered from the Ottoman experiences.[128]

Despite similarities between Davutoğlu's views and those of Cem and Özal, these politicians' stance on the West differed considerably from that of Davutoğlu, who saw an unbridgeable gap between the West and Islam. To Davutoğlu, Islamism was the main legacy of the Ottoman Empire.[129] However, the more radical views Davutoğlu advocated as an academic did not find a place in his "zero problems with neighbors" policy that guided Turkey's Middle East policy until the Arab uprisings. It served as a prelude to a more radical stance, which would be implemented when the time was ripe. To Davutoğlu, that time would come when the "illegitimate" regimes were swept out of power by Islamic actors. In Turkey, those actors had been in power since 2002 but the real power still rested in the Kemalists' hands. The Middle East too was run by its own "illegitimate" regimes. Until that changed, Davutoğlu argued, Turkey had to tread carefully.

One of the lessons Erdoğan and others in the AKP had learned from previous Islamist parties' closure by the secularists was that one had to be cautious on foreign policy matters. Necmettin Erbakan had drawn the ire of the secularist establishment with his controversial visits to Iran and Libya, which paved the way for his ousting. One of the "February 28 recommendations" the military asked Erbakan to implement after it launched its "soft" coup included an item on Erbakan's overtures to Iran. The National Security Council stated that Iran's intention to instigate instability inside Turkey had to be watched closely and policies needed to be revised to prevent Iran's interference in Turkey's domestic politics.[130]

Erdoğan's foreign policy was under scrutiny by the same circles. When his party came to power, many expected a clash with

ERDOĞAN'S STRATEGY TOWARDS HEGEMONY

Kemalists on the foreign policy front. The Erdoğan government's promotion of a deeper engagement with the Middle East, a more active role for Turkey in the Organization of the Islamic Conference and Erdoğan's vocal criticism of Israeli policies against Palestinians were particularly concerning to the Kemalists who feared Erdoğan would turn Turkey away from its traditional Western orientation.

Erdoğan played his hand wisely. To deny the Kemalists a pretext to bring down his government, avoiding a foreign policy that was antithetical to the Kemalist tradition became the trademark of his pre-uprisings regional policy. The "zero problems with neighbors policy" sought to improve Turkey's problematic relations with its neighbors while retaining the Republic's predominantly Western orientation. It deepened the country's ties to the Middle East while respecting the Kemalists' anti-Kurdish and anti-Islamist sensitivities.

Turkey's approach to the region started humbly. It was primarily driven by trade and investment, which fit the "conservative democrat" image Erdoğan was trying to build for himself and his party. To strengthen that image, Erdoğan underlined Turkey's Western identity, refrained from using Islamic symbols in public diplomacy, pursued a non-sectarian agenda and advanced relations with immediate neighbors only after securing their partnership in the fight against the PKK. Turkey's 2005 national security threat assessment document, the National Security Policy Document (NSPD), which is dubbed the country's "secret constitution," reflected Erdoğan's intention to stick to the Kemalist military's red lines in his Middle East policy. The NSPD's purpose is to identify threats to national security and define strategies. The military was a dominant actor in drafting the document but the presidency, the Ministry of the Interior, the Ministry of Foreign Affairs and the National Intelligence Service contributed to the draft which was approved by the Council of Ministers.[131] The 2005 document identified Iran and Iraq, among others, as the main foreign policy threats. The document stated that Iran's regime type as well as its nuclear program posed a grave threat to Turkish national security interests. Iraq was identified as a threat due to the presence of the PKK and the prospect of Iraq's disintegration which could pave the way for an independent Kurdish state. Erdoğan did not attempt to revise the document. Only in 2010 when he felt more confident with regard to his Kemalist rivals did the government remove Iran and Iraq as sources of threat from the NSPD. In a significant reversal, the 2010 NSPD defined these countries as allies with which Turkey should cultivate closer cooperation and a common vision.[132]

In line with the Kemalist tradition, the "zero problems with neighbors" policy refrained from meddling in the domestic affairs of regional countries. It prioritized deepening economic integration over a push for democracy. Opening up the political system or human rights considerations did not play a part in Erdoğan's Middle East policy until 2010–11. Erdoğan's stance on popular protests in Iran is a case in point. When millions of Iranians took to the streets in 2009 to protest against the re-election victory of the hard-line president, Mahmoud Ahmadinejad, arguing the elections were rigged, Turkey stood behind the regime saying it was an internal matter, and was one of the first countries to congratulate Ahmadinejad on winning the presidency.

Ankara developed cozy relations with the regions' autocrats. Erdoğan often called Syrian President Bashar Assad "my brother" and the two leaders vacationed together with their wives along the Turkish coast, as Turkey was mediating indirect talks between Syria and Israel. Erdoğan received the Qaddafi International Prize for Human Rights in 2010, months before uprisings started there.[133] Indeed, Turkey did not advance any revisionist claims regarding the borders in its immediate neighborhood before the uprisings, which had been a key principle in Kemalist foreign policy. This cautious approach helped Turkey make strides in a region which had long blamed the Ottoman Empire for its ills.

The success of the "zero problems with neighbors" policy in opening up a previously Turkey-skeptic region can be attributed to several factors. On the Arab street, Turkey with its booming economy and functioning democracy represented a model to be emulated by their own regimes. It was a Muslim-majority country and an EU aspirant run by pious leaders. Soap operas projecting a modern, yet Islam-compatible Turkish lifestyle brought what was possible for a Muslim country into their living rooms. The Turkish parliament's refusal to allow US troops to operate from Turkish soil in the invasion of Iraq contributed to Erdoğan's positive reception in the region—although Erdoğan had wanted parliament to approve the request. His denunciation of the Israeli President Shimon Peres at the World Economic Forum in Davos in 2009 in reaction to Israel's policies in Gaza turned him into a hero on the Arab street. The regimes welcomed Turkey's new activism in the region as well. Ankara sought to mediate in regional conflicts, invested in the region, played an active role in regional organizations and cultivated cordial ties with the regimes: but most importantly Ankara refrained from a "democracy promotion" agenda and Ottoman references in its public diplomacy.

The "zero problems with neighbors" policy was an important component of Erdoğan's efforts to curtail the military's power. It challenged the Kemalist military's defensive posture towards the Middle East and advanced the view that the region could offer Turkey's growing economy many opportunities without jeopardizing the country's security interests. This approach, which was welcomed by many in Turkey, desecuritized the country's Middle East policy. It prioritized trade and investment, promoted cooperation instead of conflict and focused on soft power instead of hard power. It did so without risking a major confrontation with the military.

Between 2002 and 2011, there were a few cases of policy divergence between Erdoğan and the Kemalists. The biggest risk Erdoğan took in revising policy on an issue that was vital to the Kemalists was on the Cyprus question. His support for UN-led unification efforts on the island met with strong criticism from the Kemalist power brokers, the military, the Ministry of Foreign Affairs and the presidency, which had previously resisted such international efforts. But the issue resolved itself before it became a major clash between the two rivals. The AKP-backed UN process failed when the Annan plan was approved in a referendum by a majority of the Turkish Cypriots but rejected by a majority of the Greek Cypriots.

Another foreign policy disagreement between Erdoğan and the Kemalists was over Sudan. The government's overtures to the Muslim-majority nation in the Horn of Africa, controlled by a nominally Islamist government with historic ties to the Muslim Brotherhood, drew criticism from Turkey's Western allies as well as the Kemalists at home when Erdoğan paid a visit to Khartoum in April 2006 to attend an Arab League summit. Even more troubling to many was Erdoğan's visit to Darfur where the Sudanese President Omar Hassan al-Bashir had orchestrated a massive campaign of ethnic violence that had claimed the lives of tens of thousands of civilians. The slaughter had drawn widespread international condemnation, with US Secretary of State Colin Powell calling the killings genocide.[134] As controversial as it was, Erdoğan's overture to Sudan, but more generally to Africa, at the time had little to do with Islamist ideology. It was primarily driven by economic considerations and was part of Turkey's wider plans to acquire a more significant profile in Africa as a venue for Turkish investment. Erdoğan's trip to Sudan raised eyebrows within the secularist camp but it hardly amounted to a policy revision.

Similarly, efforts to secure a larger role in the OIC were seen as an extension of Erdoğan's Islamist ideology. After intense labors, the government succeeded in securing the election of Turkish citizen Ekmeleddin İhsanoğlu as OIC Secretary-General in 2005, ruffling feathers in Kemalist circles. But Turkish efforts to enhance its influence in the OIC were not new. Ankara has seen the organization as a vehicle to garner support for its Cyprus policy since the 1960s when the Cyprus question started occupying a central place in the country's foreign policy. Despite being one of the founding members of the organization, Turkey's influence initially remained limited. But Ankara gradually expanded its involvement by financing the OIC budget in 1974, opening the Statistical, Economic and Social Research and Training Centre for Islamic Countries (SESRIC) in Ankara and the Research Centre for Islamic History, Art and Culture (IRCICA) in Istanbul in 1978–79 and chairing the Standing Committee for Economic and Commercial Cooperation (COMCEC) in 1984.[135]

As a result of the growing Turkish influence in the organization, the OIC started paying closer attention to the Cyprus question. The sixth Islamic Conference of Foreign Ministers held in 1975, for instance, hosted Turkish Cypriot leader Rauf Denktaş, who delivered his views on the Cyprus issue. In 1976, the organization recognized the "equal rights" of both ethnic groups on Cyprus and invited the Turkish Cypriots as "guests" to the conferences and upgraded them to "observer" status a few years later.[136] Turkey's efforts to become more active in the OIC continued under Turgut Özal in the 1980s. This paid off in 1991 when the OIC granted the "Turkish community of Cyprus" rights of representation on all OIC bodies. Ankara welcomed the move as "full membership in all but name."[137] Like Özal, Ismail Cem also envisioned a more active Turkish role in the OIC. Under his watch, the "OIC-EU Joint Forum: Civilization and Harmony" convened in Istanbul in February 2002.[138]

Overtures to Sudan and the search for more active participation in the OIC remained marginal matters. Erdoğan's foreign policy until 2011 did not deviate from past foreign policy moves on big ticket foreign policy items such as Israel-Palestine, Iraq, the EU, Syria and Iran. In that sense, the "zero problems with neighbors" policy was not entirely novel but it served Erdoğan's ultimate goal of weakening the military. It was both an offensive and a defensive strategy. It was defensive because it did not promote a revisionist foreign policy that would provoke a strong reaction from the military. It was in line with past efforts that sought engagement with the region to advance Turkey's interests. It was offensive because by cultivating friendly relations with Middle Eastern neighbors, it challenged the military's dominant position in foreign policy making.

Syria: The test case

Syria occupied a unique place in Erdoğan's domestic strategy. It became the test case for the policy of "zero problems with neighbors" because of the peculiar role the country had played in Turkish politics. What made Syria different from Turkey's other neighbors was the special relationship the Syrian regime cultivated with Turkey's arch enemy: the PKK. Throughout the 1980s and 90s, Syria provided military support to the PKK and sanctuary to its leader, Abdullah Öcalan. The close ties between the two increased the PKK's popularity among Syrian Kurds and made the country the most important recruiting ground for the militant group. That is why, for decades, Turkey saw Syria as one of the biggest security threats against its territorial integrity. The security risk Syria posed expanded the Turkish military's already strong influence over the country's regional and domestic politics. Generals often cited the Syrian regime's collaboration with the PKK to make the case that Turkey was under attack from enemies within and without and to legitimize their power over policy making.

The long history of fraught relations between the two countries and the impact it had on the Turkish military's sway over politics made Syria the central pillar of the "zero problems with neighbors" policy. Erdoğan hoped to build on a process of "normalization" that had begun under the previous government to desecuritize Turkey's relations with its most problematic neighbor. Mutual threats were replaced with messages of brotherly relations. Military concerns gave way to trade and investment as the key agenda of the new era. After decades of hostility, Syria became Turkey's gateway to the rest of the Arab world. This new era in bilateral ties was a success story not only for Erdoğan's regional policy but also for his domestic attempts to sideline the military.

A troubled past

The collapse of the Ottoman Empire had profound implications for Turkey's relations with Syria, which had been ruled from Istanbul for almost four centuries. The growth of Arab nationalism in the Syrian provinces in the last decades of the Empire and the 1916 Arab revolt, led by Sharif Hussein of Mecca, against the Ottomans were the main developments that had led to the construction of mutually hostile Turkish and Arab narratives. While Turks saw the Arabs as untrustworthy and back stabbers, Syrians criticized Turks for having turned their backs on Islam and blamed their own ills on "Ottoman imperialism" after gaining independence. Persecution of revolutionary Arab figures during World War I increased the anti-Turkish sentiment in Damascus, which considered itself the "beating heart" of Arab nationalism. Images of Arabs being mistreated at the hands of the Turks in popular culture fed into the animosity.[139]

This animosity grew further after France gave Turkey the Syrian province of Alexandretta (Hatay) in 1938 to secure Turkey's cooperation in the Second World War. Syria never accepted the legitimacy of the unification. In official maps and popular culture, Hatay remained part of Syria and Turkey was deemed to be the "occupier of Arab land."[140]

As the two countries embarked on projects to dam the Euphrates river for energy and irrigation purposes in the 1960s, the dispute between them grew further. The clash over water intensified in 1983 when Turkey initiated a giant irrigation and energy scheme, the Southeast Anatolia Development Project (GAP). Turkey was forced to fund the project itself after it failed to secure credit from international financial institutions due to protests from the Arab countries.[141]

Adding to the tension were the Cold War dynamics. Turkey and Syria allied with opposing fronts. Turkey was a key member in NATO's southern flank while Syria allied with the Soviet Union. To Syria, Turkey was advancing Western interests in the region at the expense of Arab interests. To Turkey, Syria's Arab nationalism provided fertile ground for the Soviets to expand their influence in the region. These long-standing grievances led to Hafez al-Assad's decision to support Turkey's enemies as a bargaining chip for water and Hatay.[142] The most consequential of those enemies was the founder of the PKK, Abdullah Öcalan.

The PKK leader flees to Syria

Just before the 1980 coup in Turkey, PKK leader Abdullah Öcalan fled to Syria to lead the group from exile. He had established the PKK in 1978 as a Marxist-Leninist organization composed primarily of Turkish Kurds to set up an independent Kurdish state in an area comprising the Kurdish regions of Turkey, Iraq, Iran and Syria. After Öcalan gave assurances to the Syrian regime that he would not mobilize Kurdish nationalism in Syria, the Assad regime agreed to provide him with refuge as well as military and financial support, as part of Assad's strategy to use the Kurds against Turkey. From then on, the PKK became the dominant issue in bilateral ties for two decades. After the PKK launched its armed insurgency against Turkey in 1984, Assad's collaboration with the group became an even bigger problem for Ankara. For Turkish decision-makers, particularly the military, Syria became a country that harbored "terrorists" fleeing Turkey.

Turkey pursued a similar strategy in response. As the Muslim Brotherhood stepped up its operations against the Syrian Baathist regime, Turkey became a safe haven for the Syrian Muslim Brotherhood members. A US Department of Defense report written in May 1982 argued that Muslim Brotherhood militants infiltrated Syria through Iraq and Turkey.[143] A Turkish official hinted in a 1989 meeting in Ankara that Turkey was supporting the Muslim Brotherhood in retaliation for Syria's support of the PKK.[144]

Besides Turkish efforts to pressure the Assad regime, there were also attempts to resolve the tension through peaceful means. Prime Minister Turgut Özal sought to improve relations with Syria through a water pipeline project. On an official visit to Damascus in July 1987, Özal signed security and economic cooperation protocols that included increasing the amount of water Syria received.[145] But Özal failed to resolve the problem. Damascus moved senior PKK members to the Bekaa valley, which was under its control at the time, but continued to aid the PKK. In response, Turkey continued to restrict the downflow of the Euphrates.

The end of the Cold War and Turkey's military alliance with Israel in 1996 emboldened Turkey to pursue more confrontational policies toward Syria.[146] There were still efforts to resolve the problems with Syria through dialogue. Ismail Cem, the Kemalist foreign minister of the DSP-led coalition government from 1997 to 2002, led these efforts. He sent a senior Turkish diplomat to Damascus in March 1997 to convey Turkey's willingness to start negotiations to resolve the bilateral problems peacefully. Cem met with his Syrian counterpart in Doha during an OIC meeting and urged the two countries to develop close economic ties to address the political problems. As a result, Syria withdrew a resolution critical of Turkey's policy on the Euphrates and Tigris Rivers.[147] Despite Cem's efforts, relations continued to decline.

ERDOĞAN'S STRATEGY TOWARDS HEGEMONY

The prospect of a military conflict started brewing in 1998 when Turkey threatened to use military force if Syria did not stop its support to the PKK. Thousands of troops were mobilized along the border. Turkish President Süleyman Demirel declared that Turkey was running out of patience and Syria would have to live with the consequences of its support for the PKK.[148] Damascus yielded to the pressure. It expelled Öcalan and signed the Adana agreement with Turkey. With the agreement, the two parties established a direct telephone link to enhance communication with each other, appointed special representatives in each other's diplomatic missions and initiated a mechanism of "monitoring of security enhancing measures and their effectiveness."[149] Syria closed down the PKK's training camps and ceased to provide logistical support to the militant group.

The Adana agreement proved to be a turning point in the two countries' long, troublesome relationship. Turkish President Ahmet Necdet Sezer's historic visit to Syria to attend Hafez al-Assad's funeral in 2000 heralded the dawn of a new era which would see an unprecedented level of cooperation between the two countries.[150] A couple of months after Sezer's visit, Turkey and Syria signed a security cooperation agreement and a memorandum of understanding restarting the Joint Economic Committee that had been inactive since 1988.[151] Erdoğan built on these past efforts to turn the bilateral ties into a strategic partnership. Kemalist circles in Turkey attributed forging close ties to the Assad regime to Erdoğan's Islamist urge to develop relations with Turkey's Muslim neighbors. But Erdoğan was pursuing a much more sophisticated strategy, one that went against any Islamist instincts he might have had.

Turkey's Islamists have had a complicated relationship with the Baathist regime in Syria, which gained prominence in the 1940s and promotes secular Arab nationalism and Arab socialism. With a 1963 military coup, the Baath party became the ruling party. The secular Baathist regime initially banned the activities of the Muslim Brotherhood in 1964 before Baathist General Hafez al-Assad who seized power in a 1970 coup, banned the movement altogether and imposed the death penalty on its members in 1980.[152] Turkey's Islamists are divided into two camps based on their views of the

Baathist regime. One camp led by Necmettin Erbakan, who held strong anti-Western, anti-Zionist views and often used anti-Semitic language, saw the Baathist regime as an important component of the "axis of resistance," a power bloc that includes Iran, Syria, Hezbollah, and Hamas and seeks to confront US and Israeli interests in the region. Therefore, when the Muslim Brotherhood ramped up its fight against the Baath regime in the 1970s, Erbakan advised the Muslim Brotherhood members who asked for his support not to launch an armed struggle against the regime, arguing this would only benefit Israel and the West.[153] Erbakan did not publicly criticize the Assad regime even after it brutally crushed a Brotherhood-led uprising in Hama in 1982. He sought to reverse Turkey's troubled relationship with Syria in the 1990s when he became prime minister.

The other Islamist camp had a completely different view. They saw the regime as "the administration of Nusayri atheist Assad."[154] The term "Nusayri" has been used by Sunni Islamists as a derogatory term toward the Assad regime and the Alawites more generally. To Sunni Islamists, including Turkish Islamists, "Nusayris" are "greater infidels than the Jews and Christians" and therefore waging "jihad" against the Assad regime is a religious duty for all Muslims.[155] This Islamist camp saw a parallel between Kemalists and Baathists. To them both were "Godless elites" who imposed a top-down program of secularism on a religious society and divided the *ummah* into what these Islamists saw as artificial nations.

The anti-communism prevalent among Turkish Islamists, particularly after the Soviet invasion of Afghanistan in 1979 inspired "jihad against communism" in the Muslim world, was another factor in the Islamist camp's negative view of the Syrian Baath regime. Due to the close relationship between Hafez al-Assad and the Soviet Union, many Turkish Islamists saw the Assad regime as a communist threat. Therefore, they supported the Muslim Brotherhood's "jihad" against the regime in the 1970s. While Erbakan refrained from publicly criticizing Assad or endorsing the Brotherhood's fight, the mouthpiece of his party, Milli Gazete, ran articles calling Assad "killer" and Alawites "infidels", and threw its full support behind the Brotherhood.[156] Erdoğan and Davutoğlu

ERDOĞAN'S STRATEGY TOWARDS HEGEMONY

were in this camp, which saw the regime as the illegitimate elites of a minority sect that had done more damage to Islam as a religion than the West. If Erdoğan was acting on Islamist urges, he would not have forged the close ties he did with Damascus. His Syria policy was part of a carefully crafted strategy to purge his opponents at home and do this in the name of democracy, economic prosperity and peaceful relations with neighbors, goals that were difficult for anyone, including the military, to oppose.

The backbone of Erdoğan's Syria policy was increasing trade and expanding markets. Davutoğlu promoted creating economic interdependence as an effective way of resolving and preventing conflicts. A Syria policy built on advancing Turkey's soft power helped Erdoğan build his image as a pragmatic leader who sought to shift the focus away from military power to finding new markets for Turkish goods. The new policy had the added benefit of helping the Islamic bourgeoisie that supported Erdoğan's rule and countering the influence of the secular business elite.

The reforms undertaken in the 1980s to liberalize the Turkish economy and implement the precepts of the Washington Consensus led to the rise of the export-oriented Anatolian Tigers. These socially and religiously conservative central Anatolian cities where companies experienced a boom in production and capital accumulation formed the core of the Islamic bourgeoisie.[157] To counter the influence of the traditional secular business elite represented by the Turkish Industry and Business Association (TÜSİAD), this burgeoning, pious, economic class established its own business association, the Independent Industrialists and Businessmen's Association (MÜSİAD) in 1990. The Islamist Welfare Party's capture of over 200 municipalities across Turkey in 1994, including those in Ankara and Istanbul with their huge budgets, strengthened this rising class. The Islamic bourgeoisie swelled the ranks of the AKP and was influential in the party's electoral success. MÜSİAD members helped the new party establish local branches and formulate its economic policy. Some twenty of them were elected as Members of Parliament for the AKP in the 2002 elections.[158] MÜSİAD, along with increasingly influential Chambers of Commerce in the booming cities of southern Anatolia and the Gülen-affiliated Confederation of Turkish Businessmen and Industrialists (TUSKON), pushed for closer political and economic ties with Syria.

Developments on the Turkey-EU front helped Erdoğan's aim of deepening ties with Syria. As Turkey started to sour on EU membership from 2005 onward, Middle Eastern markets offered an alternative. The 2008 global financial crisis, which had serious implications for employment in Turkey, strengthened this trend. The lesson learned was that a protracted crisis in the EU could slow Turkey's externally driven economic growth and Turkey had to diversify its trade and investment partnerships with the Middle East.[159]

Both Turgut Özal and Ismail Cem had put considerable emphasis on trade and investment in Turkey's regional engagements, but these past efforts faced several domestic and regional challenges. Erdoğan, on the other hand, enjoyed a favorable context to implement the policies of a "trading state." By the time he came to power, Turkey's economy had become much more integrated into the global economy and foreign trade had expanded considerably within the gross national product of Turkey. The emergence of a robust civil society with a stake in trade also facilitated Erdoğan's efforts to deepen trade ties with Turkey's neighbors. But more importantly, under Erdoğan, constituencies such as the military that had been opposed to the policies of a trading state in favor of a security-oriented approach were forced to soften their approach.[160]

As a result, Turkey-Syria relations flourished. Syria became Turkey's gateway to the wider Arab world. Turkish exports passed through Syria to reach Jordan and the Gulf. In October 2009, the Strategic Cooperation Council, composed of ministers of the two countries, met in the Syrian city of Aleppo and the Turkish town of Gaziantep. The aim of the meetings was to enhance Turkey's influence in Syria and the rest of the region through trade: a goal that was wholeheartedly supported by the Turkish business community.[161]

Bashar al-Assad's January 2004 visit to Turkey marked the first ever visit to Turkey by a Syrian president. The two leaders decided to open a consulate in Gaziantep and commercial centers in border provinces to facilitate trade between the two countries. Bashar's visit was historic for another reason. By putting his signature on documents recognizing Turkey within its current borders, the Syrian leader gave up Syria's claim over Hatay, removing a key irritant in bilateral ties from the Kemalist perspective.[162]

Prime Minister Erdoğan's December 2004 visit to Syria improved relations further. Turkey and Syria signed a bilateral free trade agreement and resolved the water issue. Erdoğan said that Syria could use more water from the Euphrates River.[163] The agreement was not only meant to enhance trade ties between Turkey and Syria but also to ensure cooperation and economic interdependence in the region. The two countries lifted visa-requirements in 2009, which increased bilateral trade. Direct foreign investment by Turkey grew to the point where some Turkish companies relocated significant proportions of their production capacity to Syria. The volume of Turkish-Syrian trade jumped from $824.1 million in 2003 to $1.84 billion in 2010. In 2011 alone, Turkish companies invested a total of $223 million in Syrian metal, food, cement, and open-sea fishing industries.[164] Turkish companies invested heavily in infrastructure projects as well, particularly in the northern Syrian city of Aleppo. They built cement plants and hotels and invested in the oil industry. The number of Syrian visitors to Turkey increased more than sevenfold between 2002 and 2011, prompting a tourist boom in the southern Turkish cities of Antakya and Gaziantep.[165]

Erdoğan could not have succeeded in forging close relations with Syria if he had crossed the military's red lines and jeopardized Turkey's security interests. Syria had already pledged to cooperate with Turkey against the PKK as part of the 1998 Adana agreement. The US invasion of Iraq aligned the two countries' security interests further. The war unleashed a massive sectarian civil war and led to the rise of al-Qaeda-linked groups and a push by Iraqi Kurds for increased autonomy. These problems, coupled with the PKK enjoying increased sanctuary in post-invasion northern Iraq, heightened the Turkish military's fears of Kurdish separatism.[166] Syria was equally worried about the destabilizing consequences of the war. During Bashar al-Assad's January 2004 visit to Turkey, he said that establishment of a Kurdish state was a red line both for

Turkey and Syria and discussed the best ways to deal with the effects of a US invasion.[167]

Turkey's secularist President Ahmet Necdet Sezer's insistence on visiting Syria in April 2005 was a testament to the fact that Erdoğan's efforts to deepen ties with Damascus had the backing of important segments of the Kemalist establishment. The visit came at a time when the Syrian regime was under increasing international pressure due to its alleged involvement in the assassination of Lebanese Prime Minister Rafik Hariri. The Bush administration was leading a campaign to isolate Syria. In response to a question about Sezer's upcoming visit, Eric Edelman, the US ambassador to Turkey, said that the international community had reached a consensus on Syria, which required Syria to withdraw from Lebanon and that the US hoped Turkey would comply with that decision.[168] President Sezer was defiant. When, after Edelman's remarks, he was asked by a journalist whether he would still go to Syria, he said "of course I will."[169]

Erdoğan's Syria policy did not break from the country's traditional Western orientation either. Erdoğan was careful not to risk further rupture with the US, which was already disappointed by the Turkish parliament's decision not to allow US troops to operate from Turkish soil to attack Iraq. Turkey's military partnership with Syria remained limited to protecting Turkey's southern border and Turkey only ramped up efforts to ease Syria's isolation after calls to pull Syria out of Iran's orbit began to be voiced in the US following the 2006 Lebanese War. In 2007–08, Turkey hosted indirect peace talks between Syria and Israel. Although Turkey's initiative did not secure a peace agreement, it paved the way for the EU and the new US administration to end their diplomatic boycott of Damascus. Erdoğan happily accompanied Bashar al-Assad when French President Nicholas Sarkozy visited Syria in 2008, breaking the international boycott. Ankara also tried to mediate between Syria and Iraq after Baghdad was struck by one of the deadliest attacks in a series of bombings in 2009. The Baghdad government blamed the Baathist exiles living in Syria and the Syrian government for harboring Iraq's enemies in their attempts to destabilize the country.[170] Turkey hosted the parties in Istanbul and offered to establish a border security mechanism to combat the PKK, al-Qaeda and Baathist forces in Iraq.

Ankara's mediating role helped Erdoğan's regional and international image and increased the Erdoğan government's strategic value to the West. Having been accepted as a mediator by both Israel and Syria boosted his clout in a region that had seen Turkey as a hostile power due to its historical legacy.

Erdoğan's pro-reform agenda along with his pro-EU posture and "zero problems with neighbors" policy helped him emerge as a Muslim democrat both at home and on the international stage. As he took gradual steps to capture key state institutions from the Kemalists, many saw him as the embodiment of a different kind of Muslim leader who rejected the previous Islamist parties' revisionist policies, liberalized the country's political system and sought friendly relations with the West. His Middle East policy was equally popular. It started humbly, largely focusing on trade and investment. The "zero problems with neighbors" policy promoted diplomacy, soft power and economic interdependence in Turkey's relations with the Middle East. Erdoğan managed to open a new chapter in a region viewed as a source of insecurity without challenging existing state strategies. Anti-Kurdish and anti-Islamist military red lines largely remained intact, and so did the Kemalists' pro-status quo posture that sought to avoid intervening in domestic affairs of regional countries. These policies proved quite popular not only at home but also in the pre-uprisings region. Erdoğan became the most popular leader in the Arab street and Turkey was seen as a constructive actor and an economic and democratic success story.[171] But more importantly, these policies provided Erdoğan with the legitimacy and the popular backing to rein in the secularist establishment.

The Muslim democrat image cultivated by Erdoğan helped him become an autocrat. By the time popular protests spread across the Arab world, Erdoğan had won the war against the military, captured key institutions from the Kemalists and concentrated power in his hands. Conservative democracy, the "zero problems with neighbors" policy and the pro-EU agenda had served their purpose. He set his eyes on a new goal: switching the country's parliamentary system to an *a la Turca* presidential system that would grant him unprecedented powers without any restraints. That goal called for an entirely new game plan.

2

ERDOĞAN TURNS TO ISLAM

What happens to the populists' war between "good people" and "evil elites" once populists become the new elite? Erdoğan's post-2011 strategy might give you an idea. One would expect Erdoğan's claim that the "silent majority" has been shut out by the secularist establishment to fail after almost a decade in power subdued the secularists and made him the establishment. But it did not. Erdoğan continued to portray himself as the victim even at the height of his power. After he eliminated his secularist rivals in the military and the judiciary, he turned to Islam to cultivate a new narrative of victimhood in which the West and its domestic conspirators were trying to undermine the Sunni Muslim community. This section explores Erdoğan's strategy of utilizing Islam to mobilize support for establishing an executive presidency and how he saw the Arab uprisings as an opportunity that would help him execute his plan.

Erdoğan's "Turkish-Islamic manifesto"

"Believe me, Sarajevo won today as much as Istanbul, Beirut won as much as Izmir, Damascus won as much as Ankara, Ramallah, Nablus, Jenin, the West Bank, Jerusalem won as much as Diyarbakır." Prime Minister Erdoğan was delivering his victory speech after his party won a third term with about 50 percent of the vote in the June 2011 general elections. He was alluding to his aspiration to be the voice of Muslims across the world. His speech struck a different tone from his past victory speeches. He sounded more confident and defiant. The speech was imbued with Islamic themes and Ottoman glory. It was the harbinger of a new chapter in Erdoğan's war.

The change in tone became more apparent at the fourth AKP convention held in September 2012. In what would have been considered a bold move a few years earlier, the AKP convention hosted the newly elected Egyptian President Mohammed Morsi, the leader of the Egyptian Muslim Brotherhood, Khaled Meshaal, leader of the Palestinian branch of the Muslim Brotherhood, Hamas, and Masoud Barzani, president of Iraq's autonomous Kurdistan region. Morsi delivered a speech thanking Erdoğan for his support during the uprisings in Egypt. The ostentatious welcome Morsi and Meshaal received at the convention was in sharp contrast to the secret reception given to Meshaal after Hamas's 2006 election victory out of fear of a secularist backlash.[1] Barzani's speech, which he delivered in Kurdish, was another indication that Erdoğan had grown confident against the Kemalists who had long objected to having official contacts with Barzani and other Iraqi Kurdish leaders, let alone allowing them to address a Turkish crowd in Kurdish.

Erdoğan's own speech during the convention confirmed this newfound confidence. It was couched in Islamic terms with frequent references to the Ottoman Empire. The speech was in marked contrast to Erdoğan's previously cautious tone. Erdoğan had broken away from Necmettin Erbakan and rejected his Islamist legacy to establish the AKP. After the party's rise to power, Erdoğan strongly emphasized his disillusionment with Islamism. It was an attempt to allay the secularists' fear that the new government would impose an Islamic lifestyle. But in the victory speech he delivered after his party won a third term, Erdoğan embraced Erbakan and pitched himself as the leader executing God's plan. His speech was interrupted by chants of "*Mücahit Erdoğan*" (Erdoğan the Islamic warrior), which had never been heard at an AKP meeting before.[2] Erdoğan, who once built his entire political survival strategy on Turkey's EU membership and talked about the EU at every opportunity, did not mention the EU except to criticize Germany and France for their Islamophobic policies. The daily *Taraf* carried the story of the AKP's fourth convention with the headline "Turkish-Islamic manifesto."[3] It was clear that Turkey under Erdoğan had entered a new era.

Gone were the days when Erdoğan trod cautiously so as not to provoke the Kemalists. He had sidelined the military, ended the Kemalist hegemony in the judiciary and consolidated power in his own hands. The most telling example of how far Erdoğan had come in curbing the military's power was the removal of an e-memorandum which was issued by the military on April 27, 2007. The e-memorandum had been posted on the Turkish Armed Forces' (TSK) website, issuing a veiled warning against the government's push for Abdullah Gül's presidency, which the military saw as a threat against the secular nature of the Republic. In August 2011, the e-memorandum was removed. Now that he had vanquished the Kemalist bastions within the state, Erdoğan was focused on switching the country's parliamentary system to an *a la Turca* presidential system that would extend his powers without checks and balances. Erdoğan ordered his party to start laying the groundwork immediately. On November 5, 2012, the ruling AKP officially introduced its proposal to parliament to create a strong presidential seat for Erdoğan.[4]

Despite the 326 seats in the 550-seat assembly captured by the AKP in elections, the party still lacked the majority to make unilateral constitutional changes. This meant Erdoğan needed allies to transform the parliamentary system into a centralized presidential one. In the past, he had relied on the pro-democracy alliance that included liberals, leftists and religious conservatives to achieve his goals. Branding his party as "conservative democratic" and pursuing a pro-reform agenda helped him mobilize these segments of society to end the country's military tutelage. But he could not justify building an autocratic regime with the conservative democratic brand. The pro-democracy alliance would not rally behind such a project either.

The chairman of the AKP's Istanbul branch, Aziz Babuşcu, succinctly summarized the party's parting of the ways with its old allies:

> Those who were partners with us in one way or another during our ten-year period of government will not be partners with us during the next ten years. The future is a period of construction. The construction period will not be to their liking. Therefore, those partners will not be with us. Those who walked together with us yesterday in one way or the other, will be partners with the forces that are against us tomorrow. Because the future that will be constructed and the Turkey that will be built will not be a future and a period which they will accept"[5]

That is why Erdoğan turned to Islam and the conservative segments of the country to build that new Turkey.

"One state, one nation, one flag and one religion"

Erdoğan gave a speech at his party's Adana convention in May 2012. The convention was taking place in the midst of the heaviest fighting between Turkey and the PKK in three decades. Commenting on the ongoing conflict, Erdoğan said "I have four red lines: one state, one nation, one flag and one religion."[6] In the past he had made similar comments to reiterate his commitment to the unitary nature of the state in response to Kurdish demands for decentralization. But his past remarks did not include "one religion." This was a reference to Sunni Islam, to which the large majority of the country belonged, but one that excluded its sizable Alevi minority. It was the clearest indication that Erdoğan sought to construct a new national identity. He wanted to socially engineer a model citizen who is pious, conscious of his Ottoman past and obedient to the state. His previous references to the country's Ottoman past and Islamic civilization had taken on a new meaning.

In the pre-2011 era when Erdoğan still felt vulnerable vis-à-vis the Kemalists, he toed the Kemalist line that saw Turkey's Muslim identity as one of the markers of Turkishness. Erdoğan and the AKP elite referred to Turkey's Ottoman past and its place in Islamic civilization as complementary to the country's Western vocation. But from 2011 on, Erdoğan redefined Turkey as a Sunni Muslim nation and a central pillar of the universal Muslim community (*ummah*). It was an attempt to challenge the Kemalist notion of nation and redefine it along lines that would suit his agenda of replacing the parliamentary system with an executive presidency. Contrary to the Kemalist conceptualization of the Turkish nation, which had viewed ethnic Turkishness as the central characteristic of Turkish national identity, Erdoğan framed Muslimhood and the Ottoman legacy as the core elements defining the nation. In his narrative, the history that defined the nation started in 1071 when the Seljuk Turks defeated the Christian Byzantines and Islamized Anatolia. The Ottoman Empire was built on this, and the Republic Mustafa Kemal established was the continuation of the glorious Ottoman state. By defining the Ottoman past as the golden age of the Turkish nation, Erdoğan's project for a Sunni Muslim nation challenged the historical basis of Kemalist nationalism, which rejected the Ottoman legacy and viewed the foundation of the Republic as the origin of the Turkish nation.

It is important to note that Islam was important in the Kemalist construction of Turkish national identity as well. Although in the early years of the Republic Turkishness was defined along secular lines, Sunni Islam was considered a de facto criterion of Turkishness. Non-Muslims, even those of Turkic descent, were not included in the nation. The Turkish-Islamic Synthesis (TIS), which was embraced as the de facto state ideology by the leaders of the 1980 coup, viewed Islam and Turkishness as central to Turkish national identity. But the main goal of the TIS was to widen the appeal of Turkishness by blending it with Islam. Erdoğan's definition was different from both the early Kemalist definition and the one advocated by TIS in the 1980s. In Erdoğan's new conception of nation, Islam was no longer a cultural feature of Turkishness but an identity that was independent of Turkishness.[7] According to this understanding, Turkishness was one among many other ethnic identities and Islam was the tie that bound different ethnic groups together.

After having rejected Erbakan's Islamist legacy, Erdoğan had now embraced a version of it. The central place Erdoğan assigned to Islam and the Ottoman Empire in the country's national identity and his fierce anti-Westernism were in line with Erbakan's Islamist tradition. But Erdoğan deployed a "thinner" understanding of

Islamism in which Islam was instrumentalized to mobilize a coalition of Islamists, pious Turks and Kurds for his political goals. Islam was stripped of its moral code, reduced to a "performative piety" and became a tool to cover up corruption and delegitimize opponents.[8] In Erdoğan's new Turkey, Islam became the main identity of the state and both state and the nation were sacralized as religious entities.[9]

According to this nationalism, Islamic and Western civilizations did not complement each other but were mutually exclusive categories. In stark contrast to his previously pro-Western posture, Erdoğan argued that under his watch, Turkey became a Muslim nation that finally freed itself from the harmful effects of hundreds of years of Westernization.[10] He often cited Islamic values to reject Western hegemony and challenge the Western-led international order. In 2013, he called for an overhaul of the United Nations, saying its Security Council had failed to address the conflict in Syria and other global challenges. He slammed the five permanent representatives of the UN Security Council (UNSC)—the UK, France, China, Russia and the US—saying "the world is bigger than five" to underline that the post-World War II international order was not adequate to address current problems.[11]

Erdoğan branded himself as the vanguard of the cross-class, multi-ethnic, morally upright and pious Sunni Muslim masses that had been systematically marginalized by the West and its domestic secular conspirators. In this conceptualization, the good majority—the "people"—were imagined to be Turkey's pious Sunni Muslims who were conscious of their Ottoman past and obedient to the state and the Muslim *ummah*. This narrative allowed Erdoğan to pitch himself not only as the protector of Turkey's Muslims but also the transnational Muslim community against the powerful, oppressive, Westernized elites. It helped him create a new chronicle of victimhood at a time when he captured all state institutions from the secularist elite, and legitimize the new status quo by presenting it as a necessary step in his "holy mission" to lead the *ummah* towards greatness.

The Arab uprisings provided Erdoğan with the perfect opportunity to burnish his image as the "protector of Muslims" and "savior of the *ummah*" and legitimize his electoral authoritarianism. Erdoğan fiercely criticized what he saw as the lack of Western support for the rise of the Islamist Muslim Brotherhood in Egypt after popular uprisings toppled the autocratic Hosni Mubarak regime. In his mind, real democracy meant the rise of Islamic identity against the culturally alienated, Westernized elite. To him, his "new Turkey" was a shining example of this democratic awakening where the "true representatives" of the pious masses came to power through elections and ended the reign of "internal colonizers." Democracy, to Erdoğan, meant re-empowerment of the Muslim masses marginalized by Kemalist authoritarianism. The ballot box was the only instrument of accountability and the sole source of democratic legitimacy. The "national will" was considered sacred and it was only expressed through the ballot box.

Under Erdoğan's electoral authoritarianism, elections became "emotional and high-stakes" events through which the voters elected a leader to become the embodiment of the nation. He often referred to "our national values," "historical values" and "our civilization." As the leader of the nation, Erdoğan defined those values, often with reference to Islam, and declared those who did not subscribe to his vision as "Islamophobic" and "enemies of true democracy." After passing a law to restrict alcohol consumption, Erdoğan defended it by referring to Islam and saying "Is there anything wrong with pursuing a policy ordered by religion?"[12] Erdoğan did not think he needed anything other than elections to legislate his own vision and impose an Islamic way of life on the rest of the country. Once the elections were over, he expected voters to become passive, obedient citizens whose only duty was to cheer everything he did. He demanded absolute obedience and gratitude for everything he had done for the nation. Society's demands were not tolerated because he, as the embodiment of the "national will", represented the "equitable and compassionate" state and determined in an absolute way what was right and fair for the entire society. Civil rights and liberties, separation of powers, and checks and balances, which are key features of democracy, meant little to Erdoğan. For him, democracy exists because the "national will" is in power.

Erdoğan pitched his efforts to centralize power as part of a historic mission. That mission was to undo the Kemalists' Westernizing reforms that forced the nation to forget its Islamic and Ottoman past. Erdoğan urged the new generation not to look to the West but to its own history to find contemporary rights and liberties.[13] By reconnecting with its past, Turkey could lead the *ummah* and become a global power. By defining Turkey as a member of another civilization, Erdoğan justified his turn away from Western-rooted universal democratic norms and push for his own version of democracy, which viewed the ballot box as the only instrument of accountability and disregarded all other autonomous institutions of the state such as the legislature or the courts.[14]

Erdoğan evoked Islam to delegitimize his opponents. Several times during campaign rallies before the 2011 elections, Erdoğan reminded the public that the leader of the pro-secular main opposition party CHP, Kemal Kılıçdaroğlu, belonged to a minority group called Alevis, a historically persecuted sect which is considered an offshoot of Shia Islam.[15] His remarks suggesting that Alevis are not real Muslims were meant to pander to the prejudices of the country's Sunni majority and reinforce the boundaries of his Sunni Muslim nation project. To Erdoğan, only those who shared his conservative Islamic values belonged to the nation. In Erdoğan's mind, even the institutions such as the judiciary had to serve the national interest and reflect the "native and national" soul of the country while making its decisions.[16] He called his followers the one and only "native and national" (*yerli ve milli*) force. Those who were opposed to him were called domestic foes. Thus, power-sharing with these "non-native" and "non-national" forces was out of question.

Erdoğan's conception pushed large segments of society out of the scope of the nation and gave the conservative segments of the country a powerful new reason to back his undemocratic practices. This new conception of national identity also allowed Erdoğan to dismiss Western criticism of his drift to electoral authoritarianism. He denounced the West for allegedly trying to undermine Turkey's democracy with its criticisms and rejected EU progress reports that pushed for inclusive and democratic practices. A Freedom House report that criticized the state of press freedom was dismissed as a colonialist exercise and those who agreed with the findings of the report were called "internal Orientalists."[17]

Erdoğan's role model in his efforts to monopolize power was a controversial sultan who ruled with an iron fist, curtailed freedoms, purged opponents, severed ties with the West and used Islam to justify his autocratic policies: Sultan Abdulhamit II. Erdoğan used the idealized memory of Abdulhamit to boost his narrative that he was the bearer of a historic mission to defend Islam against attacks by the West and restore Turkey's position as the leader of the Muslim world.

"They took down Abdulhamit, we will not let them take down Erdoğan"

Bilal Erdoğan, Erdoğan's younger son, was giving a talk at an event organized to commemorate the 100th anniversary of Sultan Abdulhamit II's death. These events commemorating Abdulhamit II had become commonplace since Erdoğan's 2011 victory. Bilal told the audience that Sultan Abdulhamit II had put a spoke in imperialism's wheels, just like the younger Erdoğan's father, who had slammed the concentration of power at the United Nations, saying, "the world is bigger than five." Bilal said that Abdulhamit's fall led to the fall of Jerusalem, dealt a blow to Muslim unity and paved the way for the colonization of Muslim countries. Abdulhamit II's removal from power, Bilal argued, unraveled "Pax Ottomana," an order that "brought peace" to the region. He ended his talk with a vow: "They took down Abdulhamit, we will not let them take down Erdoğan."

Erdoğan is often likened to Abdulhamit II by his supporters and critics alike. Abdulhamit II's legacy has been controversial in Turkey. Many, including staunch Kemalists, have vilified him as a despot who curtailed freedoms, purged opponents and jailed journalists while conservatives, particularly Islamists, have lionized him as the last great caliph-sultan and the defender of Islam against the encroachments of Western imperialism. Indeed, the parallels between the two leaders are uncanny.

Sultan Abdulhamit II came to the throne in 1876 at a time when the Ottoman Empire was experiencing a long period of decline.

Territories in the Balkans had been lost and nationalist movements that were gathering steam were threatening the multi-ethnic Empire. Meanwhile, Europe was forging ahead with industrial development, leaving the Ottomans even more vulnerable. To save the Empire, a series of Western-inspired social and political reforms, called Tanzimat reforms, were implemented. Abdulhamit II came to the throne against this background. Like Erdoğan, who promoted Turkey's EU membership and carried out liberalizing reforms in the early years of his rule, Abdulhamit II supported reforms in his first few years on the throne. He promulgated the first Ottoman constitution written by liberal Ottomans and thus established a form of constitutional democracy that provided limited electoral participation and curbed some of the Sultan's powers. He opened up powers for parliament, upheld the secularizing policies of the Tanzimat era and stuck with Tanzimat's traditional, British-focused foreign policy.

Despite their initial support for reform, both Erdoğan and Abdulhamit II ruled in more autocratic ways after they consolidated power in their own hands. They both purged those they had allied with early in their rule. After the Ottoman Empire lost territories in the Russo-Turkish War in 1877–78, Abdulhamit II thought that he had to rule with an iron fist to protect the Empire from further dismemberment. He closed down the parliament, suspended the constitution, curtailed freedoms and jailed journalists. To hold the Empire together as well as to justify his autocratic policies, Abdulhamit II turned to Islam. In the face of territorial losses, and the first indications of Arab nationalism and Western Christian domination of the Islamic world, he used Islam and his religious responsibility as caliph to unify Muslims under his leadership. Promotion of Islamic unity (İttihad-ı İslam), or Pan-Islamism, within and outside the Empire became Abdulhamit II's key survival strategy against foreign and domestic enemies.[18] By using Islamic symbols, he upheld the Islamic character of the Ottoman state and sought to generate support from Arabs and Muslims across the world. The central role he attributed to Islam helped Abdulhamit II generate legitimacy for his autocratic rule. Through his role as caliph and the defender of the faith, he sought

ERDOĞAN TURNS TO ISLAM

to form a direct sacral link with the people and avoid "inconvenient intermediaries like political parties and parliaments."[19] He relied on Naqshbandi networks to galvanize grassroots support and promote unity among the population but Abdulhamit II also tightly controlled Islamic groups to prevent them from becoming an independent focus of allegiance.[20]

Erdoğan, too, pursued a similar path once he neutralized his opponents. Immediately after he sidelined the Kemalists and brought the military, judiciary and the media under his control, he set his eyes on expanding his powers even further. He pushed for an executive presidential system that would grant him unprecedented powers and cripple all checks and balances. The most striking parallel between the two leaders is their use of Islam as a tool to justify their authoritarianism at home and to serve their foreign policy goals. Like Abdulhamit II, Erdoğan turned to Islam to mobilize support for his autocratic rule.

Erdoğan pitched himself as the authentic representative of the pious masses who were in his view scorned, oppressed and excluded by the Westernized secularist elite for decades. In his thinking, the great religion of Islam had been wiped out of the public realm due to Kemalists' westernizing reforms. It was thanks to him, he argued, that the pious masses—the authentic owners of the country—were finally liberated but there was still much to do to cement their hard-fought gains. To do that, he warned, he had to extend his powers. Otherwise, the country would face a similar fate to that of the Ottoman Empire, which Erdoğan supporters argue disintegrated after the fall of Abdulhamit II. Ahead of the referendum to switch to Erdoğan's long-held dream of an *a la Turca* presidential system, Nilhan Osmanoğlu, the greatgranddaughter of Sultan Abdulhamit II, threw her support behind Erdoğan's efforts to establish one-man rule, saying, "In order to prevent our president from being isolated just as was the case of Abdulhamit II, and to support a more powerful Turkey, and a Turkey which makes its own decisions, I support 'Yes'."[21] Erdoğan's supporters argue that he, just like Abdulhamit II, who was deposed in a 1909 coup, is surrounded by domestic and foreign enemies who seek to bring him down. Both leaders had to fight off Zionists, liberals and the

West to defend the state, the nation and above all Islam. Under such an existential threat, they claim, neither leader had the time nor the resources to continue with the reform agenda.[22] Thus, it was only natural for these leaders to become increasingly authoritarian to focus on the real task of defending Muslim existence from existential threats.

Like Abdulhamit II, Erdoğan pursued a foreign policy that aimed to unify the Muslim world under his leadership. He projected himself as the savior of the *ummah*, which had been kept weak by decades of Western imperialism. The Arab uprisings, which coincided with Erdoğan's consolidation of power and turn to Islam, provided him with an opportunity to strengthen the Islamic character of his new Turkey. Erdoğan used the idealized memory of Abdulhamit II to support his narrative that "New Turkey" and the Islamic world were under attack by the West and that he was the bearer of a historic mission to defend Islam and restore Turkey's role as the leader of the Muslim world. Appropriating this idealized Ottoman past allowed him to legitimize the Sultan-like powers he has long sought to capture.

Erdoğan, the protector of Muslims

It is important to unpack the "Islamism" in Erdoğan's post-2011 Islamist populist strategy. The Islamism Erdoğan deployed did not embody a coherent set of principles, practices and ideals. Rather, it was a superficial display of religiosity and a quest to empower the Muslims who supported Erdoğan's presidentialism project at home and protect "Muslim interests worldwide."[23] Empowering "Muslims" at home entailed catering to the demands of Erdoğan's supporters and providing them with perks. In 2011, for instance, Erdoğan changed the rules for university entrance exams that were introduced by the February 28 coup in 1997 to keep students of Imam Hatip schools out of the secular higher education system. With the new changes, Erdoğan removed the disadvantages posed to Imam Hatip graduates. In 2013, Erdoğan lifted the decades-long ban on women wearing the headscarf in state institutions. He also staffed high-level bureaucracy with Islamist supporters, gave government contracts to Islamist businessmen and transferred funds and state property to Islamist NGOs.[24]

Erdoğan's efforts to cater to his Islamist base led to fears that he might launch an Iran-style Islamist revolution that would establish a government rooted in religious law.[25] But the Islamist populist agenda Erdoğan pursued did not challenge the secular nature of the state. Rather, it secularized Islam "for the purposes of culture and memory, particularly in reinvigorating the past greatness of the Turks from the Ottoman days."[26] Erdoğan's Islamist populism was mostly in line with the decades-long Kemalist practice of controlling and co-opting Islam to mobilize constituencies, legitimize the state's authoritarian practices and contain ethnic conflict. A deeper look into the peculiar nature of Turkish secularism is warranted here to make sense of this point.

The secularism Turkey has been practicing for decades differs from other modern secular states. The French model of secularism, which is called laicism, is anti-religious. It sees the state as the ultimate arbiter of what is good for society and promotes freedom from religion. The Anglo-Saxon model of secularism, on the other hand, does not trust the state and seeks to protect religion from state interference. It promotes freedom of religion.

The Turkish model is distinct from these models. Officially, Turkey has been a secular state since 1937 but Sunni Islam has been the unofficial state religion. Secularism in the Turkish context is not about the separation of religion and politics. Instead of seeking freedom of or from religion, Turkish secularism seeks to maintain the control and use of religion via state power.[27] The aim is to create an "enlightened Islam" and serve the goals of the state. Turkish secularism's unique character is the product of Ottoman modernization and the nation-building process under Mustafa Kemal.

The Young Turks, who were predecessors of the Republican elite and first-generation agents of secularism, were influenced by French positivism and Jacobinism, which sought to create the ideal society through state-led, top-down social engineering. To strengthen the Ottoman state against Western encroachments and ethno-religious uprisings in the Balkan territories of the Empire, they embraced French faith in science and technology and the state's capacity to transform society by dismantling old institutions and practices and imposing top-down education. Unlike secularism in the Western world, which developed in response to the societal need for peace and stability, Turkish secularism was a response to the needs of the state. Both under the Ottoman Empire and the Turkish Republic, the state maintained its priority over Islam and Islam remained a tool to be utilized by the state.

Mustafa Kemal and his friends used the Jacobin theory of radical transformation to build the new Turkish nation and utilized Islam to mark the boundaries of the political community. Although Mustafa Kemal, like other Turkish modernizers, viewed Islam as an obstacle to the modernization of the state, he employed it to mobilize the masses against Western invasion. He viewed Muslimness as the glue that would tie different Muslim ethnic groups in Anatolia to the Turkish nation on which he sought to build the new Republic.[28] Thus, being a Sunni Muslim and a Turkophone became the most important markers of being a Turk in the new Turkish Republic. This ethno-religious imagination of the nation denied non-Muslims and Kurdish and Alevi citizens full membership in the political community. They have been discriminated against and subjected to violence.

One of the institutions created by the Kemalist elite to impose their vision on society was the Turkish Directorate for Religious Affairs (Diyanet). The Diyanet was established as a state institution in 1924 to not only manage and control Islam but also to help the state utilize religion for its purposes. It became the primary ideological vehicle to establish state hegemony over all religious activity and justify the Kemalist understanding of secularism.[29] Both its structure and activities reflected the Kemalist vision. Although Alevis constitute the second largest religious community in Turkey after the Sunnis, the Diyanet was created only to represent Sunni Muslims and treated Alevism as a heterodox interpretation of Islam. This denied Alevis the privileges granted by the state to Sunnis, leading Alevi calls for the abolition of the Diyanet or a change in the structure to allow for Alevi representation.

The state's control and utilization of religion continued after the country switched from a single-party rule to multi-party politics in

ERDOĞAN TURNS TO ISLAM

1945. The Kemalist elite in the CHP introduced voluntary religious classes in schools to curtail the appeal of conservative parties that pushed for more public visibility for Islam. Under the center-right Democrat Party (DP), which was elected in 1950, Islam was utilized to co-opt pious constituencies and contain ethnic conflict. Kurdish tribal leaders were co-opted under DP rule to prevent a collective Kurdish movement and promote Turkish-Kurdish rapprochement. With the beginning of armed conflict between Turkey and the PKK in 1984, the Turkish state's efforts to contain ethnic conflict via Islam accelerated. Through Imam Hatip schools in the Kurdish regions, the state promoted the idea of Turkish-Kurdish unity through Muslimness.[30]

The 1980 coup leaders' strategy to use Sunni Islam as a counterweight to radical left-wing groups in Turkey, such as Kurdish separatist and Alevi groups that were ideologically allied with Marxism, paved the way for an even closer alliance between the state and Islam. The 1970s had been marked by fighting between right-wing ultranationalists and radical left-wing groups that led to thousands of deaths in the wake of the government's inability to address the growing violence in the country. Coupled with the global threat of communism posed by the Soviet Union, the military's number one concern leading up to the 1980 military coup was the rise of the radical left in the country. The military turned to the Islamists to contain the "communist threat." Although the coup leaders viewed Islam and Islamist groups with suspicion, they also saw Islam as a tool to legitimize their repressive practices and curtail the influence of left-wing groups. To that end, the 1980 coup regime clamped down harshly on leftist organizations, diminished the power of ultranationalist organizations and prosecuted political party leaders while sparing the Islamist movement. The Islamist National Salvation Party (NSP) leaders were prosecuted after the coup but, unlike ultranationalist party leaders and leftists, no death sentence was demanded for them.

The 1980 military regime cultivated close relations with Sunni Islamic orders (*cemaat*). The goal was to secure the religious orders' support for the coup and the referendum in which Turkish society would vote on the military-drafted constitution. In return, the military would not target these groups. The agreement worked for both parties. The Islamic orders supported the coup to a large extent. Mehmet Kırkıncı, the leader of the *Nurcu* brotherhood in the eastern province of Erzurum, wrote a letter to the coup leader General Kenan Evren praising the coup and advising the military leadership to introduce compulsory religious education. Kırkıncı went on a tour across the country to tell his followers that the 1980 coup was good for the country and that they should vote "yes" in the upcoming referendum.[31] The military regime followed the advice and made religion compulsory for primary and secondary schools. It also strengthened Imam Hatip schools and built mosques in Alevi villages. General Evren cited the Quran and the sayings of Prophet Muhammed in his public speeches to rally support behind the military and advise citizens to be good Muslims by not rebelling against the state. The military also used Islam to contain ethnic conflict in the Kurdish region. Turkish military planes dropped leaflets in the Kurdish region containing verses from the Quran asking the Kurds not to rebel against the state.[32]

The military's new thinking about Islam as a tool to combat left-wing radicalism and to rally support for its repressive policies was formalized in a concept originally developed by the right-wing nationalist Intellectual Hearth (*Aydınlar Ocağı*) in the 1970s. This became the de facto state ideology after the coup: Turkish-Islamic Synthesis (TIS). Through TIS, Hearth sought to bridge the gap between the ultranationalists and the Islamists to curb the rise of radical left-wing groups. Ultranationalists and Islamists clashed over whether Islam or Turkishness should dominate Turkish identity. The former saw ethnic Turkishness as the core of Turkish identity while the latter disregarded ethnic Turkishness in favor of Islam as the core. Hearth saw Islam as the essence of Turkish culture and also as a social control mechanism that would counsel all citizens to obey state authority and resist the infiltration of "foreign ideologies" such as communism into the national culture. The goal of Hearth was to create national unity around Islam to prevent the recurrence of the 1970s' ideological clashes between the country's right-wing and left-wing segments. Despite the prominence given to Islam in Hearth's formulation of Turkish identity, Hearth did not advocate an Islamic state. Rather, it pushed for an authoritarian state that would ensure peace and stability. To the members of Hearth, Islam had to be fostered in schools but not politicized.[33]

The 1980 coup leaders adopted Hearth's TIS vision in its entirety. They still viewed ethnic Turkishness as the more important component but by stressing Islam's core place in Turkish national identity, they sought to increase Turkishness' appeal among the country's conservative segments. As the de facto ideology of the state, TIS guided the country's post-1980 education and culture policies. Hearth members assumed important positions in the state bureaucracy and participated in drafting the 1982 Constitution.[34]

By adopting TIS, the professedly secular military agreed to tactically open up space in politics and society for Islam.[35] As part of TIS, the military introduced mandatory Sunni Islam classes in state schools. Other steps included increasing Diyanet's budget and personnel, building new mosques, encouraging new religious organizations, increasing the number of places offering Quran courses, providing new opportunities for graduates of Imam Hatip schools and tolerating religious bureaucrats.[36] The coup leaders did not see the adoption of TIS as a move contradicting the Kemalist understanding of secularism. To the contrary, they viewed it as a necessary tool to prevent the politicization of Islam and the rise of radical ideologies that might threaten the state. Co-opting Islam was seen as an effective way of securing the state's supremacy over all sectors of political, social and cultural life. According to the coup leaders, the state would control religious education much more effectively if religion courses were offered at state schools. Otherwise, the thinking went, families would turn to religious brotherhoods to provide religious education for their children.

The policies Erdoğan pursued after 2011 were mostly in line with the state's use of institutions and resources to control and utilize Islam for its own purposes. After Erdoğan reached his initial goal of eliminating the Kemalist establishment as a threat to his rule, he used Islam to manufacture consent to establish an executive presidency. This did not mean Erdoğan tried to establish Islamic governance. Rather, he sought to Islamicize society by promoting "Muslim domination" in every sector of social, political, economic and cultural life and to de-secularize the state by staffing the bureaucracy with people from religious orders (*tarikat*) and religious communities (*cemaat*) that supported him. Although his control and utilization of religion was not new, Islam's expansion into social life with active promotion by the state at unprecedented levels, particularly in the fields of family, education and law, was a novelty.[37] Erdoğan transformed Diyanet into a key tool to achieve these goals. He incorporated religious orders and organizations into state institutions and paved the way for them to grow in all sectors of life. He launched new religious organizations through family-controlled religious foundations (*vakıf*) to ensure his domination in the religious field[38] and reorganized the education system in a dramatic way to "raise pious generations." All these policies formed the basis of Erdoğan's Islamist populist agenda.

Raising pious generations

"Raising pious generations" has been the hallmark of Erdoğan's Islamist populist agenda. He announced his mission shortly after his 2011 election victory. According to him, the ideal young person was one who "carries a computer in one hand and a Quran in the other."[39] To Erdoğan, it was the duty of the state to construct this ideal youth. He had criticized the Kemalists' top-down social engineering for decades but now that he had captured all state institutions, he saw no contradiction in launching his own social-engineering project. His "Quran-holding youth" stood in stark contrast to Atatürk's pro-Western, fiercely secular youth entrusted with guarding the Kemalist principles of the Republic.

Through symbolic grand events, Erdoğan sought to challenge Kemalist historiography and mobilize the youth behind a new social identity, the main component of which was Muslimness. The Ministry of Youth and Sports, which was reestablished by Erdoğan in 2011, was in charge of executing these symbolic projects. One such project was to transform mixed summer camps into gender-segregated camps. Another was an event called "The Gate to the Anatolia Manzikert" to commemorate the Battle of Manzikert in 1071 in which the Christian Byzantine army was defeated by the

ERDOĞAN TURNS TO ISLAM

Seljuq Turks and the Islamization of what is now called Turkey began. The battle of Manzikert was not a prominent event for the Kemalists, which was one of the reasons why Erdoğan appropriated it as an alternative historic marker for his own nation-building project.[40] As part of the Manzikert project, the Ministry of Youth and Sports launched a campaign to find 1,071 young men bearing the name of the sultan who had led the Seljuk armies: Alparslan. Tents resembling those used during the Manzikert war were set up and thousands of young people took part in the event.[41] The Ministry launched several such projects and widely publicized them across the country with the slogan "The Youth in the Footsteps of the Martyrs" (*Gençlik Şühedanın İzinde*), to rewrite Kemalist history and replace the commemoration of events that occupied an important place in the Kemalists' nation-building strategy.[42]

Erdoğan's most visible means of raising a pious generation has been education. Starting from 2011, he took several critical steps that dramatically reorganized the education system. Erdoğan poured billions of dollars into religious education. He significantly increased the number of Imam Hatip secondary schools, which were originally founded by the state as vocational institutions to train young men to become imams and preachers, and extended this system to lower age groups.[43] Imam Hatip schools were founded in 1924, closed down in 1931 and reinstated in the 1950s. After their reinstatement, graduates were only allowed to pursue higher education in theology faculties to prevent them from obtaining a secular education, which would have paved the way for them to seek employment in the Turkish bureaucracy. In the 1970s, the rules were changed again, letting Imam Hatip graduates enter any university depending on their performance in the university entrance exams, making imam hatip schools a parallel system of education that provided manpower for the Islamist movement.[44]

After the February 28 coup, the rules reverted to make it difficult for graduates of Imam Hatip schools to enter faculties other than theology. Prior to the coup, parents could enroll their children in any school from sixth grade onward, but the military increased compulsory schooling from five to eight years to curb the expansion of Imam Hatip schools. As intended, all these changes led to a significant drop in the number of students enrolling in these schools.

Erdoğan reversed this trend through a series of policy changes. The parliament passed a law package termed "4+4+4," which allowed students to enter vocational schools, including Imam Hatip schools, after fifth grade rather than ninth grade.[45] While before Erdoğan's reforms, religious schools were one of the options for parents, the reforms turned them into a "central institution in the education system," leaving no choice for families but to enroll their children in these schools,[46] and some students being automatically enrolled against the will of their parents. By 2015, the number of students enrolled in Imam Hatip schools had reached 1 million.[47]

The national curriculum was also Islamized under Erdoğan. At regular public schools, he increased the number of hours dedicated to religious education, introduced courses on the Quran, the life of the Prophet and the fundamentals of religion, and banned the teaching of evolution from the curriculum.[48] In the national curriculum, concepts such as human rights have been Islamized, adultery has been condemned, and the term "tolerance" has been explained in reference to the Medina Covenant, which was used by the Prophet Muhammed to govern relations between Muslims and non-Muslims.[49]

Another component of Erdoğan's plan to raise pious generations has been the unprecedented role that religious orders (*tarikat*) and religious communities (*cemaat*) have been encouraged to play in education. Even before Erdoğan, religious orders were active in the education field, opening private schools and dormitories which helped them recruit members, but their influence has grown exponentially under Erdoğan. One million students are attending schools run by religious orders.[50] Private dormitories run by religious orders make up more than half of the number in the country. The number of madrassas, Islamic religious schools, has skyrocketed in the last few years with hundreds of them operating in Istanbul and the Kurdish region. These madrassas provide education for six to ten years, accept children as young as 3 years old and have student exchange programs with schools in Iran, Iraq

ERDOĞAN TURNS TO ISLAM

and Syria. Many of the teachers in these madrassas received Islamic training in Iran and Iraq in the 1980s and 90s and are affiliated with Turkish Hezbollah, which is supported by Iran but is Sunni and different from the Lebanese Hezbollah. According to court documents, the majority of the Turkish citizens who joined ISIS received education in these schools.[51] The government encouraged the establishment of private schools, universities, kindergartens, and student dormitories run by the religious orders and funded them from taxpayers' money, while public schools remained underfunded.[52]

Paving the way for social Islam

Erdoğan's Islamist populist agenda included measures to pave the way for social Islam to infiltrate state-managed affairs and societal life. Social Islam refers to religious orders (*tarikat*) and religious communities (*cemaat*) as well as religious foundations that are not controlled by the state. These religious orders and communities played an important role in Ottoman social and political life. The Westernization and secularization reforms that started in the second half of the nineteenth century weakened their influence, and they were forced underground by the Kemalist revolution, which outlawed them in 1925. Despite the ban, from the 1950s onwards center-right governments allowed religious orders to resume some activities. The most significant of these religious orders is the Naqshbandi-Khalidi Sufi order from which the majority of Turkey's Islamic communities hail. Although Sufi orders are known to focus on mysticism and the withdrawal from public life over a strict interpretation of sharia law, the Naqshbandi order is an exception. The order follows the orthodox Sunni tradition, strictly adheres to sharia and "emphasizes the need to conquer the state from within by aligning themselves with powerful sources of capital and political actors."[53] The most well-known of these communities is İskenderpaşa, which produced the country's first Islamist party, the National Order Party led by Necmettin Erbakan in 1970. Erdoğan and other leading figures within the AKP all come from the İskenderpaşa community.

Turkey's center-right political parties have long cultivated a clientelist relationship with these religious communities. Political parties provided patronage to them in return for their electoral support. But there was no organic relationship between these parties and religious communities and these communities never played a direct political role. Instead, they often supported different political parties in every election cycle and retained their autonomy.[54] However, under Erdoğan, these religious orders and communities assumed an influential role in bureaucracy, politics, economy and society. For the first time in Republican history, religious communities have lost their autonomy and become part of everyday politics. They declare political support for Erdoğan before every election, call voting for Erdoğan's rivals *haram* (forbidden under Islamic law), advocate that their supporters back Erdoğan in any way they can and comment on everyday politics in support of Erdoğan's policies.[55] In return, Erdoğan paved the way for these religious communities to grow in all sectors of life. Many of them have established companies, schools, hospitals and student dormitories. A popular saying among conservatives refers to the predominant presence of religious communities in sectors such as construction: "Islamic fighters have become contractors" (*mücahitler müteahhit oldu*). Erdoğan backed these religious communities by giving them land, providing financial support and access to the bureaucracy. But Erdoğan's close relationship with these groups in no way meant that he fully trusted them. His strategy was to make them dependent on him financially to secure their support. But he also exploited the divisions within these communities to make sure they remained weak enough not to challenge his rule. If none of these tactics worked, the leaders of religious communities who failed to support Erdoğan were sent to prison, their properties were confiscated, and their members were harassed by state authorities.[56]

The religious community that benefited the most from Erdoğan's rule was the Gülen community. Led by the preacher Fethullah Gülen, the movement was Turkey's most powerful Islamic faction before the Erdoğan-Gülen fallout in 2013. The Gülen community is a branch of the Nurcu movement, which grew out of the Naqshibandis. The movement's main goal was "to rejuvenate faith to rebuild an ethical society where justice prevailed."⁵⁷ Thus, the followers of the Nurcu movement tried not to get involved in politics and voted for center-right parties to curb the influence of the secularist state.

Fethullah Gülen grew up in the northeastern Anatolian town of Erzurum and started his career as a preacher. He became an Islamic activist in the 1960s and was detained after the 1971 military intervention, which became a turning point in his life. In an effort to keep a low profile, he promoted building schools that provided secular education and opened student dormitories in Turkey's largest cities in the 1970s. His movement mobilized successful young people from modest backgrounds to win their loyalty and incorporate them in its ranks to spread Gülenist ideas. Gülen saw secular education as a critical tool to provide upward mobility to his followers and prepare the next generation of rulers. Islamic education was reserved for neighborhood reading groups.

The economic liberalization of the 1980s transformed the Gülen movement from a network of pious people to an "education-cum-media global movement."⁵⁸ The student dormitories became private educational institutions. The movement expanded its operations into trade, finance, industry and media, becoming one of Turkey's most powerful religious communities. Gülenists supported the co-existence of Islamic piety and free market capitalism. Religious conversation circles, known as *sohbet*, became platforms to bring together business-minded religious people. In return, they donated to the cause.⁵⁹ The movement promoted entrepreneurship and partnership among these pious businessmen and mobilized them to become involved in strategic economic sectors both to collect funds for welfare and service provision and to leverage market power.⁶⁰ To improve coordination among members, the movement established regional trade associations. In 1996, several of these associations combined their sources to open Bank Asya, one of the country's largest banks that was "interest-free." In 2005, partners in Bank Asya established the Confederation of Businessmen and Industrialists in Turkey (TUSKON), which became the country's largest private business-related organization and challenged the dominance of TÜSİAD, which was considered Turkey's secular, pro-Western business organization.⁶¹

The success of the Gülen schools in providing high-quality education legitimized the movement's efforts to expand its activities to the Balkans and the newly independent Central Asian republics in the 1990s. By the 2000s, the movement's education network had expanded to more than 100 countries.[62]

Capturing secular spaces in education, media and the market further transformed the Gülen movement. It gradually abandoned its faith-based activities and became a religio-political movement that aimed to control state bureaucracy.[63] The first target of the Gülenists was the national police force. By 2002, when Erdoğan's AKP came to power, the Gülenists had full control of the recruitment and promotion processes of the national police force. The movement used its influence over the police force to protect itself against its opponents. Gülenist police were encouraged to use intelligence, fabricate facts and blackmail those whom they thought could threaten their interests.[64]

The Gülenists' control of state institutions reached historic heights with Erdoğan's rise to power. Gülen and Erdoğan's common fear of the military united them in the campaign against the Kemalists. For Gülenists, Erdoğan could not only protect the gains they had made for decades but also offer a golden opportunity to staff bureaucracy with Gülenists and expand their control over other state institutions. For Erdoğan, the Gülenists would not only serve as support against the secular establishment but also provide manpower to bureaucracy from its pool of well-educated people and offer their vast media outlets in his service.

Alliance with the Gülenists paid off. The Gülen movement increased its sway over Turkish bureaucracy by appointing its sympathizers to key positions in various ministries, including the Ministry of Education, Ministry of the Interior and Ministry of Foreign Affairs as well as in the judiciary and military. Among higher-ranking bureaucrats, the portion of Gülenists reached 30 percent in the judiciary and 50 percent in the police force.[65] The Gülenists' influence in the education sector was particularly striking. They not only controlled the top echelon of the Ministry of Education but also educational institutions at the grassroots level. At one point the movement owned 18 percent of private dormitories and 11 percent of all private schools in the country.[66]

ERDOĞAN TURNS TO ISLAM

Gülenists became the dominant force in AKP-held municipalities as well. Using their influence over municipalities, they transferred public lands to their foundations and schools. Through their supporters in the bureaucracy, Gülenist enterprises won almost all bidding in every ministry and generated unprecedented wealth through government contracts.[67] Gülenists were also involved in the AKP's relations with foreign actors. They organized and hosted meetings between AKP officials and foreign government officials and mobilized the movement's vast network across the world to lobby on the AKP's behalf. Most of the time, the Gülenist organizations abroad played a more active role than Turkish embassies in facilitating the AKP's engagement with foreign actors.

In return for Erdoğan's efforts to pave the way for more Gülenist influence in bureaucracy and civil society, the Gülen movement threw its full support behind Erdoğan and staved off various legal and political attempts by Kemalists to get rid of the AKP. After the military's veiled threat of a military coup on April 27, 2007, and the Constitutional Court's attempt to close down the AKP in 2008, the Gülenists embarked on a process to cleanse these institutions of Kemalists. Through court cases, some of which were fabricated, they sidelined the military. Hundreds of serving and retired Kemalist military officers, including ex-military chief İlker Başbuğ, were arrested. The 2010 constitutional referendum served a similar function for the judiciary. Gülenists mobilized their supporters to actively campaign in support of the new constitution, which restructured the judiciary. The referendum heralded even more Gülenist influence in the country's courts. By 2011, Gülenists became a formidable economic and social power and the dominant force within Turkish bureaucracy.

After Gülen and Erdoğan fell out in 2013, Erdoğan filled the bureaucracy with other religious orders that declared loyalty to him. Another Naqshbandi-Khalidi offshoot, Menzil, started snatching posts in the bureaucracy, particularly in the Ministry of Health and the gendarmerie, that were formerly held by Gülenists. Menzil supporters were granted positions after they displayed loyalty to the group during job interviews. Promotions and appointments were made through references to Menzil membership.[68] Loyalists of the İskenderpaşa community, another Naqshbandi-Khalidi branch, have filled top posts in the judiciary and increased their sway over the Ministry of Education.[69] Yet another Naqshbandi branch, the Erenköy community, expanded its influence in the business community. A few religious communities that have not declared loyalty to Erdoğan and supported rival parties have been subject to harassment and closure of their organizations; in some instances their members and leaders have been jailed.

Cooperation with religious communities served Erdoğan well. With their help, Islam became ever more visible in public life. It became common practice for religious figures to express their opinions on issues ranging from the economy to foreign policy in support of Erdoğan's policies. But the alliance also helped Erdoğan, who had a strong distrust of these communities despite their alliance, increase his control over these religious groups. By incorporating them into the state structure and providing financial benefits, Erdoğan made them dependent on him and eliminated potential religious opposition to his rule at a time when he defined himself as the protector of Islam and used religion to justify public corruption and his one-man rule.

Erdoğan's efforts to use state institutions and resources to control Islam for his own purposes included other measures. New religious organizations were launched and funded by Erdoğan's family members. TÜGVA (The Service for Youth and Education Foundation of Turkey) and TÜRGEV (Turkish Foundation to Serve the Youth and Education) are two such organizations. Erdoğan's son Bilal and daughter Esra Albayrak sit on the board of these organizations, as well as smaller ones with a similar mission, and play prominent roles in their activities. These organizations are active in the education field, with many educational institutions, including kindergartens, primary and high schools, as well as university and student dorms in Turkey and abroad. Their professed goal is to execute Erdoğan's dream of "raising pious generations." Erdoğan and his wife attend these organizations' events and accept that they represent his vision for the country's youth.[70]

These organizations host lavish events including trips to holy cities in Saudi Arabia and other countries where students spend their summers free of charge. These organizations and events are funded by businessmen who are close to Erdoğan and receive government contracts in important infrastructure projects in return. In 2020, Turkish media ran a story that laid bare this clientelist relationship. In 2017, Turkish natural gas distributor BaşkentGaz, which is owned by an Erdoğan loyalist, donated 8 million dollars of tax-deductible funds to the Turkish aid organization, Kızılay, which transferred over 7 million dollars to organizations such as TÜRGEV.[71] They also have agreements with the ministries of education and family and social policies. The ministries fund the education centers set up by these organizations and disseminate religious and ideological propaganda among the country's youth. Some activities are funded by Gulf countries, leading to worries that Salafism may expand its influence in the Turkish education system and religious bureaucracy.[72]

Some of these organizations also operate outside Turkey's borders. The Maarif Foundation, which was established as an international education agency in 2016, spreads Erdoğan's brand of Islamism abroad and seeks to replace Gülenist schools operating in other countries. The administrators of the foundation carry diplomatic passports and have rights and privileges akin to those of a diplomatic attaché. The foundation controls 191 schools in 21 countries and has taken over more than 200 Gülenist schools abroad.[73]

Aside from the newly established Islamic organizations run by Erdoğan's family, Islamic civil society organizations expanded rapidly under Erdoğan's watch. They benefit from government funds and access to public projects as well as money coming from conservative capital. In turn, they supplement the public welfare system and contribute to Erdoğan's Islamic restructuring of society.[74]

Erdoğan's Islamist populist agenda extended to long-established family legal principles as well. In 2017, the Turkish parliament passed a law allowing Muslim clerics to conduct civil marriages, something only state officers in branches of the Family Affairs' Directorate had been able to conduct in the past. Erdoğan took several other steps that irked secularists. A requirement prohibiting individuals who carried out "immoral acts" before marriage from becoming Turkish citizens was added to the law.[75] Another law set the minimum age of marriage at 17, with some exceptions for girls aged 16, leading to thousands of marriages that included girls under 18. A parliamentary commission established in 2016 by the ruling AKP to study the causes of high divorce rates introduced recommendations that angered large segments of society. Among them was a widely condemned proposal to grant amnesty to some men convicted of child sex assault if they married their victims. Widespread protests forced the government to withdraw the proposal. Other proposals were introduced that allowed mediation by religious scholars in divorce cases and decriminalized the practice of couples who have a religious marriage but not a civil one registered with the state.[76]

Transforming DİYANET

The Diyanet has been influential in supporting Erdoğan's efforts to expand religion's influence in the social realm. He transformed an institution that was established as a bulwark of secularism and a check against Islamism into a key tool to inject Islam into the public arena. The Diyanet, which replaced the office of the Sheikh ul-Islam as the country's top religious authority in 1924, was the brainchild of the secularist founding elite and accommodated the policies of the secularist establishment until Erdoğan transformed the institution to reflect his vision for the country. The Diyanet hires imams, offers religious education to the public, interprets Islamic norms, and writes sermons that are read each week in the country's tens of thousands of mosques. Before its transformation under Erdoğan, the Diyanet promoted an "enlightened" version of Islam that was in line with the Kemalist elites' worldview. One of its core duties was to eliminate Islamic threats to the Kemalist nation-building project. From the 1980s onwards, the Diyanet started playing an important role in regulating Muslim practices outside Turkey's borders as well. It sent Turkish imams to Europe, Balkan countries and the Middle East to ensure radical Islamist movements did not penetrate into Turkish immigrant communities and to maintain their loyalty to the Turkish state by offering classes that promoted the Kemalist's modernized version of Islam and emphasized citizens' duties toward the state.[77]

ERDOĞAN TURNS TO ISLAM

Under Erdoğan, Diyanet grew to become one of the main bureaucratic arms of the government and adopted an Islamist worldview.[78] Its budget far exceeds that of most ministries, and it has over 120,000 employees, making it one of the largest bureaucratic institutions of the country.[79] The profile of Diyanet employees has changed as well. It was once run predominantly by secular career civil servants but under Erdoğan, openly pious people fill the posts.

Diyanet also expanded its scope of institutional responsibilities and started exerting its influence in every sector of society. The 2010 law that boosted its status from "general directorate" to "undersecretariat" paved the way for this expansion. Diyanet launched a TV channel and a radio station, that broadcast Sunni-Islam based content that is in line with Erdoğan's vision of a Muslim nation to wide audiences. It also started providing guidance on everyday matters through a free telephone hotline.

Diyanet became involved in everyday politics as well. Sermons are drafted to support the government's position on critical domestic and foreign policy matters. On key issues from the Kurdish question and non-Sunni communities to the economy and the place of women in social life, it promotes Erdoğan's policies. The president of Diyanet frequently appears on TV, delivering statements that toe the government's line. For instance, the day before the June 2015 parliamentary election, imams asked the people attending prayer in the mosque to vote for "Muslim parties" in a clear reference to the AKP. Diyanet expanded its services to youth detention centers, hospitals, and senior residences, started issuing halal certificates for food products, produced fatwas on everyday matters and opened the first religious kindergarten.[80]

Diyanet also helps suppress dissent against Erdoğan. It adheres to Erdoğan's line in critical junctures, demonizes those who are critical of him and launches programs to support Erdoğan's narrative. After popular protests against Erdoğan broke out across the country in 2013 and corruption investigations involving Erdoğan and cabinet members were instigated by pro-Gülen judges, Erdoğan declared social media to be one of the biggest public enemies, calling Twitter a "menace to society" and blocking dozens of websites including Facebook and Youtube. Diyanet pledged to "act together" with the government. Its officials drafted sermons, gave interviews and issued statements criminalizing Gülenists and hosted forums and training sessions to warn people about the dangers of social media.[81]

Diyanet became Erdoğan's most effective ideological tool to impose his vision on the country. It helped his efforts to define "the people" along Sunni Muslim and Ottoman lines and legitimize his power grab in the name of protecting Islam and Muslims across the world. This particular definition allowed Erdoğan to not only secure the support of conservative Turks but also Kurds, a critical constituency, in his quest to establish an executive presidency.

"My pious Kurdish brothers, grandchildren of Salahuddin Ayyubi"

The centrality of Islam in Erdoğan's post-2011 strategy was most apparent in the way he approached the Kurdish question. Contrary to the decades-old Kemalist policy of denying the existence of a separate Kurdish ethnic identity, Erdoğan recognized the Kurdish presence and admitted that Turkey had made mistakes in dealing with its Kurds. He promoted a peaceful resolution of the Kurdish problem. His specific conceptualization of the Turkish nation as an Islamic nation and the Kurds' place in it made this bold move possible. In this view, contrary to the old school Kemalist stance that sought to define Turkey as an ethnically homogeneous country, Turkey was a country with different ethnicities. What bound these different ethnicities together was Islam. Erdoğan often described the Kurds as the most pious ethnic group that had contributed immensely to the Islamic awakening in the country and thus were an integral part of the new Turkey as an Islamic nation.[82] Indeed, religiosity has traditionally been high among Kurds. For that reason, even the Kurdish nationalist movement, which has its roots in Marxist-Leninism, referred to Islam to expand its base.

Erdoğan's conceptualization of the nation gave him room to recognize the presence of Kurds without acknowledging them as a separate nation. To him, the Kurds have been victimized by the secularism and nationalism that were enforced by Kemalists, just as Islamists were.[83] The Kurds, like other Muslim groups, were ethnic components of his Muslim nation defined along the lines of common Muslim cultural values and a shared Ottoman legacy. In a historic speech that was considered "the manifesto of the Kurdish opening," launched by Erdoğan to grant more rights to the Kurds, he referred to a historic military alliance between Turks and Kurds against Christian Crusaders and Shiite Iran, underlying Kurds' Sunni Muslim identity:

"Weren't we the soldiers of the same army that conquered Jerusalem under the banner of Salahuddin Ayyubi, turning that place into a city of peace and calm? Weren't we those who became brothers in the army of Yavuz Sultan Selim in Çaldıran?"[84] "Brothers, please look,"

> do they not all sleep in Çanakkale side by side? Turks, Kurds, Laz, Arabs, Greeks—do they not sleep side by side? Do our martyrs not sleep side by side in Sarıkamış? In Kut-al-Amara we achieved that victory together. We founded this republic together... Diyarbakır, we are brothers. We are eternal brothers... Oh, brothers, the community praying in Ulus Mosque turns towards the same Kıblah as the people in Süleymaniye [Mosque] in Istanbul, in Selimiye [Mosque] in Edirne, and in Hacıbayram [Mosque] in Ankara. See, we have the same Kıblah. [Is there] any separation? No![85]

Erdoğan often referred to Kurds as the "grandchildren of Salahuddin Ayyubi," the Sunni Kurdish-origin sultan of Egypt who retook Jerusalem from the Christian Crusaders. He described the largest Kurdish city, Diyarbakır, as the third most important holy city after Mecca and Medina (two holy sites for Muslims) because the city is home to a number of tombs belonging to the Companions of the Prophet Muhammed. Erdoğan carried the Kurdish version of the Quran, which was translated by the Diyanet on his orders, during his rallies in Kurdish cities.[86] His criticisms against the PKK and the secular left-wing pro-Kurdish party were also framed in religious language. Erdoğan denounced them as "anti-Islamic" and the "enemy of the pious Kurds" and asked his "pious Kurdish brothers" to resist those "who insult our religion."[87]

Erdoğan's conceptualization of the nation accepts Kurdish ethnicity as a separate culture but does not allow its mobilization to demand a separate Kurdish nationhood that could challenge his plans. Therefore, Erdoğan's "one nation, one state, one flag, one religion" motto still allows him to recognize Kurdish ethnicity as long as "one religion," which is Sunni Islam, remains the primary marker of national identity.[88] In this formulation, stressing common Islamic ties is the key to addressing the Kurdish question and justified the "Kurdish openings" Erdoğan introduced.

"Great things will happen"

On his way to Iran in March 2009, President Abdullah Gül told reporters that "great things will happen on the Kurdish question." Later, it was revealed that at the time of Gül's remarks, Turkey's intelligence agency was holding secret talks with the PKK in Oslo to resolve the country's Kurdish problem. That summer, the Erdoğan-led government launched the first "Kurdish opening" which was later called the "Democratic opening." The opening was thought to be a series of reforms in state policies to address some of the Kurds' demands about their language and identity. In May, President Gül kicked off the opening by declaring "The biggest problem for Turkey is the Kurdish problem… It has to be solved." In an interview with a Turkish daily, the PKK leader in the Qandil mountains of northern Iraq, Murat Karayılan, said that PKK guerrillas were ready to lay down arms and the pro-Kurdish Democratic Society Party (DTP) could lead the negotiations for the PKK.[89]

Kurds have fought many rebellions. But the bloodiest of all began in 1984 when the PKK started an insurgency. Forty thousand lives, many of them PKK fighters, were lost in the fight between the PKK and Turkish state. During operations against the Kurdish rebels, Turkey's military and police forces killed thousands of people, including civilians, and perpetrated torture, rape and widespread destruction of property among an array of human rights abuses, dealing a severe blow to Turkey's international image. The Kurdish problem and the heavy-handed military response hindered efforts to become a fully fledged democracy. Previous governments, particularly that of Turgut Özal who was the prime minister in the 1980s, sought to resolve the conflict through peaceful means that were opposed by the Kemalist military. But this time, the military—whose image had suffered due to the Gülenist-orchestrated Ergenekon trials and its own "e-coup" attempt to prevent Gül from becoming president—did not pose such vehement opposition. The Chief of General Staff İlker Başbuğ, who warned against undermining the "unitary state," conceded that the Kurdish problem could not be resolved through military means alone.[90]

Erdoğan's Kurdish opening raised hopes. In a speech in parliament in August 2009, Erdoğan spoke of the common pains of Turkish and Kurdish mothers who lost their sons in the conflict. His interior minister, Beşir Atalay, held meetings with politicians and civil society leaders to rally their support behind the opening while Erdoğan met with the leader of the DTP, Ahmet Türk. Erdoğan's aim was first to start a public debate on the issue, rally the opposition's support behind the opening and then grant some cultural and linguistic concessions to Kurds. These included easing the remaining bans on Kurdish broadcasting, establishing Kurdish language departments in universities and changing the Turkified names of villages back to Kurdish.

Erdoğan's real goal was to tame the military and capture Kurdish votes in the 2011 parliamentary elections. The pro-Kurdish party DTP had been making steady gains. In the 2007 parliamentary elections, the DTP's predecessor party ran independent candidates to circumvent the electoral law that prevented parties with less than 10 percent of the popular vote from entering parliament, becoming the first Kurdish party to win a significant number of seats. Although the party was shut down by the courts for its alleged links to terrorism, it kept gaining ground in the Kurdish regions. In the March 2009 local elections, the DTP won ninety-nine municipalities, increasing its share from fifty-four in 2004.[91] Raising his ruling AKP's vote share among the Kurds and curbing the power of the military, which remained a powerful political force largely due to the Kurdish question, were the two main drivers behind Erdoğan's first Kurdish opening.

Two weeks after the local elections, the PKK announced a ceasefire, saying the DTP's electoral success showed that the conditions for a democratic settlement of the Kurdish problem were ripe.⁹² In October, the DTP said that a group of PKK members, as opposed to the thousands the AKP expected, would arrive at Turkey's Habur border crossing with Iraq as a goodwill gesture to show the PKK's commitment to the democratic process. On October 19, eight serving PKK members as well as 26 residents of the Mahmur refugee camp, which hosted thousands of ethnic Kurds who fled Turkey in the 1990s during the height of the PKK's war with Turkey, arrived at the Habur gate. They received a hero's welcome from thousands of Kurds, including members of parliament from the pro-Kurdish DTP, who gathered at the border, dancing, singing and carrying PKK flags. The celebrations were touted by Kurds as the victory of a decades-long struggle by the PKK for recognition of the organization as the legitimate representative of the Kurds. The PKK members even brought demands from the organization's imprisoned leader Öcalan, including concessions from the Turkish state on Kurdish political and cultural rights, before the PKK renounced violence. As per the agreement reached between Turkey and the militant group, the eight PKK members were not arrested. They continued to parade through the Kurdish region.

Turkish media's depiction of the arrival of the PKK members as a "victory of the terrorists" mobilized Turkish nationalists who took to the streets in protest and clashed with the Kurds. Erdoğan was not expecting a nationalist reaction. Opposition parties attacked the Kurdish opening as well. The leader of the main opposition CHP, Deniz Baykal, accused Erdoğan of talking to the terrorists and accused the DTP of being the political arm of the PKK. Not surprisingly, the nationalist party, MHP, joined the anti-opening camp. The chief of general staff warned the government on the military's website, saying "you cannot put martyrs who sacrificed their souls for their country and terrorists in the same corner."⁹³ Fearing further nationalist backlash, Erdoğan announced that he had postponed the planned arrival of more PKK members.⁹⁴ A few months after its launch, Erdoğan's Kurdish opening had been shut down along with the DTP. In December, Turkey's Constitutional Court voted unanimously to ban the DTP for having links to the PKK.

But Erdoğan did not give up. In September 2012, after an intense year of fighting between the PKK and Turkey, Erdoğan once again announced that peace talks with the PKK were possible. He had tamed the generals but this time he needed the Kurds to secure a majority to back his plan to switch to the presidential system. The uprising that started in Syria against the rule of Bashar al-Assad in 2011 became the catalyst for Erdoğan's second Kurdish opening. After Turkey officially joined the anti-Assad camp in the fall of 2011, the close relations between Erdoğan and Assad changed. Turkey became the organizational hub of the anti-Assad opposition. Partly in retaliation to Turkey's move, Assad allowed Kurds in exile to return to the country and gave them free rein in the country's north, leading to an autonomous Kurdish zone along Turkey's border. These developments served as a reminder to Erdoğan that failure to resolve Turkey's Kurdish problem would strengthen the hand of the Assad regime he sought to topple. This thinking, along with Erdoğan's calculation that securing Kurdish support was key to seizing more power through an executive presidency, paved the way for another round of peace negotiations with the Kurds. Turkish intelligence officials started talking to imprisoned Kurdish leader Öcalan. In September, Kurdish inmates started a hunger strike in protest against Öcalan's isolation in İmralı prison and the limited access he had to his lawyers. After talks with Turkish intelligence officials, Öcalan called on Kurdish inmates to end their strike. The inmates heeded Öcalan's plea. A delegation of the pro-Kurdish Peace and Democracy Party (BDP), which was founded as the successor party to the DTP, was allowed to visit Öcalan. Erdoğan used this to push forward the peace agenda. He proudly declared that his government had trampled on all forms of nationalisms, including Turkish and Kurdish versions.[95]

On March 21, 2013, the day of Newroz, which is the Kurdish New Year and the start of spring, a letter from Abdullah Öcalan was read in Turkish and Kurdish in Diyarbakır to a large Kurdish crowd that was carrying Kurdish flags and Öcalan banners. Pro-Kurdish BDP politicians were standing on the stage during the reading of the letter. "Today a new period is beginning," the letter read. "From a period of armed resistance, a door has been opened to democratic struggle… instead of arms, we have ideas… now it is time for our armed elements to move outside [Turkey's] borders... will you answer my call?"⁹⁶ Öcalan was calling for a ceasefire and asking the PKK to withdraw from Turkish soil. To the Kurds, the letter sounded like a farewell to the PKK. Although they were tired of war, the Kurds were still grateful to the fighters who had fought and were killed to bring about peace. They had little trust in Erdoğan, who they thought had deceived them in 2009, but Öcalan had their unwavering support.

Öcalan proposed a three-stage roadmap to resolve the conflict. The first step would be for the PKK to agree to a formal ceasefire followed by the PKK's withdrawal from Turkish soil. In return, the Turkish government would carry out reforms that would guarantee political, social and economic rights for the Kurds. Öcalan did not demand Kurdish autonomy but asked for recognition of Kurdish identity in the Turkish constitution and the strengthening of local administration. If everything went according to plan in these stages, the PKK would put down its arms.⁹⁷

Erdoğan pledged democratic reforms to address Kurdish grievances and the PKK started withdrawing from Turkey back to northern Iraq, which has been a PKK safe haven since the 1990s. After the withdrawal started, the government dispatched "wise people commissions," comprising representatives from civil society, academia, business, media and the arts, to travel around the country to explain the peace process and boost public support for the initiative. In the meantime, the government introduced a reform bill to bolster the peace process. The reform package was not exclusively about the Kurdish issue but included measures such as limiting the scope of the often-misused charge of "making terrorist propaganda," which had primarily targeted the Kurds.

Further measures were added. Many restrictions on the Kurdish languge had already been loosened. In what was considered a watershed event, Turkey's state-owned TRT had begun broadcasting documentaries and news in Kurdish in 2004. It was a symbolic yet important event in a country where even accepting that Kurds formed a separate ethnic identity was a crime in the 1980s. In 2009, TRT launched an exclusively Kurdish-language TV station, named TRT Kurdi. In the 2012–13 academic year, public middle and high schools began offering elective Kurdish classes. In another symbolic yet important step, the pledge of allegiance to the Turkish nation (*Andımız*), which was mandatory for elementary students to read out every morning before classes started and was the subject of criticism from the Kurds due to a line by Atatürk that read "how happy is the one who says I am a Turk" was removed in 2013. Other steps were taken, such as restoring the original Kurdish names of some settlements that were previously Turkified.

To Erdoğan, the second Kurdish opening was one of the main pillars of his post-2011 strategy to grab more power, and was also perfectly compatible with his "Muslim nation" project. He thought he would lose the nationalist vote because of the Kurdish opening but believed that the increase in Kurdish support would offset that loss.

Erdoğan hoped to bank on the support of religious conservatives and Kurds to establish an autocratic rule. He thought that the new Muslim nation he conceptualized and the policies he had pursued since 2011 offered enough incentives to these groups to back his project. The pious segments of the country would be pleased to see not only Islam's expansion into social life, but also their cadres filling bureaucratic posts, and the national curriculum rewritten to inject religiosity into the next generation. They would benefit financially, too, from Erdoğan's push to provide them with perks. The Kurds, Erdoğan thought, would rally behind his presidentialism project as well. After all, his Muslim nation conceptualization had changed the decades-old Kemalist denial of Kurdish identity and offered them enough room to remain part of the nation with their Kurdish identity. He thought that he could secure the Kurds' buy-in in return for recognizing their identity and addressing some of their demands. Erdoğan saw the uprisings in the Arab world as a great opportunity to help him execute his plan.

Erdoğan, the defender of Islamism

The Arab uprisings could not have happened at a better time for Erdoğan. As protests were overthrowing long-time autocratic regimes and bringing Islamists to power, Erdoğan had neutralized his Kemalist opponents, tightened his grip on the country and launched his plan to reshape Turkey. These domestic developments provided Erdoğan with both the motivation and the opportunity to implement bolder ideas in Turkey's relations with the region.

To Davutoğlu, the uprisings touched a different nerve. He thought that the winds of history were finally filling his sails. He had long argued that the regimes in the Middle East did not represent the will of the people, and thus were illegitimate. He predicted that these regimes would eventually be toppled and replaced by the authentic representatives of the people, the Islamists. When that time came, Davutoğlu argued, Turkey had to back these Islamist movements to become the leader of the region.

When popular uprisings started ousting Arab authoritarian regimes and led to the rise of Islamist movements, Davutoğlu felt vindicated. He had theorized about this for decades. Finally the Western-imposed political order in the Middle East was coming to an end under his watch and Turkey was going to help remake it. In his mind, history had proved him right. His imperial fantasy of making the Ottoman Empire's heir the leader of the Muslim world was coming true. He said that the uprisings were closing "the 100-year-old parenthesis" that was opened following the collapse of the Ottoman Empire. The people were finally bringing down a system that was artificially established by the West to divide the *ummah* and bringing to power the true representatives of the people.[98] More importantly, the uprisings were happening at the right moment for Turkey. To Davutoğlu, what kept Turkey from playing a leadership role in the Middle East were the anti-Islamic prejudices of the secularist, Westernized elite ruling the country. Now that Turkey's own Westernized, secularist, "alienated" elite was replaced by a cadre that shared the masses' piety, Turkey was ready to appreciate and bank on the historic transformation taking place in the region. Davutoğlu believed that Turkey was on its way once again to being the mover and shaker in the Middle East.

A few days after the uprisings started in Tunisia, Davutoğlu singled out principles that became key to guiding Turkey's policies.[99] The first was that change in the region was necessary and inevitable. What was happening in Tunisia was not a coincidence or an imposition by outside powers but rather "the natural flow of history." In Davutoğlu's mind, the uprisings which would pave the way for a democratic transformation should have happened decades ago, after the end of the Cold War, but the West prevented this transformation out of fear that democracy would benefit Islamic movements.[100] He thought that this delayed reaction by the people of the region to reclaim their destiny would fundamentally change the Arab states and societies as well as end Western-led regional order. He pledged that Turkey would wholeheartedly support the democratic aspirations of the uprisings. He said,

> When the revolutionary events in the Middle East began, we were determined that we would not be passive bystanders, but active agents that impacted this historic transformation of the region. Our government, therefore, made an unequivocal decision from the very first day of the Arab Spring to extend our assistance to the people of the region, so that they could enjoy the same universally acknowledged rights as their peers do elsewhere in the world. We refused to stand idly by as the basic democratic rights enjoyed by the Turkish people were denied to others by violence and oppression.[101]

Davutoğlu talked about Turkey's historical mission to lead the Middle East. "Between 2011 and 2023, we will reunite with our brothers in the lands that we lost between 1911 and 1923," Davutoğlu said.[102] He was referring to the lands the Ottoman Empire lost in the Balkans and the Middle East following the Balkan Wars and the First World War. Davutoğlu was sure that the time had come for unity of the *ummah* and pledged to "render the borders meaningless in these winds of change blowing in the Middle East, working together with the administrations that came to and will come to power."[103]

These ideas provided the intellectual framework for Erdoğan's power grab. Davutoğlu's enthusiasm to support Islamists' struggles to bring down autocratic regimes in the region fit perfectly with Erdoğan's vision to place Islam at the center of his domestic strategy. He used the ideas and the metaphors in Davutoğlu's doctrine to justify his U-turn in regional policy. In a far cry from the previous years' cautious, pro-status quo approach, Erdoğan became the defender of Islamism in the region. From the very early days of the uprisings, Turkey sided with the Muslim Brotherhood, providing political, financial, in some cases military aid as well as technical assistance.

Erdoğan's AKP and Arab Islamists have a history of friendly relations, the roots of which go back to the AKP's predecessor, the Welfare Party. Since the 1960s, Turkey's Islamist movement has sought closer ties with the regional Islamist network. This was in line with the party's foreign policy outlook that saw Turkey as the leader of the Muslim world. Necmettin Erbakan, the leader of the Welfare Party, had close family ties to key MB figures. Ibrahim al-Zayat, whose father was one of the leaders of the Egyptian Brotherhood, was Erbakan's brother-in-law and worked actively in the German branch of the National Vision movement from which the Welfare Party emerged. Other key Muslim Brotherhood members played important roles in the National Vision's European branches. Erbakan also hosted MB members from Tunisia and Egypt at his party's congresses and tried to mediate between the autocratic regimes and the Brotherhood. When ten members of the MB were sentenced to death in Egypt in 1995, Erbakan sent three of his deputies to Cairo to stop the execution and secured their release.[104] Erbakan also tried to play a mediating role during the Gulf War in 1990/91. He led a delegation of MB members from Tunisia, Sudan and Yemen and held meetings with the Gulf countries.[105]

The AKP's relationship with the Muslim Brotherhood, however, wavered depending on Erdoğan's domestic strategy. During the AKP's initial years in power, Erdoğan was cautious not to be seen as an Islamist. When the AKP's invitation to a Hamas delegation, led by its leader Khaled Meshaal, to Ankara after Hamas's victory in the Palestinian elections of January 2006 met with strong criticism from secularists at home and the Bush administration, Erdoğan toned down his party's public recognition of Hamas. Scheduled meetings with then Prime Minister Erdoğan were canceled and the delegation was hosted by Foreign Minister Abdullah Gül at the AKP's headquarters. But as Erdoğan became more confident, the Muslim Brotherhood became more prominent in

ERDOĞAN TURNS TO ISLAM

Ankara's regional policy. The uprisings which heralded the Muslim Brotherhood's electoral successes in post-revolutionary Arab countries marked the peak of Turkey's support for the group. Tunisia marked the first time Ankara's new pro-Islamist foreign policy went on display.

The uprising in the country, catalyzed by street vendor Mohamed Bouazizi setting himself on fire to protest rising living costs and corruption, happened too quickly for Turkey to react. Only after the popular demonstrations led to President Zine El Abidine Ben Ali stepping down in January after twenty-three years of rule, did Turkey issue a statement expressing its support for the democratic demands of Tunisians. According to Davutoğlu, a few days after the protests broke out in Tunisia, Turkey had made up its mind to become the standard-bearer of the revolution. Given how much Turkey had invested economically and diplomatically in the regional status quo, Turkey's decision to embrace revolutionary change was stunning.

Two weeks after Ben Ali was forced from power, Rachid Ghannouchi, the leader of the long-outlawed Islamist Ennahda Party, along with seventy other Ennahda members returned home from exile. At the airport, Ghannouchi said that critics should not compare him to the father of Iran's Islamic Revolution but to Turkey's Erdoğan.[106] It was the first sign of the upcoming Islamist solidarity between post-revolution Tunisia and Erdoğan's Turkey. In October 2011, Ennahda, which had been brutally oppressed by the Ben Ali regime for decades, won a plurality of votes in the country's first democratic elections and led a coalition government with two secular-oriented parties. From then on, Turkish-Tunisian relations became tighter. The contact between the two parties increased dramatically. Turkey's President Abdullah Gül became the first foreign president to address the Tunisian parliament after the uprisings toppled Ben Ali. He visited the Martyr's Monument, placed a wreath there in memory of those who lost their lives during the January 14 revolution and praised Ghannouchi and the Jasmine Revolution.[107]

Ennahda saw in the AKP a model to emulate. The AKP represented pragmatism and gradual "Islamization through democracy" as opposed to radical change. Ennahda leaders were stunned by how Erdoğan had marginalized Turkey's secularists through a pro-EU, pro-reform agenda. It was an appealing model, certainly more appealing than the Egyptian Muslim Brotherhood's heavy-handed approach, for a country such as Tunisia which had shared Turkey's history of French-style secularism. "The AKP will gradually make Turkey a more Muslim country, through education, building the economy, and diversifying the media," said Ennahda president Ghannouchi. "That's our model."[108]

Erdoğan and Davutoğlu were more than ready to take on the role of Islamist big brother. When the protests spread to Egypt, Erdoğan was one of the first world leaders to back the protesters. He asked Mubarak to heed his people's calls and step down. Although Egypt was a relatively more important trade partner for Turkey than Tunisia, Erdoğan and Mubarak had never seen eye-to-eye on regional issues and the two countries were competing for regional clout. The Tunisian experience had already excited Erdoğan and Davutoğlu about the prospects of an Islamist-led government. The Egyptian Muslim Brotherhood had made a decision not to be visible in the protests so as not to give the impression that it was an Islamist revolution, but Erdoğan and Davutoğlu knew that the group would have a good shot at winning the next democratically held elections. Despite the regime's repression, the MB remained the region's most successful grassroots movement that had a real connection with Egypt's rural majority. It had performed well in the country's 2005 elections. Erdoğan sent his election campaign advisors to help the Brotherhood's Mohammed Morsi in his campaign.

To capitalize on his growing stature at a time of radical change and to bolster his AKP's standing as a model for the region's Islamists, Erdoğan went on an "Arab Spring tour" to Tunisia, Egypt and Libya in September 2011. He received a hero's welcome. "Lend us Erdoğan for a month!" wrote a columnist in the Egyptian newspaper *Al Wafd*. The Brotherhood members made much of the fan turnout during Erdoğan's tour. Speaking on Egyptian television, Erdoğan called Israel "the West's spoiled child" and pledged his support for the Palestinian Authority's bid for recognition as a state at the United Nations. Reportedly, he had planned to visit Gaza on the tour to boost Hamas, but he said he had preferred to visit Mahmoud Abbas, the leader of the Palestinian Authority.[109] The MB appreciated Erdoğan's tough stance against Israel and his call for Muslim solidarity. But Erdoğan angered his hosts when he urged them to adopt secularism in their constitution and argued for a "democratic Islam."[110] A member of parliament from the AKP later said that the secularism comment was included in Erdoğan's speech to ease Western concern about "hardline Islamists hijacking the Arab revolutions."[111]

Erdoğan got his wish in Egypt. The Muslim Brotherhood's Freedom and Justice Party (FJP) won the largest number of seats in Egypt's first post-Mubarak parliamentary elections and Morsi was elected president in 2012. Davutoğlu said that post-Mubarak Egypt would become the focus of Turkish efforts. Turkey saw in Muslim Brotherhood-led Egypt a partner to lead the new post-American regional order, which ended the previous one upheld by secular autocrats. "For the regional balance of power, we want to have a strong, very strong Egypt," said Davutoğlu.[112]

Turkey stepped in quickly to bolster the Muslim Brotherhood-led government and ensure its grip on power. The newly found coziness in ties was apparent from the word go. Morsi attended the AKP's party congress a few months after being elected and President Abdullah Gül became the first foreign leader to visit the Morsi government. Ankara offered $2 billion in development aid as well as technical assistance such as 150 garbage trucks to resolve Cairo's long-lasting waste collection problem. The trade volume between the two countries increased dramatically in a year and Erdoğan signed twenty-seven bilateral agreements to boost ties in trade, transport, and police cooperation.[113]

Turkey's support of the Muslim Brotherhood government in Egypt went beyond the financial, technical, and diplomatic. Ankara also provided advice to help Morsi secure domestic and international support. Ankara suggested Egypt reduce the number of ministries from 34 to 25, carry out economic reforms and increase contacts with the international community to strengthen its legitimacy. Morsi was also urged to visit the US and Europe as soon as possible to ease Western concerns about Islamists taking power in the Arab world's most populous country.[114]

Turkey provided intelligence to the Morsi government as well. Aside from lower-level meetings between intelligence officials, Turkey's intelligence chief Hakan Fidan held meetings with Morsi three times.[115] The most critical of these meetings came two weeks before the military coup that toppled Morsi. Fidan warned Morsi about the impending coup and urged him to stand his ground rather than ease the tension by transferring some of his powers to a newly appointed prime minister.[116] Egypt's military ousted Morsi in July 2013. Erdoğan became his key defender after his overthrow. He harshly criticized the members of the UN Security Council for not condemning the coup strongly enough and started a campaign to secure Morsi's release. Pro-Morsi rallies were held in Turkey and the symbol of the Rabaa—a hand gesture with four fingers raised to symbolize Egyptian security forces' post-coup killing of up to 1000 Muslim Brotherhood supporters in Cairo's Rabaa square as well as the Arabic word for "four"—became common among AKP law makers and followers. They signaled solidarity with the Muslim Brotherhood by displaying the symbol in their social media profiles and printing it on flags, scarves, pins, and banners.[117] Erdoğan himself started making the hand gesture at public rallies.

When Morsi died in custody, Erdoğan slammed Egypt's "tyrants," called Morsi a "martyr" and ordered a prayer on his behalf in Istanbul mosques. After the coup, Turkey became a hub for Muslim Brotherhood activities. It opened its doors to Muslim Brotherhood members, hosting as many as 1,500 who launched NGOs and TV channels in Istanbul. Erdoğan's strong support for Morsi turned him into the key defender of Islamism at home and in the region. Erdoğan's firm stand defending the Muslim Brotherhood against the coup, which offered a stark contrast to the muted response by the West and those Gulf countries that threw support behind the coup plotters, burnished his image among the region's Islamists.

Turkey backed the opposition that rose up against Libyan autocrat Muammar Qaddafi as well, albeit belatedly. The presence of thousands of Turkish workers in Libya played a key role in Turkey's

ERDOĞAN TURNS TO ISLAM

delayed reaction. Ankara wanted to ensure their safe return before burning bridges with the Qaddafi regime. Turkish companies also had billions of dollars' worth of outstanding projects in the construction, engineering and energy sectors, which gave Ankara pause. Despite initial hesitation to back NATO intervention in Libya, Turkey took part in the US-led NATO operation and Erdoğan asked Qaddafi to step down. Just like in other "Arab Spring" countries, Erdoğan hoped that the rise of the Muslim Brotherhood would help his ambitions both at home and in the region.

Like other autocrats who were overthrown by popular uprisings, Qaddafi had banned the Muslim Brotherhood and put many of its members in jail. But the uprising brought the Muslim Brotherhood to the forefront of Libyan politics. From the outset, the group was involved in the uprising. After Qaddafi's overthrow, the Muslim Brotherhood emerged as Libya's largest Islamist party. In March 2012, it formed the Justice and Construction Party (JCP) and won thirty-four seats in the parliamentary elections. Turkey had backed the JCP since its inception. Davutoğlu pledged $300 million in assistance to the MB-backed Transitional National Council. Turkey's support for Libya's Islamists took on a military component in 2014. Ankara allied itself with Islamist-linked militias known as the Libya Dawn coalition and thus became part of the proxy battle that pitted Ankara against the Gulf countries' backing of the efforts of rival groups to defeat Islamist-allied groups. Islamist-allied militias formed a new government in 2014 after they captured Tripoli and forced the internationally recognized head of government to flee. Turkey's special envoy to Libya publicly met with the head of the new government before any other country. Ankara even cooperated with Libyan Islamists to topple the Assad regime after the uprisings spread there. Turkey allowed members of Ansar Al-Sharia, a jihadist organization based in Libya that was accused of carrying out the attack on the US consulate in Benghazi and killing the US ambassador, to use its territory to deliver aid to Syrian rebels in the towns of Salma and Kasab.[118]

Erdoğan's strong backing for the revolutionary changes taking place in the region and his support for the Islamists helped him at home. His stance strengthened his image as the defender of Islam and true democracy. Erdoğan and Davutoğlu couched their support for the Islamists in the language of democracy. They often argued that Ankara was backing the peoples' demand for democracy and would fully support whomever the democratically held elections brought to power. But in every country where popular uprisings overthrew autocrats, Turkey threw its support behind the Muslim Brotherhood long before elections were held and did not give much consideration to the democratic credentials of the groups it supported. To them, democracy meant Islamists coming to power. They overlooked the Egyptian Muslim Brotherhood's democratic shortcomings after it took office and urged it to stand its ground instead of giving concessions to ease the tension.

The narrative that Turkey was backing the peoples' democratic aspirations in the region also helped Erdoğan to discredit the secularist opposition at home. After the coup that toppled the Morsi government in Egypt, Erdoğan drew parallels between Turkey's long history of military coups and suppression of Islamism and quickly accused those who criticized the Muslim Brotherhood of being coup plotters.[119] Erdoğan often likened Arab autocratic regimes to the secularist main opposition party, CHP, and his own party to the revolutionaries who were overthrowing those regimes to establish real democracy. He claimed that the Arab uprisings were inspired by the AKP, calling CHP leader Kemal Kılıçdaroğlu a "Baathist", while members of his cabinet cheered the uprisings saying "Arabs are toppling their own CHP."[120]

Erdoğan's initial reaction to the uprisings expanded his appeal in the Arab world. As the mass protests rekindled the old debate on the compatibility of Islam and democracy, Turkey's unique experience as a Muslim nation and democratic state, as well as its rapid economic development, brought the issue of the "Turkish model" to the forefront of discussions about the region's future. Erdoğan became the most popular leader among Arabs and the "Turkish model" became the most desired political system.[121] For the Islamists of the region, the Turkish model represented an Islamist-rooted party's coming to power through electoral politics without having to abandon its conservative agenda. For Arab liberals, the AKP's moderation offered a third way between secular authoritarian governments and radical Islamists. It seemed to prove that institutional limitations could moderate Islamist parties and engage them in the democratic process.

Erdoğan wanted to use Islam to mobilize support for the executive presidency he wished to establish. He constructed an image as the defender of Islam, embarked on a project to make Sunni Islam the primary marker of Turkish national identity and carried out policies to cater to his religiously conservative constituency. Supporting what he saw as the "Islamic awakening" in the Arab world was a key component of Erdoğan's domestic strategy to centralize power. Once again, Syria occupied a unique place in Erdoğan's struggle to tighten his grip on the country. Post-uprising Syria offered him an opportunity to burnish his Islamist credentials, polish his image as the leader of the Sunni Muslims and delegitimize the secularist opposition at home.

3

THE SYRIAN GAMBIT

ASSAD MUST GO

Why did the Syrian war become Erdoğan's war? How did Erdoğan's struggle to build an autocracy intertwine with what started as the Syrians' battle for democracy? What were the implications of this intermingling for the thousands of Turks, Kurds and Syrians who took to the streets to demand justice, equality and freedom? The following section will seek to address these questions and shed light on Turkey's transformation from a "firefighter" into an arsonist in Syria and how "brother Assad" became "murderer Assad" in a matter of few months.

Protests erupt in Syria

"A nightingale sings in Hama and gets beheaded," said Erdoğan at an *iftar* dinner in Istanbul in August 2011. He was citing an Islamist poet who wrote poems about the 1982 Hama massacre during which then Syrian president Hafez al-Assad's security forces killed tens of thousands of Muslim Brotherhood members to crush an Islamic uprising. The massacre remained etched in the memories of Turkey's Islamists. It represented the brutality of what they called an "infidel regime." Erdoğan was worried about another

Hama. "How can we accept the repeat of that huge pain 30 years later in that wounded city in a country that we used to call our brother," Erdoğan said during *iftar*. He was referring to the al-Assad regime's offensive targeting of protesters in the streets of the opposition stronghold of Hama in which scores of people were shot dead in July. There were reports of bodies lying in the streets.[1] It was part of a nationwide offensive against the protests that started in March. The winds of the "Arab Spring" had arrived in Syria, or so Erdoğan thought.

In early March, a group of schoolboys from Deraa had been arrested for spray-painting graffiti on a high school wall that read "doctor, your turn next"—referring to Assad—"down with the regime." The boys had seen the latter slogan, which was the watchword of the revolutions in Tunisia and Egypt, on their TV. The local secret police arrested the boys and tortured them. The outrage over their mistreatment rippled across the country. Thousands took to the streets chanting anti-regime slogans. As the security forces' crackdown became harsher, thousands more joined the protests. Deraa, a town on Syria's southern border with Jordan, had become the epicenter of the Syrian uprising.

Deraa was poor and agrarian. The drought that affected the country in 2006–10 and Assad's "social market" reforms that diminished the social safety net had hit the town hard. Its mostly Sunni population was resentful towards the Alawite commander of the town's Mukhabarat, Assad's secret police.[2] As more protesters were killed, the town's outrage against the Mukhabarat grew. Protests quickly spread to other parts of the country. Protesters were outraged at the events in Deraa as well as the long-standing political and economic disenfranchisement, but local grievances specific to each area also contributed to the uprising.

President Bashar al-Assad was not worried. In January 2011, he boasted that the uprisings sweeping across the region would not spread to Syria because Syria was different in many ways from Egypt and Tunisia where autocrats were quickly overthrown. Assad was half right. Syria faced the same economic hardships, wealth disparity, political disenfranchisement and social complaints as other Arab countries that were experiencing unrest.[3] As in other countries, political power was monopolized by a small elite. Under Bashar's father, General Hafez al-Assad, who seized power in a military coup in 1970, the Baath Party was the "leader in state and society" and held the majority of seats in the parliament. Baathism, which developed in resistance against European colonialism in the Arab world and became prominent in Syria in the 1940s, is a mixture of secular Arab nationalism, Arab socialism and pan-Arabism. With a 1963 military coup, the Baath party became the ruling party. Baathist secularism was intended as a neutral form of rule in which everyone, irrespective of their religious identity, would be treated equally. The secular emphasis of Baathism was particularly appealing to different ethnic and religious communities who had been marginalized under the Ottoman Empire, while the socialist character of the regime gave economically marginalized groups hope for economic equality.[4]

Indeed, the Baath regime wanted to eliminate primordial loyalties such as sectarianism, regionalism and tribalism and promote social and economic equality. Despite early efforts to realize these goals, Hafez al-Assad and other Baathist leaders soon realized that it was impossible to secure the survival of the regime without making use of sectarian, regional and tribal ties. Hafez al-Assad made sure his allies dominated the Party's executive bodies, from which he hand-picked key administrative positions including the prime minister.[5] Although he promoted Sunni Arabs, who are the majority sect, to positions in key institutions, Hafez al-Assad packed security, military and intelligence institutions with his allies and people from his Alawite sect. The urban Sunni resentment that emerged after the takeover by lower-middle-class and poorer rural minorities kept growing, as individuals from traditionally marginalized minorities such as Alawi and Druze sects rapidly climbed social, political, and economic ladders and then discriminated against those they thought had oppressed them.[6] The dominance of Alawites in key state institutions was seen by Sunni Muslims as sectarian suppression of Sunnis by a regime they saw as anti-Islamic. This Sunni resentment led to several demonstrations and uprisings against the regime in Sunni-majority cities such as Hama.

Bashar al-Assad made several changes to the autocratic regime he inherited from his father in 2000. He replaced old regime hands with Bashar loyalists but filled key security posts with more Alawites than his father had done, which further fed Sunni resentment against the regime. That said, the Sunni frustration should not be overstated. Although sectarian resentment had been present for decades and played a role in fueling the 2011 protests against al-Assad in the later stages of the conflict, it was not prominent across Sunni and Alawi communities in Syria. The initial protests did not promote sectarian slogans, signaling that sectarian concerns were not the main source of grievance. As Christopher Phillips put it, during the early stages of the unrest, "not all Alawis sided with the regime, not all Sunnis sided with the opposition, and not all Syrians were motivated by ethno-sectarian concerns."[7] Political, economic and local issues were significantly more important.

The neoliberal reforms promoted by Bashar left people without any welfare balances, leading to an increase in poverty, unemployment and income disparity. By 2010, some 30 percent of Syrian society lived below the poverty line.[8] Particularly concerning was the state of the youth. Fifty-five percent of the population was under 24 and highly educated. Yet there were not enough jobs, making unemployment and under-employment a major problem. Compounding economic grievances was Bashar's neglect of rural areas. Removal of subsidies as well as a rise in the cost of diesel fuel hit rural areas hard. The drought that affected the country between 2006 and 2010 exacerbated the problems of the rural population that had once supported the regime. These problems were made worse by the corruption of regime officials and their exploitation of Syria's diverse ethnic and sectarian makeup.

All these factors made it impossible for Syria to escape the unrest that had started rocking the Arab world late in 2010. But peculiarities in the structure of the Assad regime made repeating the Tunisian and Egyptian scenarios in Syria, in which regimes quickly crumbled, less likely. Lacking the resources generated by oil wealth, the Assad regime deployed strategies to secure the people's buy-in. Assad courted the country's middle class and Sunni bourgeoisie as well as certain tribes through patronage networks and economic benefits. The regime also used the fear of minorities to secure their support. Alawis (12 percent of the popu-

THE SYRIAN GAMBIT

lation), Christians (8 percent), Druze (3 percent), Ismailis (1 percent) and other Shia sects (1 percent) feared that a Sunni-led regime might rule post-Assad Syria and exact revenge on minorities.[9] Assad's buy-in strategies paid off and many of these communities did not join the anti-regime protests.

Another difference between Tunisia and Egypt and Syria was the involvement of the military in the uprisings. The Tunisian army played a decisive role in removing Tunisian strongman Zine al Abedine Ben Ali by ignoring his order to shoot protesters. Similarly, the Egyptian military abandoned Hosni Mubarak at the height of the protests, leading to his overthrow. In Syria, however, the military largely remained loyal to Assad.

All these factors made toppling the Assad regime quickly a lot more difficult. But Erdoğan and Davutoğlu thought otherwise. In August, a few months after the uprising in Syria started, Davutoğlu, who assumed Assad had the backing of only the Alawite community, told Erdoğan that Assad would fall in a few weeks.[10] Western countries made similar assumptions, but they can be forgiven for not reading the regime and societal dynamics correctly. Syria had long been a black box to the Western world. It has been a pariah since 1979 when it was placed on the US list of state sponsors of terrorism. Turkey, on the other hand, shares a long border and family and historical ties with its southern neighbor. Due to the regime's decades-long policy of hosting the PKK on its soil as a trump card against Turkey, Turkish intelligence had long been active in the country. The Erdoğan and Davutoğlu duo's enthusiasm to bring about regime change and install a Muslim Brotherhood government in its place had clouded their judgement. They had watched popular uprisings remove long-term dictators in Tunisia and Egypt and the Muslim Brotherhood become the most powerful political force in those countries. If for some reason the mass protests did not topple Assad, Erdoğan and Davutoğlu thought, the West would surely intervene just like it did in Libya. Thus, Erdoğan did not want to lose more time with Assad and Ankara officially joined the anti-Assad camp in the fall of 2011.

However, Turkey's support for the anti-Assad opposition had begun much earlier. As early as April, only a few weeks after the

Syrian uprising started, the Turkish government allowed the Syrian opposition to host its first meeting in Istanbul. More robust support for the anti-regime movement followed. Turkey's backing of the Syrian opposition stood in stark contrast to the messages of brotherhood given to President Assad only a few months previously at the ground-breaking ceremony for the construction of the "friendship dam" on the Orontes River. In February 2011, then Prime Minister Erdoğan and his Syrian counterpart pledged support for the dam, along with the lifting of visa requirements for travel between the two countries, which they thought would set an example of brotherly relations for the world. Erdoğan boasted of the flourishing ties between Syria and Turkey saying, "I sat down with my brother Assad and talked about the problems and we turned Turkey and Syria into two brother nations in the region."[11] A few months later, Erdoğan was calling for his ousting. "My brother Assad" became "murderer Assad."

For Erdoğan, the U-turn was necessary to advance his domestic agenda. He had just launched a process to redefine Turkey as a Sunni Muslim nation and the central pillar of the *ummah*. He had branded himself as the vanguard of the oppressed pious Sunni Muslim masses that had been marginalized by the West and its domestic secular conspirators. He could not credibly claim to be the "savior of the *ummah*" and fail to support what he saw as a Sunni uprising against an Alawite, Baathist regime. Foreign Minister Davutoğlu provided Erdoğan with the intellectual tools he needed to legitimize the volte-face in Turkey's Syria policy.

From "firefighter" to arsonist

The uprisings in Tunisia had just started. Foreign Minister Davutoğlu was giving a talk at the Ambassadors' Conference, organized annually by the Ministry of Foreign Affairs since 2008.[12] He likened the world to a fire scene and Turkish diplomats to firefighters and added that Turkish diplomats had a duty to immediately intervene in regional crises. "If a new regional order is to emerge, we must be the first to place the first building block," said Davutoğlu. He had grand ambitions. He confidently declared that

Turkey would "ride the wave" of the Arab uprisings. But as former Turkish ambassador James Jeffrey succinctly put it, Turkey had "Rolls Royce ambitions but Rover resources."[13] As a country that had looked West since its inception, Turkey neither had "the institutional depth" nor the "material resources" to become the leader of the Middle East overnight.[14] Ten years after pledging that Turkey would "ride the wave of the Arab Spring," Davutoğlu was going to have to admit that "that wave had swallowed us all."[15] But until then, none of the extraordinary events taking place in Turkey's southern neighbor dented his bubbling confidence.

A year after the Syrian uprising started, Davutoğlu summarized the strategy he had pursued in Syria in a "four-phase strategic plan."[16] The first phase entailed engaging with the regime to force Assad to carry out reforms. When this did not work, Davutoğlu said, Turkey switched to the second phase, which involved working with the Arab League to pressure the regime to prevent a Western intervention. When that effort failed, the third phase, which involved a UN-led intervention to force Assad out, kicked in. Russian and Chinese vetoes made a UN-led intervention impossible, leading to the last phase, which involved establishing the Friends of Syria, an alliance of mainly Western and Gulf countries that sought Assad's overthrow. By laying out his "four-phase strategic plan," Davutoğlu was responding to the Turkish opposition's criticisms that Ankara had become party to the Syrian civil war too quickly. "We exerted every effort for nine months," said Davutoğlu, referring to Ankara's efforts to convince the Assad regime to carry out reforms. He was not entirely truthful.

The swift toppling of autocratic regimes in Tunisia and Egypt and the rise of the Muslim Brotherhood had raised Erdoğan and Davutoğlu's hopes that a similar scenario would soon repeat itself in Syria. From day one, toppling the regime and installing a Muslim Brotherhood-led government in Syria became the backbone of Turkey's post-uprising Syria strategy. All the phases in Davutoğlu's "plan" aimed to serve those two goals. What Davutoğlu referred to as the "first phase," which involved engaging the regime in the hopes of avoiding a regime collapse, was in fact a two-pronged strategy. While Ankara kept the dialogue channels with the regime open and encouraged reforms, it had worked towards regime change from the outset. It pushed Assad to share power with the Muslim Brotherhood. According to Western officials, Erdoğan pledged support to end the uprising if Assad included the Muslim Brotherhood in the cabinet.[17] All the while, Ankara encouraged the Muslim Brotherhood to lead opposition efforts to organize on Turkish soil, and sought to ensure recognition of the Muslim Brotherhood-dominated opposition as "the legitimate representative" of the Syrian people.

Ankara did not just allow the political wing of the Syrian opposition to use its territory as a base. It also facilitated the formation of military opposition and provided military assistance to the forces fighting against the regime as early as June 2011, months before Turkey officially joined the anti-Assad camp. The Free Syrian Army, which was formed by deserters of the Syrian Armed Forces to topple the regime, was established in Turkey. In March, after the Syrian government announced reforms such as raising wages for workers and allowing more political parties to compete in elections to meet the demands of protesters, Erdoğan called Assad to congratulate him and encourage him to carry on. But in reality, Erdoğan had long given up on Assad and was laying the groundwork for him to leave. As early as late March, a few days after Erdoğan's congratulatory call to Assad, CIA director Leon Panetta spent five days in Ankara, holding "top secret" meetings with Turkish intelligence chief Hakan Fidan as well as government and military officials. The meetings concluded that the regime was at a "critical juncture" and the Turkish side pushed for planning a regime change.[18] The meetings with the CIA director had revealed something else. Erdoğan and Davutoğlu referred to the Assad regime as "Nusayri," a derogatory term for Alawites, and defined the protests as a Sunni uprising against a "Nusayri" regime.[19] This sectarian reading of the uprising at a time when sectarian concerns were not central to the conflict was a reflection of Erdoğan's efforts to redefine Turkey as a Sunni Muslim nation and the leader of the Sunni world.

When Erdoğan and Davutoğlu realized that a swift toppling of the regime by the opposition was not going to happen, they pushed for an outside intervention. The US decision to intervene in Libya had encouraged them. They worked towards creating conditions on the ground to pave the way for a Libyan-style external intervention to topple Assad. When their efforts to secure a UN-led intervention failed due to the Chinese and Russian veto at the UN Security Council, they pinned their hopes on the Friends of Syria group to do the job.

Davutoğlu often boasted that Turkey did everything in its power to prevent a bloodbath in Syria but in reality, Turkey contributed to that bloodbath. Turkey's Syria policy exacerbated ethnic and sectarian tensions. Its support for Islamists, including radical groups, added to the jihadization of the conflict. Its military support to armed groups sped up the militarization of the uprising while its obsession with regime change derailed efforts to find a diplomatic solution in the early phase of the conflict. Turkey was surely not alone in these misguided policies, but it was the most fervent outside actor that backed the opposition. It not only provided financial and military aid but also lent its territory to Syrian rebels. Erdoğan's domestic calculations to strengthen his rule lay behind Turkey's enthusiastic support for the anti-Assad opposition. Erdoğan himself admitted on several occasions that Syria was Turkey's "domestic problem."[20] That thinking had disastrous consequences. Turkey was no longer a "firefighter"; it had become an arsonist in Syria.

Turkey becomes the patron of the Syrian opposition

The Syrian opposition convened its first international meeting at a chic Istanbul hotel in April 2011. A diverse group of people attended the meeting. Alawites, Kurds, Sunnis, Islamists, and secularists came together to declare "no religion, no sect, no ethnic group. We are all Syrian nationalists… All we want is freedom."[21] The first meeting would not go beyond a gathering for representatives of different opposition groups to get to know one another.

The second opposition meeting was also held in Turkey a month later. Participants were not impressed with Assad's limited reforms and called for his ousting. They agreed to prepare a roadmap to guide the democratic transition. The second meeting laid bare the fact that agreeing on the need for a roadmap was much easier than agreeing on the roadmap itself. To ease concerns that Islamists were leading the Syrian revolution, the Muslim Brotherhood sought to keep a low profile in these initial meetings, but they could not avoid the ideological tension.

Contrary to the first meeting where ideological differences were disregarded, they burst into the open in the second. Islamists were not happy that secularists underlined the need to separate religion from state in a post-Assad Syria. The meeting also highlighted Kurdish-Arab tension. Syria's Kurds and Arabs have had a long-running mistrust, but the Syrian uprising amplified the suspicion each ethnic group held towards the other. Turkey's policies contributed to the inter-ethnic tension. This was apparent in the second opposition meeting. Several Kurdish groups, including the Democratic Union Party (PYD), the PKK's Syrian offshoot, boycotted the meeting because it was held in Turkey, a country which could not resolve its own Kurdish problem. Other Kurdish groups that attended the meeting became frustrated. Their demands for autonomy and education in the Kurdish language prompted a strong reaction from several groups representing Arab tribes.[22]

Just a few weeks after the protests in Syria started, Turkey had already become the organizational hub of the Syrian opposition. The Muslim Brotherhood was crucial in that process. There was a large network of Syrian Muslim Brotherhood members who had fled to Turkey in the 1980s after the Hama massacre. In cooperation with Turkish Islamist NGOs such as Mazlumder, they influenced the way Turkey read the evolving dynamics on the ground. However, many of the Brotherhood's assessments of the situation were misguided. The group overstated its strength and downplayed the skepticism it faced from wide segments of the Syrian population. "Seeing the conflict in Syria through the lens of the Muslim Brotherhood was a mistake," said Abdullah Gül, who was president at the time. "I warned my friends," referring to Erdoğan and Davutoğlu, "but they didn't listen."[23] The risks of relying on the Muslim Brotherhood were going to become apparent in the months and years to come but until then the Brotherhood remained

THE SYRIAN GAMBIT

Ankara's favorite opposition group and the lens through which Turkey saw the conflict in Syria.

Turkey not only helped civilian opposition groups. Ankara supported the military opposition as well. Apaydın camp in Hatay, a Turkish town bordering Syria, became the headquarters of those who had defected from the Syrian army. Among the inhabitants of the camp were high-ranking military officers such as Colonel Riad Assad, who defected in July 2011 and established the Free Syrian Army (FSA) in Hatay to lead the military opposition operating in Syria. The Turkish government's secrecy about the Apaydın camp brought its military engagement in the Syrian conflict under scrutiny. Hurşit Güneş, a member of parliament from the main opposition CHP, complained that his request to visit the camp was turned down by Erdoğan, who scolded him by asking "are you a policeman?"[24] Güneş said Turkish authorities told him that he could visit other refugee camps but not Apaydın. He was determined not to let it go. Güneş blamed Turkey for allowing the transfer of weapons to Syria and criticized the presence of many Syrian generals at the camp who had defected but were still wearing military uniforms and directing the war from Turkish soil. "What is happening in Apaydn camp is a symbol of Turkey's misguided Syria policy," he said.[25]

The opposition's criticism that Turkey had become too involved in the conflict raging in its southern neighbor did not stop Erdoğan. On the contrary, as he doubled down on Turkey's military support to the opposition, he used the conflict to delegitimize his secularist opponents. He drew parallels between himself and the anti-Assad opposition whom he argued had embarked on a revolution to bring down a dictator and establish real democracy, while accusing the main opposition CHP of being "Turkey's Baath party." He often attacked CHP leader Kemal Kılıçdaroğlu's Alevi identity. To Erdoğan and his close circle, Syrian people were "getting rid of their own CHP." This narrative once again showed how intertwined the Syrian war and Erdoğan's struggle against his domestic enemies had become. Erdoğan used the war in the neighboring country to delegitimize his opponents and consolidate his conservative base. Seeing Syria as an extension of his domestic strategy to monopolize power had disastrous consequences for the course of the war.

Peaceful protests turn into a civil war

Until June, anti-regime protests remained largely peaceful despite the many atrocities committed by the regime against demonstrators. That changed in June and Turkey had a hand in it. In the Syrian border town of Jisr al-Shugur, many Syrian army soldiers and security people were killed, their bodies mutilated and thrown in the river. Jisr al-Shugur was a Muslim Brotherhood stronghold. Brotherhood members in the town had rebelled against the regime in the 1980s when hundreds of them were killed by Assad's security forces. Decades later, Jisr al-Shugur was once again at the forefront of anti-regime protests. Opposition activists claimed that soldiers were killed by their superiors because they were trying to defect. Others maintained that according to electronic interception of opposition communication, it was opposition members who killed the soldiers.[26] Whatever the truth, by the summer of 2011, anti-regime protests in Syria had turned into a civil war and demonstrators' peaceful call for freedom had largely been kidnapped by radical Islamists.

Turkish journalist Hediye Levent, who was working for Turkey's state-owned Anadolu Agency, was in Jisr al-Shugur at the time. She was trying to cover the story amidst competing narratives about who was responsible for the killing of Syrian soldiers. Levent found ammunition made by Turkey's Mechanical and Chemical Industry Cooperation (*Makine ve Kimya Endüstrisi Kurumu*), which consists of government-controlled factories that supply Turkish Armed Forces with military products. After she included Turkish-made ammunition in her story, she was fired immediately. In his new memoir, Ömer Önhon, Turkey's last ambassador to Syria, confirmed Levent's account.[27] Reporters from the British daily *The Guardian* had also witnessed the transfer of weapons in early June near the Turkish frontier. According to their account, five men arrived at a police station in the Syrian border village of Altima to finalize the transfer of "around 50 boxes of rifles and ammunition" from the Turkish town of Reyhanlı.[28] Turkey's state intelligence agency (MİT) helped deliver the arms.[29]

There were other indications of Turkey's military involvement in the conflict as early as June. Syrian Lt Colonel Hussein al-Harmoush was among those involved in the killing of Syrian soldiers in Jisr al-Shugur. He claimed that he was sent to suppress the protests but defected from the army because he did not want to shoot at the protesters. He later retracted these claims, saying he had not been in Jisr al-Shughur at the time of the killings and had defected four days later.[30] After the incident, Harmoush fled to Turkey and established the Free Officers Movement that called on the Syrian army to support the people, not Assad. A few months later, Harmoush was kidnapped from the camp where he was staying and handed over to Syrian intelligence by a Turkish intelligence officer. The Turkish officer was sentenced to twenty years in prison but disappeared while being transferred to another prison. Later, he told a journalist that he handed over Harmoush to Syrian authorities because he could not live with the fact that his government was providing refuge to people "who committed massacres in Syria," giving them phones and logistical support.[31] It was claimed that the officer sold Harmoush to the Syrian authorities.[32] A Free Syrian Army officer told a different story about what had happened in Jisr al-Shugur. He said that al-Qaeda-linked groups had killed the Syrian soldiers but did not want the West to think that the revolution had been hijacked by jihadi groups. So they asked Harmoush to take responsibility.[33]

Whatever the truth, Jisr al-Shugur proved to be a turning point. It shed light on how Erdoğan's support for the anti-Assad opposition had consequences far greater than Western or Gulf support for the opposition. His decision to militarily support the opposition early in the conflict became one of the key developments that "edged Syria closer to civil war."[34]

The violence in Jisr al-Shugur prompted thousands of Syrians to flee to Turkey. Erdoğan was furious at the images coming out of the town. He blamed Assad for the killings. He had already pledged that he would never allow another Hama incident in Syria, saying the images he had seen were "unpalatable" and suggested Turkey could back a UN Security Council decision against Syria.

In a letter sent to Erdoğan, Syrian opposition members referred to him as the grandson of Sultan Mehmet the Conqueror, the Ottoman Sultan who ended Christian rule in Constantinople, and pleaded for Erdoğan's help. "We will never forget your pledge that you would not allow another Hama massacre to happen in Syria," the letter said.[35] In Deraa, the birthplace of the anti-regime protests, people were carrying signs that read "We love you Erdoğan," while thousands in Damascus gathered in front of the Turkish Embassy to protest aginst Turkey's involvement in the conflict.[36]

"Assad will be toppled in a few weeks"

In August 2011, Foreign Minister Davutoğlu paid his final visit to Damascus to talk to Assad. This was meant to be Ankara's last-ditch effort to pressure Assad to carry out reforms. Davutoğlu went to Damascus like an Ottoman Pasha who governed with unlimited authority over the land under his control. He was confident of the leverage he wielded over his host. During the six-hour meeting, Assad asked for four more months to carry out democratic reforms. Davutoğlu became furious; he banged his fist on the table and yelled "you will resign."[37] Assad was defiant: "The days of the Ottoman Sultan have gone. Syria will never accept that Ottomanism replaces Arabism. Ankara will never again become the decision-making center of the Arab world."[38]

That was Ankara's last official meeting with Assad. Davutoğlu returned to Turkey and told his boss that Assad would be toppled within weeks. Erdoğan had long given up on Assad and had already become the key international patron of the Syrian opposition, but he made it official after the August meeting. To Davutoğlu, the first phase of his "four-phase Syria strategy," which involved pressuring the regime to carry out reforms, was over.

Other countries cut diplomatic ties with Assad as well. Kuwait, Bahrain, and Saudi Arabia recalled their ambassadors to Syria in August while US President Barack Obama, German Chancellor Angela Merkel, French President Nicholas Sarkozy, and British Prime Minister David Cameron issued statements calling for Assad to step down as president. These Western calls were music to Erdoğan's ears. They raised Ankara's expectation that Washington was committed to regime change in Syria. Russia and Iran, on the other hand, were enraged. They decided to increase their support to Assad.

By the fall of 2011, it had become apparent that Turkey's expectations of a Tunisian/Egyptian scenario, in which popular protests brought down the autocrats, repeating itself in Syria were misplaced. Turkey started working towards a Libyan model. In Libya, a NATO-led military intervention to protect civilians had paved the way for removing the Qaddafi regime. Before the intervention, the United Nations Security Council approved a no-fly zone. The presence of an Interim Transitional National Council (ITNC), which was the representative body of anti-Qaddafi Libyans based in the eastern city of Benghazi and was expected to form the new government after Qaddafi's fall, made the decision to launch a military intervention easier for Western governments. The expectation was that after the intervention, the ITNC would capture the remaining portion of Western Libya, topple the Qaddafi regime and quickly form a government. Ankara started laying the groundwork for a Libya-type intervention in Syria. The first task was to create a representative body like the ITNC.

In August 2011, the Syrian National Council (SNC) was established in Istanbul. Hosting the council and controlling its access to Syria, Turkey wielded great influence over the organization. Largely due to that influence, the Muslim Brotherhood played a significant role in the SNC, which prompted several groups to leave the council in protest. Turkey's insistence on a strong Brotherhood presence had already started hurting the Syrian opposition's prospects. It not only helped contribute to factionalism within the SNC and scared away potential supporters from Alawites, Christians and secularists but also confirmed Assad's narrative. Assad had long argued that the uprising was an Islamist plot that would deprive Syria's minority sects of their freedom. The Brotherhood's domination of the council resonated with that claim. An opposition leader who left the council in protest said of Turkish and Qatari support for the Brotherhood "they are setting conditions for who they arm. And those who are not Islamists or religious, they are not being supplied with guns."[39]

ERDOĞAN'S WAR

The Muslim Brotherhood's presence in the Syrian opposition was a sea change. After the 1982 Hama defeat, the Islamist insurrection was broken and many Muslim Brotherhood members fled the country, leaving its grassroots organization weakened. The Brotherhood took part in an opposition alliance in 2006 with Abdul Halim Khaddam, former vice president and crony of Hafez al-Assad, further discrediting the group.[40] Several factors helped the Brotherhood turn its fortunes around, among them Turkey's strong support for the group. But the Brotherhood's domination weakened the SNC and contributed to its demise.

There were other factors that contributed to the SNC's ineffectiveness. It was dominated by exiles, mostly based in Turkey, who were being criticized by the opposition on the grounds that they were "trying to direct the war from five-star hotel lobbies in Turkey."[41] Another weakness of the SNC was its unwillingness to engage with other opposition groups. The SNC distanced itself from leftist and Alawite opposition groups that were opposed to outside intervention and promoted a dialogue with the regime.[42] Kurdish groups largely remained distant from the SNC as well, mainly due to Turkey's high-profile role in the organization.

In September 2011, the Free Syrian Army officially announced what had been apparent to many for months. General Riad Assad, the army leader who had defected from the air force in July and fled to Turkey, said "It is the beginning of armed rebellion."[43] Turkey's plan for a Libyan scenario in Syria was in full motion. General Riad Assad said that his goals were to carve out a slice of territory in northern Syria, secure protection from the international community through a no-fly-zone, receive weapons from countries seeking Assad's overthrow and launch an attack to topple the regime. "You cannot remove this regime except by force and bloodshed," he said.[44] Syria's civil war entered a dangerous new phase.

Meanwhile, Erdoğan's efforts to overthrow the Assad regime came under increasing criticism from Turkey's opposition. A CHP delegation led by Turkey's former ambassador to Washington, Faruk Loğoğlu, paid a visit to Damascus to hold talks with Assad and other Syrian officials. According to the main opposition party, Erdoğan was making a huge mistake by becoming party to its neighbor's civil war and arming groups seeking the regime's removal. The party urged the government to take Atatürk's foreign policy approach as a model, respecting other countries' sovereignty and refraining from intervening in their internal affairs.

But to Erdoğan, Syria was another front in his war against the CHP. To him, the secularist CHP and the secularist Baath regime in Damascus were both elite, "minority" parties that did not represent the "real people." Erdoğan saw them both ruling with an iron fist, suppressing people's religiosity in the name of secularism and representing the interests of only a tiny fraction of the country. He often talked about the Alawite nature of the Assad regime and Turkish Alevi support for the CHP. Indeed, Turkey's Alevis, who are in many ways different from Syrian Alawites but like them are considered an offshoot of Shia Islam, had historically supported the CHP, thinking a secularist party would not discriminate against them based on religion. CHP leader Kemal Kılıçdaroğlu, himself an Alevi, had come under increasing attacks from Erdoğan and his Islamist circle since the start of the Syrian uprising. In Erdoğan's narrative, his rise to power had emancipated the Sunni Muslim religious masses from the oppression of the CHP and brought to power the authentic representatives of the nation. According to Erdoğan, a similar thing was happening in Syria. An "oppressive," "minority" and "godless" regime was being brought down by true Muslims and Erdoğan would fight for Syria's Muslims against their oppressors as hard as he fought against his own.

Erdoğan's fight against Turkey's secularists was not over. He had just won the elections held in 2011. His new goal was to dismantle the Kemalists' secular, Western-facing, anti-Ottoman nation project and build a national identity along Sunni Muslim and Ottoman lines in its place.[45] Supporting regional Islamists' struggle against secular, autocratic elites was part of that agenda. By backing the Syrian Muslim Brotherhood's uprising against Assad, Erdoğan was not only strengthening his narrative that he was the defender of Islam and Muslims; he was also trying to further marginalize the secularist CHP as an "illegitimate," "undemocratic" and "elite" party that sought to suppress the true will of the people. The CHP's calls to stop supporting the Syrian opposition and engage with the Assad regime fit perfectly into Erdoğan's narrative that the CHP was Turkey's Baath party. As the war in Syria raged on, Erdoğan intensified his attacks on Turkey's own Alevis and the CHP.

The country's Islamists backed Erdoğan's efforts to divide the nation along sectarian lines. To them, the post-2011 years were going to be the formative years of the new Sunni Muslim Turkish nation. Drawing the boundaries of that nation called for a "jihad against infidels, Alevis, Kemalists and everyone else who stood in the way of realizing that divine goal."[46] They saw the uprising in Syria through a similar lens. They thought it was an Islamist revolution that must be supported by Turkey at all costs. And that is exactly what Erdoğan did.

By 2012, the flow of weapons across the southern Turkish border into the hands of Free Syrian Army leaders became too obvious to hide. A command center in Istanbul had been established to coordinate supply lines in consultation with FSA leaders inside Syria. Then US defense secretary Leon Panetta said that Washington made the decision not to provide lethal assistance to the Syrian opposition, but the CIA was operating in Turkey helping the country decide which opposition fighters to arm.[47] Acceleration in the flow of weapons came after Russia and China vetoed a Security Council draft resolution demanding that both Assad forces and armed opposition groups stop the violence and reprisals. The draft resolution condemned widespread violations of human rights and called on the Syrian government to immediately implement the elements of a plan set out by the League of Arab States on January 22.

The Arab League plan called on Syria to immediately "cease all violence and protect its population; release all persons detained arbitrarily; withdraw all military and armed forces from cities and towns; and guarantee the freedom to hold peaceful demonstrations."[48] It also called for "an inclusive Syrian-led political process conducted in an environment free from violence, fear, intimidation and extremism, and aimed at effectively addressing the legitimate aspirations and concerns of the Syrian people."[49]

Erdoğan was furious about the Chinese and Russian decision to veto the Security Council draft resolution asking regime and opposition forces to stop violence. "We will not just sit back and watch the bloodshed because the UN process has been blocked," said Erdoğan. Indeed, he did not. On January 3, two Qatar Emiri Air Force C-130 transport aircraft touched down in Istanbul. They were carrying arms for the Syrian rebels and were among many cargo flights that came from Al Udeid Air Base in Qatar, a hub for American military logistics in the Middle East. Later in the year, Jordanians and Saudis stepped up their role in the arms airlift via Turkey. As Assad's forces ramped up their air operations against the rebels, particularly around the contested city of Aleppo, nearly two dozen surface-to-air missiles called MANPADS were delivered to the Free Syrian Army via Turkey.[50] According to the Syrian opposition, the decision to provide MANPADS to the rebels was taken by Turkey despite objections from the US and without the knowledge of Gulf countries.[51] They could not have been handed over to the opposition without the involvement of Turkish intelligence and security forces.

Meanwhile, the Obama administration, which wanted to tread cautiously, was growing nervous about the accelerated pace of weapons shipments to Syrian rebels by Turkey and Gulf countries. Washington was worried about weapons falling into the wrong hands. There were already reports that al-Qaeda-linked groups had got their hands on arms sent to the rebels.[52] Some US lawmakers, such as Republican Senators John McCain and Lindsey Graham, were criticizing Obama for not moving fast enough to assist the rebels and pushing the US government to become directly involved in arming Assad's opponents.[53]

To steer weapons away from Islamists, the US decided to get involved. Washington was not ready to provide lethal assistance but happy to let others arm the opposition.[54] The CIA began vetting the recipients of arms to make sure they went to moderate groups. But others argued that the US involvement in weapons shipment was more than just vetting the recipients. According to an article in the *London Review of Books* by Seymour Hersh, in early 2012, US President Barack Obama signed a secret order permitting the CIA and other US agencies to provide support that could help the rebels unseat Assad. The CIA called the back-channel supply line that was used to transfer weapons and ammunition from Libya via southern Turkey and across the Syrian border into anti-Assad groups a "rat line." Turkey's intelligence was involved in arms shipments as well.[55] Turkey was the most effective avenue to supply the Syrian opposition and Erdoğan was more than willing to make the country a weapons supply highway. According to the deal, Turkey, along with Saudi Arabia and Qatar, funded the operation while the CIA and British intelligence were in charge of funneling arms from Qaddafi's arsenal into Syria.[56]

Turkey set up a secret base near the Syrian border to help direct vital military and communications aid to Assad's opponents. The "nerve center" was in Adana, a city which was also home to an air base used by US military and intelligence agencies. The US was collaborating with Turkey in operating the nerve center and providing training and equipment to the rebels.

The Turkish government oversaw a coordinated clandestine military logistics operation. Later in the year, an impatient Erdoğan decided to accelerate the pace of air shipments of weapons to the rebels, the scale of which became unprecedented. Turkey's efforts were paying off. The weapons shipment was turning the tide of the rebels' military campaign in the northwestern city of Idlib. Rebel attacks on Assad's forces had begun driving them from parts of the countryside.[57]

While the flow of weapons to Syria accelerated, Turkey, along with France, led efforts for the establishment of the Friends of Syria Group, a cluster of countries and bodies convening periodically to discuss Syria outside the UN Security Council. For Erdoğan, the war in Syria had become his own war and he was determined not to lose. He brushed off UN-led diplomatic attempts to resolve the conflict and pushed for regime change. Kofi Annan, the UN-Arab League Joint Special Envoy for Syria, had devised a plan that promoted a political resolution to the conflict. The plan called for dialogue between the regime and the opposition. At the Friends of Syria meeting in Istanbul in April 2012, Erdoğan said that Turkey would never back a plan that would keep the regime in place. To him, the only way out was ousting Assad.

Turkey's main opposition CHP was worried about Erdoğan's hawkish stance. It argued that the Erdoğan-Davutoğlu duo's Syria policy risked drawing Turkey actively into the war. Atilla Kart, a CHP member of the Turkish Parliament, said "The use of Turkish airspace at such a critical time, with the conflict in Syria across our borders, and by foreign planes from countries that are known to be central to the conflict, defines Turkey as a party in the conflict."[58]

Erdoğan brushed off the opposition's criticism. During the party's fourth congress, Erdoğan greeted the "heroes of Syria," called Bashar al-Assad a "bloody dictator" and hit back at the main opposition party. Erdoğan said the CHP closed down mosques and banned reading and teaching of the Quran in the 1940s, and accused the party of siding with Assad due to a shared sectarian identity.[59] Listening to him in the hall where the AKP congress was being held was Mohammed Morsi, the Egyptian Muslim Brotherhood's newly elected president, as well as Khalid Meshaal, the leader of Hamas. Erdoğan was delivering what many called his "Islamist manifesto" amidst chants of *"Mücahit Erdoğan"* (Erdoğan the Islamic warrior). Supporting the "Islamic awakening" in Syria was the regional leg of that manifesto.

Too much was at stake for Erdoğan in Syria. He had made overthrowing the Assad regime a key component of the Sunni Muslim brand he was trying to craft at home. That is why he was furious when the US decided to end CIA support for weapons shipments into Syria after the killing of its ambassador to Libya by a group of Islamist militants in September 2012. The incident raised questions about the radicalization of countries shaken by the Arab uprisings.

On June 22, 2012, Turkey announced that Syrian forces had shot down a Turkish warplane over the Mediterranean, killing two crew members. The Syrians later claimed that the Turkish jet had violated Syrian airspace and their anti-aircraft gunners had downed the plane. In a speech in the Turkish Parliament after the incident, Erdoğan threatened to shoot down Syrian military jets approaching the Turkish border.[60] A few days later, Turkey-backed opposition groups announced that they had taken control of territory as far as 40 km (25 miles) inside the Syrian border. Turkey's deployment of anti-aircraft batteries up to the border and its willingness to scramble its F-16s provided cover for the rebels, creating a de facto buffer zone.[61]

However, Erdoğan wanted a no-fly zone backed by the West. He hoped that such a zone would not only give the armed opposition a secure base against the regime but also help the rebels establish a rival government to that of Assad and pave the way for a Western-backed military intervention. No-fly zones imposed by NATO and Arab allies had helped the opponents of Muammar Qaddafi overthrow him. After the jet incident, Turkey's efforts to establish a Western-backed no-fly zone intensified. Foreign Minister Davutoğlu once again raised the issue with US Secretary of State Hillary Clinton in Ankara in August. Clinton said that a major outside military intervention was necessary to impose such a zone and that the United States did not think it would help.[62] But she did not want to be dismissive of Turkey's concerns either. She suggested establishing an "operation and command" structure for the two governments to hold further discussions and coordinate their policies. With that, Washington had shunned the idea of repeating a Libya-style military intervention in Syria.[63] Erdoğan's plans had been upended by his Western allies.

Erdoğan stokes the sectarian fires

Turkish cities, particularly those on the border, were feeling the heat of Erdoğan's Syria policy. Hatay, which was once part of Syria and a shopping destination for Syrians before the outbreak of the civil war, is one such city. It sits along the Syrian-Turkish border and mirrors Syria's ethnic divides. It is home to Alawite Arabs— the same Islamic sect Syria's ruling Assad family comes from— Sunni Arabs, Armenians, Circassians, and Arab Christians as well as ethnic Turks. These communities are closely connected to those in Syria through family and tribal links.

As Erdoğan doubled down on Turkey's military engagement in the Syrian civil war, Hatay turned into a hotbed of military activity for the Syrian opposition. Apaydın camp hosted defecting Syrian military officers who daily crossed the border with ease to help the rebels' fight against the regime. Wounded rebels received treatment at Hatay's hospitals. A Turkish doctor who worked at one of the state hospitals said that they would receive hundreds of wounded "jihadists" a week and they had received orders from the hospital administration not to ask for identification cards or ask any questions. "It felt like we were serving in a war zone, but it was not our war," the doctor said.[64] Residents complained that their previously peaceful town had turned into a rest and resupply hub for the Syrian rebels. "Before the conflict began," one female university student told me, "women with shorts were a common scene on Antakya's streets, now thick-bearded men are everywhere. We are scared of leaving our homes." Salafists, or Muslim puritans, roamed the streets and boarded buses carrying fighters into Syria at night. One Turkish official working in Antakya municipality, which is part of Hatay province, said "local spies are everywhere reporting to the Assad regime on the activities of the Free Syrian Army based in Hatay."[65]

In one of the deadliest spillovers since the beginning of the uprising, fifty-three people were killed, including five children, and 146 were wounded in a car bomb in Reyhanlı, a Sunni-majority district of Hatay, in 2013. The Turkish government blamed Assad's intelligence but a Turkish public prosecutor from Adana, who was going to be removed from his post and sentenced to prison for revealing the Turkish government's military aid to al-Qaeda-linked groups in Syria, said in a written statement that Turkish officials had intelligence about the car bombing and did not act to stop the perpetrators; instead they protected them.[66]

It is difficult to verify the prosecutor's claim, but it strengthened the opposition's narrative that Erdoğan was using the Syrian war to advance his domestic agenda. In a speech after the bombing, Erdoğan lamented "fifty-three Sunni citizens have been martyred."[67] His contentious comment angered many. Protests broke out against Erdoğan in Reyhanlı. They became more frequent as Ankara became further involved in Syria's civil war and Erdoğan's sectarian rhetoric intensified. In one such demonstration in February, protesters chanted "Allah, Syria, Bashar, that's all."[68] The moment highlighted the Turkish Alevi community's unease with Erdoğan's efforts to topple the Assad regime and the sectarian spillover of the Syrian war into Turkey. They were anxious that behind Erdoğan's policy of ousting Assad lay a quest to cement Sunni supremacy in the region.

Indeed, Erdoğan had ramped up his sectarian rhetoric since the outbreak of the protests in Syria, which made the Alevi community the target of more frequent hate crimes. Several Alevi homes across the country were daubed with red paint. The incidents brought back painful memories of violence against Alevis whose homes had been similarly marked in the past. In a further sign of Erdoğan's anti-Alevi stance, at a groundbreaking ceremony, the third bridge spanning the Bosphorus was named after the ninth Ottoman Sultan, Selim I, a monarch who earned the sobriquet Selim the Grim for his severe rule. Selim I is believed to have ordered the killing of tens of thousands of Alevis. Naming the bridge after a Sultan responsible for the massacre of Alevis sparked protests from the Alevi community and the CHP.[69]

Erdoğan's sectarian rhetoric received a boost with the arrival of members of the Iranian military and Hezbollah militants in Syria to help Assad. The Syrian opposition had started alleging that Hezbollah fighters were fighting in the ranks of regime forces in 2011 but it was in late 2012 that these claims became more credible. Lending credibility to opposition claims were the US government's sanctions imposed on Hezbollah's Secretary General Hassan Nasrallah for having "overseen Hezbollah's efforts to help the Syrian regime's violent crackdown on the Syrian civilian population by providing training, advice, and extensive logistical support to the Government of Syria."[70] The Assad regime had been suffering from a shortage of manpower while the opposition, bolstered by the jihadis' military capabilities, was gaining ground against the regime's forces. Assad turned to Hezbollah and members of the Iranian military to provide manpower as well as training to build a paramilitary force. The Iran-linked groups' entrance into the Syrian theater strengthened Erdoğan's narrative that the Syrian conflict was a conflict between a "ruthless," "godless" Alevi regime and Sunni freedom fighters. The sectarian dynamic of the Syrian civil war provided Erdoğan with an ideological tool to delegitimize the Turkish opposition and promote Sunni dominance at home.

THE SYRIAN GAMBIT

Jihadis gain ground with Turkey's help

Erdoğan's efforts to turn the Turkey-based Syrian opposition groups, such as the Muslim Brotherhood-dominated Syrian National Council (SNC) or the Free Syrian Army, into the sole representatives of the Syrian opposition failed. But his attempts to arm the Syrian opposition, including radical groups, continued unabated. Turkey's de facto buffer zone along the Syrian border helped jihadist groups gain a foothold in the area. Among them was Jabhat al-Nusra, al-Qaeda's Syrian affiliate. These jihadist groups captured several border crossings on the Syrian side, raising fears in the West about the growing jihadi influence among the opposition ranks. Robert Ford, who was at the time the US ambassador to Syria, said "By the second half of 2012, some of us were warning our superiors and the White House that jihadis were taking control of eastern Syria and would link up with jihadis in Iraq."[71] Other unnamed US intelligence officials pointed to the growing al-Qaeda presence in opposition ranks and raised alarm bells about their ability to unite disconnected units and form a command and control structure that matched sophisticated operations in places like Iraq and Afghanistan.[72] A study by the London-based Quilliam Foundation, which tracks radical groups, reported that extremists were still a minority among the rebels, but their influence was growing due to the funds and weapons channeled to them.[73]

In October 2012, Secretary Clinton voiced Washington's frustration with the SNC's failure to come together with a coherent plan and the growing influence of jihadists within opposition ranks. She asked the Syrian opposition to resist extremists' efforts to hijack the Syrian revolution and called for an overhaul of the Syrian opposition's leadership. "It is time to move beyond the SNC and bring in those who are in the front lines fighting and dying," she said.[74] Shortly after her remarks, the National Coalition for Syrian Revolution and Opposition Forces, commonly named the Syrian National Coalition, which was a coalition of opposition groups, was founded in Doha, Qatar.

As hopes were waning in Western capitals, Erdoğan was trying to strike an optimistic tone. In a meeting at his party's headquarters in Ankara, Erdoğan said, "The CHP will not dare to go to Damascus tomorrow, you will see it. But we will go there in the shortest possible time, God willing, and embrace our brothers. That day is close. We will pray near the grave of Salahuddin Ayyubi and pray in the Umayyad Mosque."[75] References to Ayyubi, the twelfth-century Sunni Kurdish founder of the Ayyubid dynasty who led Muslim resistance against Christian crusaders, and the Umayyad Mosque, a center of Sunni Islam in Syria, highlighted Erdoğan's Sunni vision for both Turkey and post-Assad Syria.

Despite the confident tone, however, Erdoğan was becoming desperate. By the fall of 2012, there were already 100,000 Syrian refugees in Turkey and Ankara's defense spending was rising rapidly. The opposition's criticism of Erdoğan's Syria policy was gaining traction, particularly within the country's border regions, which had seen a dramatic increase in the number of Syrian refugees and the intensity of Syrian opposition activity. Erdoğan was desperate for an outside military intervention. A couple weeks later, Turkey's parliament endorsed a measure authorizing the military to conduct cross-border raids into Syria.[76] Members of the opposition CHP were furious. Muharrem İnce, a CHP member, said the motion would enable the government to wage a world war.[77]

Erdoğan was impatient for regime change. He had crafted his Syria policy on the premise of a swift toppling of Assad, to be replaced by a Muslim Brotherhood-led government. To bring that about, Turkey sped up its efforts. By 2012, Hakan Fidan, the Turkish intelligence chief, was directing a secret initiative to transfer weapons, money, and logistical support to the Syrian opposition.[78] By 2013, Turkey had earned a reputation as the NATO ally that backs al-Qaeda in Syria. A Human Rights Watch (HRW) report detailed an attack by fighters from several different armed groups, as well as ISIS, on Alawites, including women and children, in Latakia on August 4, 2013. Based on eye-witness and Western diplomatic accounts, the HRW report concluded that these fighters used Turkish territory to obtain weapons and stage the attack and urged the Turkish government to do more to stop arms transfers and prosecute those who were involved.[79] A 2014

UN report investigating arms transfers from Libya to Syria found that weapons came by air to the Turkish towns of Gaziantep, Ankara and Antakya and by sea to Mersin and İskenderun. They were transported into Syria by trucks.[80] Abdullah Gül, who was president at the time, admitted the government's involvement in weapons transfers to Syria. "We shared a long border with Syria, that is why I warned the government to stay away from arming the civil war," he said.[81]

Erdoğan dismissed Gül's warnings. He also dismissed Western claims that al-Qaeda-linked groups were gaining ground. "If the Syrian opposition achieves its goal, you will not find a trace of al-Qaeda in Syria," he said confidently. But Ankara had already started working with al-Qaeda affiliate Jabhat al-Nusra to organize a rebel offensive to capture Aleppo in mid-2012. Jabhat al-Nusra li-Ahl al-Sham min Mujahidi al-Sham fi Sahat al-Jihad—or simply al-Nusra—had been established in mid-2011 on the orders of Abu Bakr al-Baghdadi, the leader of the Islamic State in Iraq (ISI), also referred to as al-Qaeda in Iraq, as ISI's Syrian division. Rebel brigades within the Turkey-backed Free Syrian Army had started relying on al-Nusra to mount offensives against regime targets and Turkey allowed al-Nusra to use its territory to launch some of those attacks. In March 2014, Jabhat al-Nusra fighters took a strategic border point in Turkey's Hatay province in an attack that they launched from Turkish territory. Al-Nusra fighters later thanked Turkish authorities saying, "Turkey did us a big favor."[82] According to the fighters, Turkish officials gave them the mandate to attack and allowed them access through a heavily militarized Turkish border post, which proved essential to the success of the attack.

Erdoğan saw al-Nusra as an effective tool to unseat Assad. Indeed, by early 2013, al-Nusra had become one of the most effective fighting forces on the ground. The capture of Raqqa city in March 2013 was testament to the strength jihadi groups such as al-Nusra had gained in the opposition. While the Free Syrian Army had failed to inflict serious damage on the regime due to organizational problems, lack of military equipment, corruption, intra-opposition rivalries and competition between outside supporters, al-Nusra was gaining significant victories.

The group played a key role in the battle for control of Aleppo, Syria's largest city, winning it the admiration of the FSA-led opposition. Al-Nusra was not only confronting the regime militarily but also sought to govern the territories under its control and implement sharia law. It took control of flour production and distribution networks and established a local bus service in opposition-held territories, expanding its involvement in civil management and social services. For these reasons, Ankara criticized the US decision to designate al-Nusra as an alias for the Islamic State in Iraq (ISI) and a terrorist organization. Washington had taken the decision partly to send a message to Ankara about the need to control arms shipments to radical groups. Davutoğlu said that the decision "has resulted in more harm than good."[83] After US pressure, Ankara reluctantly designated the group as a terrorist organization in 2014 but retained its ties and support for the group. Erdoğan admitted Turkey's continued ties to al-Nusra, saying in 2016, "I talked to Putin. He requested that al-Nusra leave Aleppo. I gave instructions to my team."[84]

Enter ISIS

The Islamic State—also known as ISIS, ISIL, or Daesh—emerged from the remnants of al-Qaeda's Iraqi offshoot, al-Qaeda in Iraq (AQI), which was founded by Abu Musab al-Zarqawi in 2004. After having faded into obscurity, the group capitalized on the growing instability in Iraq and Syria and began to reemerge in 2011. In 2013, the Islamic State in Iraq announced its expansion into Syria and changed its name to the Islamic State of Iraq and Syria (ISIS). ISIS launched an offensive on the Iraqi cities of Mosul and Tikrit the following year and ISIS leader al-Baghdadi announced the formation of a caliphate stretching from Aleppo in Syria to Diyala in Iraq.[85]

ISIS's rise and its capture of large swathes of territory in Iraq and Syria laid bare how much had changed since the outbreak of peaceful protests in March 2011. The protests were led mostly by educated youth who demanded freedom, justice and dignity. They were a broad coalition that was not overtly Islamist and remained mostly peaceful. But as the conflict raged on, radical groups that sought to enforce strict Islamic laws became the dominant force in the Syrian opposition, pushing the moderate and secular forces favored by the West to the margins. The principal loser among them was the Free Syrian Army, which was backed by Turkey and the West but beset by military defeats and defections. FSA kept losing ground throughout 2014 and many of its fighters started joining radical Islamist groups. Nowhere was the jihadization of the conflict was more apparent than in ISIS's capture of much of eastern Syria in 2014. In June of that year, ISIS, which renamed itself as Islamic State, declared the northern Syrian town of Raqqa as the capital of its self-styled caliphate. In the lands under its control, ISIS forced residents to follow its strict interpretations of sharia law. Music and smoking were banned and those who did not follow the edict were either executed or forced to flee. Horrifying spectacles of violence such as public beheadings shocked the Western world.

The rise of ISIS dramatically changed the way the West viewed the Syrian civil war. President Obama had been averse to military intervention in Syria. In the summer of 2012, alarming intelligence reports suggested that Assad's forces were getting ready to use chemical weapons against the rebels or transfer them to Hezbollah. When asked about what could lead him to use military force in Syria, Obama said that moving or using large quantities of chemical weapons would cross a "red line" and "change my calculus." Obama's use of the term "red line" came as a surprise to his aides. One of them said "the idea was to put a chill into the Assad regime without actually trapping the president into any predetermined action."[86] Another asserted what Obama said was "unscripted."[87] After intelligence reports suggested that Assad had used chemical weapons in April 2013, Obama decided to make public his decision to provide military aid to the Syrian opposition. But it was the news of a catastrophic chemical weapons attack, in which sarin gas killed more than a thousand people, including children, in a suburb of Damascus, that put Obama in a difficult spot. After having received the intelligence community's "high confidence assessment" that sarin gas was used and that the Assad regime was responsible, as well as advice from close advisors including Joint

Chief of Staff, Marty Dempsey, to order a military strike, Obama leaned towards military action.

Several things changed Obama's calculus. A few days after the chemical attack, the Director of National Intelligence, Jim Clapper, told Obama that although all signs pointed to Assad ordering the chemical attack, the case was not yet a "slam dunk."[88] Growing opposition to military action in Congress as well as the administration's inability to secure the support of Western allies led Obama to seek congressional authorization to order a strike. After securing an agreement with Assad to hand over the regime's chemical weapons following diplomatic negotiations with Russia, Obama called on Congress to postpone the vote on Syria.

The rise of ISIS forced Obama's hand. To the US administration, ISIS became a more immediate threat than Assad. In 2014, Obama announced a coalition to "degrade and destroy" ISIS operating both in Iraq and Syria. Obama's strategy included military action as well as support for the Iraqi and Syrian opposition. In August, the US commenced bombing raids on ISIS positions in Iraq and had extended the raids into Syria by September. The anti-ISIS coalition included regional states such as Bahrain, Jordan, Saudi Arabia, Qatar, and the United Arab Emirates, which joined the United States in airstrikes in Syria. Turkey was reluctant to officially join the coalition. ISIS had taken forty-six Turkish citizens hostage, including diplomats from the Turkish consulate in Mosul who were captured when the jihadi group overran Iraq's second-largest city in June. Erdoğan feared retaliation against the hostages if Turkey took part in the coalition. He also raised concerns about the growing international effort to arm Kurdish fighters in Iraq against ISIS, fearing this might embolden Kurdish militants in Turkey. Erdoğan also had other reasons not to join the US-led anti-ISIS coalition. To Erdoğan and Davutoğlu, Assad posed a bigger threat than ISIS. In an interview with CNN, then Turkish Prime Minister Ahmet Davutoğlu argued that a campaign which only targeted ISIS was fruitless. "We believe that if Assad stays in Damascus with this brutal policy, if [ISIS] goes, another radical organization may come in."[89] Erdoğan wanted to leverage support against ISIS to spur the Obama administration into greater action to topple the regime.

THE SYRIAN GAMBIT

To the Obama administration, due to its location, Turkey was "absolutely indispensable" to the fight against ISIS.[90] Washington wanted Turkey to crack down on the flow of foreign fighters who had used Turkish territory to cross into Syria. The US administration also wanted to use Turkish military bases to start strikes on ISIS targets. Erdoğan had pledged support to the US-led anti-ISIS coalition but was reluctant to get involved in US efforts to root out ISIS. The tension between the two countries came to a head over the fate of a northern Syrian Kurdish town that was besieged by ISIS.

"Kobani is about to fall"

In September 2014, ISIS fighters entered the Syrian Kurdish town of Kobani, which had been under the control of PKK-linked Kurdish forces since 2012, and engaged local Kurdish fighters in street-to-street battles. The assault sent thousands of refugees fleeing across the border into Turkey. Syrian Kurds were waging a fierce battle but the jihadi group appeared on the verge of taking the town. In a phone conversation with Erdoğan, President Barack Obama pleaded for Ankara's help to save Kobani.[91] Erdoğan was reluctant. Turkey sporadically cracked down on ISIS but Erdoğan wanted to avoid direct confrontation with the jihadi group and blocked Kurds on the Turkish side from entering Syria to help their brethren. In his mind, heeding the US request would first and foremost complicate the peace talks he was carrying out with the PKK and deal a blow to his plans to establish an executive presidency.

Kobani was important for ISIS. Capturing the town would give the group control over a critical stretch of the Turkish-Syrian border that would help to expand clandestine supply routes. For Washington, the Syrian border city was vital for geopolitical and symbolic reasons. Kobani was not only a focus of the US operation against ISIS but also a test of the administration's policy of relying on airstrikes against ISIS and local ground forces to defeat the group. Kobani's fall would expose the fragility of US strategy, give the jihadi group a major boost and threaten a NATO ally, Turkey.[92]

Kobani, which was one of the three cantons that were part of the Kurdish autonomy experiment in Syria, was the symbol of

Kurdish national aspirations. The Kurds of Syria, who make up an estimated 10 percent of the population and live in the northern and eastern regions of the country, had long been marginalized and discriminated against by the Assad regime which promoted Arab nationalism. In 1962, 120,000 Kurds had been denied citizenship on the grounds that they were not born in Syria.[93] Since then, with descendants who cannot lay claim to citizenship, that number has doubled. In the 1970s, the regime confiscated Kurdish land in northern Syria and gave it to Arabs to create an "Arab belt."

Despite the long history of repression of Kurdish rights by the regime, Kurdish nationalism was not as strong among Syrian Kurds as it was among Turkey's or Iran's Kurds. Kurdish parties, which remained illegal, failed to mobilize the Kurdish community. Therefore, they confined their activities to the cultural sphere. Political autonomy or independence were not discussed. The Kurds of Syria remained relatively quiescent, except for a few brief instances. In March 2004, Syrian Kurds took to the streets throughout northern Syria to protest against the regime's treatment of Kurds. Although the protests initially appeared to be a response to the police shooting of Kurdish soccer fans who were fighting with Arab supporters of a rival team, they were the culmination of decades of repression and discrimination by the regime. The regime's use of lethal force to quell the protests led to many deaths and injuries. Hundreds were arrested after protesters burned down the local Baath party headquarters and destroyed a statue of former president Hafez al-Assad. The 2004 protests marked a turning point in relations between Syrian Kurds and the regime. The Kurds became more confident to push for their rights.

Despite their anti-regime stance, however, the Kurds of Syria did not join the Syrian opposition in large numbers following the start of the uprising in 2011, nor did they demand the fall of the regime for several months. Multiple factors influenced the Kurds' unwillingness to join the anti-Assad front. One reason was the internal divergences among the Kurds themselves. Ideological differences, personal rivalries as well as a generational divide had kept Kurdish political groups weak. There were disagreements between the Kurds and the Syrian opposition as well. The PYD, which had been established in 2003 by former members of the PKK who had been expelled from Syria in 1998 after Turkey threatened war, was one player among many in Syrian Kurdish politics. Although the party denies being the Syrian branch of the PKK, the PYD and its military wing, the YPG, are ideologically linked to the PKK, which has Marxist-Leninist roots. The PYD is a member of the Union of Kurdistan Communities (KCK), the umbrella body for groups subscribing to PKK ideology and goals.[94] Syrian opposition was made up in large part by the Muslim Brotherhood and Arab nationalists. Syrian Islamists viewed the Kurds, particularly the PYD, as their ideological enemies, while Arab nationalists were cold to the idea of granting any autonomy or even cultural rights to the Kurds in a post-Assad Syria. In the second opposition meeting held in Turkey in May–June 2011, two Arab tribal leaders rejected Kurdish demands for education in Kurdish and autonomy.[95] Tension also grew between the Syrian opposition and the Kurds over the opposition's refusal to remove the word "Arab" from the Syrian Arab Republic. The influence of outside actors was another key factor in the Kurds' hesitancy to join the Syrian opposition. Several Kurdish parties, including the PYD, refused to attend the Syrian opposition meeting held in Turkey, citing skepticism about Turkey's motivation given the country's failure to resolve its own Kurdish problem.

Assad tried hard to make sure Kurds did not join the opposition. Knowing that Kurdish support for the opposition could tip the balance against him, he granted citizenship to tens of thousands of Kurds. After Turkey openly joined the anti-Assad camp in the fall of 2011, Assad intensified efforts to cooperate with the Kurds against Ankara. He allowed PYD leader Salih Muslim to return from exile in northern Iraq and gave a free hand to the PKK to reinforce its presence in the northern part of the country. After the regime partially withdrew its forces from areas populated by Kurds to focus on other fronts, the Kurdish settlements of Kobani, Afrin and Derik came under PYD control. By the fall of 2013, the PYD and the YPG had dominated three large, non-contiguous enclaves of Kurdish-majority territory along the Turkish border. In November, the PYD proclaimed the transitional administration of

Rojava, the Kurdish name for the autonomous region of northern Syria, over these territories. For many Kurds across the region, this was a historic moment for Kurdish self-rule. To them, Rojava was more than a geographic area; it was an experiment in democracy, equality and self-rule.

These developments helped the PYD and the YPG boost their image. The Kurdish militia's rise was attributable to several factors. Its de facto alliance with the regime helped the Kurdish group capture territory without a fight; the regime's material support to PYD-held territory helped it provide services in the regions it controlled; and the PYD's organizational, ideological and military links to the PKK proved useful as well. These links increased the PYD's popularity among Kurds and helped the group militarily in its fight against ISIS. The Kurdish militia's ability to fend off jihadi militants won praise from local communities and many Kurds who had not previously supported the PYD or the autonomy project threw their support behind the group as a means of protecting themselves from jihadi attacks.

The Kurdish militia's fight against ISIS also won praise from the West. Although the PKK is officially considered to be a terrorist organization by the EU and the US, its Syrian offshoot is viewed as one of the most effective forces in the fight against jihadi groups by Western capitals. The PYD's leftist, secular ideology as well as its embrace of gender equality and freedom of religion as inviolable rights, which were enshrined in "Rojava's constitution" that was ratified in 2014, were seen as antidotes to the radical Islamist ideology of ISIS. Western press was full of praise when the Kurdish militia saved many Yazidis, the members of the largely Iraqi ethno-religious minority who were fleeing the forces of ISIS after the jihadi group overran Yazidi villages. ISIS considers the Yazidis apostates and executed Yazidi men and enslaved women as sex slaves. The Yazidis' plight prompted US airstrikes on ISIS-held positions, but it was the Kurdish militia's efforts on the ground that helped secure corridors of escape for many Yazidis. The world championed the PYD and its armed wing. Female YPG fighters on the frontline were being praised for their bravery. In an unusual photo shoot in August 2014, *Marie Claire* published pictures of female YPG fighters wearing khaki jumpsuits and holding machine guns. The *New York Times* ran a story titled "A Dream of Secular Utopia in ISIS' Backyard."

Even Turkey engaged with the PYD in the early years of the civil war despite the group's links to the PKK. Ankara encouraged the PYD and the larger Syrian Kurdish community to join the Syrian opposition it had backed during the early years of the war. However, engaging with the PYD was in sharp contrast to the policy Erdoğan would adopt from late 2015. Erdoğan's initial willingness to engage the Kurdish group was an extension of his domestic strategy of securing the Kurds' backing for the executive presidency. The Kurds were an important component of Erdoğan's new Turkey as an Islamic nation. Shortly after the uprising in Syria started, Erdoğan launched what was called a "Kurdish opening" in 2012 in an effort to resolve the Kurdish question peacefully, and the Turkish government had been party to peace discussions with the PKK from then on. This domestic background had made Ankara's engagement with the PYD possible.

Salih Muslim, the leader of the PYD, held several meetings with Turkish officials, including a 2012 meeting in Cairo with Turkey's last ambassador to Syria, who wanted to introduce Muslim to one of the leaders of the Turkey-backed Free Syrian Army.[96] He was invited to Turkey on the instruction of Foreign Minister Ahmet Davutoğlu in July 2013 and met with Under Secretary Feridun Sinirlioğlu and Deputy Under Secretary Ömer Önhon. Turkish officials urged the Syrian Kurds to back the opposition. Salih Muslim was to make a revelation that shocked many as he ended his meetings and was on his way back to Syria. He declared that Turkey had greenlighted Kurdish autonomy in Syria.[97] Muslim said that Turkish officials were not threatened by Syrian Kurdish autonomy; on the contrary, they had agreed that the Kurds had to govern themselves and that Turkey would provide help in their endeavors.[98]

In another sign of the rapprochment between Ankara and the Syrian Kurdish militia, in 2015 Turkey dispatched hundreds of ground troops, tanks, aircraft and drones to extract thirty-eight soldiers guarding a historical Ottoman tomb in Syria that had been besieged by Islamic State. The YPG opened a security corridor to

Turkish forces who went through Kurdish-held territory to relieve the garrison at Süleyman Şah's tomb and relocate its remains. Such instances of YPG-Turkish engagement would become impossible after 2015 due to a shift in Erdoğan's domestic calculations. "My last contact with Turkish officials was in 2015 when I was invited to İstanbul to coordinate between the YPG and Turkish armed forces during the Süleyman Şah operation," said Muslim.[99] Kobani paved the way for the U-turn in Erdoğan's policy toward the Kurds.

By the time ISIS started pushing into the town in the fall of 2014, global public opinion had shifted toward the PYD. American jets started hitting ISIS targets in Syria, including those around Kobani, but could not stop ISIS advances. The Obama administration sought Turkey's help in destroying ISIS. Washington asked Ankara to allow the use of an airbase in the south of Turkey for operations against ISIS and for help to rescue the people of Kobani by either directing military support across its border or sending in troops. The Kurds in Syria and Turkey were asking for Erdoğan's help as well. They wanted him to allow reinforcements to pass through Turkish territory from Iraq to Kobani and other parts of Syria. Erdoğan was reluctant.

There were several factors behind Erdoğan's foot-dragging in joining the US-led fight. At the time of the ISIS siege of Kobani, Erdoğan's government was engaged in peace talks with the PKK. In the spring of 2013, the PKK's imprisoned leader Abdullah Öcalan had called for a ceasefire and ordered PKK fighters off Turkish soil as part of the peace process between the Kurds and the Turkish government. In return, Erdoğan had pledged to grant more rights to the Kurds. He hoped to use the peace process with the Kurds to secure their backing for switching Turkey's governing system from a parliamentary system to a presidential one. Although the process was not moving as smoothly as parties had wanted, the ceasefire was largely in place and formal negotiations had commenced. Erdoğan feared that a YPG victory in Kobani would strengthen the PKK's hand in negotiations with the Turkish government, and that such a victory would boost Kurdish confidence and ethnic Kurdish nationalism, all of which would deal a blow to his plans to co-opt them.

Erdoğan also had other reasons to be hesitant about helping the campaign against the jihadi group. To him, the number one threat emanating from Syria was the Assad regime. All the other predicaments the West saw as existential problems, such as ISIS, were the byproduct of Assad's brutality and his oppression of Sunnis. If Assad were toppled, the thinking went, there would no ISIS to be worried about. Besides, to Erdoğan, ISIS was one of the most effective tools for bringing down the regime, a means that the Turkish opposition and Western governments believed Erdoğan was using very effectively. Erdoğan was engaged in a high-stakes gambit and it was making Turkish opposition and Turkey's Western allies increasingly uncomfortable.

Another reason for Erdoğan's foot-dragging to prevent a massacre in Kobani was his plan to push the Obama administration's hand. He wanted Washington to give more support to the rebels trying to unseat Assad and establish a no-fly zone in northern Syria that would help rebel efforts. He said he would not get more deeply involved in the conflict with ISIS unless the Obama administration agreed to those two things. But the US administration was reluctant to impose a no-fly zone, which would require intensive use of American air power and risk a confrontation with the Assad regime.

As tense discussions between Ankara and Washington were taking place, the Kurds in Kobani let the world know that time was running out. If they did not receive reinforcements, Kobani would fall. They asked the Turkish government to allow reinforcements to pass through Turkey from other parts of Syria on their way to Kobani. Turkish soldiers were watching ISIS advances into Kobani and the impending bloodbath from just a stone's throw away. Erdoğan was happy to let the people of Kobani face ISIS alone. Speaking to a crowd in the southern Turkish city of Gaziantep in the midst of the fighting, Erdoğan jubilantly said "Kobani is about to fall."

"US is arming terrorists"

The Obama administration was frustrated by Erdoğan's maneuvers to use the campaign against ISIS and Washington's request for access to the Turkish base İncirlik as leverage to achieve his long-term objective of regime change in Syria. "At the time, Erdoğan did not see ISIS as a threat to Turkey's national security. He saw it as an effective fighting force that could help him unseat Assad. "What he was doing was short-sighted and dangerous," said a US official who had accompanied the US delegation during their talks with Turkish officials.[100]

That concern was widely shared by Turkey's opposition, which documented that Turkey was providing ISIS with weapons, logistical support, and financial assistance, as well as medical services to wounded fighters. In an October 14, 2014 address to his party members in the parliament, Kemal Kılıçdaroğlu, the leader of the main opposition party, disclosed official documents from the Adana Office of the Prosecutor revealing that Turkey had supplied weapons to terrorist groups in Syria.[101] He also revealed transcripts of interviews with truck drivers who had carried those weapons.

> Davutoğlu calls me a traitor and asks for proof when we ask the government to stop supporting ISIS, here is the proof. A statement from the Adana public prosecutor, showing Turkey sent arms to terrorist groups. Another proof is statements from drivers who carried those arms. You call me a traitor. Who is the traitor now? Kılıçdaroğlu asked.[102]

Turkey's alleged military support to ISIS and other al-Qaeda-linked groups had become public earlier in the year. On January 1, 2014, a truck and an accompanying car were stopped by the Turkish gendarmerie on the orders of prosecutors acting on tip-offs that the truck was carrying weapons to terrorist groups in Syria. In the accompanying car were a member of Turkish intelligence and a regional official for the Islamist aid organization İHH. But before the prosecutor arrived on the scene to search the truck, the minister of the interior, Efkan Ala, had ordered the governor of Hatay and the gendarmerie to release the truck, saying it was carrying humanitarian aid to the Turkmens in Syria. Turkmens quickly rejected claims that they were receiving humanitarian aid from Turkey. The prosecutor who ordered the search was removed from his post. He later told his close circle that he barely escaped with his life that day.[103]

A few weeks later, on January 14, three more trucks were stopped in the southern city of Adana on a tip-off that they were carrying weapons to parts of Syria under the control of Salafist groups including ISIS. At the time of the search, the Syrian side of Hatay province was controlled by ISIS and a hardline Islamist group Ahrar al-Sham, which included commanders who had fought alongside al-Qaeda leader Osama bin Laden and were close to the group's current leader Ayman al-Zawahiri. Two members of Turkish intelligence were in the car accompanying the trucks. After searching the trucks, the gendarmerie found rocket parts, ammunition and semi-finished mortar shells. Erdoğan said that the trucks belonged to Turkish intelligence and repeated his government's claim that they were carrying humanitarian aid to Turkmens in Syria. Before the trucks were sent to Seyhan District Gendarmerie Command, the Adana governor intervened saying that the trucks were going to Syria on the orders of Prime Minister Erdoğan and that he would risk his life to prevent them from being searched.[104] The Turkish intelligence officers accompanying the truck got involved as well, threatening the police and physically resisting the search. The trucks were allowed to continue their journey—but the court testimonies of the prosecutors and the gendarmerie officers who faced charges of military espionage and attempting to overthrow the government told a different story.

The trucks were full of weapons and ammunition. One of the Turkish intelligence officers who was trying to prevent the gendarmerie from searching the truck said "this truck is full of weapons. If you search it, this could bring down the government tomorrow."[105] Prosecutors who ordered the trucks to be searched, as well as the gendarmerie commanders who were involved in the search, were arrested and sentenced to seventeen to twenty-six years in prison for revealing state secrets and belonging to a terrorist organization. One of the prosecutors said "something that is a crime cannot possibly be a state secret."[106] In his testimony, he said that the investigations he and his colleagues had led revealed that state officials were "unlawfully" in touch with ISIS and other terrorist groups in Syria and that video footage had confirmed that the weapons and ammunition in the trucks were transferred to the jihadi group Ahrar al-Sham on the other side of the border in October 2014.[107] The other prosecutor made similar statements highlighting Turkey's support for radical groups. He said that al-Qaeda fighters from Pakistan, Afghanistan and Iraq regularly crossed into Syria through Turkey.

Azad, brother of a former ISIS member who was born in Turkmenistan but married to a Turkish woman from the southern town of Mersin, told me how Turkish officials facilitated ISIS fighters' travel in and out of Syria.[108] Azad said that his brother was nervous before he first crossed the border into Syria but was reassured by other ISIS members that Turkish border officials would assist the crossing and that they would receive "the best care at Turkish hospitals" if they got wounded. In 2015, Azad's brother was arrested in the border town of Kilis. He had crossed into Syria numerous times through the Elbeyli district of Kilis without a problem and "with the knowledge of border officials." He and several others accompanying him were questioned by Turkish intelligence. Azad told me that Turkish officials had known his brother was fighting in the ranks of ISIS. The Kilis prosecutor ordered their arrest but they were released shortly after.

ISIS members were not only enjoying freedom of action in border towns. They were holding large gatherings in the heart of İstanbul and calling for a holy war against Assad without any objection from authorities who were known for immediately intervening in any gathering held without permission. Websites close to ISIS posted videos in which ISIS members were being trained in religious orders in places such as Ömerli, an İstanbul district, prompting opposition members of parliament to submit parliamentary questions to the minister of the interior asking whether there were ISIS training camps in İstanbul.[109]

Turkey had also become a "logistical hub" for ISIS's finances. A US Treasury report said ISIS "often gathered and sent funds to intermediaries in Turkey who smuggle the cash into Syria or send the funds to hawalas operating in the camp."[110] ISIS was making millions of dollars in oil revenue, which made it one of the wealthiest terror groups in history, with much of the oil being traded on the black market in Turkey. The oil money underpinned ISIS's operations and recruitment of new members. When the Obama administration pressured Turkey to help choke off ISIS's oil trade, Ankara claimed that it could not control the flow of foreign fighters into Syria or the flow of oil back out. But US officials argued "Like any sort of black-market smuggling operation, if you devote the resources and the effort to attack it, you are unlikely to eradicate it, but you are likely to put a very significant dent in it."[111] Ankara was unwilling to cooperate. As Colin Kahl, then Vice-President Joe Biden's national security advisor who accompanied him on official visits to Turkey to hold discussions with Davutoğlu and Erdoğan, succinctly put it: "Erdoğan therefore saw cooperation against the Islamic State as a favor to Washington, rather than something that was vital to Turkish national security. Thus, he was intent on extracting a concession in return—namely, a commitment for the U.S. military to directly confront the Assad regime."[112] During a televised interview, Brett McGurk, the National Security Council's Middle East and North Africa coordinator, said that US officials spent most of their time in Ankara because "most of the material coming to fuel the ISIS machine, frankly, was coming from across the border from Turkey into Syria... It was very frustrating because Turkey didn't take much action on the border."[113] He even suggested that Turkey was sheltering ISIS leader Abu Bakr al-Baghdadi.[114] Indeed, in 2013 alone, some 30,000 militants traversed Turkish soil.[115] Ankara had earned the reputation of being a "jihadi highway" in Western capitals as the country became a conduit for fighters seeking to join the Islamic State.

Vice President Biden expressed the US administration's frustration with Turkey when he said that Turkey had armed "anyone who would fight" Assad, a clear reference to jihadis, and that Erdoğan had admitted to administration officials that Turkey had allowed jihadis to pass through its territory to cross into Syria. Biden's remarks infuriated Erdoğan, who denied the claims, and Biden was forced to apologize. However, diplomatic niceties did not alter Turkey's reputation as the NATO ally that aided one of the most brutal terrorist groups in modern history.

A leaked tape of conversations at a high-level security meeting at the Turkish Foreign Ministry in Ankara lent credence to claims that Erdoğan's government would do anything in Syria to get its own way. On March 27, 2014, an anonymous account posted a tape in which Foreign Minister Davutoğlu, Intelligence Chief Hakan Fidan, second Chief of Staff Yaşar Güler and Foreign Ministry Undersecretary Feridun Sinirlioğlu discussed a direct military intervention in Syria.[116] On the tape, in response to Güler's insistence on the need to send arms and ammunition to Syria, Fidan admitted that Turkey had already delivered 2,000 truckloads of material. Fidan suggested using the tiny Turkish exclave in Syria, the Süleyman Şah Tomb, as an excuse for military intervention. "If we need a pretext, I will manufacture a pretext, no problem," said Fidan, adding he could send men to Syria to attack the exclave "if this is what we need to go in." Erdoğan's statements shortly after the leak gave credence to its contents.[117]

Turkey clearly turned a blind eye to ISIS activities on its soil, facilitated its militants' movements in and out of the country and took other steps to bolster the group, but there was still not enough evidence to conclude that the thousands of Turkish trucks carrying arms and ammunition to Syria were meant for ISIS. General Joseph Votel, commander of the United States Central Command at the time, said, "I do not recall any evidence that would suggest Mr. Erdoğan was arming ISIS. What did concern me was his lack of effective border control, the blind eye he turned to movement down along that border, which contributed to the buildup of ISIS fighters. We recognized that the principal route into Syria was through Turkey. Either due to a lack of competence or lack of will, Turkey was unable to stem the flow of ISIS fighters. You would think that a country like Turkey would be able to address that quickly in an effective manner."[118] General Votel added that "Turkey was supporting a lot of different groups. Some of them may have been ISIS or former ISIS or very closely aligned to it."

ISIS's siege of Kobani and the Obama administration's efforts to convince Erdoğan to help stop the ISIS advance came against a background of growing unease in the US defense and intelligence community over Erdoğan's policies toward radical jihadi groups in Syria. Erdoğan wanted to put his weight behind the US request to force the Obama administration to do more to topple Assad. But to Washington, the immediate threat was from ISIS. Besides, the Obama administration was unwilling to impose a no-fly zone. A Western-imposed no-fly zone had long been a Turkish demand. Erdoğan saw such a zone as critical to opposition efforts to oust Assad. Washington argued that it would require a significant US military commitment and could risk a military confrontation with Assad's forces. US officials also argued that the American-led coalition had already effectively imposed a no-fly zone with its rotation of flights and airstrikes so Ankara's demand for such a zone rang hollow.

Washington was worried about an impending bloodbath if the Kurdish militia in Kobani was not reinforced. Obama's patience with Erdoğan was wearing thin. The US military's Central Command had already conducted eighteen airstrikes on ISIS targets in and around Kobani but Kurds on the ground said they needed troops and arms from Turkey.[119] Secretary of State John Kerry had several phone calls with Turkish officials to convince Ankara, but to no avail.

In mid-October, President Obama made a decision that shook the decades-old strategic partnership between the two countries to the core. He authorized an airdrop to provide desperately needed medical supplies and ammunition to the Kurds fighting ISIS. The decision was made without consultation with Ankara. Obama informed Erdoğan of his decision in a phone call hours before American military aircraft dropped weapons, ammunition and medical supplies to Kurdish forces, forcing Erdoğan finally to allow Peshmerga forces from Iraq to transit Turkey into Kobani to help reinforce the YPG. The help given to the YPG by the US as well as coalition airstrikes changed the course of the battle. The YPG repelled the ISIS onslaught and Kobani was saved.

Kobani, which was once an irrelevant town, became the symbol of Kurdish national aspirations across the region. Syrian Kurds had lacked the national symbols that mobilized their brethren elsewhere. Iranian Kurds had the short-lived Mahabad Kurdish Republic that was established in 1946. Iraqi Kurds had Halabja, the site of Iraqi President Saddam Hussein's chemical weapons attacks against Kurds in 1988, which killed thousands of people. Now Syrian Kurds had Kobani.

Turkey's Kurds were equally excited about their Syrian brothers' experiment with autonomy. The US decision to airdrop weapons and ammunition to the YPG made many Kurds in Turkey believe that Kurds were at a historic juncture and they had Western support behind them. Kurdish expectations skyrocketed. However, Erdoğan's decision to allow Kurdish Peshmerga forces from Iraq to transit Turkish territory to help the YPG did not quell Kurdish anger towards Erdoğan. The protests that started during the siege of Kobani in response to Erdoğan's inaction raged on across the country, leading to many deaths. It was not just the Kurds in Turkey protesting; women's organizations, workers' syndicates, student groups and leftist organizations took to the street as well. Kurds in Kurdish-majority cities in the southeast captured government buildings. "The Turkish state lost control of Kurdish cities for the first time in recent history. Erdoğan had to plea for Öcalan's help to suppress the Kurdish uprising in Kurdish cities" said Ertuğrul Kürkçü, the honorary chair of the pro-Kurdish HDP.[120] "The prospects of a Kurdish massacre elate Erdoğan. We will never forget this," a Kurdish student from Diyarbakır said.[121]

To Erdoğan, the rise in Kurdish nationalism was anathema to his efforts to rally Kurds behind his presidentialism project under the banner of Islam. Erdoğan had hoped to secure Kurdish backing by recognizing Kurds as an integral part of the *ummah* and granting them cultural rights, but the Kurds had become too confident to settle for what Erdoğan had to offer. Western backing for the Kurds' fight against ISIS as well as the Obama administration's decision to arm the YPG boosted the Kurds' confidence. The Kobani protests had laid bare the fact that Turkey's Kurds would not back Erdoğan's efforts to grab more power. In Erdoğan's view, Obama's decision to arm the YPG had ignited a process that upended his plans to rely on Sunni Muslim solidarity to co-opt the Kurds. "Our NATO ally is arming terrorists," a furious Erdoğan said. When I related Erdoğan's words to a US official who took part in efforts to convince Erdoğan not to support radical Islamist groups in Syria, he said: "Well, he now knows how we feel."[122] It was a reference to Turkey's alleged arming of ISIS.

ISIS's capture of significant swathes of territory in Syria and Iraq as well as its exhortations to its supporters to carry out attacks against Western targets increased pressure on the Obama administration to deploy American combat ground forces. The battle for Kobani had also proven that retaking cities held by ISIS would require house-to-house fighting. Obama, who had pledged to end America's wars before he took office, was reluctant to deploy US troops. The US administration could not secure support from key states such as Turkey either. Ankara was proposing to create a Sunni force to fight ISIS but the Obama administration did not believe that those fighters were moderate enough. Washington also thought that Erdoğan and the Sunni force he would create would be focused on removing Assad rather than eliminating ISIS.

Faced with an immediate threat, the Obama administration picked what it thought to be the least bad option: arming the YPG to assist it in the fight against ISIS.[123] "President Barack Obama did not align the United States with the YPG with any enthusiasm," said Amanda Sloat, who served as the deputy assistant Secretary of State for Southern European and Eastern Mediterranean Affairs in the Obama administration.[124] It was the decision of a president who was reluctant to put boots on the ground but was alarmed by the rapid rise of ISIS. Privately, US officials admitted that the YPG was the Syrian off-shoot of the PKK. But the YPG is not formally on the terrorist organization list of the US, a legal distinction that allowed the US administration to cooperate with the group.

The US was trying to navigate difficult terrain. It had to become creative to ease Turkey's concerns about US-YPG cooperation. The US military went to the YPG, according to General Raymond Thomas, who led the US Special Operations Command at the time, and said "You've got to change your brand. What do you want to call yourself besides the YPG?" They came back a day later and "declared that they were the Syrian Democratic Forces."[125] In October 2015, when ISIS was rapidly gaining ground in Syria, the YPG joined with several Arab groups to form the Syrian Democratic Forces (SDF), which was provided with weapons by the US and supported by other Western countries such as Britain and France. The US hoped that its rebranding trick would calm Ankara down. It did not. The YPG was still the dominant force in the SDF and Ankara remained displeased. Washington ignored its NATO ally's concerns. By 2016, the US military was providing airstrikes to SDF operations against ISIS and training SDF fighters. The group had become a formidable ally to the US and secured key victories against the jihadists.

Erdoğan was furious about US cooperation with the YPG. The liberation of Kobani had become a significant symbol of Kurdish nationalism among Kurdish communities across the region. Western support had legitimized the PKK's Syrian off-shoot and earned the Kurds a lot of sympathy in the West. The Kurds' newly found image in the West led many Kurds to believe that their de facto self-rule could become permanent with Western backing. Erdoğan was convinced that the Kurds would not support his efforts to establish an executive presidency. To Erdoğan, Obama had just upended his plans to acquire unchecked powers.

The liberation of Kobani marked a turning point in Turkey-US ties as well. From the Western point of view, a NATO ally was reluctant to join the fight against an existential enemy. Many in Washington thought at best that Turkey looked the other way when ISIS operated within its borders. The US intelligence community is divided over Turkey's relationship with ISIS. Some think that Ankara actively facilitated ISIS's operations. One US official voiced Washington's frustration with Ankara's reluctance to "do its part" to crack down on the ISIS network inside Turkey and "treating wounded jihadis in Turkish hospitals." "How does it make sense to provide electricity to ISIS-held areas and cut it off when Kurds take over?" he asked.[126] He was referring to the northern Syrian town of Tel Abyad which was captured from ISIS by the YPG in 2015. Before the town was brought under YPG control, Turkish media outlets reported that Turkey continued to supply electricity to ISIS-controlled Tel Abyad from its border province Şanlıurfa, a claim denied by Turkish authorities.[127] After the YPG's capture of the town, electricity was cut off.[128]

All these events led many in Washington to believe that there was a working relationship between its NATO ally and a notoriously violent ISIS. Others in the US intelligence community do not think Turkey was sinister enough to deliberately arm ISIS.

> Did Turkey arm radical jihadi groups inside Syria? Sure. Did Turkey deliberately pick ISIS as a partner? I doubt it. Turkey was

desperate for a regime change and handing weapons to opposition groups like candy. The Turks didn't care whether those weapons went to ISIS, Al Qaeda or Nusra. They did not vet the recipients. Besides, the situation on the ground was so fluid that it was very difficult to tell who is ISIS, who is Nusra.[129]

Ankara was equally frustrated with its NATO ally. To Turkish officials, the US was arming an organization that had been waging a war against Turkey since the 1980s and had cost 40,000 lives. To many in Ankara, including members of the opposition, the Kobani incident marked the end of the decades-old Turkey-US strategic alliance.[130] The two NATO allies could never restore the eroded trust.

Erdoğan tried desperately to bring down Assad. The task of replacing a "godless" regime with a Sunni Islamist one was so crucial to his domestic agenda that he was ready to go to extremes. He accelerated Syria's descent into civil war, armed jihadi groups, turned Turkey into a major hub for jihadi activity and risked ethnic and sectarian conflict in Turkey by being a direct party to the Syrian civil war. When developments in Syria threatened one of the key pillars of his domestic strategy to switch to presidentialism, Erdoğan once again did not hesitate to take other controversial steps. To force Turkey's Kurds to back his presidentialism plans, he was willing to let their Syrian brethren die at the hands of ISIS and risk a rupture with Western allies.

4

FROM RELIGION TO NATIONALISM

The policies Erdoğan pursued in Syria had dramatic implications for the course of the war but produced mixed results for his domestic strategy. Drawing parallels between Turkey's secular authoritarian past and the Baath regime in Syria and framing the uprising as the Syrians' fight to bring down their own Kemalists helped Erdoğan build his brand as the defender of Islam and Muslims. But the rise and eventual dominance of the Syrian Kurdish militia along Turkey's southern border complicated Erdoğan's plans to secure the backing of Turkey's Kurds for his executive presidency. What went wrong with Erdoğan's plan to use Islam to generate support for establishing a centralized presidential system? What were the challenges his authoritarian vision for the country encountered? What role did the Syrian war play in complicating matters for Erdoğan? The following pages tell the story of Erdoğan's clash with key constituencies, which culminated in a historic election loss for Erdoğan in 2015, and how he snatched victory from the jaws of defeat by turning to Turkish nationalism.

"Resistance everywhere": The Gezi protests

Gezi Park—an area inside Taksim Square that hosts hundreds of sycamore trees and is one of the last remaining green spaces in central İstanbul—became the site of the main rejection of Erdoğan's project to construct an Ottoman-Islamic nation. In the summer of 2013, protesters gathered in Taksim Square in protest against the government's decision to start an urban redevelopment plan to replace Gezi Park with a giant replica of an Ottoman artillery barracks that would include a shopping mall. What began as a peaceful sit-in to save the park escalated into the biggest protest against Erdoğan's vision after the police used excessive force against the protesters. In a matter of a few days, millions across the country took to the street.

Taksim Square, a district on the European side, has always been a site of bickering over different visions for Turkey. In the 1930s, the young Republic embarked on redesigning the square to reflect its modern, secular vision. The Ottoman-era Taksim Artillery Barracks (*Topçu Kışlası*) were built in 1806 and used primarily for military purposes. The Kemalist elite demolished the barracks to cut Taksim's visual link with its Ottoman past and rebuilt it to fit secular Turkey.[1] Since then, Taksim Square, with its bars, nightclubs and galleries, has become the heart of İstanbul's secular lifestyle.

As the Ottoman capital and seat of the Caliphate, İstanbul has always occupied a special place in the psyche of Turkey's Islamists. The city reminded them of the Empire's grandeur, the demolition of the barracks by the secularist military being particularly traumatic for Islamists. It symbolized the defeat of an Empire which they idealized as the perfect Muslim state and society. Erdoğan saw Taksim Square as a site that would present his vision for society and Turkish identity, a vision that needed to be expressed visually and spatially.

The construction sector became an ideological tool to imprint Erdoğan's hegemony. By Islamizing Turkey's urban landscape, Erdoğan sought to eradicate the optical aspect of Kemalist Turkey and re-Islamize society through Ottoman symbolism. He used Ottoman art, cuisine, designs and architecture to "bring the Ottomans back." The AKP municipalities, Turkey's Mass Housing Administration (TOKİ) and construction firms close to Erdoğan were prominent in this urban transformation. Through "renewal projects," they sought to restore lost Ottoman architecture. These tacky and tasteless reproductions, which made Erdoğan's cronies rich, aimed to bring Ottoman-cum-Islamic values back into urban spaces. Countless imitation Ottoman mosques were built, and neighborhoods were demolished to build Ottoman homes and coffee shops.

Due to the charged ideological framework of the site, the planned change of Taksim Square went beyond a simple urban transformation. It became the vehicle through which different visions for the country's identity competed. To Erdoğan, the transformed site would be the ultimate visual reminder of how far Turkey has come in banishing the Kemalist tradition and re-embracing its Ottoman-Islamic roots.[2] It would symbolize the ideological hegemony of Erdoğan's "new and authentic" democracy. To those who refused to submit to Erdoğan's vision, Gezi Park and Taksim Square became "the most important symbolic venture" of resistance.[3] But that resistance did not encompass what many saw as the polar opposite of Erdoğan's Islamism: Kemalism. The protesters objected to the authoritarianism of the Kemalist tradition as well as the autocracy and paternalism of the Islamic one.[4]

Protesters were angry at the destruction of one of the few green spaces in the city. They were also furious about the way the decision for the project was taken. Erdoğan, ever more confident in his power, had completely disregarded opposing opinions, which had become the hallmark of his growing authoritarianism. After police forcefully cleared Gezi Park of a small group of protesters, a wave of anti-government demonstrations swept across the country. Over the following few months, police repeatedly used unnecessary and abusive force to prevent and disperse peaceful demonstrations. Even passive protesters who were standing silent and alone in Taksim Square were detained. The widespread use by the police of tear gas, water cannon, plastic bullets and beatings against totally peaceful protesters added to the anger, leading to figures such as the Secretary General of the United Nations to call an end to the violence. But Erdoğan threatened even more violence against the protesters if they continued. He vowed to "cleanse Gezi of terrorists" and suggested that even banging pots and pans in solidarity with the protesters would be considered a crime.[5]

It was not just the protesters who were subjected to police violence. Journalists covering the protests, doctors treating the injured and lawyers defending the protesters' rights were also arrested and subjected to police brutality. Business owners who opened their doors to protesters became the target of Erdoğan's fury, too. As Erdoğan threatened business owners and social media sites such as Twitter and Facebook, which had become important tools for protesters to coordinate among themselves, mainstream media refused to cover the demonstrations out of fear of Erdoğan. CNN Türk's decision to air a documentary on penguins during the first week of mass protests became the symbol of the self-censoring media under Erdoğan's authoritarian rule.[6]

While the police unleashed violence on protesters, Erdoğan held his own rally dubbed "Respect for the National Will" where hundreds of thousands of supporters gathered in a neighborhood miles away from Istanbul's city center. The rally was meant as a show of strength and defiance by Erdoğan's supporters. They begged for Erdoğan's permission to "crush" the protesters. They chanted "Minority, do not be confused, do not test our patience."[7] In his speech, Erdoğan lashed out not only at the protesters but also at what he called their "international collaborators." From the time the protests erupted, Erdoğan had repeatedly pointed to Israel, Western financiers, foreign press and Twitter as alleged culprits. Some of his advisors even accused Lufthansa, Germany's national air carrier, of being behind the protests to prevent Erdoğan from building a new airport in Istanbul. Others likened the protests to the "post-modern coup" that forced Islamist Prime Minister Necmettin Erbakan from power, in 1997.[8]

The Gezi protests marked a watershed event in Erdoğan's new Turkey. It was the most significant popular rejection of his authoritarian vision. The protests were unparalleled in many respects. An unprecedented number of people took to the streets in almost every city in the country in protests that lasted over two months. Many of those who took part were in their twenties, from well-off families, and had not taken part in political protests before. A significant number of protesters were children of families who supported Erdoğan and the AKP. Islamist groups also joined the protest. They were all united in their rejection of Erdoğan's use of Islam to legitimize his authoritarian rule. Some commentators called the Gezi protests "Turkish spring," inspired by the mass protests sweeping across the Middle East and North Africa, unseating authoritarian regimes in their wake. But to Erdoğan, the Turkish spring had happened a long time ago. It had brought him—the "authentic representative of the people"—and thus real democracy to power in 2002.

Missing from the protests were the country's historically most robust anti-government protesters: the Kurds. The Kurds' absence drew strong criticism from the opposition but was applauded by Erdoğan and senior figures from the AKP, who thanked the pro-Kurdish party for not taking part in the protests. In an interview with the BBC a month after the protests started cooling down, a senior figure from the PKK, Cemil Bayık, admitted that they had made a mistake by not joining the biggest anti-government protest in the history of the Republic. He said that there were several reasons for the lack of Kurdish participation: Kurds did not want to harm the peace process between the government and the PKK that had begun a few months before the protests erupted. They also did not want the government to use Kurdish participation to delegitimize the protests.[9] Kurds did not disappoint Erdoğan during the Gezi protests, but his Gülenist allies did. Gülenist media did not support Erdoğan as much as he would have liked, adding to the simmering tension between the two.

The protests became a turning point. They made Erdoğan ever more paranoid. Regional developments fed Erdoğan's paranoia as well. During the height of the anti-AKP mobilization in Turkey, a military coup toppled the first democratically elected president of Egypt, Mohammed Morsi, who served as the leader of the Egyptian Muslim Brotherhood and was a close Erdoğan ally. Erdoğan thought that the West, which remained quiet when the Egyptian military ousted Morsi, was also at work in Gezi, supporting what he saw as a coup attempt against his rule. He became suspicious of people in his close circle as well. President Abdullah Gül and Deputy Prime Minister Bülent Arınç sought to strike a less confrontational tone and met opposition MPs and some of the protesters at the heart of the original protest over Gezi Park.[10] Erdoğan saw these overtures by the people closest to him as attempts to undermine him. After the Gezi protests, Erdoğan thought the only people he could trust were family members.

Erdoğan used the Gezi protests to consolidate his post-2011 strategy of using Islamist, anti-Western rhetoric to create a sense of victimhood among the country's religious conservatives. He framed the protests as a Western plot to overthrow his government and asked his supporters to join him in what he described as the second liberation war against Western imperialists and their domestic collaborators. One incident became particularly emblematic of Erdoğan's efforts to polarize society. At the height of the protests, a woman wearing a headscarf alleged that she and her baby had been attacked by protesters who were half-naked and wearing leather gloves. She claimed they insulted her Islamic attire, ripped off her headscarf, kicked her baby, and urinated on her in İstanbul's Kabataş district. The woman, who gave interviews to pro-government media, was the daughter-in-law of an AKP mayor who was very close to Erdoğan. Erdoğan repeated her account many times during his rallies to demonize protesters and label the opposition as atheists. He claimed that he had tapes of the alleged attack that he would soon release. A few months later, a private TV network released security camera footage. No such attack had taken place. It was a fabricated story that Erdoğan used masterfully.

The Gezi protests deepened the country's polarization. Police brutality and Erdoğan's heavy-handed approach solidified the anti-Erdoğan front. The few liberals that had remained in Erdoğan's camp, in the hopes that he would bring about a peaceful resolution to the country's Kurdish problem, abandoned him after Gezi. Even the Kurds who had largely remained on the sidelines of the protests started questioning the wisdom of relying on Erdoğan, who demonstrated zero tolerance to even the slightest criticism of his authoritarian rule, to solve their problem via democratic means. The protests solidified the Erdoğan front as well. To Erdoğan and his supporters, the protesters were simply the pawns of Western imperialists and those outside forces bent on stopping the country's "holy march" to be the savior of Muslims and the oppressed across the world. They were Islamophobic, they were against the "national will," "real democracy" and everything that made Turkey "great again."

The immensity of the protests and the regional context in which they were taking place had a profound impact on Erdoğan's psyche and the way he governed. He became more paranoid, more authoritarian and divisive. Erdoğan used the Gezi protests to strengthen his narrative that his "historical mission," to remake the country to reflect its Ottoman and Islamic roots, was under assault by internal and external colonizers and that the "true nation" had to stand firmly behind him to complete what they had started. Gezi became the last straw for those who had supported Erdoğan believing he could still do good for the country's democracy. Once they were gone, Erdoğan's base became ideologically more uniform, mainly consisting of religious conservatives. This new dynamic made Erdoğan's Islamization project much more urgent to legitimize his increasingly authoritarian policies. But another watershed event spelled further trouble for his presidentialism dream.

A Muslim political feud erupts

A few months after thousands of protesters at Gezi presented the most significant challenge to Erdoğan's Sunni Muslim nation project, Erdoğan's alliance with the Gülen movement collapsed as well. It came after the long-simmering tension between the Gülenists and Erdoğan boiled over, with the arrest of dozens of people, including the detention of three sons of leading ministers, in an anti-corruption investigation in December 2013 that came dangerously close to Erdoğan himself. Erdoğan vehemently denied the corruption allegations and called them an attempt by those connected with the Gülen movement to bring down his government via a "judicial coup."

In the post-Gezi climate, the Gülen-led corruption charges strengthened Erdoğan's Gezi narrative that his government was under attack by "dark forces" and their international collaborators. He framed the investigations as another plot like the Gezi protests. Erdoğan accused the Gülenists of infiltrating the police and the judiciary to establish a "parallel state" (*paralel devlet*). The graft probe pushed Erdoğan-Gülen relations to a point of no return. Erdoğan initiated a massive anti-Gülenist purge across state institutions.[11] The Gülen movement was officially designated as a terrorist organization, the Gülenist Terror Organization or FETÖ, on the grounds that it had been trying to overthrow the government through illegal measures. Thousands of police officers, judges, and public prosecutors with alleged links to the movement were either rotated or dismissed. Pro-Gülen media outlets such as Samanyolu TV and Zaman Group as well as pro-Gülen businesses were seized. Both sides were determined to fight on. Fethullah Gülen declared his intention not to back down. "Those who don't see the thief but go after those trying to catch the thief […] let god bring fire to their houses, ruin their homes, break their unities," he cursed, while Erdoğan called Gülenists "grave robbers," "blood-sucking vampires" and "pawns of Turkey's foes."[12]

The political feud between Erdoğan and the Gülenists exposed the problems in Erdoğan's strategy of relying on his Islamist coalition to switch to a presidential system. A few weeks after the corruption probes, something dramatic happened. Erdoğan, who once declared himself as the prosecutor of the Ergenekon case which sent hundreds of Kemalist military officers to jail on bogus coup-plotting charges and ended almost half a century of military domination, said he favored fresh trials for those military officers. The move came after Erdoğan's top political advisor Yalçın Akdoğan said the prosecutors who launched the corruption probe into Erdoğan's government were the same prosecutors who framed the military officers.[13] Erdoğan's dramatic turnaround was an attempt to secure the cooperation of the few anti-Western Kemalists who still held some power in the military in his fight against the Gülenists. He publicly disowned the Ergenekon and Sledgehammer trials and released many of the active and retired military officers from jail in 2014 and 2015.[14]

However, that dramatic move was not going to save Erdoğan's presidential plans. After the crack in his Islamist coalition, the Kurds were also getting ready to leave Erdoğan's side.

FROM RELIGION TO NATIONALISM

"We will not let you become president"

The youthful Kurdish co-chair of the pro-Kurdish Peoples' Democratic Party (HDP), Selahattin Demirtaş, made his way to the podium amidst applause to deliver a talk at his party's parliamentary group meeting on March 17, 2015. He said: "I am here today to deliver the shortest remarks in the history of our party. I am here today to say one sentence. Mr. Recep Tayyip Erdoğan, as long as the HDP exists in these lands, we will not let you become president."[15] In the eastern city of Kars, an hour after Demirtaş announced the Kurds would not back his presidential plans, Erdoğan, who had been one of the boldest Turkish leaders to acknowledge and address the country's Kurdish issue, declared that Turkey did not have a Kurdish problem.[16]

Demirtaş kept his promise. In the June 2015 parliamentary elections, the HDP captured a historic 13 percent of the vote, leaping over the 10 percent parliamentary threshold, the highest in the democratic world. His party's success denied Erdoğan's AKP a parliamentary majority for the first time in thirteen years and cost Erdoğan his dream of a presidential system. Demirtaş knew Erdoğan would seek revenge. He was right. Right after Erdoğan's electoral loss, the parliament voted to strip deputies of the HDP of their immunity from prosecution, paving the way for a crackdown on Demirtaş and his fellow HDP leaders, a process that would last for years. Prosecutors filed hundreds of criminal charges against HDP leaders accusing them of links to the banned PKK. One year after Demirtaş challenged Erdoğan's grip on power, he was behind bars. By June 2015, the coalition Erdoğan thought would carry him to executive presidency had fallen apart. After the Gülenists, Erdoğan's alliance with the Kurds had broken down.

Demirtaş's rise as the biggest threat to Erdoğan's rule came against the background of negotiations between the government and the Kurds within the framework of the second "Kurdish opening" Erdoğan had launched two years earlier. The PKK had started withdrawing from Turkish territory into its safe haven in northern Iraq after Abdullah Öcalan's letter, which was read in Diyarbakır in the spring of 2013. The letter called for a ceasefire and asked the PKK to start withdrawing from Turkey in return for steps by the Turkish government to address Kurdish grievances. The process was never smooth. Despite skepticism from Kurdish leaders vis-à-vis the government's willingness to hold its end of the bargain, Kurds stuck to the deal with Erdoğan throughout the summer of 2013 when popular protests against him were sweeping the country.

In the fall of 2013, as part of the peace talks between the Turkish government and Öcalan, Erdoğan announced the long-anticipated "democratization package." The package included lifting the mandatory oath of allegiance to the Turkish nation for elementary school students; allowing the use of letters x, q and w, which are used in Kurdish but were banned in official documents; allowing female public servants to wear the headscarf; politicians to speak "languages other than Turkish" in their election campaigns; political parties to have co-chairs; and permitting education in "languages other than Turkish" in private schools. Erdoğan also said that he was open to discussions on the nationwide 10 percent electoral threshold that was originally designed by the 1980 military coup leaders to keep Kurdish parties out of the parliament.

To prevent the perception that the government was making concessions to Öcalan, AKP officials denied that the reforms in the "democratization package" were a response to Öcalan's three-stage roadmap for peace. The roadmap called for PKK withdrawal, followed by legal reforms granting the Kurds full political and language rights and ending with the PKK's laying down of arms and the reintegration of PKK militants into normal life. But the package was still seen as part of the Kurdish opening.[17] It fell far short of Kurdish expectations. Although these steps were a dramatic shift from the old Kemalist policies, in the eyes of the Kurds, they remained largely cosmetic, cultural steps that failed to meet their demands.

Turkey's Kurds have long demanded some form of decentralization. Abdullah Öcalan's proposal in the 1970s and 80s was to unify the Kurds in an independent and socialist republic. But from the late 1990s onward, he abandoned the idea of a Kurdish nation-state and promoted the constitutional recognition of Kurdish identity and accommodation of cultural and language rights within Turkey's territorial integrity. In 2005, he launched the concept of "democratic autonomy" as a solution to Turkey's Kurdish problem. Democratic autonomy entailed decentralization of Turkey's highly centralized state structures and empowerment of local government, not just in the Kurdish region but across the country. Other key Kurdish demands had been the right to mother-tongue education, electoral reform to enable fairer representation of pro-Kurdish parties in parliament, the removal of ethnic references from the constitution, which stipulates that "everyone bound to the Turkish State through the bond of citizenship is a Turk," and reforming a counter-terror law that has been used to imprison non-violent Kurdish activists.[18]

The reform package announced by Erdoğan fell far short of these demands. Neither Erdoğan nor the package made explicit reference to Kurds or Kurdish language. To Turkey's Kurds, this policy of denying them legal recognition was in line with past practices and very disappointing since it came at a time of renewed efforts to resolve the Kurdish problem peacefully. The reforms on Kurdish education were building upon past reforms that were undertaken by Erdoğan's government from 2009 onwards. With the new package, Kurds were now allowed to have education in Kurdish in private schools, but it did not address their demand for public education in Kurdish. Pro-Kurdish BDP, the HDP's predecessor, and Kurdish civil society organizations argued that the vast majority of Kurdish children were poor and did not have access to private schools.

The two items in the reform package allowing politicians to speak "languages other than Turkish" in their election campaigns and political parties to have co-chairs would not have any practical effect. There was already a practice of Kurdish politicians speaking to their Kurdish constituency in Kurdish, since the majority of them could not speak Turkish, and the pro-Kurdish party already had co-chairs. Similarly, although symbolically important, the municipalities run by the pro-Kurdish party had already created a de facto situation in the Kurdish region where local authorities used the letters q, w and x in their local correspondence and documents.

Erdoğan had announced that political parties that received 3 percent of the national vote in the last general elections would receive financial aid from the Treasury—a four-point drop from the previous 7 percent. He had also proposed lowering the 10 percent electoral threshold to 5 percent and decreasing electoral constituencies to five seats or removing them in a single-member district system to improve fairness in electoral competition.[19] The pro-Kurdish BDP, however, would not be eligible to benefit from the new criteria until after the 2015 elections. It had to run as a party instead of fielding independent candidates, a practice pro-Kurdish parties adopted to circumvent the 10 percent threshold. Doing that risked the party remaining out of the parliament if it failed to capture 10 percent of the national vote in the elections.

To Turkey's Kurds, one of the most significant items missing from Erdoğan's democratization package was revision of the penal law, including the anti-terror law. The law had been used to jail pro-Kurdish party members, activists, lawyers and journalists on trumped up terrorism charges. The deliberate vagueness of the law had paved the way for the state to prosecute anyone who simply promoted Kurdish rights such as education in Kurdish.

In the summer of 2014, Öcalan said he had run out of patience. Through his lawyers, the jailed PKK leader called on the government to carry out real reforms if it wanted to continue with the peace process. On February 28, 2015, in a joint public appearance at the Dolmabahçe Palace—the office of the prime minister in İstanbul—Deputy Prime Minister Yalçın Akdoğan, who was in charge of the Kurdish opening, and pro-Kurdish lawmakers, a lawmaker from the Kurdish party read out a message from Öcalan. Öcalan's statement urged the PKK to lay down its arms and outlined ten broad principles as a condition.

The meeting at Dolmabahçe was part of the Kurdish opening. Erdoğan was not shy about what he really wanted by pursuing the peace process with Kurds. "Are we ready to realize the goals of new Turkey, adopt a new constitution, switch to a presidential system and resolve the Kurdish issue? Give us 400 seats and let us solve this peacefully," he said in a March address in the southern city of Gaziantep.[20] Erdoğan was requesting a super majority in the 550-seat parliament for the ruling AKP so that the constitution could be changed, switching to a super-presidency. The Kurdish vote was the key. At the Dolmabahçe meeting, the government was represented by the Deputy Prime Minister Yalçın Akdoğan and minister of the interior Efkan Ala. Erdoğan was, however, involved in every detail of the meeting, from resolving the differences between the parties on the wording of the final statement to the seating arrangements during the announcement of the statements.[21]

Demirtaş's vow a few weeks after the Dolmabahçe meeting that the HDP would not make him president enraged Erdoğan. He renounced the Dolmabahçe declaration and made a statement that was considered the end of the Kurdish opening. On his way from Ukraine, Erdoğan told reporters:

> I did not find the meeting that was held there to be right. I did not think the picture of the deputy prime minister side-by-side with a parliamentary faction was appropriate... As for the 10-point statement, there is nothing in there that is about democracy, it is not a call for democracy. I will not accept that in the name of democracy.

Erdoğan's U-turn came with the realization that the Kurds would not back his bid to become an all-powerful president. The Kobani protests had been the first significant indication of that. The Kurds had become too confident to settle for what Erdoğan was willing to offer. Western backing for the Syrian Kurdish militia fighting in Kobani led to expectations of something much bigger. They thought that their century-old dream of statehood was finally coming true.[22] Erdoğan's inaction on a potential bloodbath if ISIS captured the Kurdish town alienated the Kurds further and made Erdoğan's efforts to secure their support for his agenda more difficult. Even pious Kurds, who had voted for Erdoğan since he came to power, were furious that he was willing to let ISIS capture the town. Demirtaş's "we will not make you president" declaration further exposed Kurdish disillusionment with Erdoğan. Yet, Erdoğan continued to campaign in Kurdish regions for the upcoming June general elections. He famously brandished a Kurdish Quran to a crowd in the Kurdish-majority cities of Siirt and Batman as he lashed out at the pro-Kurdish HDP. "They have nothing to do with religion. Look, the Religious Affairs Directorate, which they want to shut down, has printed the Quran in Kurdish for you,"

Erdoğan said.[23] In a last-ditch effort, he was playing the Islam card to sway Kurdish votes. It did not work.

Demirtaş ran the most progressive campaign in Turkish history. His efforts to transform the HDP from a Kurdish party to a mainstream, leftist one that would appeal to the country's non-Kurdish segments that had been traditionally skeptical of the pro-Kurdish parties paid off. He built a colorful coalition of liberals across Turkey. The party's candidates for the June 2015 general elections included socialists, Armenians, Yazidis, feminists, environmentalists, and members of the LGBT community. Demirtaş applied a gender quota to make sure each post was shared by a man and a woman and he shared his role of party chairperson with Figen Yüksekdağ.

The youthful politician charmed voters, particularly the young, with his humor, non-polarizing, peaceful rhetoric and focus on democracy and human rights. Demirtaş was everything Erdoğan was not. He played the *saz*, a traditional stringed instrument, on television; he visited students' homes, sat on the floor with them to eat lunch. He tapped into non-Kurdish voters' fear of Erdoğan's presidentialism project. His campaign slogan "we will not make you president" gave people hope for a Turkey different from Erdoğan's authoritarian, Muslim version. The months leading up the elections were bumpy. On June 5, two days before the elections, as Demirtaş was preparing to address a crowd in the HDP's final election rally in the Kurdish-majority town of Diyarbakır, two explosions hit, killing five and injuring 400 people. No one claimed responsibility for the attack.

Despite all the hardships the pro-Kurdish party had to endure, Demirtaş delivered on his promise. He did not let Erdoğan become president. The HDP captured a historic 13 percent of the vote and denied Erdoğan's AKP the parliamentary majority it had enjoyed over the last thirteen years. The AKP's loss thwarted Erdoğan's ambition to secure his party a super-majority large enough to rewrite the country's Constitution to establish a presidential system. Erdoğan had campaigned on the platform that switching to a presidential system was necessary to build a stronger "new Turkey," but voters were not convinced. Erdoğan's party lost 2.5 million votes compared to the previous general elections. Voters overwhelmingly backed the parties that opposed presidentialism. Erdoğan's loss was even more dramatic in the Kurdish-majority provinces which almost unanimously voted for the pro-Kurdish HDP.[24] His efforts to resolve the Kurdish problem through Islamic solidarity had failed. Around two million conservative Kurdish voters who had previously voted for the AKP switched to the pro-Kurdish HDP. That was Kurds' punishment to Erdoğan for his stance during the Kobani siege.

The pro-Kurdish party was not the only party that had dramatically increased its votes in June. The far-right, Turkish nationalist MHP also increased its votes by three points, moving close to its historic 18 percent in the 1999 elections when the PKK's leader Abdullah Öcalan was arrested. Many of those votes came from disgruntled AKP voters who were unhappy about the state of the economy, alarmed by the rise of PKK-affiliated Kurds in Syria and frustrated with Erdoğan's peace process with Turkey's Kurds.

Erdoğan's plan to rely on a policy of Islamization at home that would help him court conservative Turkish and Kurdish votes had failed; he had to come up with a new strategy. The hallmark of that strategy became apparent before the elections. Erdoğan ramped up his attacks against the HDP. He reverted to the security-oriented approach towards the Kurdish question, stopped talking about the Kurdish peace process and pledged to eradicate the PKK with which his government was carrying out peace talks. While attacking other opposition parties, Erdoğan refrained from publicly criticizing the ultranationalist MHP. Apparently, he had given up on the Kurds and was courting the MHP's support. In Erdoğan's mind, he had taken a big political risk by launching the peace process with the Kurds but his favor was not returned. He had not only failed to secure the Kurdish vote, but had also lost the Turkish nationalists' vote because of the peace process. In a clear sign of his new strategy, on June 26, shortly after the elections, Erdoğan pledged that Turkey would do whatever it took to prevent the establishment of a Kurdish state in northern Syria. His remarks heralded what was coming.

Despite losing its parliamentary majority, Erdoğan's AKP had still emerged from the elections as the largest party. According to the law, Erdoğan had to ask the AKP to form a coalition with other parties. If the AKP failed to do that, the president had to grant the mandate to form a coalition to the second biggest party, the secularist CHP. Erdoğan did not want to do either. A coalition government would mean the end of his dreams of a super presidency since all opposition parties, including the nationalist MHP, were opposed to it. Instead, Erdoğan wanted the AKP to form a single-party government by recapturing the parliamentary majority. That meant disregarding the June elections and calling for fresh ones. On the night of the elections, the nationalist MHP's leader Devlet Bahçeli came to Erdoğan's rescue. He announced that he would not back a coalition government and was in favor of calling for a snap election. It was a sign that Bahçeli, who was one of the staunchest opponents of the Kurdish peace process and switching to an executive presidency, had reached a bargain with Erdoğan.

"The Red Apple is our goal"

From 2015 onwards, Erdoğan often used the slogan "the Red Apple is our goal."[25] His frequent reference to the term "Red Apple" highlighted the supremacy of Turkish nationalism in his post-2015 strategy. The Red Apple is an age-old symbol of conquest in Turkish mythology. The roots of the concept go back to Turkic tribes. In their traditions, the Red Apple meant Turkish control of other ethnicities and states. After the inception of modern Turkey, the symbol was taken up by Turkish nationalists who believe that the country's cultural boundaries extend well beyond the political borders accepted by the country's founding father Atatürk after Ottoman defeat in World War I. It symbolizes Turkish imperial ambitions that aim to unite Turks across the globe to wield world hegemony.

The concept has occupied a prominent place in the ideologies of both the far-right, nationalist MHP and the nationalists on the left (*ulusalcı*). Erdoğan had never used it before he struck an alliance with nationalists in 2015. In fact, Erdoğan had often been the target of attacks from those nationalist circles since the early days of his rule. In 2003, the son of Doğu Perinçek, the leader of

FROM RELIGION TO NATIONALISM

the ultra-left, nationalist and secularist Patriotic Party, led an anti-AKP rally that included MHP and Kemalist groups. The group, called the "Red Apple coalition," was critical of Erdoğan's pro-Western and pro-Kurdish agenda as well as his alliance with the Gülenists. Over the years, nationalists increased their criticism, which peaked after Erdoğan launched the peace process with the Kurds. Devlet Bahçeli became one of the staunchest opponents of the presidential system, arguing that Erdoğan wanted to switch to an executive presidency to have a free hand in granting the Kurds autonomy.

The Kurds' decision not to back Erdoğan's executive presidency changed all that. Erdoğan gave up on the idea of resolving the Kurdish problem peacefully in return for support from the Turkish nationalists. It was a dramatic turnabout. From the Arab uprisings until the siege of Kobani, Erdoğan had employed an Islamist populist agenda and subdued Turkish nationalism to secure the backing of conservative Turks and Kurds. "We are a government that has trampled on every kind of nationalism," Erdoğan had declared.[26] Defining Kurds as an ethnic component of his Sunni Muslim nation had allowed him to pursue the Kurdish opening at home and green-light Kurdish autonomy in Syria.

The realization that he could not secure Kurdish support for his presidency as well as the fallout with the Gülenists made Erdoğan turn to the nationalists. From the nationalists' perspective, alliance with an Erdoğan who had ended the Kurdish peace process and launched a systematic campaign to root out Gülenists inside state bureaucracy became the means of saving "the nation, the state and Turkishness."[27] The nationalists who backed Erdoğan are not an ideologically uniform bloc. What brought together the far-right MHP, which is electorally the most important ally since it captured 16 percent of the vote in the June 2015 elections, and the far-left Patriotic Party, which does not command even 1 percent of the vote, is their ultranationalist, anti-Kurdish, anti-Gülenist and anti-Western worldview. Both Patriotic Party leader Doğu Perinçek and MHP leader Devlet Bahçeli see Gülenists as the puppets of the "Crusader West" and Kurds as an existential threat to the Turkish state. Although Perinçek's party is electorally marginal, its ideology, "national-patriotism" (*ulusalcılık*), which is a blend of Kemalism, socialism and Turkish nationalism, has many supporters in key state institutions, including the military, making Perinçek's support critical for Erdoğan.

After the June 2015 parliamentary elections, both Devlet Bahçeli and Doğu Perinçek threw their support behind Erdoğan. Perinçek announced that Erdoğan had become part of the "Red Apple coalition."[28] Bahçeli backed Erdoğan's efforts to block attempts to form a coalition and to call for a snap election to win back a parliamentary majority. In the five months following Erdoğan's election loss, the country slipped into a state of chaos.

"Me or chaos"

On July 20, shortly after Erdoğan's party lost its parliamentary majority, a suicide bombing hit a cultural center in the Turkish town of Suruç near the Syrian border. The attack killed thirty-two young pro-Kurdish activists, the majority of whom were Alevis, who had gathered to discuss sending aid to the Syrian Kurdish town of Kobani, which had recently been saved from an ISIS attack by Kurdish fighters. ISIS did not claim responsibility for the Suruç attack but the government blamed the bombing on the jihadi group and identified the bomber as Şeyh Abdurrahman Alagöz, a twenty-year-old university student who had recently returned from Syria and had links to ISIS. The bombing came two weeks after ISIS sympathizers threatened to retaliate against Turkey's move to arrest dozens of people believed to be linked to the group and block access to several Islamic news websites. Government critics, especially supporters of the pro-Kurdish HDP, blamed Erdoğan, arguing that he had turned a blind eye to ISIS attacks against the Kurds.

Two days after the Suruç bombing, another dramatic event took place. Two police officers were shot and killed in their homes in the border town of Ceylanpınar. Responsibility for the attack was claimed by a military organization affiliated with the PKK, which said on its website that the attack was in retaliation for the "massacre in Suruç" and accused the policemen of collaborating with ISIS. The PKK's acting leader Murat Karayılan, however, said that the decision to kill the policemen was not taken by any of the PKK's "formal units,"[29] adding that the attack was carried out by a group of Öcalan sympathizers. Ertuğrul Kürkçü, the pro-Kurdish HDP's honorary chair, said that those who killed the policemen had no formal or informal ties to the PKK and Karayılan's statement blaming the attack on Öcalan sympathizers was rushed and a mistake.[30] Several inconsistencies in the case raised further questions about the PKK's involvement in the attack. Police found fingerprints at the crime scene that belonged to another police officer but he was never questioned by the police. Five years after the incident, one police officer who arrived at the scene admitted that the police had tampered with evidence.[31] The nine suspects who were detained after the incident were all acquitted years later. The pro-Kurdish party's proposal for a parliamentary investigation into the killing was rejected by the ruling AKP and the nationalist MHP.

Erdoğan used the Ceylanpınar incident to formally end the Kurdish peace process and embark on a process of criminalizing the legitimate Kurdish opposition. A few days after the killing of the policemen, he declared that the two-year ceasefire that had been in place, despite small skirmishes, was officially over and called for the prosecution of the pro-Kurdish HDP lawmakers. Shortly after that announcement, he called for fresh elections on November 1. This was the first time in the history of the Republic that a president had called a snap poll.

Erdoğan's post-June election campaign reflected his newly emerging alliance with the nationalists. In the run-up to the June elections, Erdoğan had campaigned in Kurdish regions with a Kurdish Quran in his hands: part of his larger strategy to use Islam to secure the backing of conservatives and Kurds for his presidency. His strategy changed dramatically in the run-up to November elections. He replaced the Quran with Turkish flags. He campaigned in front of Turkish flags wrapping the coffins of soldiers who were killed in clashes with the PKK. It was a genius political move that would allow Erdoğan to snatch victory from the jaws of defeat.

Terror attacks continued. On October 10, the day when the PKK declared a conditional ceasefire ahead of the snap parliamentary elections, two suicide bombers attacked a leftist peace rally in Turkey's capital, Ankara, killing 102 and injuring more than 240. No one claimed responsibility for the deadliest single terrorist attack in the history of the country but evidence pointed to ISIS. One of the two suicide bombers was Yunus Emre Alagöz, the brother of the Suruç bomber, and like his brother, Yunus Emre had links to ISIS. Yet, the government was hesitant to lay the blame entirely on the jihadi group. Instead, Prime Minister Davutoğlu made a bizarre statement and called the attack "cocktail terrorism." He argued that two mortal enemies, ISIS and the PKK, were secretly collaborating against the Turkish government. It made little sense for the PKK to collaborate with a jihadi group to kill pro-Kurdish protesters on a day when it had declared a ceasefire. It was apparent that the government was trying to rally national sentiment against the PKK ahead of the elections.

The five months following June elections marked one of the darkest eras of Turkish history. Government critics argued that Erdoğan had unleashed the deep state to create chaos ahead of the elections. Turkey's Kurds were particularly enraged. They argued that Ankara's leniency toward ISIS was evidence of a covert alliance against Kurds both at home and in Syria. After turning a blind eye to ISIS advances in Kobani, they thought Erdoğan was now allowing ISIS to kill Turkey's own Kurds. What was more outrageous to the Kurds was that despite the ISIS attacks that had killed scores of Turkish citizens, Erdoğan still viewed the PKK and the prospects of Kurdish autonomy in Syria as bigger threats. To them, "Erdoğan is punishing us for not backing his presidency."[32]

Indeed, in an interview with CNN International's Becky Anderson aired on September 6, Erdoğan said that the PKK was Turkey's prime security priority, not ISIS. This thinking was apparent in Turkey's actions as well. In response to the ISIS attacks, Turkey finally ended its reluctance to confront ISIS, allowing the US to use İncirlik Airbase to conduct airstrikes against the jihadi group and beginning to seriously crack down on the terrorist group at home. But the government coupled its

FROM RELIGION TO NATIONALISM

attacks on ISIS with airstrikes against PKK targets in northern Iraq. Although Turkey's government had blamed the Suruç attack on ISIS, Turkish warplanes struck PKK targets in northern Iraq in retaliation. The "antiterrorism" raids rounded up a handful of ISIS supporters, many of whom were later released for "lack of evidence" while hundreds of Kurdish activists as well as members of the pro-Kurdish party were arrested on bogus terrorism charges and remained behind bars for years. Halis Bayancuk, long known as Ebu Hanzala and considered Turkey's most influential ISIS operative, for instance, was arrested after the Suruç bombing but released afterwards, while the Diyarbakır Chief Public Prosecutor's Office demanded a prison term for Selahattin Demirtaş, the man who upended Erdoğan's plans to establish a super-presidency, on charges of insulting Erdoğan and spreading terrorist propaganda. A year later, Demirtaş, along with nine other HDP lawmakers, was arrested.

Between the June and November elections, hundreds of people were killed in terror attacks. The peace process with the Kurds ended, hundreds of PKK militants, Turkish security officials and civilians were killed, HDP offices were attacked and Kurdish cities were destroyed in a military campaign launched by the government. The Kurdistan Communities Union (KCK) network, an umbrella group advocating for the PKK's agenda, declared that they had established "democratic autonomy" in the Kurdish regions. The country was going through one of the darkest episodes in its history but Davutoğlu was jubilant, announcing that the AKP was doing well in the polls.[33] Erdoğan ramped up his rhetoric that depicted Turkey as a country under assault from a coalition of foreign enemies and their internal collaborators. The HDP and PKK were the prime targets of his attacks. Gone was the man who had announced that decades of nationalist policies vis-à-vis the Kurds were over, pledged a peaceful resolution to the Kurdish problem and launched peace talks with the PKK.

As bombs exploded in Turkish cities following Erdoğan's electoral defeat in June, Erdoğan persuaded voters that they faced a stark choice between "me or chaos." More than enough voters agreed. In a matter of five months, Erdoğan's party increased its votes by nine points and recaptured a parliamentary majority in the snap elections. The results shocked even members of the AKP. Those nationalists who had switched to the MHP due to their opposition to Erdoğan's peace process with the Kurds had come back to the fold now that Erdoğan had ended it.

This nationalist backing not only helped Erdoğan win back his parliamentary majority. It helped him secure the executive presidency as well. After having been vehemently opposed to a super-presidency, Bahçeli supported the AKP's proposal for constitutional amendments to introduce a presidential system. The proposal was approved in the parliament with votes from both parties, paving the way for a referendum on the issue. The two parties joined forces to campaign for the referendum and secured a narrow victory. In 2018, they formalized their alliance by establishing the People's Alliance, an electoral alliance that helped Erdoğan secure outright victory in the first round of a presidential poll and become the country's first executive president.

Erdoğan's alliance with the nationalists replaced Islamism as the dominant component of his regime's ideology with Turkish nationalism. This new ideological orientation viewed ethnic Turkishness as the most important element of Turkish identity but stressed Islam's core place in it. Erdoğan blended nationalism with an anti-elitist, nativist populist rhetoric. This time, the "virtuous people," "the nation" were defined along ethnic, religious lines. The "corrupt elite," "the enemy" and "the terrorists" became the Kurds as well as religious minorities, the West and their domestic collaborators. He successfully exploited the country's long-standing animosity towards ethnic and religious minorities and resentment of the pro-Western elite. After the peace process with the PKK broke down in the summer of 2015, Erdoğan called for a "national coalition" against terrorism.[34] His definition of terrorism included democratically elected representatives of the Kurds, Kurdish NGOs, journalists, human rights activists and anyone who opposed his autocracy.

In a sign that Erdoğan's strategy prioritizing Islam had shifted to a game plan that sought to mobilize nationalist sentiment to secure support for his agenda, he forced Prime Minister Davutoğlu, the ideologue of the AKP's pro-Islamist foreign policy, to resign six months after the elections. There were many problems between Erdoğan and Davutoğlu including Davutoğlu's lack of enthusiasm for switching to a Turkish-style presidentialism, but his forced departure came at an important moment. It symbolized Islamism's subordination to nationalism in Erdoğan's new strategy.

The implications of Erdoğan's alliance with the nationalists were most visible in his Kurdish and Syrian policies. The PKK conflict resumed after the June elections, leading to thousands of deaths and hundreds of thousands of displacements. Erdoğan undid many of the progressive steps he had taken and reverted to the repressive Kurdish policies of previous decades. The restrictions on the Kurdish language that were loosened to secure Kurdish support were brought back. Many Kurdish cultural institutions, media organizations, language schools and associations were shut down over allegations of "connections to terrorist organizations." Even pre-schools that offered education to hundreds of Kurdish children free of charge and a children's TV channel that translated cartoons such as SpongeBob and the Smurfs were shut down.[35] The AKP removed democratically elected Kurdish mayors, replacing them with state-appointed trustees, and sent dozens of Kurdish politicians to jail on terrorism charges. The mandatory pledge of allegiance to the Turkish nation (*Andımız*) that Erdoğan removed in 2013 to court Kurds' support was reintroduced in 2018.[36]

The nationalist alliance Erdoğan cultivated in 2015 received a boost from one of the most bizarre events of Turkey's political history, with dramatic implications for domestic politics and Erdoğan's Syria policy.

"Gift from God"

At 9.00 pm on the night of July 15, 2016, General Mehmet Dişli walked into the Ankara office of General Hulusi Akar, the chief of Turkish general staff, to report that a coup was in the offing. "The military has seized power, jets are in the air, brigades are on their way," said Dişli to Akar. Akar was in disbelief. "Are you kidding me?" he asked. Lieutenant Colonel Levent Türkkan,

Akar's aide, walked in with a gun in his hand. He tried to tie Akar's hands from behind. Akar was shocked.[37] F-16s were buzzing low over the city and shaking windows while shots were being fired at army headquarters.

Meanwhile in İstanbul, Turkish army vehicles blocked a key bridge over the Bosphorus, leading to social media speculation about a potential terror attack. In other cities, coup plotters had ordered their subordinates to detain senior military leaders, block major roads and seize crucial institutions. Shortly after midnight, plotters took over the state broadcaster TRT and forced the news anchor to read a statement accusing Erdoğan of eroding Turkey's secular traditions and announce that the military had taken control to protect democracy from Erdoğan.[38]

Shortly after the plotters' statement, a shaken Erdoğan, who was vacationing with his family in the resort town of Marmaris where he narrowly escaped capture, was addressing the nation via Facetime on a Turkish anchorwoman's smartphone. Erdoğan said a small group within the military, who were incited by Gülen's "parallel state," a reference to an alleged infiltration of state bureaucracy by Gülen's followers, had attempted a coup outside the chain of command. Erdoğan called people to take to the streets to resist the coup. The Directorate for Religious Affairs instructed mosques across the country to broadcast a prayer to invite people onto the streets. Heeding Erdoğan's call, thousands of people began pouring into the streets to oppose the coup attempt. Some 250 people were killed, including many coup plotters, and 2,193 were injured. The next day, the government declared that the coup attempt had been "decisively" put down. A few days later, an emboldened Erdoğan said that the failed coup was a "gift from God" that would provide him with an opportunity to re-shape the country. He declared a state of emergency that would remain in place for two years and allow Erdoğan to rule by decree, bypassing parliamentary checks and balances, and to crack down on all dissent, not just from Gülenists.

The events on the night of the coup made little sense to the millions of people watching. It was nothing like previous coups. It was amateurish at best and there was a long list of unexplained events. There were between 8,000 to 9,000 soldiers on the street on the night of the coup, many of whom thought they were taking part in a military exercise. Yet, almost 50 percent of the military's general staff was fired immediately, raising questions about why so few soldiers had been mobilized if so many high-ranking officers took part in the coup attempt and whether there were already premade lists of those who would be fired.[39]

There were other unanswered questions. Why did the plotters stage the coup on a Friday evening when many civilians were expected to be on the street? Previous putschists had chosen the early hours of the morning. Why did they decide to block a bridge in İstanbul in one direction only? Why didn't they, as previous plotters had done, try to arrest key figures from the government such as the prime minister? But most bizarre of all, why did they bomb the parliament on a Friday night when it was not in use and inflict as little damage on the building as possible? There were also question marks about a missing block of time. By his own account, Turkish intelligence chief Hakan Fidan received a tip that a coup was in the offing at around 4.00 pm, prompting a meeting between him and Chief of the General Staff Akar. But neither of them informed Erdoğan nor took meaningful measures to prevent the coup.

Erdoğan's attribution of blame solely to the Gülenists was problematic as well. Immediately after the news of the putsch broke and long before investigation into the identities of the officers who took part began, Erdoğan announced that Fethullah Gülen and his supporters in the military were responsible. Gülen was certainly a compelling suspect. His shadowy movement, which had penetrated all levels of Turkish bureaucracy including the judiciary, had taken part in past efforts to undermine Erdoğan. It is highly likely that some Gülenists in the military took part in the revolt but there was no evidence suggesting it was purely a Gülenist affair. The only indication the government put forward was Chief of the General Staff Hulusi Akar's statement that the putschists who took him hostage suggested putting him in touch with their "opinion leader Fethullah Gülen," a fact denied by the Air Force Brigadier General who detained Akar that night. Others who have studied or followed the Gülen movement pointed out that Gülenists do not refer to Gülen as their "opinion leader" but refer to him as *hocaefendi* (respected teacher).[40] Other evidence that the government put forward to lay the blame entirely on the Gülenists was a statement from an anonymous "secret witness."[41] Many of those detained following the coup attempt admitted taking part in the putsch but denied any links to the Gülen movement. Many of the Gülenists in the military had been commissioned in 2002 when the AKP came to power, therefore they were mostly in mid-ranking positions, at colonel level and below. But according to the government, there were many generals and admirals involved in the coup attempt. That, as well as the testimonies of some Kemalist officers, contradicted the government's claim that the coup was orchestrated solely by followers of Gülen.

All these blurry events created competing narratives about the failed coup, dividing an already polarized nation. For Erdoğan and his supporters, July 15 was a pro-Western plot to destroy a leader who had embarked on steering the country on a "sacred march." For those critical of Erdoğan, the coup attempt was a "false flag" operation staged by Erdoğan himself to tighten his grip on power. A retired Turkish army general said of the botched coup, "if the Turkish army wants to bring down a government, it is perfectly capable of doing so. What we saw on July 15th were theatrics."[42] Thousands of others on social media shared the retired General's views. Postings under the hashtags #TheaterNotCoup (#Darbe DeğilTiyatro), #FakeCoup (#SahteDarbe) and #ShamCoup (#ÇakmaDarbe) became trending topics on Twitter in the days following the attempted coup.[43]

Erdoğan's reference to the coup attempt as a "gift from God" that would allow the regime to "cleanse our army of the Gülen virus" fed the "false flag" narrative. Chief of the General Staff General Hulusi Akar, under whose watch the coup attempt took place, instead of being punished for failing to foresee it, was promoted to the rank of minister of defense, feeding suspicions that Erdoğan was covering his tracks. Hundreds of captured young conscripts who allegedly were told by their superiors that they were taking part in a drill was another factor that led many commentators to question the government's narrative about July 15.

FROM RELIGION TO NATIONALISM

The main opposition CHP joined the chorus as well, arguing "The treacherous coup attempt on July 15 was a controlled coup that was foreseen, not prevented, and whose consequences were abused."[44] Others argued that the failed coup had support from the military's chain of command.[45] Turkey's Western allies expressed skepticism as well. British MPs, Germany's spy chief and US officials all said that there was no proof of Turkey's version of events. A report by Intcen, the EU's joint intelligence service, suggested that Erdoğan had planned to purge an array of soldiers before the July 15 coup attempt and that they launched the coup in haste.[46]

To this day, there are too many unknowns to make a judgement about the competing accounts surrounding the failed coup. Erdoğan turned down opposition demands to launch an independent investigation into how the coup managed to come so close to succeeding and how it eluded the attention of the country's intelligence. One thing is clear. It was indeed a "gift from God" for Erdoğan. He used the government's emergency powers to crackdown on all dissent, not just Gülenists. He launched a major purge of state institutions, including the judiciary, police and education system. He tightened his grip on power, leading to opposition party accusations that what Erdoğan had done after the failed coup amounted to a "civilian coup." The failed coup also strengthened Erdoğan's alliance with the nationalists, which helped him secure the majority he needed to finally establish a Turkish-style presidential system with him at the helm. A year after the coup attempt, Erdoğan secured a narrow victory in the constitutional referendum. One year later, he won re-election as president and assumed sweeping new powers. Thanks to the failed coup, Erdoğan consolidated a new political regime organized around the supreme power of the president with no restraints or separation of power in place.

Emergency powers, full control over the judiciary and media as well as unprecedented crackdown on the political opposition, civil society and academia helped Erdoğan change the regime and consolidate his one-man rule. Some 160,000 people were detained following the coup attempt, of which over 77,000, including military personnel, police, lawmakers, judges, prosecutors and journalists, were formally arrested for alleged links to the

Gülen movement and the PKK. More than 130,000 people, including 6,000 academics, have been purged from the public service. Some 170 generals and around 7,000 other senior military officers were arrested and many of them have been sentenced to life terms in prison. Close to 150 journalists and media workers are behind bars and the government has closed down 200 media organizations. Ten lawmakers from the pro-Kurdish HDP, including former co-chairs Selahattin Demirtaş and Figen Yüksekdağ, have been imprisoned on trumped-up terrorism charges. Enis Berberoğlu, a lawmaker from the main opposition CHP, was also arrested on espionage charges for allegedly sharing images showing the Turkish intelligence agency sending weapons into Syria. Human rights activist Osman Kavala, Amnesty International's former Turkey chairman Taner Kılıç and many others were arrested as well, on charges of trying to overthrow the government and supporting terror groups.[47]

Aside from the crackdown on dissent, Erdoğan took other alarming steps that will have more long-term consequences. Erdoğan quickly turned the failed coup into a "founding myth" to reinforce the new nationalism he sought to create after he struck an alliance with the nationalists. Contrary to his post-2011 Islamist populist agenda, which prioritized Turkey's Sunni Muslim identity and downplayed ethnic nationalism, Erdoğan's new nationalism sanctified ethnic Turkishness and infused it with a heavy dose of Sunni Islam and anti-Westernism.

To replace the country's secularist founding myth, Erdoğan and the government created their own following the failed coup. In the secularist narrative, Turkey was founded after a group of soldiers led by Mustafa Kemal Atatürk fought a war against Western powers in World War I and launched the War of Liberation. Without Atatürk, the narrative went, the country could have never become independent. This account was reinforced by textbooks, national holidays and public monuments. The post-July 15 myth created by the government portrayed Erdoğan as the embodiment of the national will, a leader heroically defending the country against the West and its "Gülenist pawns." To reinforce this myth, the coup attempt entered the country's textbooks. Millions of students start the school year with learning how the country defended itself against the Gülenists and their Western backers. In a video prepared by the Ministry of Education, July 15 is presented as one of many historical battles fought against foreign and domestic enemies. In the background, Erdoğan recites the national anthem, stressing the independence of Turkey.[48] Turks now drive across the July 15 Martyrs Bridge, walk by July 15 monuments, look at posters of people who climbed on top of the tanks on the night of the failed coup and even buy mugs and t-shirts that commemorate the botched attempt.

Erdoğan joins forces with Kemalists

A few weeks after the failed coup, in a rare appearance at a political event, General Hulusi Akar, the chief of staff, appeared in uniform before a rally of more than a million people in İstanbul, along with President Erdoğan, Prime Minister Binali Yıldırım and leaders of the Turkish opposition. Akar thanked those people who flowed into the streets on the night of the coup to oppose the putschists. The vision of unity among the people, the government and the military stood in sharp contrast to images of violence against military officers by crowds and the police just a few weeks ago. It also underscored the transformation of the relationship between Turkey's government and its military.

Not all was plain sailing for Erdoğan. He had a difficult task in the aftermath of the coup attempt. On the one hand, he had to rebuild a weakened army to ensure it could project power and meet the security challenges emanating from the PKK and ISIS. On the other hand, he had to establish his complete control over the military. To balance these conflicting demands, Erdoğan had to strike an alliance with the military's secular, ultranationalist Kemalist members, whom Erdoğan had demonized since coming to power in 2002. Without the support of the Kemalists, who were among the military's most numerous and professional, Erdoğan would struggle to replace the thousands of military officers, including nearly half of Turkey's generals, who had been purged. Fortunately for Erdoğan the Kemalists had their own agenda for cooperating with him. They wanted to repair the badly damaged image of the military and protect its core secularist ideology from further attacks, at least in the short term.[49]

After the coup attempt, Erdoğan took several steps to strip away the military's autonomy without compromising its effectiveness. The government placed the Coast Guard and gendarmerie, an internal security force, under the control of the Ministry of the Interior, and subordinated the army, air force, navy and the chief of staff to the Ministry of Defense. To inject Islam into the military and fill its institutions with Erdoğan loyalists, Erdoğan shut down military schools and allowed the graduates of Imam Hatip schools, which train state-employed preachers, to enter the armed forces. The Emergency Law system introduced after the coup as well as the switch to a presidential system tightened Erdoğan's grip on the military further.

Erdoğan's narrative that the failed coup was a solely Gülenist affair facilitated his alliance with the Kemalists by obscuring the participation of Kemalist officers in the revolt. As a sign of this Green-Kemalist alliance, ten Kemalist colonels—who had been sentenced to prison in the anti-Kemalist Sledgehammer-Ergenekon mass trials instigated by Gülenist police officers and judges with Erdoğan's support—were promoted to brigadier general and rear admiral positions. In the aftermath of the botched coup, both Erdoğan and other government officials repeatedly invoked Atatürk as a symbol of unity; Atatürk's portrait was even hung from AKP headquarters while Kemalists in the military expressed their support for the elected government.

Despite the deep divisions between the two sides over their vision for the country and the future of the military, in the short term they decided to focus on their common enemies. The military had always been opposed to Erdoğan's "Kurdish opening." But then Erdoğan joined their ranks after the pro-Kurdish party's electoral victory in June denied his party a parliamentary majority. After the ceasefire between Turkey and the PKK broke down in July, Erdoğan ramped up the fight against the PKK to rally nationalist support. Erdoğan's alliance with the Kemalist generals after the failed coup led Erdoğan to press harder in the fight against the PKK.

FROM RELIGION TO NATIONALISM

Another common enemy were the Gülenists. After many years of close alliance with the Gülenists against the Kemalists, Erdoğan now saw the Gülenists as a more immediate threat to his rule and the Kemalists as a useful partner in his fight against his former allies. The Kemalists, for their part, had always seen Gülenists as a threat to the secular foundations of the Republic. After the Sledgehammer/ Ergenekon trials, which mostly targeted anti-Gülen, Kemalist generals, Kemalist hatred for the Gülen movement grew. As Erdoğan's aggressive effort to cleanse state institutions of Gülenists intensified, ultranationalist Kemalists filled those ranks.

The Erdoğan-Kemalist alliance's third common foe was the West. The bungled putsch had brought anti-Western sentiment, which was already on the rise in Turkey due to US cooperation with the Syrian Kurdish militia in the fight against ISIS, to a new high. Erdoğan slammed the US and the EU for failing to show solidarity with Turkey over the coup attempt and accused the US of supporting the putschists. A Turkish newspaper reported that an American academic and former State Department official had instigated the coup from a hotel on an island near İstanbul, where he was attending a workshop on Iran. The same newspaper ran a front-page headline claiming the US had tried to assassinate Erdoğan on the night of the coup. Several of Erdoğan's cabinet ministers repeated these claims on the night of the coup and in the days after.

Turkey's Western allies had in fact condemned the coup attempt but also raised concerns about the scale of the crackdown in the aftermath. The European Parliament advised temporary suspension of accession talks with Turkey due to the government's "disproportionate repressive measures." US officials had other concerns. They were worried that the purges in the military, which overwhelmingly targeted officers who had worked closely with the US, were hurting the fight against ISIS. But Turkish officials continued to blame the US for being behind the coup attempt, a perception widely shared by Turkish society. In a poll conducted on Twitter, a pro-government newspaper asked which part of the US government was behind the failed coup. The CIA came in first with 69 percent, the White House came in second with 20 percent.[50]

One of the reasons for the popularity of this conspiracy theory was the fact that Fethullah Gülen, the alleged mastermind of the coup, had been living in the US in self-exile since 1999. A former CIA official and a former American ambassador to Turkey helped Gülen receive a green card, leading many Turks to believe that Gülen was a CIA agent. Turkey had requested Gülen's extradition long before the coup attempt. After Gülenists in the police initiated a corruption investigation into Erdoğan's close circle, which saw three members of cabinet quit, Erdoğan accused Gülen of plotting to topple him and undermine Turkey with concocted graft accusations and secret wiretaps. After the failed putsch, Ankara repeated its extradition request but US officials turned it down arguing Turkey had to provide hard evidence linking Gülen to the failed coup. As a result, anti-Americanism skyrocketed in Turkey.

Anti-American sentiment had been intense in the military too, especially since the Sledgehammer/Ergenekon trials which mostly targeted anti-Gülen generals who promoted a strategic reorientation in Turkey's foreign policy away from NATO and toward Russia. Those generals were part of the Eurasianist clique within the military. Eurasianists often highlight the rapprochement between Ankara and Moscow during and after the Turkish War of Independence, which they consider an "anti-imperialist dialogue" between Mustafa Kemal Atatürk and Vladimir Lenin. They promote an anti-Western and pro-Russian re-orientation in Turkish foreign policy.[51] This pro-Russian rethinking of Turkey's geopolitical identity sought to shape Erdoğan's foreign policy during the early years of his rule but failed to become a significant force due to Erdoğan's pro-Kurdish, pro-Western stance and his close alliance with the Gülenists. Eurasianism made a comeback after frustration with the US reached new heights following US-YPG cooperation, Erdoğan clashed with the Gülenists and ended the peace process with the Kurds. Many of its proponents threw their support behind Erdoğan after his nationalist turn following the 2015 elections. The failed coup strengthened this alliance. As part of Erdoğan's post-coup purge, the government fired several hundred Western-educated, pro-NATO senior military officers and replaced some of them with Eurasianist colonels who

FROM RELIGION TO NATIONALISM

had been sentenced to prison terms in the Sledgehammer/ Ergenekon trials. These developments strengthened the anti-Western clique in the military.

The Islamist populist strategy Erdoğan banked on after his 2011 election victory failed to deliver the expanded powers he wanted, after popular resistance to his Sunni Muslim authoritarian vision and fallout with his Islamist allies and the Kurds shook his rule. In response, he turned to nationalism. The coup attempt expanded the scope of Erdoğan's nationalist alliance to include the ultranationalist Kemalists in the military. This alliance opened a new chapter in Erdoğan's war to stay in power. This time, Kurds were the arch enemy. Some of the most destructive battles of that war were fought in Syria.

5

ATTACKING KURDS TRUMPS TOPPLING ASSAD

Erdoğan's Islamist populist agenda at home had turned Turkey into the main patron of the anti-Assad opposition. With Erdoğan's nationalist turn, toppling Assad took a back seat to curbing Kurdish gains, paving the way for a tacit cooperation with the Assad regime Erdoğan had so fervently sought to unseat in return for Assad's acquiescence for Turkey's military campaign against the Syrian Kurds. What were the implications of Erdoğan's nationalist shift for the war in Syria? How did it impact on the anti-Assad opposition's fight against the regime? What did this shift mean for Turkey's relations with Assad's allies such as Russia and Turkey-US bilateral ties? Most importantly, what was the human toll of this change on the people of Syria? The following section will seek to address these questions.

Turkish tanks cross into Syria

On August 24, 2016, a month after the failed coup, Turkish tanks, supporting ground forces and hundreds of Turkey-backed Syrian opposition fighters advanced into Syrian territory. The military operation into northern Syria, dubbed Operation Euphrates Shield, was Turkey's first military incursion into the country since the conflict started. Major General Zekai Aksakallı, the Special Forces commander who was praised for his action in resisting the coup attempt, was leading the operation. According to the official Turkish announcement, the aim of Operation Euphrates Shield was to eliminate ISIS presence from Jarabulus and Al-Rai along Turkey's border but the real target was the Kurdish militia, the YPG. Targeting the group was an extension of Erdoğan's anti-Kurdish stance at home.

Just a few days before the incursion, the Syrian Democratic Forces (SDF) had captured Manbij, a northern Syrian town west of the Euphrates River, from ISIS with US-led coalition support. Ankara had long warned the YPG, the dominant force in the SDF, and the US that YPG presence west of the Euphrates River was its redline. Turkey feared that the capture of Manbij would help the YPG extend the boundaries of the defacto autonomous Kurdish region across the west bank of the Euphrates River and link up with the Kurdish enclave in Afrin, further to the west. A contiguous Kurdish autonomous zone along Turkey's southern border was the Turkish nationalists' nightmare scenario. To prevent that, Turkey wanted to capture Jarabulus and other ISIS-held territory that lay between the Kurdish cantons of Afrin and Kobani and move on to Manbij.

Erdoğan had long wanted to intervene in Syria but the Turkish military, traditionally skeptical of deployment of troops outside of its borders, had put the brakes on that ploy. The idea of a Turkish military intervention was first introduced in 2012 when Turkey was urging the Syrian rebels to march on Aleppo, and reintroduced several times in the following years. Plans were made and presented to the military by Turkey's Intelligence Agency (MİT), whose head was a close Erdoğan ally and had become a key player in the country's Syria policy. The goal of the initial intervention plan was to create a safe zone for the rebels that would allow them to launch more effective assaults against the regime. But the Turkish military was reluctant. Among those who ferociously opposed intervention into Syria was Army Chief of Staff General Necdet Özel.[1] There were many other senior personnel within the military who were opposed to Erdoğan's Syria plans, such as Brigadier General Semih Terzi. The reasons for Terzi's opposition to a military incursion into Syria are not known but many in the

ATTACKING KURDS TRUMPS TOPPLING ASSAD

Turkish military were critical of Erdoğan's Syria policy, particularly Turkey's support for radical Islamist groups in Syria.[2] They were worried about the risks of such intervention. They did not want to send Turkish troops into harm's way and argued that there were not enough moderate rebels to efficiently perform the operation of liberating the territories in northern Syria.

Opponents of a military incursion had other concerns as well. They did not want to risk a confrontation with Russia.[3] Russia had militarily intervened in Syria and deployed the S-400 missile defense system in 2015, giving Moscow control over Syrian airspace. Air cover was essential for any ground operation, but Turkey and Russia were not on good terms. Relations had been strained over Turkey's downing of a Russian fighter jet in 2015, leading to a halt in all Turkish air operations over Syria. Erdoğan tried to push back against the military's foot-dragging, but to no avail. After the failed coup, however, the Turkish military was in no position to resist Erdoğan's demands. Brigadier General Semih Terzi, who joined the coup attempt against Erdoğan on July 15, was shot dead on the night of the putsch. Others were purged. To the remaining Kemalist officers within the military, a military incursion into Syria that aimed to curb the influence of the Kurdish militia was an opportunity to repair the military's badly damaged image. The thaw in Turkey-Russia relations after Erdoğan issued an apology for downing the Russian jet in June also influenced the military's decision to go ahead with the incursion.

Operation Euphrates Shield epitomized how much things had changed in Turkey in a matter of a few years. The peace process with the Kurds had ended abruptly: Erdoğan was now in alliance with those who considered Kurds their arch enemies. Salih Muslim, the co-leader of the PYD who was in Turkey at the invitation of Foreign Minister Davutoğlu and had helped the Turkish military operation to evacuate the Süleyman Şah tomb, was banned from entering the country. Turkey issued an arrest warrant for Muslim and announced it would seek an Interpol Red notice for him shortly after Turkey's military incursion. The military, which was once a thorn in Erdoğan's side, had been brought under his full control with the coup attempt.

Operation Euphrates Shield was the most significant foreign policy implication of these new domestic power dynamics. It also reflected the shift in Ankara's relations with Moscow and Washington. Turkey had been the most ardent supporter of the anti-Assad opposition, providing military, political and diplomatic support. Ankara's efforts to topple the regime had placed Turkey on the opposing front to Assad's closest ally, Moscow. But Operation Euphrates Shield heralded the beginning of a new era where all these dynamics changed. Ousting the regime was no longer Ankara's priority. After years of adamantly opposing the idea, Erdoğan was now suggesting that the Syrian president could have a role to play in a future political transition.[4] Crippling Kurdish ambitions for autonomy had replaced unseating Assad through Islamist proxies as Erdoğan's top priority. That goal required working with the regime and Moscow. Through a series of measures following the launch of the operation, Ankara strengthened Assad's hand, both militarily and politically, and cultivated a close alliance with Russia at the expense of its Western partners.

From "patron of the revolution" to "sellout"

At the height of the siege by ISIS forces in the northern Syrian town of Kobani, Erdoğan held a phone conversation with US President Barack Obama. Erdoğan was furious about the US president's efforts to help the Syrian Kurds fighting against ISIS. "Why is Kobani so important for you?" asked Erdoğan. "It is Aleppo, not Kobani, that is strategically important."[5] This sentence captured the gap between the two NATO allies' priorities in Syria. At the time, Erdoğan's number one goal in Syria was getting rid of Assad, and defending Aleppo against regime offensives was key to achieving that goal. He was desperately trying to convince the American president, who was more worried about the threat ISIS posed to US interests than the regime in Damascus, that unseating Assad should take priority over all else. As the change in Erdoğan's domestic strategy forced a shift in his Syria priorities, Erdoğan found himself in a similar spot to Obama: overthrowing Assad, thus protecting Aleppo against regime offensives, could take a backseat to other strategic priorities. Just like Obama, Erdoğan was now looking to northern Syria, not Aleppo, to achieve his strategic goals in Syria. Turkey's Operation Euphrates Shield showed the shift in Erdoğan's priorities in the war-torn country.

As his strategy of co-opting the Kurds to establish a presidential system gave way to attacking them to achieve that same goal, Erdoğan revised his Syria policy accordingly. He was now focused on denying the Syrian Kurds a contiguous autonomous region along Turkey's border. So dramatic was Turkey's about-face that Erdoğan, who was once considered the "biggest patron of the Syrian revolution," became a "sellout" in the eyes of some key opposition figures who worked closely with Turkey.[6] Burhan Galyon, the first chairman of the İstanbul-based umbrella organization of the Syrian opposition, the Syrian National Coalition, expressed his frustration with Turkey in his memoir, pointing to the many mistakes Turkey made in the conflict, that strengthened the Assad camp and undermined the revolution.[7] Abu Ahmed, a commander for one of the opposition factions who fought in Aleppo against Assad's forces, was another name voicing the uneasiness in opposition ranks concerning Erdoğan's shifting priorities. He said "dirty, secret deals between Ankara and Damascus gave Erdoğan the Kurds but sacrificed the revolution."[8]

Indeed, the developments on the ground following Turkey's military incursion pointed to a troubling trend for the anti-Assad opposition. The operation itself was an indication that Turkey was cozying up to Assad's biggest ally. Ankara would be able to launch the operation after Moscow's green light. As the two countries had fought on opposite fronts of the Syrian war for years, their newfound cooperation came as a surprise to many, particularly Turkey's NATO allies.

There were other signs of dramatic changes in Erdoğan's Syria policy. Every Turkish military operation was concurrent with a major Russia-backed Syrian government offensive, leading many to believe that there was some form of "land swap" deal between Ankara and Damascus that allowed territorial exchanges to Ankara to curb Kurdish advances and Damascus to capture territory from the opposition.[9] To many, Aleppo's fall to Assad's forces in 2016, which was largely seen as a sign that the regime had won the war, was part of that deal.

Before the war, Aleppo was the country's largest city and industrial capital. Shortly before the 2011 uprisings, "an economic renaissance was underway, fueled by thousands of small factories on the city's outskirts," wrote Robert Worth, a *New York Times* journalist who covered the story of the city's fall.[10] Turkey played a critical role in that renaissance. A trade deal between Ankara and Damascus contributed largely to the city's fortunes. Mohamed Al Maree, a businessman from Aleppo, told me in a 2013 meeting in Turkey's southeastern city of Gaziantep how trade between the two countries before the uprising helped his business grow. "But things have changed dramatically," he added. "Turkey's legacy in Aleppo used to be booming trade and tourism. Now it is Turkish-made ammunition and Turkey-backed fighters who are bent on destroying everything great about this city."[11]

Al Maree was referring to the battle for Aleppo that was considered the "heart of the revolution."[12] The battle had begun in 2012 when Turkey-backed rebels launched an offensive with an unprecedented barrage of shellfire from the city's countryside and took half of the city. So intense was the attack that rebel commanders and residents expected a swift opposition victory. But the offensive stalled shortly after the rebels captured the city's eastern neighborhoods. To recapture rebel-held territory, the regime started bombing the area. But the rebels continued to advance, putting Assad's forces under pressure in northwest Syria. Turkey was instrumental in the rebels' military successes in Aleppo by providing weapons, training, logistical support and its territory as a base for many rebel factions, including the al-Qaeda-linked Nusra Front, which was designated as a terrorist group by the US and Turkey. Worried about the rebel advances, Russia militarily intervened in 2015 and put the rebels on the back foot. By that time, civilian casualties due to regime and rebel offensives had reached such heights that Aleppo had turned into a "global byword for savagery."[13] A month before Turkey's first military incursion, the regime launched another offensive and managed to fully encircle eastern Aleppo for the first time, but the siege was broken by a rebel counterattack.

ATTACKING KURDS TRUMPS TOPPLING ASSAD

When Turkey launched Operation Euphrates Shield, the battle for Aleppo was ongoing. The rebels and regime forces were controlling different parts of the city but the battle had largely reached a stalemate. Shortly after Turkey's incursion, Assad forces intensified their attacks on Aleppo. As the Turkish operation expanded from Jarabulus to Azaz in September, the Assad regime announced its final offensive on the city.[14] In December, after years of fighting and months of bitter siege, the rebels agreed to withdraw in a ceasefire brokered by Turkey and Russia. The ceasefire ensured the safe exit of civilians and rebels out of Aleppo. Assad's forces regained all of Aleppo while rebels were forced to flee what was once their largest stronghold and were boxed in to the northwestern province of Idlib, with no strategically significant urban areas under their control.

Erdoğan, who once called Aleppo strategically the most significant place that rebels had to remain in control of at all costs, called the agreement that led to the fall of the city to Assad forces a "historic opportunity" that should not be squandered.[15] Erdoğan's about-face was dramatic. In less than a year, Ankara shifted from being the main supporter of the Aleppo resistance against Assad to helping Assad recapture the "heart of the revolution." Ankara did this through several steps. As the regime's siege of Aleppo was intensifying, it convinced the rebel factions it was backing to withdraw to Idlib. Erdoğan acknowledged Turkey's part in the regime takeover of Aleppo in an October speech to local administrators in Turkey. Erdoğan said that Putin had requested his help to convince the Nusra Front, one of the most effective fighting forces in Aleppo against the regime, to withdraw from Aleppo. "I advised my friends accordingly," said Erdoğan.[16]

Erdoğan took other measures to help the regime offensive in Aleppo. After the launch of Operation Euphrates Shield, Turkey withdrew its support from the armed opposition groups in Aleppo that it had been backing for years. Some of the rebel brigades were withdrawn from Aleppo to take part in the Turkish operation to the north, further weakening the rebels' ability to confront the regime offensive. A senior official from the Turkey-backed Turkmen Sultan Murad brigade, which was one of the groups pulling out of

Aleppo, said the work on enlisting fighters in Turkey's fight in the north was already under way.[17] He continued that fighters from Aleppo would join Turkey's operation to capture al-Bab, a northern city critical to Turkish efforts to block Kurdish expansion.

These developments showed that Ankara allowed Aleppo to fall in return for a green light from Damascus and Moscow to attack the Kurds.[18] Following the fall of Aleppo, Russia and the Assad regime launched an offensive against ISIS in al-Bab, indirectly helping Turkish efforts to capture the city, strengthening the view voiced by rebel commander Abu Ahmet that Erdoğan had "sacrificed the revolution" to be able to attack the Kurds.

Indeed, the regime's capture of Aleppo, which was the rebels' last major urban redoubt and often dubbed "Syria's Stalingrad" in reference to the 1942–43 Battle of Stalingrad that marked the turning point of the Second World War, reconfigured the Syrian battleground. After rebels took control of half of the city in 2012, Aleppo had become an opportunity for them to prove that they could offer an alternative in urban government to Assad. The city's recapture by Assad's forces effectively ended the Syrian opposition's prospects for the control of urban centers and the country as a whole. It persuaded many Syrians that the Assad regime, despite all its cruelty and corruption, was their "best shot at something close to normality."[19] The international community, too, seemed to have resigned itself to Assad's rule after the city's fall. The world's attention turned away from Assad's cruelties and years of bloodshed to the capturing of ISIS's capital Raqqa. In many ways, the recapture of Aleppo by the regime was both a military and an ideological turning point that strengthened Assad's hand. It was ironic that Erdoğan had a key role in that.

Erdoğan continued to help the regime consolidate its power and Moscow cement its influence over the war.

"Don't forget Syria, don't forget Aleppo"

In December of 2016, several months after Turkey's military incursion into Syria began, a dramatic event took place that showed how important Erdoğan's cooperation had become to the Assad

ATTACKING KURDS TRUMPS TOPPLING ASSAD

regime's goals. On the night of December 19, Russia's ambassador to Turkey, Andrei Karlov, was giving a talk at an art gallery in Ankara. A man in a dark suit, who was later identified as a twenty-two-year-old off-duty police officer, shot him dead shouting "God is great. Don't forget Syria, don't forget Aleppo."[20] Erdoğan said the assassination was a provocation meant to derail the two countries' regional and economic cooperation and blamed Gülenists, who had taken part in the coup attempt a few months earlier. If the incident had happened a year before, it would have caused a strong reaction, even sanctions, from Moscow on the scale that followed the Turkish downing of a Russian jet in 2015, but this time Russia's response was measured. Moscow accepted Ankara's condolences. Putin even repeated the Turkish government's line by blaming the "destructive forces that had infiltrated into the Turkish state," an expression used by the Turkish government to refer to Gülenists, for the killing.[21]

There was a simple reason for Moscow's restraint. Putin wanted to keep Erdoğan onboard to turn the military victory in Aleppo into a diplomatic triumph. He was working on a Syrian peace roadmap of his own. In a December phone call with Erdoğan, he had invited him to Astana (now Nur-Sultan), the capital of Kazakhstan that is within the Russian zone of influence, to a series of talks that would "bring armed groups together in order to forge a military agreement that results in a political accord."[22] UN-led Geneva talks had stalled due to the Assad regime's objections to the composition of the opposition delegations, the role of the Syrian Kurds and the demands that Assad step down at the end of a transition process. Putin said his initiative was meant to complement the process spearheaded by the UN and the US, but the UN was uneasy. For Putin, it was the perfect time to launch his rival peace initiative. Erdoğan had given up his obsession with regime change. Instead, he was signaling that he could accept some role for Assad in the transition.[23] Putin was confident that Erdoğan would take part in arrangements that would allow Assad to stay in power and convince the opposition to do the same as long as Turkey was allowed to continue its operations targeting the Syrian Kurdish militia.

There were other factors that worked in favor of Putin's attempts to launch his own Syria peace initiative. Ankara's relations with Washington were strained due to the latter's cooperation with the Syrian Kurds in the fight against ISIS. The coup attempt had made things worse. Although the US military supported Turkey's Operation Euphrates Shield, the military incursion—which pitted Turkey against the US-backed YPG—was likely to drive a further wedge between the two NATO allies. The fall of Aleppo was the icing on Putin's cake. After the fall of the city changed the military and psychological balance of the war, he was ready to embark on a project that would help him pitch himself as a peacemaker after a fifteen-month bombing campaign.

Erdoğan had clear-cut expectations from Astana. In the lead-up to the talks, he made it clear that participation of the YPG in the talks was a red line. He also wanted assurances that the territory lost by ISIS would be regained by Turkey-backed rebels, not the YPG. Al-Bab was one of the most important ISIS-controlled territories in the north and critical to Turkey's efforts to contain Kurdish expansion. But Turkey's operation to capture the city had stalled partly due to lack of support from the US. Erdoğan saw Astana as an important occasion to secure the help of Damascus and Moscow in al-Bab.

In January 2017, Turkey, Iran and Russia met to hold the first round of Astana peace talks. It was the first time that rebels and the Assad regime had gathered at the negotiation table since the civil war began.[24] The three countries agreed to set up a trilateral monitoring body to enforce the ceasefire that had been brokered by Turkey and Russia the previous month, but neither the regime nor the rebels signed the agreement. Iran, Russia and Turkey expressed their commitment "to the sovereignty, independence, unity and territorial integrity of the Syrian Arab Republic as a multiethnic, multireligious, nonsectarian and democratic state," and their belief "that there is no military solution to the Syrian conflict and that it can only be solved through a political process."[25] The agreement put pressure on Turkey to separate the rebel groups it supported from jihadist groups, which had enjoyed strong support from Ankara and had been instrumental in Erdoğan's efforts to unseat Assad. The Nusra Front, which was one of them, was excluded from the ceasefire.

ATTACKING KURDS TRUMPS TOPPLING ASSAD

The Astana process had an immediate dividing impact on the already divided Syrian opposition. A day after the Astana talks wrapped up, clashes broke out between Jabhat Fateh al-Sham (JFS), a group formerly known as Nusra Front, and Ahrar al-Sham in Idlib. These two groups were the most powerful rebel forces that had fought side by side against the regime, but after Astana they turned on each other.[26] The attack by JFS was an attempt to eliminate rebel groups that had lent credibility to the Astana process. Ahrar al-Sham had both moderate and Salafist factions within its ranks but it was considered moderate by Russia and received strong support from Ankara. Although it did not attend the Astana talks, JFS criticized groups such as Ahrar al-Sham for the fall of Aleppo and accused the group of sharing its coordinates in Syria to help US drone strikes in Idlib that had killed scores of its fighters.[27] The infighting between different rebel groups left the province divided between areas controlled by Salafists and Western-backed factions and further weakened the already divided opposition.

Unlike the rebel groups that protested against Astana, those that were at the table had high expectations. They were misled into thinking that Russia would pressure the regime to accept a political compromise.[28] The Astana process had one key goal for Russia: keeping Assad in power. Although officially launched in 2017, the Kremlin had started working towards Astana in 2015 when it convened Turkey-backed armed groups and Assad's representatives. The idea was not to secure compromises from Assad or hold real negotiations between the parties but to put forth the idea that there were opposition groups that were not anti-Assad to bolster the regime's legitimacy and lock in Assad's military gains with Ankara's help.[29]

Russia used several mechanisms to help Assad, localized cease-fires being one of them. Once they were established, the regime regrouped its forces and launched offensives elsewhere. The Aleppo ceasefire, brokered by Turkey and Russia, was the first such endeavor which helped Assad's forces evict rebel forces from the city before it was fully captured by the regime. Other mechanisms that were introduced by Russia and implemented with Turkey's help such as creating de-escalation zones, separating rebel groups from jihadis or forming "reconciliation committees" all facilitated the regime's consolidation of power.

In May 2017, Turkey agreed to Russia's plan to establish "de-escalation zones" in Syria as part of the Astana process. The plan called for delineating zones where frontlines between the regime forces and rebels would be frozen. It would develop four zones of ceasefire for six months in heavily contested areas around western Syria. Turkey's foreign ministry said that the scope of the zones would include the whole of Idlib province; parts of Latakia, Aleppo and Hama provinces; parts of Homs province; parts of Damascus and the East Ghouta region; and also parts of the southern Daraa and Quneitra provinces.[30] Northern Syria was excluded from the de-escalation zones, allowing Turkey to continue campaigns in this region and undermine the rise of Kurdish autonomy on its border. Russia and Damascus reassured everyone that Assad's air force would halt flights over designated areas if all sides respected the ceasefire. The wording sounded like a genuine attempt to stop the bloodshed, but in reality it was an attempt to undermine the opposition. A year after agreeing to establish de-escalation zones, the regime captured the majority of those areas.

Moscow introduced the idea of creating "de-escalation zones" to freeze large geographic regions to allow the regime, which up to that point had to expend most of its energy on holding onto its territories within western Syria, to focus its limited resources in areas elsewhere. The clause that excluded jihadi groups from the ceasefire agreement and the need to separate them from other rebel groups provided the regime and Russia with justification to violate the ceasefire in areas where there were jihadi groups.[31] Once the regime captured areas from the rebels, "reconciliation committees" were launched to convince rebel groups to surrender and lay down their weapons. Rebel groups that refused to agree to the terms of the reconciliation committee were forced to leave, often to Idlib. Some rebel groups affiliated with the Turkey-backed Free Syrian Army that agreed to the terms were even integrated into the Syrian regime forces.[32]

The Astana process became the most effective Russian strategem to bolster Assad. It divided the opposition, boxed in rebels in Idlib and helped the regime reclaim territory. By December 2017, the Syrian Army had launched a campaign to secure the entire western portion of the Euphrates River.[33] By 2018, less than three years after Russia militarily intervened in Syria, Moscow had helped its ally in Damascus recapture over 60 percent of the country's territory. The international press was abuzz with headlines like "After 7 years of war, Assad has won in Syria"[34] and "How Bashar al-Assad won the War in Syria."[35]

Turkey, one of the sponsors of the Astana process, played a key role in Assad's military and diplomatic gains against the opposition. The change in Erdoğan's domestic strategy made this possible. As part of that new strategy, a relentless war against the Kurds, targeting not just the PKK but also Kurdish civil society, activists, journalists and elected Kurdish politicians, replaced the peace process with the Kurds. Erdoğan's war against the Kurds shifted his Syria policy as well. The days when Turkey did everything to support the Syrian revolution and topple Assad were gone. Turkey also gave up on the idea of US-Turkish cooperation in Syria that would serve its interests. Instead, Turkey began cooperating with Assad and his Russian allies in return for their acquiescence in Ankara's campaign against the Syrian Kurdish militia. Operation Euphrates Shield epitomized this new thinking.

Seven months after its launch, Turkey declared that it had successfully ended Operation Euphrates Shield. The operation captured around 800 square-miles of territory stretching from Azaz in the west through al-Bab to Jarabulus on the Euphrates River. In the Euphrates Shield zone (ESZ), Turkey took measures that amounted to creating a "de facto client state."[36] With its own troops and the allied rebel factions, Turkey dominated the security sector in the ESZ. It established local councils, which are administrative bodies in charge of managing issues at the local level ranging from collecting revenues, repairing roads and infrastructure to running the civilian registry. Theoretically, these local councils are subordinate to the Syrian Interim Government but are controlled by Turkey. The Turkish governors of Kilis and Gaziantep have the final authority over them. Turkey selects their members and pays the salaries of local councilors and civil servants as well as the armed groups operating in the ESZ. Gaziantep mayor Fatma Şahin's visit to Jarabulus in the ESZ a few weeks after it was liberated from ISIS heralded the beginning of Turkey's nation-building efforts in northern Syria. Turkey's Disaster and Emergency Management Authority (AFAD), Turkey's Ministry of Health and Turkish companies had already started working in the ESZ, digging wells, setting up medical tents and laying lines from the Turkish border to supply electricity to the zone's residents.[37] Mayor Şahin promised to do more to integrate the newly liberated territories into Turkey. Indeed, Turkey has become the main governing authority in the area, controlling all aspects of the economy, society and politics. It has established schools, hospitals, even a branch of its postal service; Turkey's Religious Affairs Directorate has renovated hundreds of mosques; Turkish businesses and Turkish goods are everywhere in the ESZ, all pointing to the rapid "Turkification of all aspects of civic life" in the territories captured by Turkey and its Arab allies.[38]

Pro-Erdoğan media portrays Turkish occupation of northern Syria as a success story which has provided security and public services in an area gripped by chaos, violence and human suffering. Turkey's involvement in the ESZ has indeed improved economic activity and provided some relief but it has also created serious problems for ESZ residents. Turkey-backed rebel factions include radical groups that are accused of human rights abuses. These factions are only accountable to Turkey and many of them are motivated by financial gains. United Nations war crime investigators said some of the Turkey-backed factions operating in northern Syria were engaged in looting civilian property, rape, kidnapping and torture.[39] They often target Kurdish civilians and appropriate their homes and businesses. Overall, the security situation in the ESZ has worsened due to human rights abuses committed by Turkey-backed groups and infighting within their ranks over the control of resources.

From Erdoğan's point of view, Operation Euphrates Shield was a success, albeit smaller than was originally intended. Retaking Jarablus, Dabiq and al-Bab from the jihadists gave Turkey control over a large chunk of territory in northern Syria and thwarted the YPG's plans to stitch together a semiautonomous region in north-

ATTACKING KURDS TRUMPS TOPPLING ASSAD

ern Syria. Erdoğan had initially warned that the offensive would push the Kurdish militia out of Manbij and move south to Raqqa. But neither happened due to US objections. The US was determined to work with the YPG to retake Raqqa and would not tolerate a Turkish operation against Manbij, where US Special Forces working with the YPG against ISIS were stationed. Yet, Erdoğan's nationalist allies were happy. Public support for the operation was at 70 percent.[40] The Turkish military's badly damaged image due to the failed coup had been partially restored. Turkish media, including media outlets that were critical of Erdoğan, were full of praise for the army and the nationalist alliance that had made the operation possible. Business opportunities for Erdoğan's cronies were the icing on the cake. Turkish businessmen in the construction sector who are close to Erdoğan as well as the Turkish Cooperation and Coordination Agency (TİKA), the key government agency in charge of real estate investments, were undertaking major infrastructure projects in the ESZ.[41]

The wind of the operation filled Erdoğan's sails. He was ready to move onto his next target to keep the momentum going.

"We will return Afrin to its rightful owners"

On January 20, 2018, airstrikes started pounding the Kurdish-majority northwestern town of Afrin as Turkey launched its second military incursion into Syria. The city had been controlled by the YPG since the Assad regime withdrew from Kurdish-majority areas to focus on fighting elsewhere early in the civil war. After it came under the control of the Kurdish militia, Afrin became one of the three cantons under Kurdish self-administration, which later became known as the Autonomous Administration of North and East Syria, or Rojava, the self-proclaimed autonomous region in northern Syria. Afrin had remained unscathed through much of the Syrian war and a safe place for refugees. Turkey's operation, dubbed Operation Olive Branch, changed all that. The operation forced thousands of Kurds to flee their homes. Arab families fleeing regime offensives elsewhere were resettled in Kurdish residences, raising accusations against Turkey of forced demographic change.

Multiple reports indicated looting and kidnapping by Turkey's allies in the city. But according to Erdoğan, who falsely stated that Afrin was an Arab-majority town, Turkey was "returning Afrin to its rightful owners."[42]

Turkish officials said Turkey wanted to create a 30-kilometer deep "secure zone" and that the operation was important for Turkey's security and Syria's territorial integrity.[43] Erdoğan's real goal, however, was different. He had long wanted to oust the YPG from Afrin and please his nationalist allies at home. "When asked where they were going, they said they were going to the Red Apple," Erdoğan said of Turkish troops taking part in the operation.[44] Reference to the Red Apple was meant to galvanize nationalists and frame the operation as part of Turkey's quest to project military power into lands formerly ruled by the Ottoman Empire.

A few days before the Turkish operation, the US had announced that it was going to create a 30,000-member border force with the YPG and its allied Arab militias to secure northern Syria. The US military walked back on the announcement shortly after but Devlet Bahçeli, the leader of the far-right MHP and Erdoğan's close ally, was infuriated. Ankara used the announcement as a pretext to justify its longstanding plan to intervene in Afrin. In preparation for the offensive, Turkey re-organized the rebel factions that took part in Operation Euphrates Shield to form the Syrian National Army (SNA). Ankara's goal was to establish its own mercenary proxy force that would serve Erdoğan's goals in Syria. Indeed, the SNA became less of a rebel group fighting against the Assad regime to liberate Syria and more of Erdoğan's proxy in his fight against the Syrian Kurdish militia.[45] Turkey paid the salaries of SNA fighters and Turkish intelligence directed their operations. In two months, Turkey and the SNA captured Afrin.

Erdoğan framed the operation as a national struggle against an existential enemy, calling it an extension of Turkey's war with the PKK at home. His message struck a chord with a public whose fear of Kurdish separatism had skyrocketed with the developments in Syria. The operation received overwhelming support from Turkish society, with 90 percent of the population backing it.[46] Public support for the Afrin operation was stronger than for Operation

ATTACKING KURDS TRUMPS TOPPLING ASSAD

Euphrates Shield because, unlike the first operation that captured territory from ISIS, the Afrin operation directly targeted the YPG-held areas. The operation drew strong praise from Turkish nationalists as well. Erdoğan's ally Bahçeli vowed to fight on the frontlines in Afrin. Members of his party petitioned the Military Recruitment Office to volunteer in the operation.[47] Turkish troops in tanks rolling across the border to battle with Kurds flashed the ultranationalist sign, showing how politicized the Turkish military had become after the failed coup and how closely aligned Erdoğan and nationalists in the military were on Syria.[48]

Erdoğan got what he wanted from the incursion. Before the operation, polls showed that economic concerns were a top priority for Turkish voters. Even AKP supporters were worried about unemployment and high inflation. The operation stirred nationalist sentiment and diverted public attention away from the country's economic troubles. Turkish media and public opinion rallied around Erdoğan, who was up for reelection in a few months. Imams in mosques held public prayers for a military victory. The country's singers, writers and actors rushed to post their support for the operation. Even opposition parties fell in line. Those who did not support the operation were named and shamed on national TV and many were detained.

Erdoğan used the Afrin operation to exploit the surging anti-Americanism in the country as well. The military incursion happened against the background of strained bilateral ties partly due to US cooperation with the Syrian Kurdish militia. The US urged Turkey to exercise restraint in Afrin and pledged to continue to work with the YPG but the messages coming out of Washington ahead of Turkey's operation suggested the US was not willing to risk further escalation of tension with Turkey. Before the operation started, the US signaled that it would not intervene if Ankara followed through with the promised military intervention. Despite Washington's acquiescence to Turkey's maneuvers, Erdoğan continued to stir anti-Americanism. After the operation commenced, he slammed the US for working with "terrorists" and criticized NATO for failing to support Turkey's incursion. His anti-Western remarks resonated with large segments of the country. Even those critical of Erdoğan agreed that the operation was necessary because the US was backing the PKK. Opinion polls suggested that 90 percent of Turkey's public shared this view.[49]

Operation Olive Branch served Erdoğan well at home, but it further weakened the anti-Assad opposition. Just like Turkey's first military intervention, the Afrin operation was part of an understanding between Turkey and Russia in which Putin allowed Erdoğan to go after the Kurds in Syria and Erdoğan pressured the rebels to give up territory to the regime in return. Russia controlled Afrin's airspace and had deployed troops in the area as part of a 2017 agreement to protect the YPG from Turkish attacks. Before the operation, Turkey dispatched its military chief Hulusi Akar to Moscow to seek Putin's approval to launch an air campaign in Afrin. Russia convinced Assad that it would benefit from the Afrin operation and pressured the Kurds to transfer territory they controlled in Afrin to the regime in return for security guarantees.[50] After the Kurds rejected the offer, Russia opened Afrin's skies and pulled its troops out of the town.[51] The Kurds saw the Russian move as a "betrayal." From the Russian point of view, however, it was part of a perfect strategy to secure the Assad regime's survival.

By allowing Turkey to launch Operation Olive Branch, Russia and the Syrian regime got what they wanted in two critical places: Idlib and Eastern Ghouta. Russia did not want a military escalation in Idlib, the last rebel stronghold, because such an escalation would further weaken Assad's army and force Russia to join the fight on the frontlines. By approving Turkey's Afrin operation, Russia received concessions from Ankara in Idlib and prevented a military confrontation.

The regime gained ground thanks to Turkey's Afrin operation. On the day of the attack, the Syrian regime announced that it had captured the Abu-Duhur airport in Idlib from opposition forces.[52] By late 2017, Assad's forces had significantly escalated the siege of the Damascus suburb of Eastern Ghouta where Turkey-backed armed groups such as Muslim Brotherhood-linked Faylaq Ar-Rahman were battling against the regime. Concurrent with the Afrin operation, Assad's forces launched their final offensive on Eastern

ATTACKING KURDS TRUMPS TOPPLING ASSAD

Ghouta, which was at the time a "de-escalation zone" under the guarantee of Turkey, Russia and Iran. Despite its guarantor status, Turkey's response to the regime's offensive was muted. Three weeks after Turkey-backed opposition forces captured Afrin, the Syrian regime negotiated a reconciliation agreement with rebels in Eastern Ghouta to surrender and turn over their weapons. Turkey mediated the agreement.[53] The rebels were forced to leave Eastern Ghouta and relocate to Afrin. The regime had won another key battle with Turkish support. Erdoğan was willing to give even more to the regime. After Kurdish and regime sources announced that a deal had been struck between the two for the Syrian army to go into Afrin, Turkish Foreign Minister Mevlüt Çavuşoğlu said that Turkey would not mind Syrian troops entering Afrin if the goal was to "cleanse" the town of the Kurdish fighters.[54] Ankara's message was unmistakable. The Kurds had become Erdoğan's number one target.

"Nothing is ours anymore"

The Turkish operation had devastating implications for Afrin and its residents. Afrin had remained unscathed through much of the war with people fleeing clashes elsewhere in the country taking refuge in the Kurdish-majority city. Turkey's operation opened a new phase where the city became the focal point of Arab-Kurdish conflict, demographic engineering and war crimes by Turkey-backed rebels against locals.

Turkish officials claimed that the goal of the operation was to eliminate "PKK/PYD terrorism" but Turkey and its allies' actions on the ground suggested that Turkey's operation had other motives. One of the first acts of Turkish forces and their Arab proxies after they swept in the city was to tear down the statue of the blacksmith Kawa, a central figure in Kurdish culture, in the center of Afrin, signaling that Turkey's incursion was as much about suppression of Kurdish identity.[55] This was a clear message to the Kurdish residents of Afrin about Erdoğan's intentions. Thousands fled to YPG-held areas. Some who stayed in the city were forced to flee by Turkey-backed forces that accused them of having links to the Syrian Kurdish militia. According to local groups, the Kurdish population fell by some 60 percent following the operation.[56] In addition to internally displaced thousands of Kurds, Turkey resettled Arab families, mostly those of Turkey-backed fighters, from elsewhere in their place. Many of these Arab families were from the Damascus suburb of Ghouta, where rebels surrendered after Turkey mediated a reconciliation agreement between the armed groups it backed and the Assad regime. Human rights organizations accused Turkey of carrying out demographic change and forced displacement to change the balance of Afrin's population from predominantly Kurdish to majority Arab.[57]

Turkey-backed Arab militias that included several Islamist groups such as the National Liberation Front committed other rights abuses against Kurdish locals as well. A UN report on Afrin suggested that armed groups "committed the war crimes of hostage-taking, cruel treatment, torture, and pillage." According to the report, "numerous cases involving arbitrary arrests and detentions by armed group members also included credible allegations of torture and ill-treatment, often targeting individuals of Kurdish origin, including activists openly critical of armed groups and those perceived to be so."[58]

Several Turkish, Kurdish and Syrian Arab sources alleged that Turks with ties to Turkey's ruling AKP made a profit out of the pillage carried out by warlords in Afrin.[59] Reports of looting even extended to Afrin's olive orchards. Several opposition party members of the Turkish parliament said that tens of thousands of tons of olive oil from Afrin had been moved into Turkey.[60] The Turkish mMinister of agriculture's response confirmed reports. The minister said, "As a government, we don't want the PKK to make money" from the olives and "We want the revenue from Afrin to come to us in the area we control. Until now, [only] 600 tons of produce has come to our side. It is truly shameful talking about this [small quantity] when there are 200,000 tons of olive oil available."[61] Salah Mohammed, an Afrin exile, summed up the looting: "Lands are being confiscated, farms, wheat, furniture, nothing is ours anymore; it's us versus their guns."[62] The UN report on the situation in Afrin after Turkey's operation quotes witnesses who say that as Turkey-backed armed groups carried out all these atrocities and criminal acts, Turkish soldiers in the vicinity looked on.

The atrocities committed by Turkey's Arab allies in Afrin exacerbated Kurdish-Arab ethnic tension in Syria. There had already been a long-standing mistrust between the two owing to the repressive policies carried out by the Baath regime against Kurds, but the Syrian war made things worse. The fight against ISIS allowed the Syrian Democratic Forces (SDF), in which the Kurdish militia YPG plays a dominant role, to control a large chunk of territory in the north. Millions of people live in SDF-controlled territories and most of them are Arabs. Due to the SDF's unwillingness to share power with Arabs in the Arab-majority cities it controls and the human rights abuses it has committed, discontent has been growing among Arabs.[63] Turkey's military incursions that pitted Arab rebel groups against Kurdish groups have heightened ethnic tension.

Afrin stood as a testament to what was left of the Syrian revolution. The Turkey-backed Syrian opposition's revolutionary zeal had given way to a quest for financial gain and criminality. Turkey, once hailed as a model for Arab Spring countries and a patron of the revolution, had become an occupier and turned its back on the revolution to advance Erdoğan's anti-Kurdish agenda. In the territories that it controlled, Ankara was experimenting with nation-building, demographic engineering and cultural imperialism. This was most visible in Afrin.

Operation Olive Branch ousted the YPG from Afrin and turned a Kurdish-majority town into an Arab-majority one under the strict control of Turkey. "Turkish flags are flying all over Afrin," said Ahmad Khaled, a thirty-year-old high school teacher in Afrin.[64] After capturing the town, Turkey dissolved the governance structures created and managed by the YPG and established its own. It set up local councils, which were overseen by the governor of the Turkish town of Hatay, to provide public services. It appointed civil servants. It formed and trained military police to provide security. It set up the Chamber of Commerce and Industry, and introduced infrastructure similar to that of the ESZ. Turkey Turkified the curricula in the schools it opened, sending in Turkish teachers who were tasked with providing Sunni Islamic education in Turkish and Arabic. In pro-Erdoğan circles the narrative was Turkey had "liberated" Afrin from "terrorists" and established a "safe zone."[65] According to Afrin's Kurdish residents, Turkey was an occupier, and the reality of Erdoğan's "safe zone" was one of constant fear of rape, torture, kidnapping and death.[66]

"Atatürk would roll in his grave"

"How did we get here?" asked a senior Turkish diplomat who had spent most of his career in the Middle East.

> We are violating every single principle Atatürk set forth for Turkey's Middle East policy. We first tried to topple the regime in a neighboring country by arming radical Islamist groups. Then we changed our minds and decided to empower that very regime that we so desperately tried to overthrow. Then we invaded parts of that country and became occupiers of Arab lands. Along the way, we pissed off pretty much everyone. If Atatürk saw what we are doing in Syria, he would roll in his grave.[67]

The diplomat was voicing the unease about Erdoğan's Syria policy among Turkey's senior diplomats, but no one dared to criticize the policy openly. Many were worried about getting too bogged down in the "Syrian mess" and "handing over a huge Syria problem to the next generation."[68] Indeed, Turkey's military incursions into Syria would have lasting consequences for both countries and had changed dynamics on the ground. Both operations corroborated the beliefs of those who suspected a "land swap" deal between Ankara and Damascus that allowed territorial exchanges to Ankara to curb Kurdish advances and Damascus to capture territory from the opposition. Erdoğan helped the regime recapture Aleppo, the opposition's last major urban stronghold, in return for Damascus and Moscow's acquiescence to Turkey's Operation Euphrates Shield. He did this by withdrawing Turkey's support from the opposition fighting against Assad in Aleppo, convincing them to surrender to the regime in a ceasefire Turkey brokered and enlisting them in his fight against the Kurds in the north. Turkey's Operation Olive Branch against the YPG in Afrin helped

ATTACKING KURDS TRUMPS TOPPLING ASSAD

Assad gain more ground. In return for opening Afrin's airspace to Turkey and withdrawing its troops from the area, Russia secured concessions from Ankara in Idlib. On the day of the operation, Assad's forces captured a key airport in the town from the opposition. More importantly, regime forces captured Eastern Ghouta through a "reconciliation agreement" with the rebels that was moderated by Turkey.

Erdoğan weakened the anti-Assad opposition further. He turned the rebels into Turkey's mercenary proxy force that was tasked "less to liberate Syria than to protect Turkish interests."[69] The Syrian National Army that was established, funded and managed by Turkey did not fight a single battle against the regime in the territories captured by Turkey and its allied forces in the north.[70] Its primary task was to capture lands run by the YPG and prevent the Kurdish militia's advances. Later, these Syrian fighters played a significant role in Erdoğan's policy ambitions outside of Syria. Ankara contracted thousands of them as well as Syrian refugees living in Turkey to fight alongside the UN-backed Government of National Accord (GNA) in Libya for a monthly wage of $2,000 and the promise of Turkish citizenship.[71] The Turkey-backed Syrian mercenaries' involvement in the Libyan war tipped the balance for pro-GNA forces. Also, Turkey deployed Syrian mercenaries to another war zone to shore up Erdoğan's foreign policy objectives. When fighting erupted between Armenia and Azerbaijan in 2020, Turkey sent Syrian mercenaries to bolster forces in Azerbaijan, a country with which Erdoğan had cultivated a close alliance. Using Syrian mercenaries served Erdoğan well, offering him a way to strengthen his foreign policy objectives without mobilizing Turkey's own forces—but it weakened the anti-Assad opposition further.

By becoming party to the Russia-led Astana process, which was designed to keep Assad in power, Erdoğan dealt another blow to the Syrian opposition. All the mechanisms of Astana, which were wholeheartedly supported by Erdoğan helped the regime consolidate its military gains and deepen the divisions within the opposition. Thanks to them, by 2018, Assad had captured over 60 percent of the country's territory.

Erdoğan "sold out the revolution" to be able to go after the Kurds.[72] The Euphrates Shield and Olive Branch operations did exactly that. They dealt a blow to the rebels' fight against the regime and empowered Assad. Meanwhile, Turkish incursions not only thwarted Kurdish plans for autonomy but added a new chapter to the Kurds' long history of persecution and marginalization. Thousands were forced to flee their homes, lost their lives or became refugees in their own lands. Turkey established "de facto client states" in the territories it captured in northern Syria with the stated goal of eliminating terrorism and bringing peace and stability. Instead, Turkey's involvement opened a new front in previously stable areas. It exacerbated Kurdish-Arab tension, led to a violent insurgency by those whose lands were appropriated, increased violence due to infighting among the radical groups backed by Ankara and unleashed a humanitarian crisis.

Turkish operations were not only a sign of a new chapter in Erdoğan's war for his political survival, they also heralded a new era in relations with the US and Russia.

"A country we call an ally"

For more than six decades, the Turkey-US relationship was defined as a strategic partnership. It was forged at the outset of the Cold War to check Soviet expansionism and endured many crises throughout its long history. The Syrian war, however, dealt the strategic partnership a fatal blow. Erdoğan's foot-dragging in joining the fight against ISIS and President Obama's reluctance to send US troops to confront the jihadist group led to the fateful US decision to arm Turkey's arch enemy. As the Kurdish militia won battle after battle against ISIS, cooperation with it became "the least bad option" available to a US president who had zero appetite to increase the US's military footprint in the region. Some of his aides disagreed. During discussions about whether to arm the YPG, an Obama aide advised the president against it, saying, "if we do this, relations with Turkey will never be the same again."[73] From Obama's point of view, it was Erdoğan's actions that had left no other option but to partner with the YPG. According to

ATTACKING KURDS TRUMPS TOPPLING ASSAD

the most optimistic view in the administration, Erdoğan had turned a blind eye to ISIS and contributed to its rise. Others in the administration such as Brett McGurk, Obama's envoy to counter ISIS, had a darker view of Erdoğan. In an article he penned in 2019, he suggested that Turkey might have been sheltering ISIS leader Abu Bakr al-Baghdadi.[74] Erdoğan was less than enthusiastic when the US requested the use of Turkish airbase İncirlik to attack ISIS. When he finally agreed to open up the airbase, it was mostly to check Kurdish expansion. From Washington's perspective, while the US administration scrambled to put forth alternative plans to defeat ISIS with Turkey's help, Erdoğan tried to leverage the fight against ISIS to force Obama to pursue a Syria policy aligned with his own objectives.

The Turkish view was dramatically different. Except for the pro-Kurdish HDP, all political parties and the public at large viewed Obama's decision as the ultimate betrayal. Turkey had legitimate security concerns. It had fought a PKK insurgency for decades and lost thousands of lives. The war in Syria further complicated Turkey's fight against the PKK. The establishment of a PKK-controlled de facto Kurdish autonomous region in northern Syria presented fresh challenges. Obama decided to arm the PKK's Syrian offshoot against this background. Despite assurances from US officials that the US partnership with the Kurdish militia was "temporary, transactional and tactical," many Turks saw the move as the latest in Western efforts to carve out an independent Kurdish state and undermine Turkey.[75]

Erdoğan capitalized on this mood. He used the anti-American and anti-Kurdish sentiment that received a boost with US-YPG cooperation to advance his domestic agenda. He doubled down on his efforts to criminalize Turkey's legitimate Kurdish opposition. He made his intention clear when he proposed to widen the definition of terrorism a day after a 2016 bomb attack in the Turkish capital Ankara that killed thirty-seven people. No group claimed responsibility for the attack but then Prime Minister Davutoğlu put the blame on the PKK. Erdoğan said he saw no difference between "a terrorist holding a gun or a bomb and those who use their position and pen to serve the aims" of terrorists.[76] That wide definition allowed Erdoğan to jail democratically elected pro-Kurdish HDP lawmakers, including the party's co-chairs, Kurdish civil society activists and human rights defenders. It helped his crackdown on the media and freedom of speech. Turkish newspapers, opposition politicians, and columnists who did not wholeheartedly support Turkey's military incursions into Syria or his attacks against legitimate Kurdish opposition were silenced. Even foreign journalists were deported on terrorism charges.

US-YPG cooperation came in handy for Erdoğan's ambition to draw support for his long-held dream of establishing a presidential system. While campaigning for the constitutional referendum to transform the parliamentary system into a powerful executive presidency, Erdoğan pledged new military incursions into Syria. "We will pull ourselves up by our bootstraps if the US continues to cooperate with the YPG," he said.[77] He spoke at length about the growing terrorism threat bolstered by the US and promised that the country would better tackle the issue if it switched to a presidential system.[78]

Erdoğan won the 2017 constitutional referendum, albeit narrowly, with the backing of nationalists. His anti-American and anti-Kurdish narrative struck a chord. The number of those who saw the US as a top national security threat and favored a confrontational policy vis-à-vis the US had spiked in the aftermath of Kobani.[79] Waves of attacks against Kurdish homes and businesses in Turkey had peaked after Washington's decision to arm the Syrian Kurds. Kurds were attacked and gunned down on the street for speaking Kurdish, their businesses were assaulted and the pro-Kurdish HDP's offices were set on fire. The unease with US-YPG cooperation among wide sectors of Turkish society was most apparent in the overwhelming support Turkey's Afrin operation received, with 90 percent saying the operation was necessary because the US armed the PKK.

Anti-American and anti-Kurdish sentiment continued to rise. A few weeks before Operation Euphrates Shield, YPG-led Syrian Democratic Forces captured Manbij from ISIS. The city, located on the western bank of the Euphrates river, was a key transit point and a critical supply line for ISIS. The US wanted to use the SDF to clear Manbij but Turkey rejected the plan, fearing YPG presence in the town would enhance Kurdish efforts to unify the Kurdish cantons. After the Turkish struggle to capture Manbij failed, the SDF moved into the city and cleared it of ISIS. Erdoğan had repeatedly said that a YPG presence west of Euphrates was a red line— and it had been crossed.

To ease the tension, the Obama administration promised that the YPG would move back, east of the river, but some YPG fighters remained, heightening Turkish fears that the Kurds would soon control the entire border. Despite the tension between the two NATO allies and the fact that Turkey gave no warning of Operation Euphrates Shield, the US provided air and special operations forces to support Turkey's incursion.[80] But the relationship continued to deteriorate. Erdoğan was already furious that the Obama administration had not been fast enough to condemn the coup attempt against him. The US's refusal to extradite Fethullah Gülen, who had been residing in Pennsylvania since the late 1990s, on the grounds that Turkey did not provide hard evidence linking him to the failed coup strained ties further.

Erdoğan thought that things would get better once Obama was out of the picture. On the campaign trail, Donald Trump had promised to take the US out of extended military entanglements. Erdoğan hoped that he would find a more sympathetic ear on the Syrian Kurds in Trump's White House. His hopes were dashed shortly after Trump took office. The new US president endorsed his predecessor's policies and approved an Obama, era plan to arm the YPG in preparation for the battle to retake Raqqa, the capital of ISIS's self-proclaimed caliphate and its last bastion in Syria, from the jihadi group, despite strong objections from Erdoğan. The Trump administration had hoped that Erdoğan would soften his objection to arming the YPG after winning the constitutional referendum that would give him vast powers, but that assumption failed to appreciate how much Erdoğan had to rely on the nationalists to realize his domestic goals. Pursuing anti-Kurdish policies at home and in the region was the Erdoğan-nationalist alliance's most important currency. Erdoğan had recaptured the parliamentary majority his party lost in a matter of a few months thanks to that.

Attacks against the Kurds had helped him win the referendum as well. Erdoğan had no intention of giving that up as long as it worked. He sent General Hulusi Akar, then commander of the Turkish armed forces, Hakan Fidan, Turkey's intelligence chief and Ibrahim Kalin, the presidential spokesperson to Washington to talk Trump out of arming the YPG. It did not work.

To mollify Erdoğan, American officials assured the Turks that the supply of arms would be limited to what was needed to carry out specific operations and any excess equipment would be retrieved. They also pledged that they would monitor the weapons to make sure they were not used against Turkey and that most of the fighters involved in the Raqqa operation would be Arabs. None of these pledges eased Erdoğan's frustration.

Raqqa, ISIS's nominal capital, was captured by the Syrian Kurdish militia with US support. At its height, ISIS held about one-third of Syrian territory. By December 2017, it had lost 95 percent of the lands it controlled, leading to expectations in Ankara that US-YPG cooperation would soon end. But the US continued to work with the Kurdish militia. As the group's mission against ISIS was drawing to a close, the US was getting ready to give them a new assignment. A few days before Operation Olive Branch, the Turkish offensive into Afrin, Washington announced that it was working with its Syrian Kurdish allies to set up a new border force of 30,000 personnel to patrol Syria's borders with Turkey and Iraq.[81] Although, the US immediately backed away from the idea saying the plan was poorly conceived and would not proceed as outlined, this did not assuage Erdoğan. The announcement reflected divisions within the Trump administration over how to craft a new Syria policy after the fight against ISIS ended. The announcement, coupled with Secretary of State Rex Tillerson's speech in California unveiling the administration's new Syria policy a few days earlier, had made it clear to many in Washington how confused Trump's Syria policy was. In his speech, Tillerson had signaled the continued presence of the US in Syria, saying it was necessary to push back against Iranian influence in Syria, prevent an ISIS comeback and to have a say in the resolution of the Syrian conflict.

ATTACKING KURDS TRUMPS TOPPLING ASSAD

To Erdoğan, everything was clear. He thought that the defeat of ISIS would not lead to a US withdrawal from Syria or end to its cooperation with the Syrian Kurds. He was enraged. "A country we call an ally is insisting on forming a terror army on our borders," he said in a speech in Ankara. "What can that terror army target but Turkey? Our mission is to strangle it before it's even born."[82] A few days later, Turkey launched its long-signaled Operation Olive Branch into Afrin. US officials had warned Turkey against it, saying the operation would derail the fight against ISIS, but the initial response from Washington was not critical of the operation. This led many to think that it was greenlighted by Washington to prevent a further drift in relations with Turkey. On the day of Turkey's action, General Joseph Votel, the head of US Central Command, said that Afrin was not part of US operations in Syria, while Secretary Tillerson and Defense Secretary Jim Mattis acknowledged Turkey's "legitimate security concerns." According to a White House readout, President Trump delivered the bluntest message to his Turkish counterpart in a phone call after the operation. He urged Turkey to "deescalate, limit its military actions and avoid civilian casualties."

Trump was already angry at Erdoğan for keeping a North Carolina pastor, Andrew Brunson, in jail on charges of espionage since 2016. The pastor had been accused of orchestrating a coup against Erdoğan and was facing up to thirty-five years in prison. Brunson's detention was politically motivated. On several occasions, Erdoğan had suggested a swap with the US in exchange for Fethullah Gülen. Trump took a personal interest in securing the evangelical pastor's release. When Erdoğan ignored Trump's pleas, Washington announced further tariffs on Turkish imports and imposed sanctions on two Turkish ministers, whom Washington says were instrumental in the arrest of Brunson. The US move hit Erdoğan where it hurt the most: Turkey's already struggling economy. After Trump's decision, the Turkish lira collapsed.

By late 2018, bilateral ties between the countries had deteriorated so badly that Erdoğan had to engage in hostage diplomacy with its NATO ally, the US was arming Turkey's arch enemy, and the American president was imposing sanctions and threatening to destroy the Turkish economy. The strong anti-American sentiment in Turkey was matched by bipartisan anti-Erdoğan sentiment in the US. Erdoğan was seen as the man who backed ISIS, killed Kurds and jailed his political opponents. The trust between the long-time allies had been eroded beyond repair. The Syrian war had ignited the fuse. After six decades, the US and Turkey were "strategic allies" in name only and Erdoğan was looking for a new friend.

"My dear friend Putin"

"Unilateral actions against Turkey by the United States will undermine American interests and force Turkey to look for other friends and allies," wrote Erdoğan in a *New York Times* article shortly after US sanctions.[83] The article was a veiled threat to leave NATO and get cozy with its historical enemy: Russia. Leaving NATO seemed like a distant prospect, but Erdoğan had already taken steps to cultivate close ties with Moscow. The Syrian war was the main driver behind the rapprochement.

The war had an interesting impact on Turkey-Russia relations. It first brought the two countries to the brink of war, then paved the way for the closest partnership in the history of bilateral ties. The milestone year was 2015. In September, Russia militarily intervened in Syria to shore up Assad who was faring poorly in the war largely thanks to Turkish support for the anti-Assad opposition. A month after Russian intervention, tension between Turkey and Russia came to a head when Turkey downed a Russian jet in the Syrian border area for violating its airspace. In retaliation, Russia announced a package of economic sanctions, that took a heavy toll on the Turkish economy. Erdoğan was also worried about a Russian military retaliation. Patriot missiles had been deployed along the Turkish-Syrian border since 2013 when Turkey asked its NATO allies for help in protecting against the escalating war in Syria, but Germany and the US were planning to withdraw the missiles after reassessing the threat stemming from the war. After the jet incident, Erdoğan urgently called a NATO meeting to discuss contingency plans in preparation for collective defense and ask its NATO allies to maintain the missile defense system in Turkey. Despite Erdoğan's appeals, Washington and Berlin went ahead with the withdrawal, strengthening views in Ankara that the US-led alliance was not committed to Turkey's security. The decision to withdraw Patriots came a few months after the US air-dropped weapons to the YPG and less than a month after Turkey opened its air bases to US jets, launching attacks against ISIS targets. The sense of betrayal in Ankara was running amok. Then came the coup attempt. In Erdoğan's view, Washington was neither fast nor clear enough to condemn the putsch while Putin phoned him immediately and offered the support of Russian Special Forces deployed on a nearby Greek island.[84]

Frustration with the US as well as Russian military intervention in Syria changed Erdoğan's calculations. Erdoğan resigned himself to the fact that US goals in Syria were not going to align with his. Even if they did, to Erdoğan a US that was eyeing an exit from Syria mattered little. The real power to be reckoned with was Russia. In addition to air power, Moscow had built up substantial ground forces, deployed its latest air defense missile system, secured permanent control of strategic air bases and started building new ones in Syria. This suggested a strong Russian commitment to protect its ally in Damascus and maintain a permanent presence in the country. If Turkey were to do anything on the ground, it needed Russian cooperation. Cultivating a close partnership with Moscow would strengthen Erdoğan's hand at home. This would signal to the United States that Turkey had other options, a message that would play well with the strong anti-American sentiment among the public. More importantly, a closer partnership with Moscow would please the Eurasianists in Erdoğan's nationalist alliance.

There was one key problem though: Russia's relationship with the Kurds. Kurds had historically played a critical role in Russian efforts to exert its influence in the Middle East. The Soviet Union established close relations with Turkey's Kurds as a trump card to pressure NATO member Turkey. The PKK was established as a Marxist-Leninist and Kurdish nationalist organization and received material and political support from Moscow.[85] More recently,

Moscow had worked with the PKK's Syrian offshoot, the YPG, in Syria. After Turkey shot down the Russian military jet in 2015, Russia allowed Syrian Kurds to open a diplomatic mission in Moscow. Moscow provided military aid to the YPG in western Syria and training to Kurdish forces in Afrin. The two conducted joint operations against ISIS and Russian warplanes provided air cover for the YPG while the Kurdish forces protected Russian forces on the eastern side of the Euphrates in return. Russian help to Syrian Kurds extended to the diplomatic realm as well. Moscow proposed a draft constitution that included Kurdish autonomy in Syria. While Erdoğan lashed out at the United States for its cooperation with the Syrian Kurdish militia, he remained mute when it came to Russian support for the YPG because he saw better prospects for convincing Putin not to back the Kurds than he did with the US administration and expected higher returns from an alliance with Moscow.[86]

All these considerations opened a new phase in Turkey-Russia ties. Months after Turkey downed the Russian jet, Erdoğan finally bowed to Putin's demand that Erdoğan issue an apology for the incident. In a letter to the Kremlin, Erdoğan expressed regret to the Russian president and said that he was ready to do everything possible to restore ties.[87] In St Petersburg, on his first foreign trip after the coup attempt, Erdoğan thanked his "dear friend Putin" for his rapid offer of help on the night of the coup. The warm meeting between the two leaders stood in vivid contrast to recent hostilities in Syria. It heralded the opening of a new chapter.

The highlight of the new relationship was Erdoğan's decision to purchase the S-400 surface-to-air defense system, one of Russia's most sophisticated pieces of military equipment. Negotiations over the purchase started shortly after the coup attempt against Erdoğan and the deal was finalized the following year, making Turkey the first NATO country to own Russia's most sophisticated system. From Washington's point of view, the S-400s became the mother of all problems in relations with Turkey. The US argued that the Russian system was incompatible with NATO technology and a threat to the Euro-Atlantic alliance. Turkey had ordered about 100 F-35 fighter jets from the US and Turkish companies were making parts of the jet. American officials feared that operating both F-35s and the Russian system might allow Russia to gain access to the highly classified technical characteristics of the F-35 aircraft. Washington warned Turkey that it could not have both. If Ankara went ahead with the deal, its purchase of the F-35s would be jeopardized, Turkey would be expelled from the F-35 production program and Washington would impose further sanctions. But Erdoğan was adamant. He said that he chose the Russian system because the US refused to sell its own Patriot air defense system to Turkey. Other Turkish officials argued the Russians offered a better price and better terms to share technology, a key Turkish demand. But none of those arguments reflected reality.

There has been no indication of Russia giving any of its sophisticated S-400 technology to Turkey. Erdoğan's claim that the US was not willing to sell Patriots to Turkey was simply not true. Since 2009, Raytheon, the maker of the Patriot, and the US Department of Defense had offered Turkey several sales packages that came close to meeting Turkish demands, including technology transfer. The Turkish president was not truthful about the financial driver of his decision either. The Russian system would cost Turkey a lot more than the Patriots. Turkey reportedly paid $2.5 billion for the S-400s but would lose over $9 billion in revenue when the US expelled Turkey from of the F-35 program. This was on top of the $1.5 billion Turkey had made as an advance payment to buy F-35s and the potential US sanctions that Washington threatened to impose if Ankara went ahead with the deal.

According to two senior US defense officials who helped the Department manage defense ties with Turkey, it was Erdoğan who derailed the Patriot negotiations.[88] He sought to leverage cooperation against ISIS to drive down the price and secure Washington's approval for a technology transfer. As Ankara's frustration with Washington grew, purchasing the Russian system became Erdoğan's way of making "the Americans pay a price for supporting the Kurds and refusing to play ball on Gülen."[89]

According to a senior US military official serving in Ankara, a combination of factors drove Erdoğan's decision. Signaling to the US that it had other options was one of them.[90] The deal also allowed Erdoğan to feed his patronage network, something the US official said would not be possible under a Patriot deal. Vecdi Gönül, former minister of defense under whose watch Turkey flirted with the idea of buying a Chinese defense missile system in 2013, confirmed this angle. In response to drivers behind Erdoğan's plans to buy the Chinese system despite Western objections, he said, "as an analyst I understand why you are trying to explain his motives by looking at the larger geostrategic context, but the answer is much simpler than you think: if the deal went through, the people around him (Erdoğan) would have made lots and lots of money."[91]

According to the US military official, Erdoğan had another reason to choose a Russian rather than a Western missile defense system. He wanted to protect himself against a future coup. He was particularly wary of a rogue air force plot. Turkish air force pilots made a major contributions to the coup attempt, bombing the Turkish parliament and threatening the plane in which Erdoğan was flying on the night of the coup. "He does not trust his own air force," he said. Turkey operates American-made aircraft and the S-400s are designed to shoot them down. The Patriots, on the other hand, have built-in mechanisms to avoid friendly fire against other NATO aircraft.

In July 2019, the first shipment of the Russian-made S-400 air defense missile system landed in Turkey amid great fanfare. Turkish TV channels live-streamed the landing of the missile parts. Turkey's Defense Ministry announced via Twitter that the first component had arrived at the Murted Air Base in Ankara. Columnists, analysts, and TV commentators—pro- and anti-Erdoğan alike—hailed the delivery of the missile system as the "country's liberation from the West."[92] The public was behind the decision as well. According to a survey, 44 percent of respondents supported Erdoğan's decision to purchase the Russian system, while only 24 percent said otherwise.[93]

In response to delivery of the missile system, the US removed Turkey from the F-35 fighter jet program and imposed sanctions that would have long-term effects on Turkey's defense sector. To many, choosing the Russian system made little sense given all the cost it imposed on Turkey's economy, defense sector and Turkey's ties with the West but to Erdoğan, it seemed like a great move at the time. The factors that were mentioned by US officials probably played a role in Erdoğan's decision-making, but the key driver behind the decision was Erdoğan's realization that he could not trust the US and needed Russia to realize his goals in Syria. That is primarily why he sought closer ties with Moscow. Purchasing the S-400s consolidated Turkish-Russian rapprochement, which served Erdoğan well in Syria. By the time the first shipment landed, Turkey had launched two military incursions into the war-torn country and thwarted Kurdish aspirations for autonomy with Russian blessing.

Operations Euphrates Shield and Olive Branch marked the beginning of a new era in Turkey's domestic politics and foreign policy. The Kurds became enemy number one. The "strategic ally" US turned into the patron of "terrorists." The historic rival Russia became a "strategic partner." "The murderer Assad" developed into a necessary actor for Erdoğan's efforts to curb Kurdish gains in Syria.

These military operations were not simply a reflection of Erdoğan's anti-Kurdish nationalism. They also reinforced that nationalism and helped Erdoğan consolidate his alliance with the anti-Kurdish bloc in politics, society and bureaucracy. These military incursions served Erdoğan well in the short term but had devastating implications for Syrians. They did not eliminate terrorism as Erdoğan claimed, nor did they bring peace and stability to the areas captured. On the contrary, the operations opened new fronts in previously stable areas, aggravated ethnic tensions between the Kurds and Arabs, triggered a violent insurgency by those whose lands were appropriated by Turkish-backed forces and escalated violence as infighting began among Turkey-backed rebel groups. The operations unleashed a humanitarian crisis, particularly in Kurdish areas where thousands were forced to flee their homes, lost their lives, or became refugees in their own lands. Erdoğan did not care as long as the war on the Kurds secured him votes. There came a time when it did not.

6

ERDOĞAN'S NATIONALIST GAMBLE BACKFIRES

Anti-Kurdish nationalism did wonders for Erdoğan. In return for unleashing a bloody war against the Kurds at home and in Syria, he secured nationalists' backing to recapture the parliamentary majority his party lost in 2015, win the referendum to switch to a presidential system in 2017 and assume sweeping new powers in 2018. However, at one point, the nationalism Erdoğan had promulgated for years turned against him and cost him dearly at the ballot box. With that, Erdoğan's descent began. How did that happen? What caused an autocrat to lose elections? What role did the Syrian war that helped Erdoğan build his autocracy play in his decline? This section will try to answer these questions.

"If we lose İstanbul, we lose Turkey"

In 2017, Erdoğan said "if we lose İstanbul, we lose Turkey." In 2019, his party lost the mayoral elections in İstanbul, twice. That was not all. Erdoğan's AKP suffered a loss in almost all major cities, including the capital Ankara. Erdoğan was not on the ballot but he campaigned as if he were. He held over a hundred rallies across the country in which he used strong nationalist rhetoric. On the campaign trail, he cataloged a series of conspiracy theories. He claimed that the elections were not just about electing mayors and local officials but were also a fight against an existential threat Turkey was facing from foreign-backed enemies. He declared participants of the International Women's Day rally "invaders" and threatened to "crush them" with police force and the military.[1] He announced that the Turkish military had launched a strike against PKK targets in northern Iraq. He showed his supporters a video of an anti-Muslim attack in Christchurch, New Zealand, in which the shooter attacked people in two mosques and killed dozens. Erdoğan claimed the attacks were part of an attack on Turkey and warned "anti-Muslim Australians" that they would be "sent back in coffins" like their grandfathers who fought in the 1915 Gallipoli campaign in which thousands of Australian and New Zealand troops were killed by Ottoman forces.[2]

Neither the conspiracy theories nor the nationalist rhetoric managed to divert voters' attention away from the country's mounting problems. Concern over the economic, social and political problems was so strong that local issues, which usually drive voters' preferences in municipal elections, took a back seat and the elections turned into a referendum on Erdoğan's leadership. In several big cities, the opposition secured comfortable majorities against Erdoğan's party. In İstanbul, Ekrem İmamoğlu, the opposition CHP candidate, won by a razor-thin majority.

İmamoğlu did what many thought impossible. He defeated Erdoğan's hand-picked candidate in Erdoğan's hometown despite the massive state resources mobilized against him and broke the Islamist parties' twenty-five-year grip on the city. İmamoğlu was not a well-known figure in Turkish politics before the 2019 elections. He became mayor of İstanbul's middle-class Beylikdüzü district in 2014. He ran a low-profile campaign condemning Erdoğan's divisive politics and promoting working together to tackle pressing problems such as urban poverty and youth unemployment. His positive rhetoric, pious background, and his easy rapport with the people on the street broadened his appeal. He managed to draw votes from diverse constituencies, including the city's Kurds who were unhappy with Erdoğan's crackdown on the pro-Kurdish party and working-class Erdoğan supporters who were hit hard by economic recession.

ERDOĞAN'S NATIONALIST GAMBLE BACKFIRES

Losing almost all big cities was a stunning defeat to a leader who had won almost every election since coming to power. Losing İstanbul hit Erdoğan particularly hard. İstanbul is Turkey's biggest city and financial capital. Erdoğan was born and raised there and rose to political prominence as the city's mayor in the 1990s. The city had been controlled by Erdoğan's party since then. İstanbul's vast financial resources helped Erdoğan and his allies establish a well-honed system of political patronage, which spread to everything from construction to health and culture. Through this network, Erdoğan had secured the loyalty of the business elite and used their resources to consolidate his power. Losing İstanbul risked disrupting this network and losing a significant source of revenue to the opposition at a time of great economic difficulty.

With stakes so high, Erdoğan challenged the results in several cities. In İstanbul, he pushed for a recount over alleged irregularities. After the recount failed to reverse the opposition win, Erdoğan ordered a rerun. This move quickly changed the post-election mood. The opposition win was a breath of fresh air for those long resigned to the fact that the ballot box did not matter anymore, and that Erdoğan was invincible. Nullification of the İstanbul election and calling for a new vote, however, strengthened the pessimistic view that Erdoğan would do anything not to lose the city a second time. They were wrong.

In the repeat election that was held three months later, İmamoğlu won by even a bigger margin, almost sixty times greater than in March. İmamoğlu's second and more decisive victory was the greatest electoral defeat of Erdoğan's political career. The opposition's win dented Erdoğan's aura of invincibility and breathed new life into the long-stagnant opposition. Many thought it was the beginning of the end for Erdoğan.[3]

"Erdoğan is starving his own people to feed the Syrians"

According to public opinion polls, two factors were responsible for Erdoğan's defeat: economic problems and growing anger over Syrian refugees. Economic problems and unemployment had climbed to the top of Turkish voters' concerns and many people, including Erdoğan supporters, blamed the president's misguided policies for the country's economic woes. When local elections were held, inflation was nearly 20 percent, unemployment was nearly 15 percent, the lira stood at 5.7 to the dollar and the economy had fallen into its first recession in a decade.[4] The country's economic turmoil was fueled by a massive currency crisis following the economic sanctions imposed by the US government over Turkey's detention of pastor Andrew Brunson.

Erdoğan blamed Turkey's economic ills on foreign powers but the origin of the country's worst economic crisis in two decades lay in the structural contradictions of Erdoğan's neoliberal populism. The populist policies Erdoğan pursued on the economic front, such as providing clientelist aid and cheap consumer credit, helped him centralize power but the key vulnerability of this strategy was its dependence on low interest rates and favorable global economic conditions. As those conditions started changing, Erdoğan's economic miracle began failing, leaving many low- and middle-income families without access to consumer credit and with enormous debt they had accumulated under Erdoğan.

Making matters worse was Erdoğan's usurpation of vast powers, which had come under increased scrutiny as poverty spread across the country, with an overwhelming majority of the Turkish public saying their trust in the government's economic policies had declined.[5] While campaigning for the presidential system, Erdoğan had promised that accumulation of authority under the new system would make decision-making on critical matters such as the economy a lot smoother and more efficient. Yet, Erdoğan's vast powers had proven to be a liability when it came to addressing the country's mounting economic problems. Unlike his early years in government when economic decision-making was deferred to technocrats, Erdoğan was now surrounded by sycophants. Financial institutions had been hollowed out and key figures who were responsible for advising the government on the economy and who had challenged problematic economic decisions were all gone, leaving Erdoğan without the independent thinkers necessary to assure global markets and investors.

Economic problems hardened the public's attitudes toward some 4 million Syrian refugees living in the country. Respondents to a poll listed the Syrian refugees as the third most important problem facing the country after economic and unemployment concerns. It was the first time since Turkey started accepting refugees from Syria that the issue had risen that high on the list.[6] Indeed, the influx of millions of refugees to Turkey has been one of the greatest challenges posed by the Syrian war. Erdoğan pursued an open-border policy after the conflict in Syria started, turning the country that has never considered itself a nation for non-Turkish migration into a primary destination for Syrian refugees in a matter of few years. Turkey extended generous assistance and provided expansive services in refugee camps, including primary and secondary schools, community centers, supermarkets, and playgrounds. Refugees were given refrigerators and stoves, and in some cases TVs and air conditioners. They were provided with cash cards and a monthly allowance. Even those refugees living outside camps survived on Turkey's largesse.[7]

Initially, Turkey's religious and nationalist circles were not opposed to Ankara's generous support of the Syrian refugees. They bought into Erdoğan's "compassionate Islamist" narrative that called for Sunni Muslim solidarity against the "Alawite Shiite" oppression perpetrated by the Assad regime. Erdoğan called the refugees *muhacir*, or religiously oppressed, a term which originally referred to the first Muslims who migrated with Prophet Muhammad from Mecca to Medina to escape religious persecution. He called those who welcomed Syrian refugees *ensar*, or helpers, referring to the people of Medina who helped the Prophet and his followers.[8] This narrative of Sunni Muslim solidarity gained traction after a double car bombing that killed fifty-one people on May 11, 2013, in Reyhanlı, a town on the Syrian border which was an entry point for Syrian refugees fleeing the conflict. Locals quickly blamed the refugees for the deadly attack while Erdoğan pointed the finger at the Assad regime. He said,

> Brothers, you have opened your arms to our 25 thousand siblings from Syria. Now, do not pay heed to those who strive to expel them from here. They are part of our [religious] fraternity. They came here because they trust and believe us [...] We will be *ensar*, we will open our arms, we will never give credence to this discord and unrest.[9]

ERDOĞAN'S WAR

The "compassionate Islamist" narrative fit Erdoğan's post-2011 agenda which used Islam to cement his power and was received well among the Turkish religious-nationalist right. As late as 2016, when Turkey hosted close to 3 million Syrian refugees, only a fraction of society said that they did not want to live in the same city as Syrians while an overwhelming majority said they had no problems with the refugees.[10] But as the Turkish economy tipped into recession, resentment toward refugees, even among Erdoğan's own base, grew stronger. Terrorism associated with the Syrian war strengthened anti-refugee sentiment. By 2019, a large segment of society did not want to live in the same city as Syrians and wanted them to go back to their own country.[11]

Particularly concerning to Erdoğan was the growing anti-refugee sentiment among nationalists, whose support has proven critical to him since 2015. A growing number of nationalists saw refugees as an economic burden, a security threat and a danger to the ethnic make-up of the country. The unease within the nationalist base became visible in the 2018 elections. The ruling AKP lost votes to the nationalist MHP due to Erdoğan's generous refugee policy. The most stridently anti-refugee party, İYİ Party, which splintered from the MHP, gained ground in provinces where agricultural and unskilled construction workers were hit hard by Syrian refugees working in the Turkish informal sector. Yet, this anti-refugee sentiment did not have a dramatic impact on Erdoğan and his party's electoral fortunes until 2019. The AKP performed worse in the 2018 elections than the November 2015 elections but the party did not lose a significant number of votes in provinces where the refugee issue loomed large. Opinion polls taken months before the 2018 elections found that the refugee issue fell behind economic and security problems and concerns over the country's education system as the country's top predicaments.[12] Things started changing dramatically from 2018 onwards. The sharp economic downturn in 2018 hardened public attitudes against refugees. Incidents of intercommunal violence particularly in the metropolitan areas of Istanbul, Ankara and Izmir increased dramatically, leading to many deaths.

Anti-refugee sentiment cuts across party lines. Working-class Turkish citizens complain that Syrian refugees receive aid from the government while Turkish citizens are receiving second-class treatment. Utku Şen, who works for a telecommunications company in the southern town of Mersin, where there is a large Syrian community and anti-refugee sentiment runs high among the locals, said "Erdoğan is starving his own people to feed the Syrians."[13] Kurds resent the warm welcome Syrian refugees are getting from the Turkish government while they lack basic rights such as access to public education in Kurdish. Erdoğan's emphasis on "Islamic brotherhood" with Syrian refugees angers Turkey's Alevis and secular constituency, who blame him for the Sunnification of Turkish society. Both Kurds and Alevis think that Erdoğan is trying to change the ethnic and sectarian composition of border cities by resettling large numbers of Sunni Arabs in the Kurdish-majority southeast. Kurdish seasonal workers complain that they are losing jobs to Syrians. Others argue that Syrians drive up rent, undercut wages and free ride on Turkish taxpayers' money. Turks who are opposed to Erdoğan see his efforts to grant citizenship to Syrians, 1.5 million of whom will be eligible to vote if granted citizenship, as a move to expand his voter base. Even AKP municipalities and Erdoğan supporters are critical. An AKP-run municipality in İstanbul that hosts a large Syrian refugee community has banned renting homes to Syrians.

Differences in culture and lifestyle between Syrians and Turks have contributed to anti-refugee sentiment, especially in conservative border towns. These towns have seen a dramatic increase in polygamy and divorce rates. Turkish women are worried about Turkish men divorcing their wives to marry young Syrian refugee women. The fast-changing demographics in these border towns exacerbate feelings of insecurity and loss of local culture among the host community. The cultural clash between the Turkish and Syrian communities is also common in Western metropolises. Syrian refugees tend to live in the same neighborhoods as their compatriots and form parallel societies isolated from the local Turkish population. This segregation feeds mutual hostilities, leading locals to think that Syrians have no intention of integrating into Turkish culture. Some Turks argue that Syrian neighborhoods are prone to crime and violence.

Until recently, public concern over refugees had not been part of a national debate largely because the media are controlled by Erdoğan and opposition parties did not pick up on the issue to mobilize voters. Growing public protest against refugees, however, has changed that. The issue became a hot campaign topic ahead of the 2018 elections. Opposition parties blamed what they saw as Erdoğan's misguided Syria policy for the presence of millions of Syrians in the country and called for their return to Syria. Meral Akşener, the head of the nationalist İYİ Party, pledged to send them back. Other İYİ Party officials blamed Syrians for the recession. A newly elected mayor from the main opposition CHP cut aid to the refugees. The CHP's 2018 presidential candidate Muharrem İnce criticized Erdoğan for letting refugees go back home for the Muslim holiday of Eid Al-Fitr and then return to Turkey, arguing if they could go home to visit, they could go home to stay. Ekrem İmamoğlu, the CHP's candidate for İstanbul mayor, joined the chorus. Within hours of his election victory, the hashtag "SuriyelilerDefoluyor," or "Syrians are getting the hell out" began trending on Twitter.

The 2019 elections were a wakeup call for Erdoğan. The loss his party suffered was an indication of the level of bitterness against refugees among the Turkish public. Erdoğan got the voters' message and recalibrated his policies. Restrictions on Syrian refugees were tightened after the elections. Shortly after the İstanbul election rerun, Turkish authorities began arresting Syrians. Police officers conducted spot-checks in public spaces, metro stations and businesses. Thousands of Syrians were detained and coerced into signing forms saying they would like to return to Syria before they were bussed to the border. They were forcibly deported from İstanbul to Syria, including to the volatile northwestern town of Idlib. The government ordered hundreds of thousands of Syrians who were registered outside İstanbul to leave the city. Erdoğan modified his Syria policy as well. Sending Syrians back to Syria became his number one priority.

Nationalism strikes back

Turkish nationalism has been a powerful force in Turkish politics since the inception of the Republic and has been invoked by almost

ERDOĞAN'S NATIONALIST GAMBLE BACKFIRES

all factions in the political spectrum. Erdoğan long resisted the temptation. Until 2014, he opposed ethnic divisions thinking that co-opting the Kurds would be a better move for his electoral fortunes. When Kurds refused to back Erdoğan's plans to acquire sweeping new powers, Erdoğan launched a war on them. Since then, Erdoğan, who once claimed to have "trampled" on nationalism, has been riding it to stay in power. Anti-Kurdish nationalism became the glue that kept his diverse coalition of religious conservative, Islamist, center-right, far-left and nationalist currents together. Anti-Kurdish policies accompanied by anti-Western rhetoric that urged the nation to unite against the supposed domestic and foreign enemies bent on destroying the Turkish state managed to keep the public's focus away from the country's mounting problems and rallied support behind the man who pledged to "fight till the last drop of his blood" to defend the nation. The war in Syria gave nationalism a huge boost and consolidated Erdoğan's alliance with the nationalists.

Erdoğan won election after election thanks to Turkish nationalism. The support lent to Erdoğan by the nationalists changed his political fortunes in 2015 during snap elections that were held a few months after Erdoğan's party lost the parliamentary majority. Alliance with the nationalists once again proved critical in the 2018 elections, granting Erdoğan the presidency and a parliamentary majority. But the 2019 local elections showed that nationalism was no longer doing the trick for Erdoğan. On the contrary, it had started hurting his electoral fortunes. The nationalism that Erdoğan had systematically stoked against the country's Kurds since 2015 turned against him when it found a new target in Syrian refugees. As economic problems worsened and refugees started leaving the camps and becoming more visible in big cities, Erdoğan, who had turned the country into the world's biggest refugee host nation, came under attack, particularly by nationalists.

In the summer of 2021, a group of young nationalists calling themselves "Angry Young Turks" put up banners across the country reading "The Border is Our Honor." When asked what they were angry about, they cited the presence of millions of Syrians living in the country and called for their return to their homeland.

Compounding their worries about Syrian refugees was the influx of thousands of Afghans fleeing over land through Iran to Turkey following the takeover of their country by the Taliban. The nationalist activists were arrested but opposition parties took up the cause. The CHP and the nationalist İYİ Party quickly hung similar banners across the country. The move became widely popular, with half of Erdoğan's own voters, two thirds of his nationalist allies and more than 90 percent of opposition voters agreeing with the activists' message that Turkey needed to do more to protect its borders against refugees.[14] The incident was a testament to the shifting priorities of the nationalists. The Kurdish question has dominated their agenda for decades but Syrian refugees are now becoming a more pressing problem.

This anti-refugee sentiment has not only hurt Erdoğan's electoral fortunes. His nationalist ally, the MHP, has lost ground as well. Although the party increased its votes in the 2019 local elections, thanks to the votes it captured from disgruntled AKP voters who wanted to punish Erdoğan but did not want to leave the ruling bloc all together, support for the party gradually started declining after that. Party leader Devlet Bahçeli's reluctance to criticize Erdoğan's refugee policy has been influential in that decline. Many MHP supporters complain that Bahçeli's unconditional support for Erdoğan is jeopardizing the ethnic make-up of the country.[15] The growing discontent within the party burst into the open in 2017. A group of dissidents who were critical of the party becoming a rubber stamp for Erdoğan's one-man rule launched the İYİ Party.

The İYİ Party has become the country's most strident anti-refugee party. It is also the fastest growing, with its support dramatically rising since the 2019 local elections. The party's rise is eating into Erdoğan's conservative, nationalist base. Party leader Meral Akşener is the most dynamic opposition leader, touring the country frequently to take the pulse of the street, talk to local businesses and voice the electorate's economic frustrations. Economic concerns and growing public outrage with Syrian refugees are the two main factors driving the party's popularity. In the 2019 elections, it gained ground in provinces where grievances against Syrian refugees run deep. Anti-refugee sentiment will only grow stronger in

ERDOĞAN'S NATIONALIST GAMBLE BACKFIRES

the run-up to the next elections, boosting the İYİ Party's electoral fortunes and hurting Erdoğan's further.

The rise of the nationalist İYİ Party's star, while the MHP's is in decline, exposes an uncomfortable truth for Erdoğan: the strategy of relying on Turkish nationalism to tighten his grip on power has run its course. But Erdoğan does not have that many options, so he is trying hard to save his nationalist alliance. To prevent the MHP's sagging popularity from hurting his chances in the next elections, Erdoğan announced that the country's 10 percent electoral threshold, which parties must pass to get into the parliament, will be lowered to 7 percent.[16] The move is intended to help the MHP, whose voter share is below the 10 percent threshold according to polls. He also extended an invitation to the İYİ Party leader to join the ruling nationalist bloc.

There is no quick fix for the rising anti-refugee sentiment. It is likely to get worse as the country's economic problems grow. The lack of a legal framework to integrate refugees politically, socially and economically into Turkish society makes matters worse. Despite the Turkish government's warm welcome, the Syrians in Turkey do not enjoy formal refugee status. After the first Syrian refugees started crossing into Turkey in 2011, Turkey focused on providing humanitarian aid and establishing refugee camps in the border provinces because the government assumed that the Syrians' stay would be short and temporary. As the conflict dragged on, Turkish officials came to realize that reforming the existing system became a necessity to address the Syrian refugee question.

Syrian refugees were granted the right to stay in Turkey temporarily by the Law on Settlement, which was established in 1934 and updated in 2006. However the law restricted the right of permanent settlement, a designation that leads to citizenship, only to persons of Turkish descent and culture. In 2013, the Turkish parliament passed a law that established a legal framework for protecting and aiding asylum seekers. A year later, Turkey adopted new regulations that accorded Syrian refugees secure legal status in the country for the first time. These new regulations provided them with ID cards and allowed them to access services such as healthcare and education. Despite these progressive steps, refugees still lack official refugee status, which would entitle them to benefits like housing, public relief and various social services. They are not allowed to work or move without authorization either. Education is equally problematic with almost half the school-age Syrian children who live outside the camps unenrolled. Taking steps to offer long-term solutions to these problems requires recognizing that Syrian refugees are in Turkey to stay but Erdoğan fears a domestic backlash if he openly admits that they are not returning home.

#NoVotesForYou

Erdoğan faces a myriad of other problems. His stinging electoral defeat in 2019 cracked his aura of invincibility and emboldened critical voices. Those in the business community, current members of the AKP, and people who had backed Erdoğan every step of the way since the inception of the party started voicing their frustration more vocally. Even those in the bureaucracy began to prepare for a "post-Erdoğan" Turkey.[17]

Weeks after the elections, Ahmet Davutoğlu, who served as foreign and prime minister before falling out with Erdoğan in 2016, produced a fifteen-page manifesto blasting Erdoğan.[18] He blamed the alliance with the MHP, and the new executive presidency that gave way to one-man rule, for the party's embarrassing defeat, arguing that alliance with nationalists replaced the party's "liberal and reformist ethos" with a statist and security-oriented approach. The manifesto was a scathing critique of Erdoğan and the ruling AKP, which Davutoğlu had been part of since its launch. A few months after the rerun elections in İstanbul, he launched his own party. Ali Babacan, the former deputy prime minister who had recently resigned from the party over "deep differences" with the party direction, established his own shortly after Davutoğlu. Other AKP heavyweights such as Bülent Arınç became more vocal in their criticism of Erdoğan. Kemal Öztürk, one of Erdoğan's former advisors and a columnist for the pro-government newspaper Yeni Şafak, criticized in his column the decision to order a rerun in İstanbul. When the newspaper declined to run his critical piece, he quit and joined a monthly Islamist publication.[19] Even

ERDOĞAN'S NATIONALIST GAMBLE BACKFIRES

Erdoğan's hardcore Islamist allies joined the chorus. Abdurrahman Dilipak, an Islamist ideologue who has long supported the AKP, argued the party had succumbed to greed. Another prominent Islamist who served as a member of parliament for the opposition Islamist Felicity Party said that pious people had been subjected to even harsher oppression under the Islamist-rooted AKP than they had suffered under the secularists.[20] Still others in the party expressed their criticism more quietly.

> Ordering a rerun in İstanbul was a really bad call. Some of us thought that he knew what he was doing but apparently, he did not. The sad truth is that he lost his populist touch. It saddens me to say this, but I think it is the beginning of the end.[21]

A string of developments following the elections reinforced this view. Poll after poll showed that a growing number of Erdoğan supporters were unhappy with the way things were. To register their discontent, many started voting for Erdoğan's ally, the nationalist MHP. Others abandoned the ruling coalition altogether to support the opposition nationalist İYİ Party. A large pool of voters left the Erdoğan–Bahçeli bloc but they are not yet ready to throw their support behind the opposition. They remain undecided. Erdoğan's personal popularity, which had traditionally been a lot stronger than that of his party, took a hit. Those who said that they could not imagine someone other than Erdoğan leading the AKP fell dramatically.[22] The Interior Minister Süleyman Soylu, who had taken a hard line against Syrian refugees, was the top prospect, particularly among young conservatives.[23] It was the first time in Erdoğan's almost two decades in power that his popularity among his own supporters had dropped this much.

The resignation of Berat Albayrak, Turkey's unpopular finance minister and Erdoğan's son-in-law, reinforced the view that despite a façade of unity, there were cracks in Erdoğan's iron grip on power. Albayrak announced his resignation in a letter he posted on Instagram in which he cited health reasons for his resignation, thanked his wife and parents, but barely mentioned his boss. The letter made reference to the infighting in the party and ended with an ominous plea for help from God. Albayrak's resignation came amidst months of mounting economic problems and a currency in freefall. Over the years, Albayrak had accrued vast influence and made many enemies. His handling of the economy had come under increasing criticism too, even from within the ruling party. At a time of economic crisis, Albayrak often boasted that Turkey was outperforming rival economies and made light of the dire state of the central bank's foreign currency war chest and the Turkish lira, which had lost about a third of its value against the US dollar since the start of 2020. Yet, Erdoğan, who had sidelined critical voices and was often briefed only by his son-in-law about the state of the economy, stood by him.

Over the years, Erdoğan's growing paranoia forced him to retreat into a close circle of family members. Despite warnings from other AKP heavyweights against it, Erdoğan put his son-in-law in charge of the country's finances and shielded him from growing criticism. Many thought that Erdoğan was grooming him as his political heir. But election losses and mounting economic problems were a wakeup call for Erdoğan to the true state of the country's economy. Erdoğan suddenly realized that he could not bear the brunt of having his son-in-law as the finance minister, which unnerved investors and markets and angered many in his own base at a time when Erdoğan faced mounting challenges from his opponents and allies alike.

Albayrak's resignation showed that Erdoğan was at his most vulnerable. He had lost the most critical constituencies, the Kurds being one of them. They make up 18 to 20 percent of the electorate. The crackdown on Kurds both at home and in Syria took a toll on Erdoğan's standing. Even the conservative Kurds who had traditionally backed Erdoğan and other right-wing politicians who came before him complained that Erdoğan's anti-Kurdish policies went too far. İhsan Arslan, one of the Kurdish founders of the AKP and a member of parliament from the Kurdish city of Diyarbakır, was an exemplar case. He had been a close friend and ally to Erdoğan for many years and taken part in the Kurdish peace process. But he was very critical of Erdoğan's post-2015 nationalist transformation.[24] Arslan's vocal criticism was a reflection of the growing unease with Erdoğan's policies among conservative Kurds.

Erdoğan's unwillingness to help break the siege of Kobani when it was surrounded by ISIS forces, as well as the conviction of many

ERDOĞAN'S NATIONALIST GAMBLE BACKFIRES

Kurds that Erdoğan was directly aiding ISIS against Kurdish fighters, led to an erosion of Erdoğan's support among Kurds. Local elections once again showed how critical that support is for an election victory. In İstanbul, Kurds make up about 15 percent of the roughly 10.5 million eligible voters. Their support for Ekrem İmamoğlu proved critical for the opposition victory.

Another key constituency is the country's young generation and Erdoğan's popularity has taken a hit there as well. "Raising pious generations" has been the landmark of his Islamist populist agenda but the growing unease among Turkey's youth with Erdoğan's brand of Islamic conservatism, even among the children of pro-AKP families, suggests that Erdoğan's efforts to shape the next generation in his image has failed. Polls indicate that religiosity in the younger generation has declined dramatically, with far fewer describing themselves as "religiously conservative." Growing numbers of young people, even those attending Imam Hatip schools, are rejecting Islam altogether. According to a workshop organized by the Ministry of National Education, many students in Imam Hatip schools are abandoning Islam and consider themselves deists—people who believe in a divine being but don't adhere to the tenets of Islam. Young people's disillusionment with Islam and Erdoğan goes hand in hand. Islam is seen by many as an instrument stripped of its moral code and used to cover up corruption and Erdoğan's one-man rule, pushing young people to search for other sources of moral authority.[25]

Erdoğan's growing authoritarianism and the curtailment of freedoms are other reasons why the country's young generation has turned against him. According to a 2018 poll, a large majority of the young generation values the freedom their peers enjoy in the West and want to move abroad to live in free and more prosperous societies.[26]

Young Turks are also worried about unemployment. Youth unemployment has reached unprecedented levels, a staggering 29 percent, and young people do not think Erdoğan is willing to implement sound economic policies to alleviate the problem. The quality of education is another major concern. Education has become Erdoğan's main tool to raise a pious generation. He has poured billions of dollars into religious education, replaced standard subjects with courses on Islam and significantly expanded the number of Imam Hatip schools. The majority of Turkey's youth believe that they need to move to a Western country to get a decent education. Young people doubt that their college degree will land them a decent job because of the spread of nepotism under Erdoğan. They complain about the lack of merit-based hiring in private and public sectors.

The youth revolt against Erdoğan has intensified in the last few years. During an online address to youth, thousands of students who joined the YouTube livestream disliked the video. They expressed their anger using the comments section and told him that he would not get their votes. The video received hundreds of thousands of dislikes and the hashtag #OyMoyYok—no votes for you—became a trending topic on Turkish Twitter. Erdoğan's office disabled the video's comments and Erdoğan announced plans for new regulations to control social media platforms or shut them down entirely. Erdoğan's appointment of a political ally as rector at a prestigious İstanbul university became another platform for Turkey's disillusioned and unemployed youth to vent their frustration.

With half of the country's population below the age of thirty-two, what young people think has significant political ramifications. Local election results were a testament to that. A majority of the country's new generation backed opposition party candidates and played a critical role in the opposition victory. An estimated 7 million Turks born around the millennium will vote in the 2023 presidential and parliamentary elections, making them the next kingmakers. Erdoğan has been trying to woo the youth but his chances of winning them over remain slim.

Compounding Erdoğan's problems is his sagging popularity among another key constituency: Turkey's business community, particularly the country's more than 3 million small and medium-sized enterprises (SMEs). Backing from the small business owners had been the bedrock of Erdoğan's political support and key to his electoral successes. These businesses have been hit the hardest by Covid 19 pandemic restrictions and the uncertainty around

ERDOĞAN'S NATIONALIST GAMBLE BACKFIRES

Erdoğan's monetary policy. In 2020 alone, hundreds of thousands of them filed for bankruptcy and many more have unofficially closed. Even big businesses are struggling. After the 2019 elections, members of TÜSİAD, the country's largest business organization that had largely remained silent in the face of Erdoğan's authoritarian turn, started voicing rare criticism of the government's economic policy. They say that the erosion in the rule of law, repressive tactics against the opposition, the widespread corruption, confusing monetary policy, the anti-Western foreign policy and Turkey's isolation on the global stage have all contributed to the country's economic troubles. TÜSİAD members called for a return to democracy to attract investors and put the country's economy on the right track.[27]

There is discontent within army ranks as well. The Turkish military had thrown its full support behind Erdoğan and his Syria policy after the failed coup, to prove its loyalty and fix its damaged reputation. After years of opposition, military leaders finally approved an operation into Syria a month after the coup attempt. Some high-ranking members of the army were not comfortable with going into Syria without a clear exit strategy and relying solely on "Russian goodwill," but these concerns were not voiced in the highly tense atmosphere of post-coup Turkey. Erdoğan's election loss, however, emboldened critical voices in the country's armed forces as well. As a sign of disagreement with Erdoğan's Syria policy, five generals who served in critical posts in Syria sought to resign. The Defense Ministry said the generals requested early retirement due to health and family reasons, but long-time military analysts argued that the early retirement requests were a gesture of disapproval for Erdoğan's Syria policy, which risked the lives of Turkish soldiers and was out of touch with the operational reality on the ground.[28]

Erdoğan's Syria policy came under closer scrutiny after a fugitive, ultranationalist crime boss, Sedat Peker, who was once a die-hard Erdoğan supporter, started releasing videos from his alleged base in the United Arab Emirates, making scandalous allegations about Erdoğan's close circle. Peker, who was convicted of mob-related activity in the past and is wanted again by the Turkish police, was a very popular figure in nationalist circles, and he used his popularity to rally nationalist support for Erdoğan's 2018 election campaign. But they had a falling out. In a series of videos, Peker leveled accusations of rape, corruption, drug dealing, and even murder against officials close to Erdoğan. In one of his most controversial claims, Peker claimed he had sent steel vests and other equipment to Syrian Turkmens and that SADAT, a private military company founded by a retired general who served as an advisor to Erdoğan, had added trucks carrying weapons to those in Peker's convoy.[29] But according to Peker, SADAT's weapons were sent to the al-Qaeda affiliate al-Nusra. Peker also claimed that figures close to Erdoğan were involved in commercial activities with radical Islamist groups such as Hayat Tahrir al-Sham on the Syrian side of the border.

Peker's allegations rekindled the debate on Erdoğan's misguided Syria policy at a time when he was already under pressure because of Syrian refugees. Peker's videos, which were watched by millions, resonated strongly with many nationalist and pious Turks, including AKP members. They further dented Erdoğan's flagging popularity. Erdoğan's approval ratings hit record lows and the combined support for the AKP and its ally MHP is well below the 50 percent mark that is necessary to win elections in the presidential system Erdoğan introduced. Pollsters argue that for the first time in Erdoğan's almost two decades in power, voters who ditched the AKP are unlikely to be won back.[30]

"Erdoğan shot himself in the foot"

Much of the AKP's governing elite blames alliance with the MHP for Erdoğan's dwindling support. Some argue that the anti-Kurdish agenda has gone too far, and that without Kurdish backing the prospects of securing a comfortable majority remain grim.[31] Others complain the MHP wields disproportionate political power, most of the time to the disadvantage of Erdoğan and the ruling AKP. They worry that the decline in the MHP's support would hurt Erdoğan's prospects further in the upcoming elections.

The most widely expressed criticism inside the AKP is the newly introduced executive presidency. Erdoğan "shot himself in the foot" by replacing the country's parliamentary system.[32] Although the new presidential system placed unprecedented power in Erdoğan's hands, it also made it more difficult for him to win elections. Under the parliamentary system, Erdoğan could form single-party governments with a vote share well below the 50 percent plus one that is necessary to win in the new presidential system. In 2002, for instance, although the AKP captured only around 34 percent of the vote, it controlled 66 percent of the seats in the parliament largely due to the 10 percent electoral threshold that left all parties that could not clear the threshold out of the parliament. Under the presidential system, Erdoğan must capture more than 50 percent of the votes to win reelection. With poll support dropping, he relies on the MHP to preserve an electoral majority, and dependence on the ultranationalist party has come at a cost. More and more people in the ruling party's circles quietly argue that alliance with the ultranationalists is hurting the party's brand and dealing a blow to Erdoğan's electoral fortunes.

The presidential system has posed another problem for Erdoğan. For years, Turkey's notoriously divided opposition made it easier for Erdoğan to win election after election. But the presidential system has unintentionally unified them. Under the new system, if a candidate is unable to capture more than 50 percent of the vote in the first round of presidential elections, the top two contenders enter a run-off, which forces political parties to form electoral alliances. Turkey's opposition is deeply divided along ideological lines. They are split among Turkish and Kurdish nationalists, secularists and Islamists. But their rejection of the executive presidency has provided common ground. Thanks to the introduction of a new law that allows parties to create electoral alliances, the secularist CHP, the nationalist İYİ Party, the Islamist Felicity Party and the Democrat Party cast their differences aside to form a united front, the Nation's Alliance, ahead of the 2018 presidential and parliamentary elections. The pro-Kurdish HDP was formally excluded from the alliance, but the party asked its supporters to vote for the opposition alliance's candidates. The opposition's 2019 election victory proved that Erdoğan had unwittingly created the biggest electoral challenge to his rule.

Public opinion, too, has turned against the presidential system. It was never widely popular to begin with. The 2017 referendum endorsing the change passed by a narrow margin but widespread allegations of fraud marred its legitimacy. Public displeasure with the new system grew as the country plunged into an economic recession and Erdoğan failed to respond to a myriad of problems from rising inflation and unemployment to a surging Covid 19 pandemic and environmental disasters. A growing majority of people, including those in Erdoğan's close circle, blames the concentration of power in one man's hands for the country's ills, with support for the executive presidency dropping from 51 to 34 percent since 2017.[33]

Erdoğan took several steps to shore up his flagging popularity. To court religious-conservative supporters, he sought to co-opt key personalities and organizations from the Islamist Millî Görüş movement, from which Erdoğan and the core of the AKP had sprung. He withdrew Turkey from an international treaty on preventing violence against women, known as the İstanbul convention, at a time when violence against women soared. The treaty underlines gender equality and obliges state authorities to take steps to prevent gender-based violence, but many conservatives in Turkey say it undermines the family structures that are key to a functioning society and urged Erdoğan to quit the pact. Responding to decades-long demands from Islamists, Erdoğan ordered Istanbul's Hagia Sophia, an ancient Orthodox church that became a mosque after the Ottoman conquest in 1453 but in 1935 was converted into a museum by modern Turkey's secularist founder Mustafa Kemal Atatürk, to be turned back into a Muslim place of worship.

Erdoğan tried to reach out to the Kurds as well to salvage his withering popularity among this electorally critical constituency. In the summer of 2021, he paid a visit to Diyarbakır, the spiritual capital of Turkey's Kurds, where he owned up to the failed Kurdish opening for the first time since he formed an alliance with the nationalist MHP in 2015. He blamed the PKK and the pro-Kurdish HDP for its failure and said that he stood behind the words he uttered in his historic 2005 Diyarbakır speech in which he said the Kurdish problem was his problem. Erdoğan pledged to address a long-time Kurdish demand. He promised to convert the Diyarbakır prison, where thousands of Kurdish men and women were imprisoned and tortured, into a cultural center. The horrific forms of abuse committed in the prison fueled the rise of the PKK and the prison has come to represent the bloody history of the Kurdish struggle for rights.

The Kurds are unlikely to be swayed by these symbolic gestures. Nor are the religious conservatives Erdoğan has been courting likely to lift his electoral fortunes. Erdoğan's troubles run too deep for any quick fix. One of the most intractable problems he is facing is that of Syrian refugees. The issue is seen as one of the country's top problems by a large segment of the population and expected to be a leading campaign topic in the next elections. According to polls, half of Erdoğan's supporters, about two thirds of his nationalist allies and more than 90 percent of opposition voters worry about the growing number of refugees and think Erdoğan should do more to protect the borders.[34]

Facing growing challenges and dwindling support for his ruling alliance, Erdoğan has dramatically changed his tune on refugees. He once asked Turkish citizens to accept Syrian "Muslim brothers and sisters" with open arms, raised the prospect of granting Syrian refugees Turkish citizenship and boasted about hosting millions of Syrians. He now complains that Turkey cannot become the world's "refugee warehouse" and vows to send them back. The most recent shift in Erdoğan's Syria policy reflects that urgent need. His new "red line" in Syria is another refugee flow. The primary goal of Turkey's post-election military incursions is to secure territory that could be used as safe zones where Turkey's Syrian refugees can be relocated.

Local elections marked a turning point in Turkey's domestic and Syria policies. Election results forced a rethink of some of the premises that had dominated Turkish politics until then. For instance, election results prove that the ballot box still matters in Erdoğan's "new Turkey." Erdoğan is not invincible. Turkish opposition is not as inept as many have thought. Erdoğan's magic formula of playing the nationalist card is not only running out of steam but is fast becoming a force to shake his rule. Erdoğan is losing his grip on power and his Syria policy is partly responsible for that.

7

SYRIANS MUST GO

Is this the last chapter in Erdoğan's war? Is his two-decade rule coming to an end? Those who long for a liberal democratic country where everyone's rights and freedoms are officially recognized and protected, and the exercise of political power is limited by the rule of law, certainly hope so. They are encouraged by the opposition's 2019 victories. In many ways, Erdoğan is in a more difficult spot today than he was then. He is pressed by a crashing currency, soaring inflation and declining popularity. Making matters worse is the growing backlash against Syrian refugees. Domestic conditions are ripe for an opposition victory but one of the many worries Erdoğan's opponents have is whether foreign policy will once again come to his rescue. Will the war in Syria offer Erdoğan some relief from his domestic troubles, as it did in the past? Erdoğan is surely trying to use the war in Syria to advance his domestic agenda, again.

A few months after his party's humiliating election defeat, Erdoğan unveiled a plan he hoped would help solve two of his most urgent problems: a sinking economy and the growing domestic backlash against Syrian refugees. In a September 2019 speech at the United Nations General Assembly, Erdoğan held up a map of northern Syria setting out an ambitious proposal to resettle millions of refugees. The map showed a proposed safe zone that would stretch 30 kilometers into Syrian territory spanning the Turkish-Syrian border. Erdoğan said that 1 million Syrians would be housed in the northeast, an area controlled by US-allied Kurds, and another 2 million could settle there once the Turkish army took control. Erdoğan's proposal included a $27 billion project to build hundreds of thousands of homes, hospitals, football pitches, mosques, schools and other facilities in northern Syria. The plan was one of the largest public construction projects on foreign-occupied land in modern history. Erdoğan hoped a building boom in Syria would not only solve his refugee problem but also boost the country's economy. Years of economic growth under his rule had been fueled by a surge in construction. Economic recession, however, hit the industry hard. Erdoğan's proposal to build towns and villages in northern Syria created so much excitement in the sector that shares in cement companies with production plants in regions close to the Syrian border started rising shortly after his announcement.

The question was where to find the money to fund this mega construction project. Erdoğan hoped to secure financial and political support from the United Nations and key European states, but Western countries were reluctant. His plan heightened concerns that Turkey would forcefully deport Syrians to an area that remained unsafe and that it would alter the demographics of the region by resettling Syrians from the Sunni areas of western Syria in the Kurdish northeast. Erdoğan was desperate. Ignoring warnings from the UN, Turkey started shuttling refugees across the border into northeastern Syria despite the dangerous security conditions in the area. Erdoğan also threatened European countries that he would "open the gates" for refugees who wanted to cross Turkey's borders to enter Europe if Europe did not support his plan to establish a safe zone. A few months later, he made good on that threat. Thousands of refugees amassed at Turkey's border with Greece. Many of them were bussed to the border by Turkish officials. Allowing refugees to cross into Europe marked a dramatic departure from previous policy, which stemmed the tide of refugees to Europe in return for financial aid as part of a 2016 deal with the European Union. It showed how desperately Erdoğan needed to address the refugee question. In early October, several months after his party's election loss, Erdoğan took action by ordering an invasion of northeast Syria.

SYRIANS MUST GO

"Operation Peace Spring: Ethnic cleansing by another name"

On October 9, 2019, Turkish troops and their Syrian rebel allies started pounding the Syrian Kurdish militia with artillery before starting a cross-border ground operation. President Erdoğan announced that Turkey had launched a military incursion, dubbed Operation Peace Spring, into northeastern Syria to eliminate a "terror corridor" along Turkey's southern border and establish a safe zone to enable the return of the Syrians taking refuge in Turkey.

For months, Erdoğan had pushed the Trump administration to create a jointly controlled safe zone. He was encouraged by Trump's announcement that ISIS had been defeated and that he would pull out all 2,000 US troops from Syria. Almost a year passed after that announcement with US troops still in Syria and the US administration pushing back on Erdoğan's safe zone idea. The Pentagon and US officials in the region were urging the White House not to abandon the Kurds who had played such a decisive role in the fight against ISIS. Days before the Turkish operation, however, Erdoğan got what he wanted: a green light for the offensive from Trump. A White House statement on the phone conversation between the two leaders declared "Turkey will soon be moving forward with its long-planned operation into Northern Syria. The United States Armed Forces will not support or be involved in the operation, and United States forces, having defeated the ISIS territorial 'Caliphate,' will no longer be in the immediate area."[1] Following the statement, the US military began moving its forces away from the Kurdish-controlled region to clear the way for Ankara.

The White House announcement blindsided not just the US's Kurdish allies but almost everyone—senior officials at the Pentagon, State Department and the White House, lawmakers on the Hill and US allies in Europe and the Middle East. It prompted a furious backlash from the Democrats and senior members of Trump's own Republican Party. Senator Lindsey Graham, a fierce Trump loyalist, tweeted: "Pray for our Kurdish allies who have been shamelessly abandoned by the Trump Administration. This move ensures the reemergence of ISIS."[2] Others said allowing a Turkish military operation across the border could lead to a massacre of Kurds and

US withdrawal could open the way for Russia and Iran to move into the abandoned area.

Trump denied that he had given Erdoğan a green light for the incursion. He cited an unconventional letter he wrote to his Turkish counterpart on the day of the operation, urging him not to be a "tough guy" and to negotiate with the Syrian Kurdish militia instead of launching the incursion. A little more than a week after the incursion started, Trump imposed sanctions on Turkish officials for their part in the invasion and announced that he was reimposing steel tariffs on Turkey and would halt trade negotiations with the country. The war in Syria had dealt another blow to Turkey-US ties.

The Kurds' trust in the US had been shattered. After US forces left, one of the world's most powerful armies unleashed a brutal attack that crushed Kurdish defenses. To fend off a wider Turkish assault, the Kurds struck a deal with the Assad regime allowing Damascus and allied Russian forces to move into Kurdish-controlled areas that the regime had quit years ago, including the flashpoint city of Manbij. Once again, thanks to Turkey's actions, the Assad regime emerged as one of the big winners and Russia as the chief power-broker as it pushed for a post-conflict political settlement.

The Turkish and allied forces' combat against the Syrian Kurdish militia raged for ten days until US Vice President Mike Pence secured a ceasefire at a meeting with Erdoğan in Ankara. The deal gave the Kurdish forces 120 hours to pull their forces back thirty kilometers from a 120 km long strip stretching from the town of Tel Abyad to Ras al-Ain. This area was much smaller than Erdoğan had in mind. He hoped to establish a much larger safe zone along the whole border to repatriate millions of Syrian refugees residing on Turkish soil.

Hours before the US-brokered ceasefire between Turkish and Kurdish-led forces was due to expire, a second ceasefire agreement was reached between Turkey and Russia. According to the deal, Turkey would control the strip of territory between Tel Abyad and Ras al-Ain and Kurdish forces were given 150 hours to complete their withdrawal from the area. Once completed, Turkey and Russia would run joint patrols to prevent potential clashes between Turkey and its Syrian rebel allies and the Assad forces that had moved to the Kurdish-controlled areas.

SYRIANS MUST GO

Although Erdoğan declared the operation a military and diplomatic success, Turkey came under fire over accusations of war crimes and other violations during the operation. More than 200,000 civilians, the majority of them Kurds, were displaced as a result of the Turkish military incursion. Amnesty International said that Turkish military forces and allied rebels carried out serious violations during the operation that amounted to war crimes, including summary killings and unlawful attacks that killed and injured civilians.[3] The killing of Hevrin Khalaf, a prominent young female Syrian-Kurdish politician, was one of them. Members of Ahrar al-Sharqiya, which is part of the Turkey-backed Syrian National Army, stopped her SUV, removed her from the car, broke her jaw and leg, and dragged her by her hair until the skin of her scalp detached before repeatedly shooting her until she died.[4]

In a leaked internal memo, William V. Roebuck, US special envoy for the anti-ISIS campaign in Syria, called the Turkish operation "ethnic cleansing by another name."[5] Roebuck criticized the Trump administration for not doing enough to stop the Turkish incursion that led to "what can only be described as war crimes and ethnic cleansing."[6] Roebuck said that the Turks cited border concerns to justify attacking the Syrian Kurdish forces but asserted that "the border stayed quiet on the Syrian side the entire time" until Turkey violated it with the invasion.

Turkey's operation drew strong public condemnation from regional countries and from the West. The Arab League called it an "invasion" against an Arab state. The EU urged Ankara to halt the operation immediately and declared that it would not pay for the safe zone that might be created. Several EU members including Germany, the Netherlands and France imposed an arms embargo in response to Turkey's military action. The Turkish operation triggered angry reactions in Washington as well. Pentagon officials, along with Republican and Democratic lawmakers were alarmed at the prospect of a Kurdish massacre. Republican Senator Lindsey Graham and Democratic Senator Chris Van Hollen launched a bipartisan effort to impose economic sanctions on Turkey. Facing pressure from his Republican allies, President Trump, who had greenlighted the incursion, turned against the operation as well. He threatened to destroy the Turkish economy if Ankara "doesn't play by the rules" and later imposed sanctions on Turkish officials.

Of the three Turkish military incursions into Syria, Operation Peace Spring became the main public relations headache for Erdoğan. But domestically, the operation served its purpose. It eased public resentment over Erdoğan's Syria policy as Turkish-funded NGOs began construction on thousands of homes in northern Syria and the first bus carrying seventy Syrian refugees living in Turkey arrived in newly captured Ras al-Ain. Erdoğan's popularity received a boost, with some three-quarters of Turks supporting the incursion.[7] His approval rating rose to 48 percent, its highest level since the currency crisis that had rocked the Turkish economy a year before.[8]

The operation secured another key goal for Erdoğan. It drove a wedge into the opposition coalition. The secularist CHP had formed an official alliance with the nationalist İYİ Party, and unofficial alliances with the Islamist Felicity Party (Saadet) and the pro-Kurdish Peoples' Democratic Party (HDP) before the 2019 local elections. These maneuvers dealt a huge electoral blow to Erdoğan and the AKP. Ever since, Erdoğan has intensified his efforts to criminalize the HDP and fracture the opposition alliance. The military incursion helped those endeavors. The operation was endorsed almost unanimously by opposition parties, which saw it as a necessary move to fight the PKK and resettle the Syrian refugees. The pro-Kurdish HDP was the only major opposition party that was against the mission, putting it at odds with other parties in the opposition bloc.

The upward tick in Erdoğan's poll numbers following the incursion turned out to be short-lived. The invasion did not fix the country's economic troubles. Nor did it solve Erdoğan's refugee problem. His so-called safe zone that would host millions of refugees was too difficult to establish. But Erdoğan was bent on trying. Turkey made significant investments in the region to attract refugees. As in other areas captured during previous Turkish incursions, Turkey oversaw the establishment of local councils closely linked to neighboring Turkish provinces in the Tel Abyad-Ras al-Ain area. The region is administered by the governor of the

SYRIANS MUST GO

southeastern Turkish town of Urfa. Turkish civil servants help local councils provide basic services and infrastructure and train local police forces. Turkish-funded NGOs built tens of thousands of houses in the territories Turkey controls. Turkey reopened the Tel Abyad customs gate, which was closed after the Kurdish-led SDF captured the town, and opened a new gate in Ras al-Ain to boost trade with the region. Local infrastructure was connected to the Turkish electricity grid and the Turkish postal service operates in the area.[9]

Turkish officials announced that hundreds of thousands of Syrian refugees had moved from Turkey to the region, although the UNHCR estimated a much smaller number, and that more refugees would be resettled in the months to come.[10] Despite the rosy assessment by Turkish officials, several factors have made Erdoğan's safe zone plans almost impossible to implement. Given the country's economic recession, Turkey is in no position to fund the billions of dollars required for the project. Neither Gulf nor European countries stepped up to help alleviate the cost. Western countries are already concerned about the hundreds of thousands of people who were internally displaced by the operation. The UNHCR reports nearly 180,000 Syrian Kurds, including some 80,000 children, were forced to leave their homes due to the Turkish assault. Turkey started settling Sunni Arabs from outside the border region in the abandoned regions. Western countries do not want to fund Turkey's efforts to demographically engineer a Sunni Arab majority in Kurdish regions. The biggest problem facing Erdoğan's ambitious safe zone project is the Syrian refugees themselves. Refugees living in Turkey do not want to move into a war zone: they want to stay in Turkey or move to Europe. Forcefully repatriating refugees to dangerous countries violates international law, making it even more difficult for Erdoğan to secure international backing for his project.

The temporary boost Erdoğan received at home came at a great cost to the Syrians. The Turkish operation compounded Syria's already dire social conditions, leading to the displacement of thousands of civilians and exacerbating the safety and well-being of the area's 3 million residents. Two million of them depend on aid from humanitarian agencies. Many humanitarian agencies had to limit or suspend their operations due to the incursion.[11] The UN Commission of Inquiry for Syria (COI) reported that Turkey-backed rebels committed the war crimes of hostage-taking, cruel treatment, rape of minors and torture.[12] In addition, Turkish-backed forces refused to allow the return of Kurdish families displaced by the operation, burned down their houses, looted agricultural equipment and occupied their property.[13]

The atrocities committed by Turkey-backed groups were not the only cause of insecurity in the area. Turkey's operation divided northeastern Syria into several pockets controlled by groups hostile to each other, making the region one of the most combustible in Syria's civil war. Clashes between Turkey-backed rebels and Kurdish-led Syrian Democratic Forces (SDF) intensified following Turkey's operation. Turkish forces and their Syrian allies regularly violated ceasefires and attacked SDF positions in Kurdish-controlled areas. The PKK retaliated by launching an insurgency campaign. Following the Turkish occupation, it carried out car bombings and assassinations to target Turkish and allied forces around Ras al-Ain, killing over a dozen and wounding many Turkish and allied forces.

The increased infighting among Turkey-affiliated armed groups over power-sharing and resources fueled the conflict further. These groups' scant regard for the safety of the local population caused civilian casualties and serious damage to civilian infrastructure.[14]

The Turkish operation had a detrimental impact on the fight against ISIS as well. The Turkish and allied forces' attack on the SDF distracted the anti-ISIS coalition's most effective fighting force on the ground from its mission. A report by the Defense Intelligence Agency said that ISIS exploited Turkey's operation and subsequent drawdown of US troops to increase its attacks by 20 percent.[15]

Operation Peace Spring was primarily Erdoğan's response to the growing backlash against Syrian refugees, whose presence and a badly faltering economy ired voters and led to a substantial election loss. But the operation failed to resolve Erdoğan's refugee problem. Establishing a large enough safe zone in northern Syria to resettle millions of refugees proved tougher than he had expected.

SYRIANS MUST GO

As the fighting in Idlib intensified and anxiety grew in society at the prospect of another wave of refugees arriving at the Turkish border, Erdoğan turned his attention from the northeast to the northwestern town of Idlib.

"We are ready to die"

In his address to party members on February 15, 2020, Erdoğan issued an ultimatum to the Assad regime to pull its forces back to the borders set out in the 2018 Sochi agreement. He was referring to the regime's Russian-backed offensive in the last rebel enclave of Idlib, a northwestern town that sits on the Turkish border and is home to more than 3 million civilians.[16] The province is important to the Assad regime. It is traversed by vital highways and capturing them would allow the regime to reconnect areas that are important for the economic stabilization of the country. The regime's offensive had caused one of the biggest waves of displacement in the nine-year war. After weeks of aerial bombing, tens of thousands of people had fled north towards the Turkish border, stoking fears in Turkey of a new influx of refugees. Tensions escalated further between Ankara and Damascus after a deadly exchange of fire killed several Turkish and regime troops. Erdoğan warned that if regime forces did not withdraw by the end of the month, Turkey would launch a military operation. "We are ready to die for this, if need be," Erdoğan said.[17] Idlib became the new front in Erdoğan's war.

    The province became the last rebel bastion after Turkey reached an understanding with Damascus and Moscow that paved the way for the crumbling of opposition strongholds elsewhere in the country. It is one of the four de-escalation zones established in Astana. The three countries agreed to cease hostilities in Idlib and deploy observer forces to monitor compliance. Under the terms of the agreement, Turkey deployed troops to twelve observation posts in the town to monitor de-escalation and ensure the rebels' compliance with the ceasefire. Turkey also committed to containing and eventually eliminating the dominant rebel group in Idlib, Hayat Tahrir al-Sham (HTS), which is a former al-Qaeda affiliate and considered by Russia, Turkey and others to be a terrorist organization.

At the time, Turkey's primary goal in Idlib was to prevent the Kurdish YPG's potential expansion into the town. The lines of control established by Turkish troops in Idlib were meant to allow the troops to monitor and contain the YPG's actions in its stronghold of Afrin in the north.[18] As domestic opposition to Syrian refugees grew, however, Idlib took on new importance in Erdoğan's Syria policy. He called Turkey's military campaign in Idlib Turkey's "new War of Independence," referring to the military campaign by the Turkish National Movement after parts of the Ottoman Empire were occupied following its defeat in World War I.[19] That was how crucial establishing a safe zone in Syria was to Erdoğan. There were millions of civilians living in Idlib and they had nowhere but the Turkish border to flee in the event of a regime offensive. Preventing such an offensive on the northwestern town became one of Erdoğan's top priorities in Syria from 2019 onwards.[20]

Erdoğan relied on Russia to achieve that goal. Assad had vowed to retake "every inch of Syria" from his foes but Ankara hoped Moscow would rein him in. Russian President Putin and Erdoğan, however, were not on the same page in Idlib. Disagreements between the two countries emerged shortly after the two reached a deal in Astana. Strikes by pro-regime forces continued after the agreement. Russia and Assad claimed that they were targeting HTS and other alleged terrorist groups that were excluded from the ceasefire agreement and accused Turkey of failing to take steps against the jihadi groups. Turkey blamed Russia and the regime for failing to comply with the ceasefire.

In September 2018, Putin and Erdoğan negotiated a new deal in Sochi to iron out differences and stave off an imminent attack by regime forces. Russia agreed to take measures to avoid any attacks on Idlib; Turkey pledged to secure the withdrawal of heavy weapons and "radical terrorist groups" from a 15–20 kilometer-wide strip between rebel- and regime-controlled areas in Idlib.[21] Although the Sochi agreement halted an imminent regime offensive, it failed to address the most fundamental problem. Russia and Turkey's ultimate goals in Idlib are diametrically opposed to each other. Russia wants Assad to eventually recapture Idlib. Instead of supporting a large-scale regime offensive that would expose Moscow to more international criticism, Putin has been securing smaller territorial gains through ceasefire agreements with Turkey. Erdoğan's worst nightmare is a regime takeover of Idlib. He agrees to Russian-brokered ceasefires to prevent that. But the regime uses those ceasefires to secure more territory, putting Erdoğan in a bind.

Divergence over the fate of Hayat Tahrir al-Sham further complicates Turkey's mission impossible. Russia expects Turkey to weaken and eventually eliminate the jihadi group but from Turkey's point of view doing so would be shooting itself in the foot. Ankara is worried that the military operation required to drive the "radicals" out might send a new wave of refugees to its borders, and that weakening an effective fighting force against the regime might facilitate a regime takeover.

These discrepancies have given the parties an excuse to violate the ceasefires. In February 2019, Russia began conducting airstrikes on Idlib and backed the regime's ground offensive in April. Resumption of attacks displaced close to a million civilians and led to deadly clashes between Turkish and regime forces, killing several Turkish soldiers. The most dramatic escalation of violence came a year later. On February 27, 2020, an airstrike struck a Turkish mechanized infantry battalion in Idlib, killing at least thirty-six Turkish soldiers and wounding dozens. The attack sent shockwaves through Turkey. It was Turkey's deadliest single day since its first military intervention in Syria in 2016 and the Turkish army's single biggest loss of life on foreign soil since the 1974 intervention in Cyprus.

"Why are our soldiers in Syria?"

The attack on Turkish troops came against a background of escalating fighting and worsening humanitarian conditions in northwestern Syria. The Assad regime and its allies had launched an offensive against Hayat Tahrir al-Sham and Turkey-backed rebels in Idlib and neighboring Aleppo in December. By late February, the regime had captured the full length of the strategically important M5 highway, taken more than a hundred rebel-held towns and villages, and encircled Turkish observation posts in some areas. In the fighting, more than ten Turkish military personnel were killed. In response, Turkey significantly ramped up its military presence in Idlib, sending in thousands of troops and bolstering its support to rebels including providing shoulder-fired missiles that were used in a rebel attempt to shoot down a Russian military aircraft.

The direction of the regime's offensive suggested that Assad forces were preparing to seize the M4 Aleppo-Latakia highway. If the regime were to succeed, it would recapture more than half of the remaining rebel-controlled areas in northwestern Syria. The Russian-backed regime offensive had a devastating human toll. Schools, hospitals and vital civilian infrastructure were targeted to put pressure on the civilian population, leading to almost 2,000 civilian deaths and displacement of nearly 1 million people.

Turkey and its rebel allies launched counterattacks to push regime forces away from their observation posts and retook Saraqeb, a key Idlib crossroads town that the rebels had lost in February. Losing the strategically important town reversed one of the main gains of the regime's offensive. The killing of thirty-six Turkish soldiers came after Saraqeb's recapture by the rebels.

After the attack on Turkish troops, social media was blocked in Turkey to prevent widespread coverage of the incident. The Turkish government kept quiet for hours. Even Erdoğan, who typically never misses an opportunity to appear in front of the cameras, disappeared from public view. Twelve hours after the incident, in an apparent effort to avoid further public criticism of his Syria policy, he let the governor of the border province of Hatay do the talking instead. But as the death toll rose, so did public outrage. Angry crowds gathered in front of the Russian consulate in İstanbul to condemn Moscow for the deaths of the soldiers. When Erdoğan finally appeared in front of the cameras, he sounded out of touch. He began his speech with a reference to the 2013 popular protests against his rule, then praised martyrdom, blamed the Assad regime for the attack, cracked jokes and then went on to talk about the country's great economic performance.

SYRIANS MUST GO

Erdoğan's speech drew widespread criticism for being insensitive at a time of national mourning. Main opposition leader Kemal Kılıçdaroğlu said he was deeply hurt by Erdoğan's speech, pledged that there would be no more martyrs if the opposition came to power and asked what Turkish soldiers were doing in Syria.[22] It became clear that the safe zone Erdoğan had pledged to set up in northern Syria to resettle refugees was not going to materialize. "Why are our boys dying in Syria then? To clean up the mess Erdoğan made?" asked a former Erdoğan supporter.[23] The opposition's narrative that the Syrians living in Turkey were the result of Erdoğan's missteps in war-torn country was gaining traction among large segments of the country. The solution put forward by the opposition to solve the country's refugee problem was mending ties with Assad so that a negotiated settlement could take place and refugees could safely return to their country.

The opposition's mounting criticism put Erdoğan in a tight spot. His disconnected speech after the killing of the soldiers reflected his struggle to put a positive spin on a disastrous policy. But the reality is that the Syrian war, which once provided a great opportunity for Erdoğan to advance his domestic agenda, has become one of the major challenges of his two-decade rule. And nowhere is that more obvious than in Idlib.

"What will protect us against Russia?"

One of the uphill battles Erdoğan faces in Syria is managing relations with Russia. Frustration with US policy, Russia's military intervention in Syria, and his domestic alliance with the nationalists have all made cooperation with Moscow a necessity for Erdoğan. Since 2016, he has taken steps to cultivate closer ties with Putin. But Erdoğan has the weaker hand in this relationship: he needs Putin's blessing to get anything done in Syria. That is why Erdoğan blamed the Assad regime for the killing of the Turkish soldiers in Idlib. But Turkish military officials admitted that it was Russia that had launched airstrikes on the Turkish convoy. According to Turkish soldiers deployed in the area, the attack was a deliberate attempt to kill Turkish troops. Russians knew Turkish troops were there and despite several warnings from Turkish officers to their Russian counterparts, Russia targeted the area many times before the deadly airstrike.[24] To Turkish military officers on the ground, the most infuriating part of the incident was what the Russians did after the attack. They refused to allow Turkey to secure a safe passage to extract the dead and wounded, forcing Turkey to evacuate by ground. Russia's reluctance to allow Turkey to use Syrian airspace to transfer the wounded drove up the casualty count.

After the attack, as Turkey was mulling over a response to the killing, Russia announced that it had dispatched two state-of-the-art warships to the Middle East. After the pronouncement, Erdoğan appealed to the US for support. He asked the US to deploy two Patriot batteries on Turkey's southern border to help Turkey repel the Russia-backed regime forces' attack in Idlib. Pentagon officials were reluctant to support what they saw as a "reckless move."[25] They thought it would set a precedent and would not change the dynamics on the ground. A Turkish special operations veteran summed up Erdoğan's dilemma. "Everyone says the S-400s will protect us against the West but what will protect us against Russia?" he asked.[26] After years of carefully cultivating what he said was a strategic alliance with Russia to strengthen his hand in Syria, Erdoğan found himself vulnerable and alone.

The Turkish government never launched an investigation into the killing of the Turkish soldiers. Nor did it make public the jet radar records from the day of the incident. The official Turkish line was that it was the Assad regime, not Russia, that killed the Turkish soldiers. Erdoğan could not afford a confrontation with Moscow at a time when he desperately needed Putin's cooperation in Idlib. Nearly 1 million Syrians fleeing clashes were heading toward the Turkish border. Turkey's observation posts had been surrounded by regime forces. Only Putin could deliver the badly needed cease-fire. The pro-Russia clique within the Turkish military backed Erdoğan's decision to avoid confrontation with Moscow.

Putin was eager to temper tensions as well. He did not want a complete rupture in relations with Turkey. Understanding the difficult position in which Erdoğan found himself domestically after the killing of the Turkish soldiers, he allowed Erdoğan to save face.

SYRIANS MUST GO

Turkey launched a military incursion into Idlib a few days after the attack on its troops. The new operation, dubbed "Operation Spring Shield," was Turkey's fourth incursion in Syria. It lasted only a few days. Turkish jets shot down multiple regime jets and helicopters and launched an expanded campaign of drone strikes against regime targets. According to the Turkish Ministry of Defense, 3,000 regime soldiers were killed, three Syrian jets and eight helicopters were shot down, over 2,000 tanks and military vehicles were destroyed and numerous airfields, command posts and weapons production facilities were disabled.[27]

As war raged on in Idlib, thousands of Syrians living in Turkey were gathering at the Greek-Turkish border. Many of them had been bussed by the Turkish government from refugee camps to Turkey's border with Greece. After the Russian attack on Turkish troops in Idlib, Erdoğan decided to make good on a longstanding threat. He announced that his country's borders with Europe were open for millions of Syrian refugees to leave. The move was meant to ease public anxiety about the possible refugee wave from Idlib and pressure European countries to back Turkey's policy in Syria. It did not work.

After a chaotic few days that kept everyone on tenterhooks, Erdoğan went to Moscow to meet with Putin. Following more than six hours of talk, the two leaders announced that they had agreed to a ceasefire in Idlib. The three-point agreement stipulated the establishment of a 7-mile "safety corridor" along the M4 highway, which would be patrolled by Turkish and Russian forces.[28] The pro-Erdoğan circles touted the agreement as a huge success for Ankara but the opposition saw it as a humiliation. A video circulated by Russian media showed Erdoğan and the delegation accompanying him on his visit to Moscow being kept waiting by Putin. Erdoğan became tired at some point and took a seat before being ushered into the room. The video went viral and triggered an uproar in Turkey. The leader of the main opposition CHP summed up the public mood: "Russia martyred our 33 soldiers. What did you do while our soldiers were being martyred? You ran to Putin. Instead of him coming to you, you went to him. This hurts my pride. On top of that, they made you wait in front of the door."[29]

ERDOĞAN'S WAR

"We don't want our soldiers and policemen to get martyred in Syria"

Erdoğan faced criticism on his return for coming home empty-handed. Although he secured his main goal of preventing an imminent new wave of refugees, it was certain to be a temporary relief. There was no change in regime plans to retake Idlib and Russia was still bent on supporting it. This meant that sooner or later, when fighting resumed, Erdoğan would find himself in the same difficult position. And he did. Like previous ceasefires, the one agreed on in Moscow turned out to be short-lived. Fighting started again soon afterward.

The ceasefire secured in Moscow was a disappointment for another reason. It failed to meet a key Turkish demand. Erdoğan had asked the regime to withdraw to the borders set out in the Sochi agreement before Turkey would stop its offensive. The agreement did not meet that demand. On the contrary, like previous ceasefire agreements, the accord reached in Moscow consolidated the regime's military gains by allowing it to preserve the territories it had captured in the three-month offensive. While Assad came out stronger from the deal, Erdoğan was in a much weaker position. Months-long fighting had shown that the observation posts Turkey set up to project power had become a liability. In the absence of air cover, Turkish troops and observation posts were vulnerable to attack by pro-regime forces. Erdoğan's hand was weakened diplomatically as well. His calls for US support fell on deaf ears. His decision to open the gates for refugees angered Europeans. Putin, whom Erdoğan called a friend, did not hesitate to kill Turkish troops when his interests called for it and Erdoğan could do nothing other than swallow it.

Most importantly, Erdoğan continued to hemorrhage support at home. Support for him dropped by ten points even among his loyal backers.[30] His poll numbers hit an all-time low in the months following Turkey's military operation in Idlib.[31] For the first time in several years, in a poll more respondents said Erdoğan would lose than said he would win.[32] Neither the incursion nor opening the gates to refugees eased public anxiety over millions of Syrians living in the country. It is still one of Turkish voters' top concerns.

SYRIANS MUST GO

According to surveys, in addition to domestic problems, Erdoğan's military interventions in Syria, which dragged Turkey into political crises with the United States and European Union, cost support. An increasing number of people started questioning Turkey's military presence in the neighboring country. Only 30 percent of the Turkish public thought that Turkey's military presence in Idlib was a "necessity."[33] It was a dramatic drop from the public support given to Turkey's previous military incursions in Syria.

Erdoğan began losing the backing of another important constituency. He had secured the military's backing following the failed coup. But that support began to wane as the military became more and more uneasy about Erdoğan's Syria policy. Many who were fighting on the frontlines thought that Erdoğan paid little attention to the dynamics on the ground and risked the lives of Turkish soldiers.[34] His sole focus was on consolidating his rule at home. Restlessness in the military grew after the Moscow ceasefire. Shortly after Erdoğan and Putin negotiated a halt in fighting, pro-regime offensives began and Turkey found itself in the same vicious cycle of violence. Some senior military personnel were worried that by committing to eventually eliminating radical groups such as Hayat Tahrir al-Sham in Idlib, Turkey took a big risk. Others thought that relying on Russia to realize Turkey's goals in Syria was a big mistake.[35] These misgivings were thrust into the open when Turkey's top generals in charge of the country's military operations in Syria sought early retirement amidst escalating tensions in Idlib. Many thought that the generals' decision was a protest against Erdoğan's reckless policies that led to the killing of the Turkish troops.[36]

The main opposition CHP capitalized on the burgeoning discontent with Erdoğan's Syria policy. Its call for mending ties with the Assad regime to solve Turkey's refugee problem grew louder. In a surprise move, the party voted against a motion that extended the government's mandate to send troops to Syria and Iraq to carry out cross-border operations. The CHP's decision not to back the motion came after Erdoğan vowed to launch yet another military incursion into Syria to clear the Kurdish militias from the border areas. The party's opposition to the motion was a dramatic move.

It had backed previous incursions into Syria so as not to alienate its nationalist base, which viewed the military moves as necessary to curb Kurdish advances. But as Erdoğan's Syria policy became more unpopular in light of the Syrian refugees' extended presence, the party recalibrated its stance. To explain the change, the CHP leader said, "We don't want fighting in Syria… we don't want more refugees… we don't want our soldiers and policemen to get martyred in Syria."[37] Party officials said several reasons including concern over the safety of Turkish troops stationed in Syria and the damning evidence of war crimes committed by Turkey-backed Syrian rebels led to a change in the party's stance.

The CHP's nationalist ally İYİ Party voted in favor of the motion. Party officials, however, said they did so for the safety of Turkish troops and that the yes vote "should not be interpreted as a support to the government's Syria policy."[38] A long-lasting solution, they argued, could only be achieved through "dialogue with Assad."[39] Despite the different votes cast by the opposition coalition's two most important parties, the opposition is united in its criticism of Erdoğan's Syria policy.

Turkey's opposition parties are presenting an increasingly united front in other areas as well, despite their gaping political and ideological differences. They are hoping to replicate their success in local elections. That is Erdoğan's nightmare. To exploit the ideological differences in the opposition alliance, Erdoğan once again turned to Syria. He threatened to stage an operation in Kobani to clear the border of Kurdish militias. Picking Kobani as Turkey's next target in Syria made sense from Erdoğan's point of view, since the town struck a chord in the psyche of both Kurdish and Turkish nationalists. A Kurdish victory there simultaneously boosted both nationalisms. The Turkish nationalists felt threatened by the international support the Kurdish militia received during the Kobani siege. They thought the Kurds were on the verge of establishing an independent Kurdish state backed by Western support. Similar perceptions boosted nationalism among Turkey's Kurds as well. To them, the battle for Kobani marked a historic moment. Many thought that their long-held dream of statehood was finally coming true. Erdoğan used the spike in Turkish and Kurdish

SYRIANS MUST GO

nationalisms to deepen societal anxieties and recapture the parliamentary majority his party lost in the June 2015 elections. By launching an all-out war against the Kurds both at home and in Syria, he secured the backing of the Turkish nationalists. Erdoğan once again pins his hopes on the war against the Kurds. By launching a military incursion into Kobani, he is hoping to drive a wedge between the Kurds and the rest of the opposition. This strategy has worked in the past but it has run its course. Today, there is a dramatically different domestic context. Turkish nationalists are not as homogenous as they were in 2015. The Kurdish question remains a key issue to them, but it is not the only one. Economic problems, Syrian refugees, Erdoğan's authoritarianism and systemic corruption all drive their voting behavior. That is why there is growing nationalist opposition to Erdoğan. It is led by the İYİ Party, which splintered from Erdoğan's nationalist ally MHP and has become the fastest-growing party in the country. This change in the nationalist base makes it harder for Erdoğan to appeal to them solely with an anti-Kurdish agenda.

There is another factor that complicates Erdoğan's plan to launch a Syria incursion against the Kurdish militia to secure the nationalists' backing. Opposition parties finally understand that Erdoğan's Syria policies have sought to serve only one goal: advancing Erdoğan's domestic agenda. After voting against the parliamentary motion extending the government's mandate to send troops to Syria and Iraq, CHP officials underlined this point.[40] A CHP lawmaker said his party voted against the motion because they did not want to be part of Erdoğan's game of using the Syrian war to expand his power at home.[41] The party's vote marks a turning point. Erdoğan has long sought to depoliticize foreign policy. By defining it as a matter of survival for the Turkish state, he sought to shield his foreign policy moves from criticism. It worked. Opposition parties, except for the pro-Kurdish HDP, largely stood by Erdoğan's foreign policy decisions. His military incursions into Syria were endorsed by the opposition. The main opposition CHP's vote, therefore, marks a watershed moment. It paves the way for others to do the same, making it difficult for Erdoğan to instrumentalize the Syrian war to reap political benefits at home.

ERDOĞAN'S WAR

Idlib: The closing chapter of Erdoğan's war?

Erdoğan once said Syria was a domestic matter for Turkey due to the long border, and the historical and cultural ties the two countries share.[42] As the Syrian war progressed, Erdoğan's remarks became more pointed. The civil war in the neighboring country became part and parcel of Erdoğan's domestic battle against his enemies. He used the war to legitimize and implement his domestic agenda. As that agenda shifted, so did Turkey's role in Syria. A once pro-status quo power became an "advocate of democracy." Then it turned into the country fanning the flames of civil war and finally an "occupier of Arab lands." Despite the zigzags in his Syria policy, Erdoğan has always had one primary goal in the war-torn country: to consolidate his rule. His quest to remain in power came at a great cost to the people of both countries. Idlib, the last bastion in the Syrian civil war, is a testament to that. It represents everything that has gone wrong with Erdoğan's Syria policy.

Idlib is the rebels' last stronghold and the largest al-Qaeda safe haven since 9/11.[43] At the height of the civil war, rebels controlled large swathes of territory including key towns such as Aleppo. But today they are boxed in to the northwestern town of Idlib and have joined the ranks of the radicals. A majority of the mainstream opposition abandoned the fight against Assad and are now fighting Erdoğan's wars in Syria, Libya, and even in Azerbaijan. Erdoğan's actions were influential in this state of affairs. Ankara contributed to the escalation of violence and Syria's descent into civil war by backing the revolutionary fervor of the rebels early on in the conflict. It bolstered the radicals among their ranks, providing military, logistical and financial aid. After reaching an agreement with Damascus and Moscow, Ankara left the rebels high and dry. It helped the regime surround them in Idlib and recapture some of the territory controlled by rebels in their last stronghold. The revolutionaries who were once bent on bringing down Assad with Erdoğan's help are now fighting against Erdoğan's Kurdish enemies in the north or dying in Libya or Azerbaijan as mercenaries on Turkey's payroll.

Idlib is also a snapshot of how Syria transformed Turkey's foreign relations, particularly with the US and Russia. Post-uprising

Syria has become the graveyard of Turkey's strategic alliance with the US. Ankara's support to radical jihadi groups and its foot-dragging in joining the fight against ISIS dealt the first blow to the alliance. The Obama administration's decision to arm the PKK's Syrian off-shoot knocked it down. The fatal blow came when Erdoğan decided to purchase the S-400 Russian missile defense system in 2016. Since then, Erdoğan has been trying to cultivate a "strategic partnership" with Russia. From his point of view, that was a wise move. Years of Turkish efforts failed to convince Washington to pursue a more forceful policy to bring Assad down. When Washington finally decided to act, it was to arm Turkey's arch enemy. It was time for Ankara to chart an independent course. After all, it was Russia that had called the shots in Syria since 2015 when it militarily intervened in the country. Erdoğan hoped to strengthen his hand vis-à-vis Moscow and Washington by cozying up to Putin. He ended up having a weaker hand with both.

Russia's killing of dozens of Turkish soldiers in Idlib showed Erdoğan that there were limits to pivoting towards Putin, particularly in Syria. Moscow might have allowed Ankara to launch several military incursions into Syria but only because it served Russia's larger goal of securing a victory for Assad. If Ankara's actions undermine that goal, Putin will not hesitate to remind Erdoğan of his red lines, even if that means a military confrontation with Turkey. The Russian attack on Turkish troops in Idlib was the latest reminder of that. Erdoğan got the message. His reluctance to directly blame Russia for the attack and backing down on his previous demand that regime forces withdraw to the borders agreed in 2018 showed once again that in Syria, Erdoğan was at the mercy of Putin.

What makes the tension with Russia more problematic for Erdoğan is that he does not have the West on his side either. Erdoğan's years of anti-Western rhetoric and reckless foreign policy moves left a sour taste in the mouths of Western leaders. After the Russian attack on Turkish troops, Turkey turned to the West for help. Erdoğan asked the US to deploy Patriots to deter Russia but his request was turned down.

Idlib also serves as a window into how Turkey's pro-Muslim Brotherhood policy strained ties with regional countries. The

United Arab Emirates and Saudi Arabia were particularly ascerbic regarding Erdoğan's post-uprising regional policies. The Syrian war became an eye-opener for those countries. It exposed how far Erdoğan would go to advance his agenda. As a sign of this tension between Turkey and the Gulf countries, days before Erdoğan and Putin negotiated the ceasefire deal in Idlib, Mohammed bin Zayed (MBZ), the crown prince of Abu Dhabi, sent an envoy to Damascus to reach an agreement with Assad. Reportedly, MBZ agreed to pay Assad billions of dollars to reignite the offensive. After the ceasefire deal was reached, MBZ tried to convince Assad to break it.[44] By encouraging Assad to relaunch the offensive, MBZ hoped to distract Turkey from the battle for the Libyan capital Tripoli, where the two countries backed opposing sides.

Idlib sums up the humanitarian toll caused by Turkey's involvement in Syria. As the regime intensifies its attacks against rebels in the civil war's last stand, Idlib is bound to emerge as the worst humanitarian crisis of the ten-year war. There are over 3 million civilians, many of them women and children, stuck in Idlib. Hundreds of thousands of them are internally displaced people. Turkey is applauded for averting a humanitarian tragedy in Idlib by preventing an all-out regime offensive on the town, but Turkey's actions throughout the civil war have contributed to the dire conditions in which those civilians now find themselves.

Idlib serves as a synopsis of Erdoğan's missteps both in Turkey and Syria. Erdoğan's actions have taken a massive toll on the Syrian people. Turkey's military incursions have heightened ethnic tensions between Turks and Kurds, and Kurds and Arabs. The civil war Erdoğan inflamed has killed over 350,000 thousand people, displaced millions. Turkey's intervention has forced thousands of Kurds out of their homes and sown the seeds of future conflict by orchestrating demographic change and carrying out Turkification policies in northern Syria. His policies have had devastating implications for Turkey as well. Because of Erdoğan's policies, there are now well-established Salafi networks in Turkey, threatening to radicalize the traditionally moderate Turkish Islam. ISIS cells inside Turkey will remain a security threat for the foreseeable future. Turkey's costly occupation of Syrian land has taken its toll on

SYRIANS MUST GO

Turkey's struggling economy. Most importantly, Turkey's social fabric has changed forever. The presence of 4 million Syrian refugees in a country that has failed to provide equal citizenship to its largest minority, the Kurds, will continue to pose serious social, economic and political challenges to future generations.

CONCLUSION

How will history judge Erdoğan? His die-hard supporters think that he will be remembered as a hero. He is the "voice of the oppressed," and the "hope of the *ummah*." He ended the military tutelage that oppressed the pious segments of the country and restored religious values to public life. He lifted the decades-long ban on wearing the headscarf in universities, civil service jobs and government offices. Even women serving in the military may now wear headscarves with their uniforms.

The economic boom the country enjoyed under Erdoğan elevated many, including his religiously conservative supporters, from poverty into the middle class. The unprecedented upward economic mobility that the conservative segments of society enjoyed led to the formation of a smug urban middle class. This new Islamic bourgeoisie has access to a luxurious life. They live in luxury gated communities, drive luxury cars, vacation in luxury hotels catering to a pious lifestyle. Muslim fashionistas appear on the cover of high-fashion magazines and YouTube channels. For these segments of the country, Erdoğan represents freedom from the decades-long oppression they had had to endure under Turkey's radical secularism and opportunities that were not available to them before Erdoğan came to power.

Erdoğan's critics have a radically different view of him. They see him as a dictator in the making who rode the wave of democracy until he captured absolute power. Turkish democracy was far from perfect before Erdoğan but the assault on rights, liberties, rule of law and institutions has never been as grave as it has been under him. He has systematically emasculated independent media, waged a merciless campaign to silence his critics, jailed pro-Kurdish lawmakers and journalists and sacked tens of thousands of civil servants, academics, military personnel and police on dubious terrorism charges. Anyone who criticizes Erdoğan is vulnerable. Even children who mock the president on social media are investigated.

Erdoğan's secular opponents see many of his actions and rhetoric as a sign of creeping Islamization in a once resolutely secular country. Erdoğan's intention to "raise pious generations" led to a restructuring of the country's education system, which has dramatically increased the number of religious schools and the amount of compulsory religious education. State bureaucracy has been filled with members of religious orders that support Erdoğan. The extensive influence and power the Directorate for Religious Affairs, Turkey's top religious body, has acquired under Erdoğan's watch, Erdoğan's narrative that women's sole vocation should be motherhood, and his ban on alcohol sales during Covid lockdowns all feed his opponents' fear for Turkey's secular foundations.

There are staunch Islamists in the opposition ranks as well, who argue that Erdoğan gave Islam and Islamism a bad name by using religion to cover up corruption and justify authoritarianism. They argue that the government's promotion of unfettered consumerism, stripping Islam of its moral code and reducing it to shallow displays of religiosity have led to the young generation's rejection of Islam. Many leading Islamists argue that the tyranny they endured under Erdoğan is worse than the oppression they faced under the Kemalist elite. Accompanying these issues are complaints about a construction-driven crony capitalism that benefited a few companies close to Erdoğan. Erdoğan's mega infrastructure projects pay scant regard to the environment. His building spree remade Turkey's urban skylines and public infrastructure but destroyed the country's forests, beaches and green valleys to keep Erdoğan's cronies in the construction sector happy. Many Turks see the ecological catastrophe Erdoğan's policies have caused as something that will haunt future generations. Increasing repression and worsening working conditions have forced Turkey's brightest to flee the country.

CONCLUSION

Scores of academics, doctors and young people see no future in Erdoğan's new Turkey and prefer to live somewhere else, leading to the biggest brain drain in the country's history. Despite having radically different views of life under Erdoğan, supporters and opponents of Turkey's strongman agree on one thing: his Syria policy has changed the social fabric of Turkey forever. Nationalists worry about the changing ethnic make-up of the country and fear that, just like Kurds, Syrians too might demand autonomy in the not-so-distant future. Secularists are anxious about their way of life being threatened by the Syrians who they think do not conform to Turkish societal norms. Minorities such as Kurds and Alevis are upset about what they view as the many privileges Syrian refugees enjoy while they lack basic rights. Even Erdoğan's pious base turned from compassion to grievance towards the refugees as economic hardships grew. They blame the Syrians for the rising crime rate. They accuse them of driving wages down, and rents up, and of stealing jobs from locals. Indeed, millions of Syrian refugees living in Turkey may be Erdoğan's most lasting legacy. In his two decades in power, Erdoğan has done unprecedented damage to Turkey's institutions, rule of law and democratic norms. But many of them can be undone if Erdoğan is out of the picture and a popularly backed process of reforms is launched. The refugee issue, however, will continue to haunt the next generations and pose serious social, economic and political challenges in a country that has long struggled to provide equal citizenship rights to its largest minority.

What about the Syrians? How will they remember Erdoğan? It depends on whom you ask. To a Kurd in Afrin who lost everything due to Turkish occupation of their land, Erdoğan is just another cruel, Middle Eastern dictator. A Syrian who backs the Assad regime probably views him as an occupier of Arab land while others on the opposition front might see him as a hero who backed the people's revolution against a brutal dictator. An overwhelming majority of Syrian refugees are grateful that Erdoğan opened the country's doors to millions of them. But there are also those who resent the role Erdoğan played in their country's descent into civil war.[1] The short life of Alan Kurdi, the two-year-old Syrian Kurdish refugee boy who drowned attempting to reach the Greek island of Kos, summarizes that role.

The boy on the beach

On September 2, 2015, a Turkish police officer discovered the body of Alan Kurdi on a sandy beach near the Turkish resort of Bodrum. His cheek was pressed against the sand and his sneakers were still on his feet. He looked as if he were sleeping peacefully. Except the heart-wrenching story of his short life and tragic death was a stark reminder of one of the worst humanitarian crises of our time. His body had washed ashore after the overcrowded boat carrying him and his family capsized. The boat was headed towards the Greek island of Kos, where the family would attempt to enter Europe and ultimately travel to Canada, in search of a safer life. The picture of Alan's dead body sparked outrage across the world over the global handling of the migration crisis. The image of the dead toddler lying alone on a beach captured international headlines. It was shared, published and viewed millions of times. Then it was forgotten. A couple months after his party lost the 2019 municipal elections, Erdoğan held up the picture of Alan at the United Nations General Assembly summit in New York and blamed the West for the little boy's death. Erdoğan's effort to keep this image alive in order to shine a light on the plight of Syrian refugees would have been noble if his own actions had not paved the way for their misery. Alan's life and death are testament to how much Turkey's involvement in the Syrian war contributed to the tragedy of millions like him.

Alan Kurdi was born into a Syrian Kurdish family. The family lived in Damascus until the clashes started late in 2011. Until then, Damascus had been largely spared the unrest in other cities. A rocket-propelled grenade attack on the offices of the Baath Party by the Turkey-backed Free Syrian Army (FSA) in November changed that. It was the first strike at the heart of the regime's base. The rebel commanders who led the attack were part of the Free Syrian Army, whose central command was located in a camp in Turkey's southern border province of Hatay, where they had

CONCLUSION

been receiving training, weapons and logistical support from Turkey. In Rukn al-Din, the Damascus neighborhood where the Kurdi family lived, Turkey-backed rebels started recruiting young men between the ages of eighteen and forty to join the rebel groups. Abdullah, Alan's father, had a wife, Rehanna, and a baby boy, Ghalib. He did not want to take one side or the other, nor risk his life or the lives of his family, as he told his sister who lived in Canada.[2] Shortly afterwards, clashes between rebel groups and the regime forces in Abdullah's neighborhood intensified with the Kurdi family being caught in the crossfire. One morning, after a long night of constant gunfire, an explosion shook the Kurdi family's home, forcing them to leave Damascus for Kobani, where the family was originally from.[3]

Abdullah could not find work in Kobani and started commuting to Damascus. Clashes between the Syrian opposition and the regime in nearby Aleppo were beginning to escalate. The battle for Aleppo was marked by widespread violence against civilians and the targeting of schools and hospitals, both by pro-regime and rebel forces. Civilian casualties were about to reach such heights that Aleppo was going to turn into a "global byword for savagery."[4]

One day, when Abdullah was returning from Damascus to his family in Kobani, a group of rebel fighters captured him near Aleppo. "You are a Kurd and all Kurds are *kafreen* (non-believer)," yelled the long-bearded men.[5] They took Abdullah to an abandoned house and tortured him for a week. Before they let him go, they pulled out his teeth, one by one. Abdullah knew that traveling inside Syria had become too dangerous. He decided to leave his wife and son Ghalib in Kobani and find work in Turkey. He picked up whatever job he could find for only a few dollars a day. As Abdullah was struggling to make money in Turkey, his second son, Alan, was born in Kobani in June 2013. Kobani had been a safe place for Abdullah's family, but that changed shortly after Alan's birth. As Turkey-backed radical groups intensified their fighting in Aleppo and began to attack cities closer to Kobani, the Kurdi family was forced to flee again. Rehanna and the boys arrived in Turkey safely to join Abdullah, but they were soon forced to travel again. When Abdullah could not pay the rent, the family was evicted and Abdullah had no choice but to send his wife and his boys back to Kobani.[6]

Shortly after their return to Kobani, ISIS forces began to advance through the countryside and surrounded the town. As they captured hundreds of neighboring villages, they raped, mutilated and beheaded civilians. Once again, Rehanna and the boys were forced to uproot. They joined thousands of other families who fled across the border into Turkey. Many refugee families had to survive landmines planted along the escape route and battle with security forces on the Turkish side of the border. Despite US airstrikes and Kurdish resistance, ISIS appeared to be on the verge of taking the town. President Barack Obama was trying to convince Erdoğan to help save Kobani. Erdoğan refused. He did not want to help the US in the fight against ISIS and blocked Kurds on the Turkish side from entering Syria to help their brethren. The Kurdi family and thousands of others started fleeing from the impending massacre. After ISIS advanced to within a few kilometers of Kobani, Erdoğan finally opened the border. As the Kurdi family was about to begin a new life as refugees, their Kurdish brethren in Turkey were taking to the streets across the country to protest against Erdoğan's inaction.

The Kurdi family settled in İstanbul. Like most other Syrians in Turkey, they were not granted refugee status but recognized as "guests." This status makes it difficult for Syrians to work legally in the country, driving most of them into the underground economy and leaving them open to exploitation. Abdullah's sister, Tima, said that "a refugee's life was in many ways just as brutal as life in a war zone," after visiting her refugee family in Turkey.[7] Abdullah and his family became victims of the temporary status they were granted in Turkey. To sustain his family, Abdullah started working on construction sites for approximately $17 per day. Lack of employment rights and sound legal protection, the strong anti-refugee sentiment in the country and the low-paying, exploitative work made life extremely difficult for them. The arduous living conditions and impossibility of legally exiting Turkey due to their "guest" status forced Abdullah to make the decision to cross illegally into Greece. His goal was to take his family first to Europe and then on to Canada. It was not an easy decision. He had two toddlers and a wife who did not know how to swim. Every day, they would hear terrifying stories of refugees drowning while trying to cross the Mediterranean in search of a better life. Abdullah and Rehanna decided that they had no other option. With Tima's financial help, Abdullah paid thousands of dollars to smugglers to carry them across the Mediterranean.

The family made several attempts to cross the Mediterranean but were thwarted by bad weather or caught by the Turkish police. The Kurdi family made its final attempt in the early hours of September 2, 2015, from the Turkish coastal town of Bodrum, in close proximity to the Greek island of Kos. Alan, Ghalib, Rehanna and Abdullah set out on a small boat. The trip was meant to last about thirty minutes. Abdullah thought the journey would be safe, because the water was calm.[8] But the captain had overloaded the small boat with nearly twelve passengers. Within five minutes of leaving Bodrum, the boat hit choppy waters.[9] The captain panicked and swam back to the shore, leaving Abdullah in charge of the boat. The boat capsized. They were only 500 meters from the shore. "I was holding my wife's hand… but my children slipped through my hands… One by one, they all died," said Abdullah.[10] The Turkish photographer who took the picture of Alan's lifeless body said the beach was like a "children's graveyard."[11]

Erdoğan blames the West for turning the Mediterranean into a cemetery. He is not wrong. Europe's inhumane refugee policy, draconian approach to irregular migration, dismal record on racism and growing anti-Muslim sentiment all inflict horrific humanitarian suffering on refugees. But none of them has played as critical a role as Erdoğan in laying the groundwork for their suffering. Turkey was the first country to provide military support to the anti-Assad opposition. By arming both the moderate and radical jihadi factions in the opposition, Turkey accelerated the country's descent into civil war. With Turkish support, the opposition captured large swathes of territory. Then Ankara withdrew its support from the fight against Assad and paved the way for a regime takeover of opposition-held territory, leading to the internal displacement of thousands of people and great human suffering.

Turkey's military incursions sowed the seeds of further violence and worsened the situation.

When the conflict in Syria started, Erdoğan said that he would never turn a blind eye to the suffering of the Syrian people and asked Assad to step down without spilling any more blood, without causing any more injustice, for the sake of peace.[12] But his own actions have caused tremendous suffering. Baby Alan and millions of others like him who were forced to flee their homes in search of safety were not only victimized by a brutal regime in Damascus and radicals who hijacked people's struggle for a dignified life but also a neighboring autocrat's shifting strategies to consolidate power.

Syria has always served as a window into Erdoğan's game plan. From his first years in office when he was struggling against the military through his fight against the Kurds and the nationalists in the opposition, Syria has not only been a front but also a weapon in Erdoğan's war against opponents. During his initial years in power, Syria helped him build his image as a conservative democrat. After the war broke out, Syria aided his efforts to cast himself as the defender of Sunni Muslims and delegitimize the secularist opposition at home. During later years, Erdoğan used Syria to burnish his nationalist credentials and criminalize the Kurdish opposition.

A Syria at war helped Erdoğan construct his autocratic rule. It played a key role in his ambition to consolidate his alliance with the nationalists and acquire unchecked powers. It helped him legitimize the war he launched not only against the PKK but also against the legitimate Kurdish opposition at home. Other opposition parties were forced into silence as well. Framing Turkey's military presence as part of the country's war against the PKK forced opposition parties to line up behind Erdoğan's Syria policy. Those who criticized his actions in Syria were labeled terrorists, fired from their jobs and sent to jail. When Erdoğan faced trouble at the polls, Turkey's military incursions into Syria came to his rescue. They diverted public attention away from mounting economic, social and political problems and boosted Erdoğan's popularity.

While the steps Erdoğan took in Syria helped his domestic agenda, they changed the two countries forever. His actions fueled, radicalized and prolonged the civil war and caused immense human

CONCLUSION

suffering. Turkey's military presence and its experiment with institution building in the territories it controls will have a lasting impact on Syrian politics and society. Erdoğan's policies also exacerbated the polarization of Turkish society along ethnic and sectarian lines. There are well-established Salafi networks inside Turkey that will have an effect on an otherwise moderate Turkish Islam. The country will struggle either to integrate the millions of Syrian refugees or face mounting economic, political and social problems. But most importantly, the missteps Erdoğan took in Syria have revived the mutual prejudices of Turks and Arabs about each other.

Erdoğan's strategy of using war in a neighboring country to consolidate power has run its course. The Syrian war is no longer full of opportunities for him. His Syria policy has become his Achilles heel. The nationalist backlash against Syrian refugees has peaked. The number of those who think Turkey's military presence in Syria is too costly is growing by the day. Even die-hard Erdoğan supporters think that Turkey should not have become involved in its neighbor's civil war. The deepening economic crisis is likely to make Erdoğan's Syria policy one of the top campaign issues in the next elections.

The war in Syria is drawing to a close. What about Erdoğan's war? Given the mounting challenges he faces at home and declining popularity, could this be the last chapter in his two-decade struggle to keep his hands on the levers of power? Or will foreign policy come to his rescue, again? Will he find another foreign war to fuel his personal ambitions? It is difficult to tell whether all the challenges he is facing will bring Erdoğan down but one thing is certain: foreign policy will remain a key weapon in his war for survival.

NOTES

INTRODUCTION

1. Cas Mudde, *Populist Radical Right Parties in Europe* (Cambridge: Cambridge University Press, 2007).
2. Bilge Yabanci, "Populism as the Problem Child of Democracy," *Southeast European and Black Sea Studies* 16, no. 4 (2016).
3. Esen Kirdis, "The Role of Foreign Policy in Constructing the Party Identity of the Turkish Justice and Development Party," *Turkish Studies* 16, no. 2 (2015): 178.
3. Lisel Hintz, *Identity Politics Inside Out: National Identity Contestation and Foreign Policy in Turkey* (New York: Oxford University Press, 2018).
3. Lisel Hintz, *Identity Politics Inside Out: National Identity Contestation and Foreign Policy in Turkey* (New York: Oxford University Press, 2018).

1. ERDOĞAN'S STRATEGY TOWARDS HEGEMONY

1. Reuters, "Istanbul Mayor, an Islamist, Is Given 10-Month Jail Term," *New York Times*, April 22, 1998, https://www.nytimes.com/1998/04/22/world/istanbul-mayor-an-islamist-is-given-10-month-jail-term.html.
2. Halil Ibrahim Yenigun, "The New Antinomies of the Islamic Movement in Post-Gezi Turkey: Islamism vs. Muslimism," *Turkish Studies* 18, no. 2 (2017): 230.
3. Ergun Özbudun, "From Political Islam to Conservative Democracy: The Case of the Justice and Development Party in Turkey," *South European Society and Politics* 11, no. 3–4 (2009).
4. "Gündemde 'Türban' Yok," *Radikal*, November 26, 2002, http://www.radikal.com.tr/politika/gundemde-turban-yok-652521/.
5. "İşte Akp'nin Öncelikleri," *Radikal*, November 17, 2002, http://www.radikal.com.tr/ekonomi/iste-akpnin-oncelikleri-651602/.

6. Özbudun, "From Political Islam to Conservative Democracy."
7. "Party with Islamic Roots Wins Landslide Victory in Turkish Elections—2002–11–04," *VOA*, October 26, 2009, https://www.voanews.com/a/a-13-a-2002-11-04-20-party-66270217/539753.html.
8. Michael A. Reynolds, *Echoes of Empire: Turkey's Crisis of Kemalism and the Search for an Alternative Foreign Policy*, Analysis Paper Series No. 26 (Washington, DC: The Saban Center for Middle East Policy at Brookings, 2012), https://www.brookings.edu/wp-content/uploads/2016/06/25-turkey-reynolds.pdf.
9. Ümit Cizre and Menderes Çınar, "Turkey 2002: Kemalism, Islamism, and Politics in the Light of the February 28 Process," *South Atlantic Quarterly* 102, no. 2–3 (January 2003): 309–332.
10. Deborah Sontag, "The Erdogan Experiment," *The New York Times Magazine*, May 11, 2003, https://www.nytimes.com/2003/05/11/magazine/the-erdogan-experiment.html.
11. Esen Kirdiş, "Islamic Populism in Turkey," *Religions* 12, no. 9 (2021): 6.
12. Ümit Cizre, *Secular and Islamic Politics in Turkey: The Making of the Justice and Development Party* (London: Routledge, 2011), 71.
13. Omer Taspinar, *Kurdish Nationalism and Political Islam in Turkey: Kemalist Identity in Transition* (London: Routledge, 2004), 154.
14. Ibid.
15. Stephen Kinzer, "Tirade by Qaddafi Stuns Turkey's Premier," *New York Times*, October 9, 1996, https://www.nytimes.com/1996/10/09/world/tirade-by-qaddafi-stuns-turkey-s-premier.html.
16. Hakan M. Yavuz, "Turkish-Israeli Relations through the Lens of the Turkish Identity Debate," *Journal of Palestine Studies* 27, no. 1 (1997): ??
17. Celia J. Kerslake, Kerem Öktem and Philip Robins, *Turkey's Engagement with Modernity: Conflict and Change in the Twentieth Century* (New York: Palgrave Macmillan, 2014), 107.
18. M. Hakan Yavuz, "Political Islam and the Welfare (Refah) Party in Turkey," *Comparative Politics* 30, no. 1 (October 1997): 63–82.
19. Taspinar, *Kurdish Nationalism*, 157.
20. Ersin Kalaycıoğlu, *Turkish Dynamics: Bridge Across Troubled Lands* (New York: Palgrave Macmillan, 2007), 159.
21. Ihsan D. Dagi, "Transformation of Islamic Political Identity in Turkey: Rethinking the West and Westernization," *Turkish Studies* 6, no. 1 (2005): 9.
22. Ihsan D. Dagi, "Rethinking Human Rights, Democracy, and the West: Post-Islamist Intellectuals in Turkey," *Critique: Critical Middle Eastern Studies* 13, no. 2 (2004): 3.
23. Dagi, "Rethinking Human Rights," 1.
24. Mehmet Metiner, *Yemyeşil Şeriat Bembeyaz Demokrasi* (İstanbul: Doğan Kitap, 2004).
25. Ümit Cizre-Sakallıoğlu and Menderes Çınar, "Turkey 2002: Kemalism, Islamism, and Politics in the Light of the February 28 Process," *South Atlantic Quarterly* 102, no. 2–3 (January 2003).

26. Yalçın Akdoğan, *Ak Parti ve Muhafazakar Demokrasi* (Ankara: Alfa Yayınları, 2004).
27. Dagi, "Rethinking Human Rights," 5.
28. Ibid.
29. Ümit Cizre and Ali R. Usul, "The Justice and Development Party and the European Union: From Euroscepticism to Euro-Enthusiasm and Euro-Fatigue," in *Secular and Islamic Politics in Turkey: The Making of the Justice and Development Party*, ed. Ümit Cizre (London: Routledge, 2008).
30. Owen Boycott, "Islamic Party Wins in Turkey," *The Guardian*, November 7, 2002, https://www.theguardian.com/world/2002/nov/07/turkey.owenbowcott.
31. Ümit Cizre, "The Justice and Development Party and the Military: Recreating the Past after Reforming it?" in *Secular and Islamic Politics in Turkey: The Making of the Justice and Development Party*, ed. Ümit Cizre (London: Routledge, 2008), 138.
32. Özlem Denli, *Liberal Thought and Islamic Politics in Turkey: Converging Paths* (Baden: Nomos Verlagsgesellschaft, 2018), 208.
33. Cizre, "The Justice and Development Party," 140.
34. Ibid., 142.
35. "Cyprus Country Profile," *BBC News*, October 19, 2020, https://www.bbc.com/news/world-europe-17217956.
36. Andreas Theophanous, "Revisiting the Cyprus Question and the Way Forward," *Turkish Policy Quarterly*, March 14, 2017, http://turkishpolicy.com/article/841/revisiting-the-cyprus-question-and-the-way-forward.
37. Ayşe Aslihan Çelenk, "The Restructuring of Turkey's Policy Towards Cyprus: The Justice and Development Party's Struggle for Power," *Turkish Studies* 8, no. 3 (2007).
38. Cizre, "The Justice and Development Party," 142.
39. Çelenk, "The Restructuring of Turkey's Policy Towards Cyprus," 351.
40. "Atina'yı Sevindirdi," *Milliyet*, November 6, 2002, https://www.milliyet.com.tr/dunya/atina-yi-sevindirdi-5199036.
41. Cizre, "The Justice and Development Party," 143.
42. Amberin Zaman, "Turkey's Anniversary Wrapped in Bitterness over Scarves," *Los Angeles Times*, October 30, 2003, https://www.latimes.com/archives/la-xpm-2003-oct-30-fg-scarves30-story.html.
43. Metin Heper, "The Justice and Development Party Government and the Military in Turkey," *Turkish Studies* 6, no. 2 (2005): 223.
44. Gareth Jenkins, *Political Islam in Turkey: Running West, Heading East?* (New York: Palgrave Macmillan, 2016), 173.
45. Ibid., 173.
46. Alphonso Marsh, "Turkey 'May Drop Adultery Ban'," *CNN*, September 14, 2004, https://edition.cnn.com/2004/WORLD/europe/09/14/turkey.adultery/index.html.

47. "Verheugen Warns Turkey on Adultery Law," *DW*, September 10, 2004, https://www.dw.com/en/verheugen-warns-turkey-on-adultery-law/a-1324102.
48. Ümit Cizre, "Introduction: Creating Public Interest, Sensitivity and Engagement as Part of Security Sector Reform," in *Democratic Oversight and Reform of the Security Sector in Turkey: 2005/2006 Status Report*, ed. Ümit Cizre (Piscataway, NJ: Transaction Publishers, 2008), 8.
49. *Turkey Transformed: Authoritarianism and Islamization Under the AKP* (Washington DC: Bipartisan Policy Center, October 2015), https://bipartisanpolicy.org/download/?file=/wp-content/uploads/2019/03/BPC-Turkey-Transformed.pdf, 42.
50. Ibid.
51. "Şahin V. Turkey," Global Freedom of Expression, Columbia University, October 31, 2017, accessed April 23, 2022, https://globalfreedomofexpression.columbia.edu/cases/sahin-v-turkey/.
52. Marcie J. Patton, "AKP Reform Fatigue in Turkey: What Has Happened to the EU Process?," *Mediterranean Politics* 12, no. 3 (2007): 344.
53. Katinka Barysch, "Turkey and the European Union: Don't Despair," *Centre for European Reform*, November 27, 2006, https://www.cer.eu/in-the-press/turkey-and-european-union-don%E2%80%99t-despair.
54. Nicholas Watt, "Ankara Needs Cultural Revolution to Join EU, Says Chirac," *The Guardian*, October 4, 2005, https://www.theguardian.com/world/2005/oct/05/turkey.eu.
55. Patton, "AKP Reform Fatigue," 345.
56. Ibid., 340.
57. Carol Migdalovitz, *Turkey's 2007 Elections: Crisis of Identity and Power*, CRS Report for Congress (Washington, DC: Congressional Research Service, June 12, 2007), https://fas.org/sgp/crs/mideast/RL34039.pdf.
58. "Tarihi Mesaj," *Milliyet*, April 15, 2007, https://www.milliyet.com.tr/gundem/tarihi-mesaj-256855.
59. "Org. Büyükanıt basın toplantısı yaptı," *Samanyolu Haber*, April 12, 2007, http://www.samanyoluhaber.com/gundem/Org-Buyukanit-basin-toplantisi-yapti/162202/.
60. "Sezer'in konuşmasının tam metni," *Hürriyet*, April 13, 2007, https://www.hurriyet.com.tr/gundem/sezerin-konusmasinin-tam-metni-6329346.
61. Julian Borger, "Turkish PM Drops Out of Presidential Race to Placate Army," *The Guardian*, April 24, 2007, https://www.theguardian.com/world/2007/apr/25/turkey.julianborger.
62. Paul de Bendern, "One Million Turks Rally Against Government," *Reuters*, April 29, 2007, https://www.reuters.com/article/us-turkey-president/one-million-turks-rally-against-government-idUSL2910950920070429.
63. "Excerpts of Turkish Army Statement," *BBC*, April 28, 2007, http://news.bbc.co.uk/1/hi/world/europe/6602775.stm.

NOTES pp. [32–38]

64. Uyari Yıldız, "Ne şeriat, ne darbe demokratik Türkiye," *The Daily Star*, April 29, 2007, http://arsiv.sabah.com.tr/2007/04/29/haber,26BBC21FA3D442 84B09236590FBF7346.html.
65. Hasan Cemal, "Muhtira ve Seçim!," *Milliyet*, May 13, 2007, https://www.milliyet.com.tr/yazarlar/hasan-cemal/muhtira-ve-secim-199319.
66. "E-memo Night Was 'Nightmare': Çiçek," *Hurriyet Daily News*, April 28, 2012, https://www.hurriyetdailynews.com/e-memo-night-was-nightmare-cicek-19472.
67. Ibid.
68. "Gül 27 Nisan Bildirisine Karşı 'Sert Tepki Verelim' Dedi, Erdoğan, 'Askerin Tepkisini Çekeriz' Diyerek Karşı Çıktı," *T24*, May 16, 2016, https://t24.com.tr/haber/gul-27-nisan-bildirisine-karsi-sert-tepki-verelim-dedi-erdogan-askerin-tepkisini-cekeriz-diyerek-karsi-cikti,340669.
69. Aydın Gülden, "Dolmabahçe'Nin 135 Dakikası," *Hürriyet*, September 25, 2011, https://www.hurriyet.com.tr/kelebek/dolmabahcenin-135-dakikasi-18820847.
70. Some polls suggested the e-memorandum boosted AKP's support by three to five points.
71. Gareth H. Jenkins, *Between Fact and Fantasy: Turkey's Ergenekon Investigation, Silk Road Paper* (Washington, DC: Central Asia Caucasus Institute & Silk Road Studies Program, August 2009), https://www.silkroadstudies.org/resources/pdf/SilkRoadPapers/2009_08_SRP_Jenkins_Turkey-Ergenekon.pdf, 29.
72. Gareth H. Jenkins, "Illusion's End: Erdoğan and Turkey's Coming Economic Chill," *Institute for Security and Development Policy*, June 20, 2018, https://isdp.eu/publication/illusions-end-erdogan-turkeys-coming-economic-chill/.
73. Daron Acemoglu and Murat Ucer, "The Ups and Downs of Turkish Growth, 2002–2015: Political Dynamics, the European Union and the Institutional Slide" (Working Paper 21608, National Bureau of Economic Research, Cambridge, MA, October 2015).
74. Uümit Akcay, "Neoliberal Populism in Turkey and Its Crisis" (Working Paper No. 100/2018, Institute for International Political Economy Berlin, 2018).
75. Acemoglu and Ucer, "The Ups and Downs."
76. Ümit Cizre Sakallioğlu, "The Anatomy of the Turkish Military's Political Autonomy," *Comparative Politics* 29, no. 2 (January 1997): 154.
77. Jenkins, *Between Fact and Fantasy*, 41.
78. Ersel Aydinli, "Ergenekon, New Pacts, and the Decline of the Turkish 'Inner State'," *Turkish Studies* 12, no. 2 (2011): 9.
79. Jenkins, *Between Fact and Fantasy*, 10–11.
80. *Turkey Transformed*, 46–47.
81. Jenkins, *Between Fact and Fantasy*, vii.
82. *Turkey Transformed*, 47.
83. Ibid., 47.
84. Jenkins, *Between Fact and Fantasy*, 83.

85. "Ergenekon Davası: Deniz Baykal 'Avukatıyım', Tayyip Erdoğan 'Savcısıyım' Demişti," *T24*, April 21, 2016, https://t24.com.tr/haber/ergenekon-davasi-deniz-baykal-avukatiyim-tayyip-erdogan-savcisiyim-demisti,337233.
86. Jenkins, *Between Fact and Fantasy*, 82.
87. "HSYK Makes a Series of Surprising Appointments," *Daily Sabah*, March 30, 2011, https://www.dailysabah.com/turkey/2011/03/31/hsyk-makes-a-series-of-surprising-appointments.
88. Ali Bayramoğlu, "Zekeriya Öz Neden Görevden Alındı?," *Yeni Şafak*, September 4, 2019, https://www.yenisafak.com/yazarlar/alibayramoglu/zekeriya-oz-neden-gorevden-alindi-26738.
89. Ahmet Sever, *İçimde Kalmasın: Tanıklığımdır* (İstanbul: Destek Yayınları, 2018).
90. Gareth H. Jenkins, "Turkey's Constitutional Amendments: One Step Forward, Two Steps Back?," *The Turkey Analyst*, March 29, 2010, https://www.turkeyanalyst.org/publications/turkey-analyst-articles/item/206-turkeys-constitutional-amendments-one-step-forward-two-steps-back?.html.
91. "Başsavcının Elindeki Son Dosya Fethullah Gülen," *NTV*, February 16, 2010, https://www.ntv.com.tr/turkiye/bassavcinin-elindeki-son-dosya-fethullahgulen,TijexqOfdUyin2MAdAeXpw.
92. Aslı Bâli, "Courts and Constitutional Transition: Lessons from the Turkish Case," *International Journal of Constitutional Law* 11, no. 3 (January 2013): 667.
93. Bâli, "Courts and Constitutional Transition."
94. Jenkins, "Turkey's Constitutional Amendments."
95. Bâli, "Courts and Constitutional Transition."
96. Jenkins, "Turkey's Constitutional Amendments."
97. Bâli, "Courts and Constitutional Transition."
98. "2010 Referandumu: 'Evet', 'Hayır' Ve 'Boykot' Cepheleri Ne Demişti?," *T24*, April 5, 2017, https://t24.com.tr/haber/2010-referandumu-evet-hayir-ve-boykot-cepheleri-ne-demisti,397466.
99. Personal observation of the author who visited Turkey ahead of the vote.
100. "Turkish Reform Vote Gets Western Backing," *BBC News*, September 13, 2010, https://www.bbc.co.uk/news/world-europe-11279881.
101. Ibid.
102. "Turkish Interior Ministry Orders German Charity Scandal Probe," *DW*, September 20, 2008, https://www.dw.com/en/turkish-interior-ministry-orders-german-charity-scandal-probe/a-3658865.
103. "Deniz Feneri kavgası büyüyor," *DW*, September 13, 2008, https://www.dw.com/tr/deniz-feneri-kavgas%C4%B1-b%C3%BCy%C3%BCyor/a-3642996.
104. Delphine Strauss, "Dogan Hit by Record $2.5bn Tax Fine," *Financial Times*, September 8, 2009, https://www.ft.com/content/e91d2bac-9c9f-11de-ab58-00144feabdc0.
105. Jenkins, *Between Fact and Fantasy*.
106. M. K. Kaya and Svante E. Cornell, "Politics, Media and Power in Turkey," *The Turkey Analyst*, June 4, 2008, https://www.turkeyanalyst.org/publica-

tions/turkey-analyst-articles/item/126-politics-media-and-power-in-turkey.html.
107. Zia Weise, "How Did Things Get So Bad for Turkey's Journalists?," *The Atlantic*, August 23, 2018, https://www.theatlantic.com/international/archive/2018/08/destroying-free-press-erdogan-turkey/568402/.
108. Stefan Dege, "Turkey's Constitution Guarantees Press Freedom—But That's Not the Whole Story," *DW*, March 1, 2017, https://www.dw.com/en/turkeys-constitution-guarantees-press-freedom-but-thats-not-the-whole-story/a-37768976.
109. Lisel Hintz, Identity Politics Inside Out: National Identity Contestation and Foreign Policy in Turkey, (New York: Oxford University Press, 2018).
110. "2007 CHP Election Manifesto," *Cumhuriyet Halk Partisi*, https://chp.org.tr/yayin/2007-secim-bildirgesi.
111. Philip Robins, "Turkish Foreign Policy since 2002: Between a 'Post-Islamist' Government and a Kemalist State," *International Affairs (Royal Institute of International Affairs 1944–)* 83, no. 1 (March 2007): 292.
112. Patton, "AKP Reform Fatigue," 343.
113. Ahmet Davutoğlu, "The Clash of Interests: An Explanation of the World (Dis)order," *Journal of International Affairs* 2, no. 4 (1998).
114. Ahmet Davutoğlu, *Civilizational Transformation and the Muslim World* (Kuala Lumpur: Brill, 1994); Ahmet Davutoğlu, *Alternative Paradigms: The Impact of Islamic and Western Weltanschauungs on Political Theory* (New York: University Press of America, 1994).
115. Birol Başkan, "Turkey's Pan-Islamist Foreign Policy," *The Cario Review of Global Affairs*, Spring 2019, https://www.thecairoreview.com/essays/turkeys-pan-islamist-foreign-policy/.
116. Ahmet Davutoğlu, *Stratejik Derinlik: Türkiye'nin Uluslararası Konumu* (Istanbul: Küre Yayınları, 2001), 53.
117. Dietrich Jung, "Turkey and the Arab World: Historical Narratives and New Political Realities," *Mediterranean Politics* 10, no. 1 (2005): 6.
118. Ibid.
119. Meliha Altunışık, "Worldviews and Turkish Foreign Policy in the Middle East," *New Perspectives on Turkey* 40 (2009): 173.
120. Altunışık, "Worldviews and Turkish Foreign Policy," 171.
121. Orna Almog and Ayşegül Sever, "Hide and Seek? Israeli–Turkish Relations and the Baghdad Pact," *Middle Eastern Studies* 53, no. 4 (2017): 3.
122. Altunışık, "Worldviews and Turkish foreign policy," 173.
123. Clyde Haberman, "Turkey's Top Officer Quits, But Only Hints Why," *New York Times*, December 4, 1990, https://www.nytimes.com/1990/12/04/world/mideast-tensions-turkey-s-top-officer-quits-but-only-hints-why.html.
124. Cengiz Çandar, *Turkey's Mission Impossible: War and Peace with the Kurds* (Lanham, MD: Lexington Books, 2020), 97.
125. Ibid., 182.
126. Ibid.

127. Altunışık, "Worldviews and Turkish Foreign Policy."
128. Hakan Yavuz, *Nostalgia for the Empire: The Politics of Neo-Ottomanism* (Oxford: Oxford University Press, 2020), 165.
129. Behlül Özkan, "Turkey, Davutoglu, and the Idea of Pan-Islamism," *Global Politics and Strategy* 54, no. 4 (2014): 128.
130. H. Ksebalaban, *Turkish Foreign Policy: Islam, Nationalism, and Globalization* (Palgrave Macmillan, 2016), 140.
131. Ali Tekin and Aylin Güney, eds., *The Europeanization of Turkey: Polity and Politics* (New York: Routledge, 2020), 117.
132. "Kırmızı kitabın tehdit unsurları değişiyor…" *T24*, August 24, 2010, https://t24.com.tr/haber/kirmizi-kitabin-tehdit-unsurlari-degisiyor,93061.
133. "Erdogan to receive 'Gaddafi Human Rights Prize' in Libya," *The Jerusalem Post*, November 26, 2010, https://www.jpost.com/breaking-news/erdogan-to-receive-gaddafi-human-rights-prize-in-libya.
134. "Powell Calls Sudan Killings Genocide," *CNN*, September 9, 2004, https://www.cnn.com/2004/WORLD/africa/09/09/sudan.powell/.
135. Günter Seufert, *Turkey's Cyprus Policy in the Context of Nicosia's Presidency of the European Council*, SWP Comments 34 (Stiftung Wissenschaft und Politik/ German Institute for International and Security Affairs, October 2012).
136. Ibid., 5.
137. Ibid.
138. Altunışık, "Worldviews and Turkish Foreign Policy," 185.
139. Meliha Altunisik and Özlem Tür, "From Distant Neighbors to Partners? Changing Syrian–Turkish Relations," *Security Dialogue* 37, no. 2 (2006): 231.
140. Altunisik and Tür, "From Distant Neighbors," 231.
141. Ibid.
142. Christopher Phillips, "Into the Quagmire: Turkey's Frustrated Syria Policy" (Briefing Paper 2012/04, Chatham House, London, 2012): 35.
143. Behlül Özkan, "Relations Between Turkey and Syria in the 1980s and 1990s: Political Islam, Muslim Brotherhood, and Intelligence Wars," *Uluslararası İlişkiler* 16, no. 62 (2019): 16.
144. Özkan, "Relations Between Turkey and Syria," 16.
145. Hasan Kösebalaban, *Turkish Foreign Policy: Islam, Nationalism and Globalization* (New York: Palgrave MacMillan, 2011), 125.
146. Phillips, "Into the Quagmire," 3.
147. Altunışık, "Worldviews and Turkish Foreign Policy," 183.
148. Özlem Tür, "Turkish-Syrian Relations—Where Are We Going?," UNISCI Discussion Papers 23 (May 2010): 163–175.
149. Altunisik and Tür, "From Distant Neighbors," 238.
150. "Şam'a büyük jest," *Hurriyet*, June 13, 2000, https://www.hurriyet.com.tr/dunya/sam-a-buyuk-jest-39160970.
151. Tür, "Turkish-Syrian Relations," 63.
152. "The Muslim Brotherhood in Syria," *Carnegie Endowment for International Peace*,

February 1, 2012, https://carnegieendowment.org/2012/02/01/muslim-brotherhood-in-syria.
153. Oüzkan, "Relations Between Turkey and Syria," 19.
154. Ibid., 20.
155. Ibid., 11.
156. Oüzkan, "Relations Between Turkey and Syria," 13.
157. Kemal Kirişçi, "The Transformation of Turkish Foreign Policy: The Rise of the Trading State," *New Perspectives on Turkey* 40 (2009): 43.
158. Denli, *Liberal Thought and Islamic Politics*, 205.
159. Emidio Diodato, "Turkey in Progress: Foreign Policy, Geopolitics and Democracy," in *Turkey and the European Union: Facing New Challenges*, eds. Firat Cengiz and Lars Hoffman (New York: Routledge 2014), 94.
160. Kirişçi, "Trading State," 43.
161. Damla Aras, "Turkish-Syrian Relations Go Downhill: The Syrian Uprising," *Middle East Quarterly* 19, no. 2 (Spring 2012): https://www.meforum.org/3206/turkish-syrian-relations.
162. Tür, "Turkish-Syrian Relations," 139.
163. John A. Shoup, *The History of Syria* (Santa Barbara, CA: ABC-CLIO, LLC, 2018), 139.
164. Aras, "Turkish-Syrian Relations Go Downhill."
165. Ibid.
166. Frederic Wehrey, Dalia Dassa Kaye, Jessica Watkins, Jeffrey Martini and Robert A. Guffey, *The Iraq Effect: The Middle East After the Iraq War* (Santa Monica, CA: RAND Corporation, 2010), 149.
167. Tür, "Turkish-Syrian Relations," 129.
168. "ABD: Suriye'ye bastırın," *Radikal*, March 15, 2005, http://www.radikal.com.tr/yorum/abd-suriyeye-bastirin-740902/.
169. "Cumhurbaşkanı Sezer: 'Suriye'ye Gideceğim'," *VOA*, March 16, 2005, https://www.amerikaninsesi.com/a/a-17-2005-03-16-voa10879 87402/840942.html.
170. Martin Chulov, "Baghdad Car Bombs Blamed on Syria and Islamists by Iraqi Government," *The Guardian*, December 8, 2009, https://www.theguardian.com/world/2009/dec/08/bagdad-car-bombs-iraq.
171. 2010 poll conducted by University of Maryland and Zogby International, https://www.brookings.edu/wpcontent/uploads/2016/06/0805_arabic_opinion_poll_telhami.pdf.

2. ERDOĞAN TURNS TO ISLAM

1. Senem Aydın-Düzgit, "The Seesaw Friendship Between Turkey's AKP and Egypt's Muslim Brotherhood," *Carnegie Endowment for International Peace*, July 24, 2014, https://carnegieendowment.org/2014/07/24/seesaw-friendship-between-turkey-s-akp-and-egypt-s-muslim-brotherhood-pub-56243.

NOTES

2. "BAŞBAKAN RECEP TAYYİP ERDOĞAN AK PARTI 4. GENEL KONGRE 30.09.2012 FULL KAYIT 6 SAATLİK," Mersin Gündem, October 8, 2008, Youtube video, 5:50:17, https://www.youtube.com/watch?v=NyHnNqHuPLo.
3. "Başbakan'dan Türk-İslam vurgusu," Demokrat Haber, October 1, 2012, https://www.demokrathaber.org/siyaset/basbakandan-turk-islam-vurgusu-h12171.html.
4. "AKP's Proposal to Create Strong Presidential Seat," Hürriyet Daily News, November 7, 2012, https://www.hurriyetdailynews.com/akps-proposal-to-create-strong-presidential-seat-34099.
5. Ergun Özbudun, "AKP at the Crossroads: Erdoğan's Majoritarian Drift," South European Society and Politics 19, no. 2 (2014): 158.
6. "'Tek millet, tek devlet, tek din, tek bayrak'," Evrensel, May 5, 2012, https://www.evrensel.net/haber/28424/tek-millet-tek-devlet-tek-din-tek-bayrak.
7. Cenk Saraçoğlu and Özhan Demirkol, "Nationalism and Foreign Policy Discourse in Turkey Under the AKP Rule: Geography, History and National Identity," British Journal of Middle Eastern Studies 42, no. 3 (2015): 307.
8. M. Hakan Yavuz, "Understanding Turkish Secularism in the 21th Century: A Contextual Roadmap," Southeast European and Black Sea Studies 19, no. 1 (2019): 19.
9. Yavuz, "Understanding Turkish Secularism," 19.
10. Menderes Çınar, "Turkey's 'Western' or 'Muslim' Identity and the AKP's Civilizational Discourse," Turkish Studies 19, no. 2 (2018): 177.
11. Razi Canikligil, "'Dünya 5'ten büyüktür' kampanya oldu," Hürriyet, September 26, 2014, https://www.hurriyet.com.tr/dunya/dunya-5-ten-buyuktur-kampanya-oldu-27276792.
12. Özbudun, "AKP at the Crossroads," 157.
13. Sedat Ergin, "Muhteşem Yüzyıl dizisine neden kızıyor?," Hürriyet, November 30, 2012, https://www.hurriyet.com.tr/muhtesem-yuzyil-dizisine-neden-kiziyor-22044035.
14. Özbudun, "AKP at the Crossroads," 162.
15. Taylan Büyükşahin, "'Sizin inancınızı binlerce kişi aynı anda hiç yuhaladı mı?'," T24, June 18, 2012, https://t24.com.tr/haber/sizin-inancinizi-binlerce-kisi-ayni-anda-hic-yuhaladi-mi,206585.
16. Cendzi Candar, "Erdogan Takes on Central Bank, Judiciary," Al-Monitor, April 16, 2014, https://www.al-monitor.com/originals/2014/04/erdogan-faces-central-bank-judiciary.html.
17. Çınar, "Turkey's 'Western' or 'Muslim' Identity," last page on note 57.
18. William Armstrong, "The Sultan and the Sultan," History Today, November 8, 2017, https://www.historytoday.com/miscellanies/sultan-and-sultan.
19. Selim Deringil, The Well-Protected Domains: Ideology and the Legitimation of Power in the Ottoman Empire 1876–1909 (New York: I.B. Tauris, 2011), 17.
20. Ibid., 63.

NOTES

21. Yavuz, *Nostalgia for the Empire*, 152.
22. Ibid., 149.
23. Yenigun, "The New Antinomies," 242.
24. Ibid.
25. Soner Cagaptay, "Turkey Faces Its Iran 1979 Moment," *Wall Street Journal*, July 17, 2016, https://www.wsj.com/articles/turkey-faces-its-iran-1979-moment-1468797632.
26. Yavuz, "Understanding Turkish Secularism," 19.
27. Yavuz, "Understanding Turkish Secularism," 9.
28. Yavuz, "Understanding Turkish Secularism," 9.
29. Ahmet Erdi Özturk, "Turkey's Diyanet Under AKP Rule: From Protector to Imposer of State Ideology," *Southeast European and Black Sea Studies* 16, no. 4 (2016): 2.
30. Sinem Adar, "Understanding Religion in (New) Turkey," *Jadaliyya*, March 14, 2018, https://www.jadaliyya.com/Details/36307.
31. Mehmed Kırkıncı, "1980 Öncesi ve İhtilal Hatıraları," accessed 23 December 2021, http://mehmedKırkıncı.com/index.php?s=article&aid=82.
32. Oral Çalışlar, "Kenan Evren...," *Hürriyet*, May 11, 2015, https://www.hurriyet.com.tr/yazarlar/oral-calislar/kenan-evren-28969147.
33. Banu Eligür, *The Mobilization of Political Islam in Turkey* (New York: Cambridge University Press, 2010), 99.
34. Ibid., 59.
35. Ibid., 277.
36. William Armstrong, "The Mobilization of Turkish Islamism," *Hürriyet Daily News*, https://www.hurriyetdailynews.com/opinion/william-armstrong/the-mobilization-of-turkish-islamism-64129.
37. Adar, "Understanding Religion."
38. Salim Çevik, "Erdoğan's Comprehensive Religious Policy: Management of the Religious Realm in Turkey," *SWP Comment* 12 (March 2019), https://www.swp-berlin.org/10.18449/2019C12/.
39. Ahmet Topal and Sinan Uslu, "Başbakan'dan gençlere tavsiyeler," *İhlas Haber Ajansı*, December 27, 2012, https://www.iha.com.tr/haber-basbakandan-genclere-tavsiyeler-256118/.
40. Demet Lüküslü, "Creating a Pious Generation: Youth and Education Policies of the AKP in Turkey," *Southeast European and Black Sea Studies* 16, no. 4 (2016): 641.
41. Ibid., 641.
42. Ibid., 642.
43. Gonul Tol and Ayça Alemdaroğlu, "Turkey's Generation Z Turns Against Erdogan," *Foreign Policy*, July 15, 2020, https://foreignpolicy.com/2020/07/15/turkey-youth-education-erdogan/.
44. Svante E. Cornell, "Headed East: Turkey's Education System," *Turkish Policy Quarterly* 16, no. 4 (Winter 2018): 48.

45. Ibid.
46. Ibid.
47. Cornell, "Headed East," 49.
48. Tol and Alemdaroglu, "Turkey's Generation Z."
49. Ayhan Kaya, "Islamisation of Turkey Under AKP Rule: Empowering Family, Faith and Charity," *South European Society and Politics* 20, no. 1 (2015): 12.
50. "Prof. Dr. Esergül Balcı, "1 milyon öğrenci tarikatların elinde" diye konuştu," *AvruptaHaber.net*, February 25, 2018, http://www.avrupahaber.net/prof-dr-esergul-balci-1-milyon-ogrenci-tarikatlarin-elinde-diye-konustu-2210h.htm.
51. Ibid.
52. Ibid.
53. Birol Yeşilada, "The Refah Party Phenomenon in Turkey," in *Comparative Political Parties and Party Elites: Essays in Honor of Samuel J. Eldersveld*, ed. Birol Yeşilada (Ann Arbor: University of Michigan Press, 1999), 137.
54. Çevik, "Erdoğan's Comprehensive Religious Policy."
55. "Cübbeli, 'İmamoğlu'na oy vermek haramdır'," Kaç Saat Oldu, June 23, 2019, Youtube video, 1:17, https://www.youtube.com/watch?v=7kjg1SSNUNk.
56. Çevik, "Erdoğan's Comprehensive Religious Policy."
57. Hakan Yavuz, "A Framework for Understanding the Intra-Islamist Conflict Between the AK Party and the Gülen Movement," *Politics, Religion & Ideology* 19, no. 1 (2018): 19.
58. Ibid., 19.
59. Tugba Bozcaga and Fotini Christia, "The Geography of Gulenism in Turkey," *Foreign Policy*, March 18, 2019, https://foreignpolicy.com/2019/03/18/the-geography-of-gulenism-in-turkey/.
60. Elizabeth Özdalga, "Transformation of Sufi-Based Communities in Modern Turkey: The Nakşibendis, the Nurcus, and the Gülen Community," in *Turkey's Engagement with Modernity*, eds. Celia Kerslake, Kerem Öktem and Philip Robins (London: Palgrave Macmillan, 2010), 85.
61. Joshua D. Hendrick, "Media Wars and the Gulen Factor in the New Turkey," *Middle East Report* 260 (2011): https://merip.org/2011/08/media-wars-and-the-gulen-factor-in-the-new-turkey/.
62. Ibid.
63. Hakan Yavuz, "A Framework," 11.
64. Ibid., 20.
65. Bozcaga and Christia, "The Geography of Gulenism."
66. Ibid.
67. Hakan Yavuz, "A Framework," 22.
68. Killian Cogan, "Erdogan's Purges Have Replaced One Islamic Sect With Another," *Foreign Policy*, January 15, 2020, https://foreignpolicy.com/2020/01/15/erdogans-gulen-gulenist-purges-have-replaced-one-islamic-sect-with-another-menzil/.
69. Ruşen Çakır, "Ruşen Çakır ve İsmail Saymaz tartışıyor: Tüm yönleriyle tarikat

NOTES

ve cemaatler," *Medyascope*, September 15, 2020, https://medyascope.
tv/2020/09/15/rusen-cakir-ve-ismail-saymaz-tartisiyor-tum-yonleriyle-tarikat-ve-cemaatler/.
70. Çevik, "Erdoğan's Comprehensive Religious Policy."
71. "Ensar, Kızılay aracılığıyla aldığı bağışı TÜRGEV'in ABD'deki vakfına aktarmış," *Diken*, January 31, 2020, http://www.diken.com.tr/ensar-kizilay-araciligiyla-aldigi-bagisi-turgevin-abddeki-vakfina-aktarmis/.
72. Cornell, "Headed East," 53.
73. Evrin Güvendik, "Maarif Continues Legal Battle Against FETÖ Schools Abroad," *Daily Sabah*, August 17, 2019, https://www.dailysabah.com/war-on-terror/2019/08/17/maarif-continues-legal-battle-against-feto-schools-abroad.
74. Özge Zihnioğlu, "Islamic Civil Society in Turkey," *Carnegie Europe*, October 4, 2018, https://carnegieeurope.eu/2018/10/04/islamic-civil-society-in-turkey-pub-77375.
75. Kareem Shaheen and Gokce Saracoglu, "Turkish Marriage Law a Blow to Women's Rights, Say Activists," *The Guardian*, November 14, 2017, https://www.theguardian.com/world/2017/nov/14/turkish-marriage-law-a-blow-to-womens-rights-say-activists.
76. Ibid.
77. Özturk, "Turkey's Diyanet," 8.
78. Ibid.
79. "Turkey's Top Religious Body Spends 2.5 Times of What Foreign Ministry Spends," *Duvar English*, December 19, 2019, https://www.duvarenglish.com/domestic/2019/12/19/turkeys-top-religious-bodys-spending-2-5-times-of-foreign-ministrys/.
80. Nil Mutluer, "Diyanet's Role in Building the 'Yeni (New) Milli' in the AKP Era," *European Journal of Turkish Studies* 27 (2018): https://journals.openedition.org/ejts/5953.
81. Özturk, "Turkey's Diyanet," 12.
82. Şener Aktürk, "One Nation Under Allah? Islamic Multiculturalism, Muslim Nationalism and Turkey's Reforms for Kurds, Alevis and Non-Muslims," *Turkish Studies* 19, no. 4 (2018): 10.
83. M. Hakan Yavuz and Nihat Ali Özcan, "The Kurdish Question and Turkey's Justice and Development Party," *Middle East Policy Council* XIII, no. 1 (Spring 2006): https://mepc.org/journal/kurdish-question-and-turkeys-justice-and-development-party.
84. Aktürk, "One Nation Under Allah," 10.
85. Saraçoğlu and Demirkol, "Nationalism and Foreign Policy Discourse," 309.
86. Aktürk, "One Nation Under Allah," 10.
87. Aktürk, "One Nation Under Allah," 12.
88. Saraçoğlu and Demirkol, "Nationalism and Foreign Policy Discourse," 309.
89. Alexander Christie-Miller, "The PKK and the Closure of Turkey's Kurdish Opening," *Middle East Report Online*, August 4, 2010, https://merip.org/2010/08/the-pkk-and-the-closure-of-turkeys-kurdish-opening/.

90. "Peace Time?," *The Economist*, August 27, 2009, https://www.economist.com/europe/2009/08/27/peace-time.
91. Christie-Miller, "The PKK and the Closure of Turkey's Kurdish Opening."
92. Christie-Miller, "The PKK and the Closure of Turkey's Kurdish Opening."
93. Ibid.
94. Gareth H. Jenkins, "Turkey's 'Kurdish Opening' Faces New Challenges," *The Turkey Analyst*, October 26, 2009, https://www.turkeyanalyst.org/publications/turkey-analyst-articles/item/185-turkeys-kurdish-opening-faces-new-challenges.html.
95. Selçuk Şenyüz, "Erdoğan: Milliyetçilik Ayak Altında," *Hurriyet*, February 18, 2013, https://www.hurriyet.com.tr/gundem/erdogan-milliyetcilik-ayak-altinda-22621388.
96. Jenna Krajeski, "Peace Comes to Turkey," *The New Yorker*, March 24, 2013, https://www.newyorker.com/news/news-desk/peace-comes-to-turkey.
97. Selin Bölme and Müjge Küçükkeleş, "Turkey's Recent Kurdish Opening: opportunities and the Challenges Ahead," *OpenDemocracy*, April 23, 2013, https://www.opendemocracy.net/en/turkeys-recent-kurdish-opening-opportunities-and-challenges-ahead/.
98. Baskan, "Turkey's Pan-Islamist Foreign Policy."
99. "Davutoğlu'ndan 'Arap Baharı' dersi," *Hürriyet*, November 18, 2011, https://www.hurriyet.com.tr/gundem/davutoglundan-arap-bahari-dersi-1927435.
100. Michel Nawfal and Cengiz Çandar, "Turkish Foreign Minister Ahmet Davutoğlu: New Arab Legitimacy or Regional Cold War?," *Journal of Palestine* 42, no. 3 (Spring 2013): 99.
101. Ahmet Davutoglu, "Zero Problems in a New Era," *Foreign Policy*, March 21, 2013, https://foreignpolicy.com/2013/03/21/zero-problems-in-a-new-era/.
102. "'Kaybettiğimiz topraklarda buluşacağız'," *Haber Türk*, January 21, 2012, https://www.haberturk.com/gundem/haber/708252-kaybettigimiz-topraklarda-bulusacagiz.
103. Baskan, "Turkey's Pan-Islamist Foreign Policy."
104. "Dünyanın lideri," *Milli Gazete*, April 10, 2014, https://www.milligazete.com.tr/haber/898094/dunyanin-lideri.
105. Aydın-Düzgit, "The Seesaw Friendship."
106. "Islamist Leader Ghannouchi Returns to Tunisia after 22 years in Exile," *France 24*, January 30, 2011, https://www.france24.com/en/20110130-tunisia-rached-ghannouchi-islamist-leader-returns-exile-ennahda-party-london.
107. "Gül praises Ghannouchi's success," *Hürriyet Daily News*, March 10, 2012, https://www.hurriyetdailynews.com/gul-praises-ghannouchis-success-15715.
108. Monica Marks, "Tunisia's Islamists and the 'Turkish Model'," *Journal of Democracy* 28, no. 1 (January 2017): 106.
109. David D. Kirkpatrick, "Premier of Turkey Takes Role in Region," *New York*

NOTES pp. [117–127]

Times, September 12, 2011, https://www.nytimes.com/2011/09/13/world/middleeast/13egypt.html.
110. "Islamists Criticize Turkish Premier's 'Secular' Remarks," *The Wall Street Journal*, September 15, 2011, https://www.wsj.com/articles/SB10001424053111904491704576570670264116178.
111. A key AKP figure who accompanied Erdoğan on his Arab Spring tour told this to the author in January 2012.
112. Anthony Shadid, "Turkey Predicts Alliance with Egypt as Regional Anchors," *New York Times*, September 18, 2011, https://www.nytimes.com/2011/09/19/world/middleeast/turkey-predicts-partnership-with-egypt-as-regional-anchors.html.
113. Aydın-Düzgit, "The Seesaw Friendship."
114. "MİT müsteşarı Mursi'yi darbe konusunda uyarmış," *Türkiye Gazetesi*, August 23, 2013, https://www.turkiyegazetesi.com.tr/gundem/66479.aspx.
115. Ibid.
116. Marks, "Tunisia's Islamists," 107.
117. Ibid.
118. Aaron Stein, "Turkey's Proxy War in Libya," *War on the Rocks*, January 15, 2015, https://warontherocks.com/2015/01/turkeys-proxy-war-in-libya/.
119. Aydın-Düzgit, "The Seesaw Friendship."
120. "Erdoğan: Sen 'Baas'çısın Kılıçdaroğlu," *Denge*, April 25, 2012, http://www.dengegazetesi.com.tr/service/amp/Erdoğansen-baascisin-kilicdaroglu-74755h.htm.
121. Gönül Tol, "The 'Turkish Model' in the Middle East," *Middle East Institute*, December 14, 2012, https://www.mei.edu/publications/turkish-model-middle-east-0.

3. THE SYRIAN GAMBIT: ASSAD MUST GO

1. Nour Ali, "Syrian Tanks Kill Protesters in Hama," *The Guardian*, July 31, 2011, https://www.theguardian.com/world/2011/jul/31/syria-tanks-hama-assault.
2. Christopher Phillips, *The Battle for Syria: International Rivalry in the New Middle East* (New Haven, CT: Yale University Press, 2016), 49.
3. Ibid., 42.
4. Ibid., 43.
5. Ibid.
6. Nikolaos van Dam, *Destroying a Nation: The Civil War in Syria* (London: I.B. Tauris, 2017), 61.
7. Phillips, *The Battle for Syria*, 48.
8. Ibid., 47.
9. Phillips, *The Battle for Syria*, 52.
10. "Kulis: Esad reform için dört ay istemiş, Davutoğlu yumruğu masaya vurmuş,"

311

Diken, October 29, 2017, http://www.diken.com.tr/kulis-esad-reform-icin-dort-ay-istemis-Davutoğlu-yumrugu-masaya-vurmus/.
11. Recep Tayyip Erdoğan, "Tarih:15.08.2010 Yer: Gaziantep / Erdoğan: 'Kardeşim Esat'," herkesicinCHP, September 23, 2012, YouTube video, 2:10, https://www.youtube.com/watch?v=T_4im5VBc9M.
12. Zeynep Gürcanlı, "Davutoğlu: Türk diplomatlar itfaiye eri," *Hürriyet*, January 3, 2011, https://www.hurriyet.com.tr/gundem/davutoglu-turk-diplomatlar-itfaiye-eri-16669775.
13. "What Lies Beneath Ankara's New Foreign Policy," *WikiLeaks*, January 20, 2010, https://wikileaks.org/plusd/cables/10ANKARA87_a.html.
14. Phillips, *The Battle for Syria*, 35.
15. "Davutoğlu: Cumhurbaşkanı'nın tabiri beni utandırdı," *Gazete Duvar*, January 22, 2020, https://www.gazeteduvar.com.tr/politika/2020/01/22/Davutoğlu-cumhurbaskaninin-tabiri-beni-utandirdi.
16. Abdülkadir Selvi, "Esad gitmezse Suriye bölünür," *Yeni Şafak*, March 23, 2012, https://www.yenisafak.com/politika/esad-gitmezse-suriye-bolunur-374082.
17. "AKP'den Esad'la "Müslüman Kardeşler'i yönetime alın" pazarlığı," *SolTV*, September 29, 2011, https://haber.sol.org.tr/dunyadan/akpden-esadla-musluman-kardesleri-yonetime-alin-pazarligi-haberi-46878.
18. Yahya Bostan, "CIA Başkanı'ndan 'çok gizli' ziyaret," *Sabah*, April 26, 2011, https://www.sabah.com.tr/gundem/2011/04/26/cia-baskanindan-cok-gizli-ziyaret.
19. Ibid.
20. "Erdoğan: Suriye bizim iç meselemiz," *BirGün*, August 8, 2011, https://www.birgun.net/haber/Erdoğan-suriye-bizim-ic-meselemiz-59465.
21. Fehim Tastekin, *Suriya: Yikil Git, Diren Kal!* (Istanbul: Iletisim Yayinlari, 2015), 72.
22. Tastekin, *Suriya*, 85.
23. Zoom interview with Abdullah Gül, April 28, 2021.
24. "Apaydın herhangi bir kamp değil," *Cumhuriyet*, September 2, 2012, https://www.cumhuriyet.com.tr/haber/apaydin-herhangi-bir-kamp-degil-368034.
25. Ibid.
26. van Dam, *Destroying a Nation*, 87.
27. Ömer Önhon, "Büyükelçinin Gözünden Suriye" Remzi Kitabevi, 2021.
28. Martin Chulov, Ewen MacAskill, and John Densky, "Saudi Arabia Plans to Fund Syria Rebel Army," *The Guardian*, June 22, 2012, https://www.theguardian.com/world/2012/jun/22/saudi-arabia-syria-rebel-army.
29. Turkish journalist Fehim Tastekin said in a radio interview that a member of MIT who worked closely with the intelligence chief Hakan Fidan had told him personally about MIT's involvement in the arms deliveries. Kisa Dalga Podcast, "SURİYE'DE SİLAH VE TİCARET GERÇEKLERİ," 1 June, 2021, https://kisadalga.net/podcast/detay/suriye-silah-ve-ticaret-gercekleri_7433#.YLV-9XaDEFo.twitter.

30. "Syria Army Defector Hussein Harmoush in TV 'Confession'," *BBC*, September 16, 2011, https://www.bbc.com/news/world-middle-east-14945690.
31. Tastekin, *Suryiya*, 92.
32. "Eski MİT'çiye 20 yıl hapis," *Sözcü*, October 9, 2013, https://www.sozcu.com.tr/2013/gundem/eski-mitciye-20-yil-hapis-386588/.
33. Alptekin Dursunoglu, *Suriye'de Vekalet Savaşı* (Istanbul: Önsöz Yayıncılık, 2014), 866.
34. Phillips, *Destroying a Nation*, 75.
35. "800 bin Suriyeli'ye hazırız," *Habertürk*, June 11, 2011, https://www.haberturk.com/dunya/haber/638822-800-bin-suriyeliye-haziriz.
36. "Şam'da protesto," *Milliyet*, June 13, 2011, https://www.milliyet.com.tr/gundem/sam-da-protesto-1401819.
37. Ahmet Takan, "Davutoğlu masaya yumruğunu neden vurdu?," *Yeniçağ*, October 29, 2017, https://www.yenicaggazetesi.com.tr/yazi-arsivi-395434h.htm.
38. Samuel Segev, "Arabs Spurn Ottoman Overtures," *Winnipeg Free Press*, October 4, 2011, https://www.winnipegfreepress.com/opinion/analysis/arabs-spurn-ottoman-overtures-131034778.html.
39. Samia Nakhoul, "Fragmented Syria Opposition Emboldens Assad," *Reuters*, March 28, 2012, https://www.reuters.com/article/us-syria-opposition/fragmented-syria-opposition-emboldens-assad-idUSBRE82R0UT20120328.
40. Phillips, *Destroying a Nation*, 108.
41. Author's conversation with an opposition member in Gaziantep in May 2013. He was conveying to me the criticisms they were receiving from opposition on the ground.
42. Phillips, *Destroying a Nation*, 107.
43. Liz Sly, "In Syria, Defectors Form Dissident Army in Sign Uprising May be Entering New Phase," *The Washington Post*, September 25, 2011, https://www.washingtonpost.com/world/middle-east/in-syria-defectors-form-dissident-army-in-sign-uprising-may-be-entering-new-phase/2011/09/24/gIQA-Kef8wK_story.html.
44. Ibid.
45. Lisel Hintz, *Identity Politics Inside Out: National Identity Contestation and Foreign Policy in Turkey*, (New York: Oxford University Press, 2018).
46. Author's interview with a mufti in Mersin, July 22, 2013. He said he had not voted for Erdoğan before because "he was not Islamist enough" but decided to support him in 2011 because he had "gone back to his roots to serve God."
47. Chulov, MacAskill, and Densky, "Saudi Arabia Plans to Fund Syrian Rebel Army."
48. United Nations Department of Public Information, "Security Council Fails to Adopt Draft Resolution on Syria as Russian Federation, China Veto Text Supporting Arab League's Proposed Peace Plan," *United Nations*, February 4, 2012, https://www.un.org/press/en/2012/sc10536.doc.htm.
49. Ibid.

50. Reuters Staff, "Syrian Rebels Acquire Surface-to-Air Missiles: Report," *Reuters*, July 31, 2012, https://www.reuters.com/article/us-usa-syria-missiles/syrian-rebels-acquire-surface-to-air-missiles-report-idUSBRE86U1T920120731.
51. Dursunoglu, *Suriye'de Vekalet Savaşı*, 414.
52. Mark Hosenball, "Obama Authorizes Secret Support for Syrian Rebels," *Reuters*, August 1, 2012, https://www.reuters.com/article/us-usa-syria-obama-order-idUSBRE8701OK20120802.
53. Ibid.
54. Josh Rogin, "Inside the Administration's 'New' Approach on Syria," *Foreign Policy*, August 1, 2012, https://foreignpolicy.com/2012/08/01/inside-the-administrations-new-approach-on-syria/.
55. Justin Vela, "Exclusive: Arab States Arm Rebels as UN Talks of Syrian Civil War," *Independent*, June 13, 2012, https://www.independent.co.uk/news/world/middle-east/exclusive-arab-states-arm-rebels-un-talks-syrian-civil-war-7845026.html.
56. Seymour M. Hersh, "The Red Line and the Rat Line," *London Review of Books* 36, no. 8 (April 2014): https://www.lrb.co.uk/the-paper/v36/n08/seymour-m.-hersh/the-red-line-and-the-rat-line.
57. C. J. Chivers and Eric Schmitt, "Arms Airlift to Syria Rebels Expands, With Aid From C.I.A.," *New York Times*, March 24, 2013, https://www.nytimes.com/2013/03/25/world/middleeast/arms-airlift-to-syrian-rebels-expands-with-cia-aid.html.
58. Ibid.
59. "Başbakan Erdoğan'ın konuşmasının tam metni," *T24*, September 20, 2012, https://t24.com.tr/haber/basbakan-Erdoğanin-konusmasinin-tam-metni,214180.
60. Jon Hemming and Khaled Yacoub Oweis, "Syria Helicopter Flights Test Turkey's Wrath," *Reuters*, July 2, 2012, https://www.reuters.com/article/us-syria-crisis-turkey-border/syria-helicopter-flights-test-turkeys-wrath-idUSBRE86112Z20120702.
61. Ibid.
62. Karin Brulliard, "Turkey Faces Questions on Syria Policy," *The Washington Post*, September 7, 2012, https://www.washingtonpos.com/world/middle_east/turkey-faces-questions-on-syria-policy/2012/09/07/3c9ae47e-f7db-11e1-8398-0327ab83ab91_story.html.
63. Hadeel Al Shalchi, "U.S., Turkey to Study Syria No-Fly Zone," *Reuters*, August 11, 2012, https://www.reuters.com/article/us-syria-crisis/u-s-turkey-to-study-syria-no-fly-zone-idUSBRE8610SH20120811.
64. From my interview with a Turkish doctor who worked at a state hospital in Antakya. He wanted to remain anonymous due to concerns that he might lose his job for criticizing the government's Syria policy. The interview was conducted on July 23, 2013.
65. Ibid.

66. Tastekin, *Suriya*, 288.
67. Constanze Letsch, "Syrian conflict Brings Sectarian Tensions to Turkey's Tolerant Hatay Province," *The Guardian*, September 3, 2013, https://www.theguardian.com/world/2013/sep/03/syria-crisis-threatens-turkish-tolerance.
68. Peter Kenyon, "Along Syrian Border, Turks Torn By Divided Loyalties," *NPR*, March 15, 2012, https://www.npr.org/2012/03/15/148677100/along-syrian-border-turks-torn-by-divided-loyalties.
69. "3. Köprü'nün adına büyük tepki!," *Sözcü*, May 29, 2013, https://www.sozcu.com.tr/2013/gundem/3-koprunun-adina-buyuk-tepki-302933/.
70. Charles Lister, *The Syrian Jihad: Al-Qaeda, the Islamic State and the Evolution of an Insurgency* (Oxford: Oxford University Press, 2016), 88.
71. Hannah Allam, "Warnings of Jihadists among Syria's Rebels Came Early, Were Ignored," *The Charlotte Observer*, August 13, 2015, https://www.charlotteobserver.com/news/nation-world/world/article31034067.html.
72. Lister, *The Syrian Jihad*, 84.
73. Deborah Amos, "Syrian Rebels Fear Radicals May Hijack Revolt," *NPR*, September 19, 2012, https://www.npr.org/2012/09/19/161350798/syrian-rebels-fear-radicals-may-hijack-revolt.
74. "Clinton: Syria Opposition Must Beware of Efforts to 'Hijack the Revolution'," *Haaretz*, October 31, 2012, https://www.haaretz.com/clinton-calls-for-overhaul-of-syria-s-opposition-leadership-1.5195659.
75. "Premier Vows to Pray in Damascus Mosque 'Soon'," *Hürriyet*, September 6, 2012, https://www.hurriyetdailynews.com/premier-vows-to-pray-in-damascus-mosque-soon-29505.
76. "Turkish Parliament Passes Syria Cross-Border Motion," *Hürriyet*, October 4, 2012, https://www.hurriyetdailynews.com/turkish-parliament-passes-syria-cross-border-motion-31639.
77. Ibid.
78. Adam Entous and Joe Parkinson, "Turkey's Spymaster Plots Own Course on Syria," *WSJ*, October 10, 2013, https://www.wsj.com/articles/SB10001424052702303643304579107373585228330.
79. "'You Can Still See Their Blood'," Human Rights Watch, October 10, 2013, https://www.hrw.org/report/2013/10/10/you-can-still-see-their-blood/executions-indiscriminate-shootings-and-hostage#.
80. Phillips, *Destroying a Nation*, 137.
81. Zoom interview with Abdullah Gül on April 28, 2021.
82. Ruth Sherlock, "Turkey 'Aided Islamist Fighters' in Attack on Syrian Town," *The Telegraph*, April 14, 2014, https://www.telegraph.co.uk/news/worldnews/europe/turkey/10765696/Turkey-aided-Islamist-fighters-in-attack-on-Syrian-town.html.
83. Stephen Starr, "A Deeper Look at Syria-Related Jihadist Activity in Turkey," *Combatting Terrorism Center* 7, no. 8 (August 2014): https://ctc.usma.edu/a-deeper-look-at-syria-related-jihadist-activity-in-turkey/.

NOTES

84. "Ilımlı denilen muhalifler kafa kesip yürek yiyor!," *BirGün*, December 22, 2016, https://www.birgun.net/haber/ilimli-denilen-muhalifler-kafa-kesip-yurek-yiyor-140406.
85. "Timeline: the Rise, Spread, and Fall of the Islamic State," *Wilson Center*, October 28, 2019, https://www.wilsoncenter.org/article/timeline-the-rise-spread-and-fall-the-islamic-state.
86. Peter Baker et al., "Off-the-Cuff Obama Line Put U.S. in Bind on Syria," *New York Times*, May 4, 2013, https://www.nytimes.com/2013/05/05/world/middleeast/obamas-vow-on-chemical-weapons-puts-him-in-tough-spot.html.
87. Ibid.
88. Ben Rhodes, "Inside the White House During the Syrian 'Red Line' Crisis," *The Atlantic*, June 3, 2018, https://www.theatlantic.com/international/archive/2018/06/inside-the-white-house-during-the-syrian-red-line-crisis/561887/.
89. Michael Crowley, "Crisis in Syrian City Exposes Fissure in Obama's Anti-ISIS Coalition," *Time*, October 10, 2014, https://time.com/3491192/obama-isis-kobani/.
90. Helene Cooper, "Turkey is Courted by U.S. to Help Fight ISIS," *New York Times*, September 8, 2014, https://www.nytimes.com/2014/09/09/world/europe/turkey-is-courted-by-us-to-help-fight-isis.html.
91. Mark Landler, Anne Barnard, and Eric Schmitt, "Turkish Inaction on ISIS Advance Dismays the U.S.," *New York Times*, October 7, 2014, https://www.nytimes.com/2014/10/08/world/middleeast/isis-syria-coalition-strikes.html.
92. Denise Hassanzade Ajiri, "Why is the Battle for Kobane So Important?," *The Christian Science Monitor*, June 27, 2015, https://www.csmonitor.com/World/Global-News/2015/0627/Why-is-the-battle-for-Kobane-so-important.
93. J. Michael Kennedy, "Kurds Remain on the Sideline of Syria's Uprising," *New York Times*, April 17, 2012, https://www.nytimes.com/2012/04/18/world/middleeast/kurds-remain-on-sideline-in-syrias-uprising.html.
94. Cengiz Gunes and Robert Lowe, *The Impact of the Syrian War on Kurdish Politics Across the Middle East*, Research Paper (London: Chatham House, July 2015), https://syria.chathamhouse.org/assets/documents/20150723SyriaKurdsGunesLowe.pdf, 4.
95. Tastekin, *Suriya*, 85.
96. Zoom interview with Salih Muslim on April 6, 2021.
97. Cengiz Çandar, "Has Turkey Made U-Turn on Syria's Kurds?," *Al-Monitor*, July 29, 2013, https://www.al-monitor.com/originals/2013/07/turkey-changes-position-on-syrian-kurds.html#ixzz6rxhptony.
98. Zoom interview with Salih Muslim on April 6, 2021.
99. Ibid.
100. Interview with the former Obama administration official on the sidelines of a conference in California on March 8, 2018.

NOTES

101. "Kılıçdaroğlu: 'Davutoğlu belge istiyordun, al sana belge," *Cumhuriyet*, October 14, 2014, https://www.cumhuriyet.com.tr/video/video/130347/Kilicdaroglu__Davutoğlu_belge_istiyordun__al_sana_belge_.html.
102. "Kılıçdaroğlu IŞİD'e giden silahların belgesini gösterdi," *Samanyolu Haber*, October 14, 2014, http://www.samanyoluhaber.com/gundem/Kilicdaroglu-ISIDe-giden-silahlarin-belgesini-gosterdi/1064168/.
103. Tastekin, *Suriye*, 284.
104. Tastekin, *Suriye*, 286.
105. Ibid., 288.
106. "Devletin IŞİD'le teması vardı," *Cumhuriyet*, May 9, 2015, https://www.cumhuriyet.com.tr/haber/devletin-isidle-temasi-vardi-273117.
107. Ibid.
108. Author interview with the brother in 2015.
109. "İstanbul'da piknik yapıp cihat çağrısında bulundular," *CNN Turk*, Last updated December 11, 2018, https://www.cnnturk.com/video/turkiye/istanbulda-piknik-yapip-cihat-cagrisinda-bulundular.
110. Gregory Sullivan, "Operation Inherent Resolve—Summary of Work Performed by the Department of the Treasury Related to Terrorist Financing, ISIS, and Anti-Money Laundering for First Quarter Fiscal Year 2021," US Department of the Treasury, January 4, 2021, https://oig.treasury.gov/sites/oig/files/2021-01/OIG-CA-21-012.pdf.
111. David E. Sanger and Julie Hirschfeld Davis, "Struggling to Starve ISIS of Oil Revenue, U.S. Seeks Assistance From Turkey," *New York Times*, September 13, 2014, https://www.nytimes.com/2014/09/14/world/middleeast/struggling-to-starve-isis-of-oil-revenue-us-seeks-assistance-from-turkey.html.
112. Colin Kahl, "The United States and Turkey Are on a Collision Course in Syria," *Foreign Policy*, May 12, 2017, https://foreignpolicy.com/2017/05/12/the-united-states-and-turkey-are-on-a-collision-course-in-syria-trump/.
113. @Ahval_en, Twitter Post, January 22, 2019, 8:14am, https://twitter.com/ahval_en/status/1087699975927140357?s=20.
114. Brett McGurk, "Opinion. Baghdadi's Death Underscores What We've Lost by Abandoning Syria's Kurds," *The Washington Post*, October 27, 2019, https://www.washingtonpost.com/opinions/baghdadis-death-underscores-what-weve-lost-by-abandoning-syrias-kurds/2019/10/27/117c6688-f8db-11e9-8906-ab6b60de9124_story.html.
115. Ahmet S. Yayla and Colin P. Clarke, "Turkey's Double ISIS Standard," *Foreign Policy*, April 12 2018, https://foreignpolicy.com/2018/04/12/turkeys-double-isis-standard/.
116. Hakan Fidan, "Başçalanın Seçim Güdümlü Savaş Planı 1–1," secim gudumu, March 26, 2014, YouTube video, 8:56, https://www.youtube.com/watch?v=c-1GooSDwJ8.
117. "Erdoğan, Suriye'ye dair ses kaydını doğruladı," *Evrensel*, March 27, 2014,

https://www.evrensel.net/haber/81071/Erdoğan-suriyeye-dair-ses-kaydini-dogruladi.

118. Interview with General Joseph Votel, December 2, 2021.
119. Landler, Barnard, and Schmitt, "Turkish Inaction on ISIS Advance Dismays the U.S."
120. Skype interview on April 16, 2021.
121. Phone interview with Hasan Atik on October 10, 2014.
122. An off-the-record meeting held by the Middle East Institute on December 2, 2014, with a US defense official.
123. Amanda Sloat, "The U.S. Played Down Turkey's Concerns about Syrian Kurdish Forces. That Couldn't Last," *The Washington Post*, October 9, 2019, https://www.washingtonpost.com/outlook/2019/10/09/us-downplayed-turkeys-concerns-about-syrian-kurdish-fighters-that-couldnt-last/.
124. Ibid.
125. Ruby Mellen, "A Brief History of the Syrian Democratic Forces, the Kurdish-Led Alliance That Helped the U.S. Defeat the Islamic State," *The Washington Post*, October 7, 2019, https://www.washingtonpost.com/world/2019/10/07/brief-history-syrian-democratic-forces-kurdish-led-alliance-that-helped-us-defeat-islamic-state/.
126. Interview with a US intelligence official, Washington, DC, April 20, 2017.
127. "Türkiye'den Tel Abyad'a yol ve elektrik hizmeti," *Türkiye Gazetesi*, November 12, 2019, https://www.turkiyegazetesi.com.tr/dunya/662205.aspx.
128. Erk Acarer, "En büyük tehlike IŞİD," *BirGün*, June 17, 2015, https://www.birgun.net/haber/en-buyuk-tehlike-isid-82936.
129. Interview with a US intelligence official, 23 October, 2019, Washington, DC.
130. Meeting with a Turkish Ministry of Foreign Affairs official in Ankara on June 25, 2015.

4. FROM RELIGION TO NATIONALISM

1. Nikos Moudouros, "Rethinking Islamic Hegemony in Turkey through Gezi Park," *Journal of Balkan and Near Eastern Studies* 16, no. 2 (2014): 189.
2. Lisel Hintz, Identity Politics Inside Out: National Identity Contestation and Foreign Policy in Turkey, (New York: Oxford University Press, 2018).
3. Moudouros, Rethinking Islamic Hegemony, 190.
4. Ibid., 193.
5. "Gezi Park Protests: Brutal Denial of the Right to Peaceful Assembly in Turkey," Amnesty International, 2013, https://www.amnesty.org/download/Documents/12000/eur440222013en.pdf.
6. "Gezi Park Protests."
7. Pari Dukovic and Raffi Khatchadourian, "Ghosts of Gezi," *The New Yorker*, https://projects.newyorker.com/portfolio/gezi/.
8. Piotr Zalewski, "Protocols of the Interest Rate Lobby," *Foreign Policy*, June 27,

2013, https://foreignpolicy.com/2013/06/27/protocols-of-the-interest-rate-lobby/.
9. Mahmut Hamsici, "Cemil Bayık: 'Gezi'de yanlışlar yaptık'," *BBC*, August 29, 2013, https:// www.bbc.com/turkce/haberler/2013/08/130828_cemil_bayik_3_gezi_cemaat.
10. Daniel Dombay, "Turkish Protesters Call for Police Chiefs' Dismissal," *The Financial Times*, June 5, 2013, https://www.ft.com/content/11e0ec00-cdf1-11e2-8313-00144feab7de.
11. Hakki Tas, "A History of Turkey's AKP-Gülen Conflict," *Mediterranean Politics* 23, no. 3 (2018): 6.
12. Ibid., 7.
13. Tim Arango, "Turkish Leader Disowns Trials That Helped Him Tame Military," *New York Times*, February 26, 2014, https://www.nytimes.com/2014/02/27/world/europe/turkish-leader-disowns-trials-that-helped-him-tame-military.html.
14. Tas, "A History of Turkey's AKP-Gülen Conflict," 7.
15. Selahattin Demirtaş, "Selahattin Demirtaş: Seni başkan yaptırmayacağız," Al Jazeera Turk, March 17, 2015, YouTube video, 0:37, posted by Al Jazeera Turk, March 17, 2015, https://www.youtube.com/watch?v=FwKUBhyny8Y.
16. Recep Tayyip Erdoğan, "Cumhurbaşkanı Erdoğan: "Türkiye'nin Kürt Sorunu Yoktur," Haberler.com, 2015, Dailymotion video, 5:40, 2015, https://www.dailymotion.com/video/x2jrp1m.
17. Dilek Kurban, "Not a Roadmap for Peace: Erdoğan's Democratisation Package Defies Kurdish Expectations," *German Institute for International and Security Affairs*, November 2013, https://www.swp-berlin.org/fileadmin/contents/products/comments/2013C35_kun.pdf.
18. "Turkey's Election Reinvigorates Debate over Kurdish Demands," *International Crisis Group*, June 13, 2018, https://www.crisisgroup.org/europe-central-asia/western-europemediterranean/turkey/b88-turkeys-election-reinvigorates-debate-over-kurdish-demands.
19. Kurban, "Not a Roadmap for Peace."
20. "Erdoğan: 400 milletvekilini verin ve bu iş huzur içinde çözülsün," *T24*, March 7, 2015, https://t24.com.tr/haber/cumhurbaskani-Erdoğan-gaziantepte-konusuyor,289267.
21. "Erdoğan's Denial of 'Dolmabahçe Agreement' Sparks Row," *Hurriyet Daily News*, July 20, 2015, https://www.hurriyetdailynews.com/Erdoğans-denial-of-dolmabahce-agreement-sparks-row-85656.
22. Interview with Ramazan Tunc from the pro-Kurdish Kurdish Democratic Regions Party (DBP), April 25, 2015, Diyarbakır.
23. Tulay Cetingulec, "Erdogan Spins Kurdish Quran as Political Tool," *Al-Monitor*, May 8, 2015, https://www.al-monitor.com/originals/2015/05/turkey-kurds-kurdish-koran-makes-political-debut.html#ixzz6uUmJiygO.
24. "Turkey Divided and Conquered: How the AKP Regained Power," *Bipartisan*

319

Policy Center, January 2016, https://bipartisanpolicy.org/download/?file=/wp-content/uploads/2019/03/BPC-National-Security-Turkey-Divided-and-Conquered.pdf.

25. "'Yeni Türkiye, Artık Milletimizin 'Kızıl Elma'sıdır'," TCCB, May 6, 2015, https://tccb.gov.tr/haberler/410/32596/yeni-turkiye-artik-milletimizin-kizilelmasidir.html.

26. Daren Butler, "Analysis: Move to Ban Kurdish Party Shows Erdogan's March to Nationalism," Reuters, March 19, 2021, https://www.reuters.com/article/us-turkey-politics-kurds-Erdoğan/analysis-move-to-ban-kurdish-party-shows-Erdoğans-march-to-nationalism-idUSKBN2BB1CZ.

27. "Millet ve devlet için evet diyeceğiz," Milliyet, Last updated January 29, 2017, https://www.milliyet.com.tr/siyaset/millet-ve-devlet-icin-evet-diyecegiz-2386675.

28. "Perinçek Erdoğan'ın Kızıl Elma'ya dahil olduğunu ilan etti," Evrensel, November 7, 2015, https://www.evrensel.net/haber/264585/perincek-Erdoğanin-kizilelmaya-dahil-oldugunu-ilan-etti.

29. "PKK yöneticisi Karayılan: Ceylanpınar'daki iki polis resmi birimlerimizce öldürülmedi," Diken, June 8, 2015, https://www.diken.com.tr/pkk-yoneticisi-karayilan-ceylanpinardaki-iki-polis-resmi-birimlerimizce-oldurulmedi/.

30. Skype interview with Ertugrul Kurkcu, April 16, 2021.

31. "Ceylanpınar'da 2 polisin öldürülmesine ilişkin önemli iddia: Bir polis delillerle oynadıklarını itiraf etti," T24, July 20, 2020, https://t24.com.tr/haber/ceylanpinar-da-2-polisin-oldurulmesine-iliskin-onemli-iddia-bir-polis-delillerle-oynadiklarini-itiraf-etti,891773.

32. Ertugrul Kurkcu, Skype interview, April 16, 2021.

33. "Davutoğlu işaret etmişti: 7 Haziran—1 Kasım tarihleri arasında neler yaşandı?" Gazete Duvar, August 24, 2019, https://www.gazeteduvar.com.tr/gundem/2019/08/24/davutoglu-isaret-etmisti-7-haziran-1-kasim-tarihleri-arasinda-neler-yasandi.

34. Bilge Yesil, "Performing Nationalist Populism in Turkey: An Exploration of Anti-Western, Anti-Elite and Muslim Conservative Undercurrents," Celebrity Studies 11, no. 2 (2020): 10.

35. Constanze Letsch, "In Turkey, Repression of the Kurdish Language is Back, With No End in Sight," The Nation, December 21, 2017, https://www.thenation.com/article/archive/in-turkey-repression-of-the-kurdish-language-is-back-with-no-end-in-sight/.

36. Saygi Ozturk, "Andimiz' la ilgili önemli karar," Sözcü, September 21, 2018, https://www.sozcu.com.tr/2018/yazarlar/saygi-ozturk/andimizla-ilgili-onemli-karar-2640895/.

37. "Mehmet Dişli Hulusi Akar'ı yalanladı: Akın Öztürk ve Hulusi Akar'la birlikteydim," Sol, July 26, 2016, https://haber.sol.org.tr/toplum/mehmet-disli-hulusi-akari-yalanladi-akin-ozturk-ve-hulusi-akarla-birlikteydim-163520.

38. "Turkey Coup: Top Officers Given Life Terms in Mass Trial," *BBC*, April 7, 2021, https://www.bbc.com/news/world-europe-56663221.
39. Henri Barkey, "Opinion: One Year Later, the Turkish Coup Attempt Remains Shrouded in Mystery," *The Washington Post*, July 14, 2017, https://www.washingtonpost.com/news/democracy-post/wp/2017/07/14/one-year-later-the-turkish-coup-attempt-remains-shrouded-in-mystery/.
40. Gareth H. Jenkins, "Myths and Mysteries: Six Months on from Turkey's Curious Coup," *The Turkey Analyst*, January 26, 2017, https://www.turkeyanalyst.org/publications/turkey-analyst-articles/item/572-myths-and-mysteries-six-months-on-from-turkey's-curious-coup.html.
41. Ibid.
42. Author phone interview with a recently retired general, August 18, 2016.
43. Kristin Fabbe and Kimberly Guiler, "Why There Are So Many Conspiracy Theories about the Turkish Coup," *The Washington Post*, July 19, 2016, https://www.washingtonpost.com/news/monkey-cage/wp/2016/07/19/why-there-are-so-many-conspiracy-theories-about-the-turkish-coup/.
44. "Turkey's Main Opposition CHP Reiterates in Report July 15 Was 'Controlled' Coup Attempt," *Stockholm Center for Freedom*, June 12, 2017, https://stockholmcf.org/turkeys-main-opposition-chp-reiterates-in-report-july-15-was-controlled-coup-attempt/.
45. "Eski Tuğgeneral: Darbe girişimi, Genelkurmay Başkanı ile MİT Müsteşarı'nın bilgisi ve kontrolü dahilinde oldu," *T24*, May 24, 2017, https://t24.com.tr/haber/eski-tuggeneral-darbe-girisimi-genelkurmay-baskani-ile-mit-mustesarinin-bilgisi-ve-kontrolu-dahilinde-oldu,405733.
46. Leela Jacinto, "Turkey's Post-Coup Purge and Erdogan's Private Army," *Foreign Policy*, July 13, 2017, https://foreignpolicy.com/2017/07/13/turkeys-post-coup-purge-and-Erdoğans-private-army-sadat-perincek-Gülen/.
47. "A Look at Turkey's Post-Coup Crackdown," *AP News*, August 30, 2018, https://apnews.com/article/dbb5fa7d8f8c4d0d99f297601c83a164.
48. Mustafa Akyol, "'New Turkey' Finds Founding Myth in Failed Coup," *Al-Monitor*, September 22, 2016, https://www.al-monitor.com/originals/2016/09/turkey-july-15-coup-attempt-founding-myth.html#ixzz6voIIvpNFD.
49. Gonul Tol and Omer Taspinar, "Erdogan's Turn to the Kemalists," *Foreign Affairs*, October 27, 2016, https://www.foreignaffairs.com/articles/turkey/2016-10-27/Erdoğans-turn-kemalists.
50. Tim Arango and Ceylan Yeginsu, "Turks Can Agree on One Thing: U.S. Was Behind Failed Coup," *New York Times*, August 2, 2016, https://www.nytimes.com/2016/08/03/world/europe/turkey-coup-erdogan-fethullah-gulen-united-states.html.
51. Emre Ersen, "The Return of Eurasianism in Turkey: Relations with Russia and Beyond," in *Turkey's Pivot to Eurasia: Geopolitics and Foreign Policy in a Changing World Order*, eds. Emre Ersen and Seckin Kostem (New York: Routledge, 2019), 34.

5. ATTACKING KURDS TRUMPS TOPPLING ASSAD

1. Metin Gurcan, "Assessing the Post-July 15 Turkish Military," *The Washington Institute for Near East Policy*, 2019, https://www.washingtoninstitute.org/media/1147, 4.
2. Interview with a Turkish colonel who served in Syria, Washington DC, September 23, 2019.
3. Raziya Akkoc, "Turkey 'Planned Syria Operation for over 2 Years'," *Yahoo! News*, August 25, 2016, https://news.yahoo.com/turkey-planned-syria-operation-over-2-years-183841565.html.
4. "Erdogan, Merkel Say Syrian Transition Could Include Assad," *Al Arabiya News*, Last updated May 20, 2020, http://english.alarabiya.net/en/News/middle-east/2015/09/24/Merkel-says-Assad-must-be-involved-in-Syria-talks.html.
5. Yıldız Yazıcıoğlu, "Erdoğan: ' Kobani Değil Halep Stratejiktir'," *VOA*, January 6, 2015, https://www.amerikaninsesi.com/a/Erdoğan-halep-degil-kobani-stratejiktir/2587499.html.
6. Interview with an FSA commander who fought in Aleppo in 2016.
7. Cengiz Çandar, *Turkey's Mission Impossible: War and Peace with the Kurds* (Lanham, MD: Lexington Books, 2020), 198.
8. Author's phone interview, 12 February, 2017.
9. "'Land Swaps': Russian-Turkish Territorial Exchanges in Northern Syria," Center for Operational Analysis and Research, November 14, 2019, https://coar-global.org/2019/11/14/land-swaps-russian-turkish-territorial-exchanges-in-northern-syria/.
10. Robert F. Worth, "Aleppo After the Fall," *New York Times*, May 24, 2017, https://www.nytimes.com/2017/05/24/magazine/aleppo-after-the-fall.html.
11. Face-to-face meeting in Gaziantep, July 2013.
12. Michael Martin and Andrew Tabler, "Why the Fall of Aleppo Marks a Turning Point in Syria's War," *NPR*, transcript of show All Things Considered, December 17, 2016, https://www.npr.org/2016/12/17/505996757/why-the-fall-of-aleppo-marks-a-turning-point-in-syrias-war.
13. Robert Worth, "Aleppo After the Fall."
14. "'Land Swaps': Russian-Turkish Territorial Exchanges in Northern Syria."
15. Louisa Loveluck and Andrew Roth, "Cease-Fire Brokered by Russia and Turkey Begins Across Syria," *The Washington Post*, December 30, 2016, https://www.washingtonpost.com/world/cease-fire-to-begin-across-syria-starting-at-midnight-syrian-army-says/2016/12/29/91ca960c-cdbe-11e6-a747-d03044780a02_story.html.
16. "Erdoğan ve Putin ile o konuda mutabakata vardılar," *Sabah*, October 19, 2016, https://www.sabah.com.tr/gundem/2016/10/19/erdogan-ve-putin-ile-o-konuda-mutabakata-vardilar.
17. Nick Tattersall and Humeyra Pamuk, "After Aleppo, a Chapter Closes on

Turkey's Ambitions in Syria," *Reuters*, December 15, 2016, https://www.reuters.com/article/us-mideast-crisis-syria-turkey-idUSKBN14422U.
18. "'Land Swaps': Russian-Turkish Territorial Exchanges in Northern Syria."
19. Worth, "Aleppo After the Fall."
20. Tim Arango and Rick Gladstone, "Russian Ambassador to Turkey is Assassinated in Ankara," *New York Times*, December 19, 2016, https://www.nytimes.com/2016/12/19/world/europe/russia-ambassador-shot-ankara-turkey.html.
21. "Putin: Yıkıcı güçler Türk devletine derinden sızmış," *BBC*, December 23, 2016, https://www.bbc.com/turkce/38417058.
22. Fabrice Balance, "Will Astana Displace Geneva in the Syrian Peace Process?" *Washington Institute for Near East Policy*, January 20, 2017, https://www.washingtoninstitute.org/policy-analysis/will-astana-displace-geneva-syrian-peace-process.
23. Anne Barnard and Hwaida Saad, "First Day of Syria Peace Talks Quickly Descends into Quarreling," *New York Times*, February 2, 2017, https://www.nytimes.com/2017/01/23/world/middleeast/syria-astana-talks-russia-turkey.html.
24. Hamidreza Azizi, "Why Are Syrian Rebels Stepping up Efforts to Isolate Iran?," *Al-Monitor*, February 1, 2017, https://www.al-monitor.com/originals/2017/02/iran-syria-rebels-astana-meeting-alloush-saudi.html#:~:text=February%201%2C%202017%20For%20the%20first%20time%20since,and%20further%20push%20it%20toward%20a%20political%20settlement.
25. Anne Barnard and Hwaida Saad, "Iran, Russia and Turkey Agree to Enforce Syria Cease-Fire, but Don't Explain How," *New York Times*, January 24, 2017, https://www.nytimes.com/2017/01/24/world/middleeast/syria-war-iran-russia-turkey-cease-fire.html.
26. Dylan Collins, "Idlib's Rebel Split: A Crossroads for Syrian Opposition," *Al Jazeera*, February 2, 2017, https://www.aljazeera.com/features/2017/2/2/idlibs-rebel-split-a-crossroads-for-syrian-opposition.
27. Ibid.
28. Meeting with a Turkish official from the Ministry of Foreign Affairs, March 2019, Ankara.
29. Balance, "Will Astana Displace Geneva."
30. Bassem Mroue and Zeina Karam, "Russia, Iran, Turkey Sign on 'De-escalation Zones' in Syria," *AP News*, May 4, 2017, https://apnews.com/article/4f0f4b38c0374d46bdcb2184065cd0c4.
31. Balance, "Will Astana Displace Geneva."
32. Mona Alami, "Russia's Local and Regional Approach to Syria," *Carnegie Endowment for International Peace*, July 31, 2018, https://carnegieendowment.org/sada/76952.
33. Tom Perry and Suleiman Al-Khalidi, "Assad's March East Compounds West's Syria Dilemma," *Reuters*, August 17, 2017, https://www.reuters.com/article/

us-midcast-crisis-syria-analysis/assads-march-east-compounds-wests-syria-dilemma-idUSKCN1AX0H1.
34. Mara Karlin, "After 7 Years of War, Assad Has Won in Syria. What's Next for Washington?," *Brookings*, February 14, 2018, https://www.brookings.edu/blog/order-from-chaos/2018/02/13/after-7-years-of-war-assad-has-won-in-syria-whats-next-for-washington/.
35. Daniel R. DePetris, "How Bashar Al-Assad Won the War in Syria," *The National Interest*, August 24, 2017, https://nationalinterest.org/feature/how-bashar-al-assad-won-the-war-syria-22035.
36. Max Hoffman and Alan Makovsky, "Northern Syria Security Dynamics and the Refugee Crisis," *Center for American Progress*, May 26, 2021, https://www.americanprogress.org/issues/security/reports/2021/05/26/499944/northern-syria-security-dynamics-refugee-crisis/, 10.
37. Gregory Waters, "Between Ankara and Damascus: The Role of the Turkish State in North Aleppo," *Middle East Institute*, June 20, 2019, https://www.mei.edu/publications/between-ankara-and-damascus-role-turkish-state-north-aleppo.
38. Hoffman and Makovsky, "Northern Syria Security Dynamics," 29.
39. Stephanie Nebehay, "U.N. War Crimes Experts Urge Turkey to Rein in Rebels in Syria," *Reuters*, September 15, 2020, https://www.reuters.com/article/us-syria-security-un/u-n-war-crimes-experts-urge-turkey-to-rein-in-rebels-in-syria-idUSKBN2662O5.
40. Metin Gurcan, "Can Turkey Afford New Battlefront in Iraq?," *Al-Monitor*, April 4, 2017, https://www.al-monitor.com/originals/2017/04/turkey-syria-what-next-after-euphrates-shield.html.
41. Sinem Adar, "Turkish Intervention in Syria Heightens Authoritarianism in Turkey and Fragmentation in Syria," *Middle East Report Online*, July 14, 2020, https://merip.org/2020/07/turkish-intervention-in-syria-heightens-authoritarianism-in-turkey-and-fragmentation-in-syria/.
42. Recep Tayyip Erdogan, "Erdoğan: 'Afrin'i Gerçek Sahiplerine Teslim Edeceğiz'," Türkiye Gazetesi, January 21, 2018, YouTube video, 8:36, https://www.youtube.com/watch?v=m_GMBYKuFWY.
43. Associated Press, "AP Explains Turkey's 'Operation Olive Branch' in Afrin, Syria," *VOA*, January 22, 2018, https://www.voanews.com/a/ap-explains-turkeys-operation-olive-branch-afrin-syria/4219146.html#:~:text=Codenamed%20%22Operation%20Olive%20Branch%2C%22%20it%27s%20the%20latest%20chapter,a%2030-kilometer%20%2820-mile%29%20deep%20%22secure%20zone%22%20in%20Afrin.
44. Stuart Williams, "Turkey's Chase for the 'Red Apple'," *New Lines Magazine*, January 13, 2021, https://newlinesmag.com/essays/turkeys-chase-for-the-red-apple/.
45. Hoffman and Makovsky, "Northern Syria Security Dynamics," 22.
46. Dorian Jones, "Turkey Poll Shows Strong Support for Ankara's Military

NOTES

Campaign in Syria," *VOA*, February 14, 2018, https://www.voanews.com/a/turkey-polls-show-strong-support-for-ankara-military-operations-in-syria/4254881.html.

47. "MHP İl Başkanlığı, askere gitmek için askerlik şubesine dilekçe verdi," *Milli Gazete*, October 13, 2019, https://www.milligazete.com.tr/haber/3192557/mhp-il-baskanligi-askere-gitmek-icin-askerlik-subesine-dilekce-verdi.
48. "Afrin operasyonunda 3. gün: 1 asker hayatını kaybetti," *Evrensel*, Last updated January 23, 2018, https://www.evrensel.net/haber/343861/afrin-operasyonunda-3-gun-1-asker-hayatini-kaybetti.
49. Erin Cunningham, "In Turkey, Soaring Support for Syrian Offensive and Rising Anti-Americanism," *The Washington Post*, February 4, 2018, https://www.washingtonpost.com/world/middle_east/turkish-support-for-offensive-soars-standing-of-longtime-ally-america-tumbles/2018/02/03/0612e970-06a2-11e8-aa61-f3391373867e_story.html.
50. Amberin Zaman, "Suriyeli Kürt yetkililer: ABD buna nasıl seyirci kalabilir?," *Diken*, January 20, 2018, https://www.diken.com.tr/suriyeli-kurt-yetkililer-abd-buna-nasil-seyirci-kalabilir/.
51. Leonid Issaev, "Why is Russia Helping Turkey in Afrin?," *Al Jazeera*, January 29, 2018, https://www.aljazeera.com/opinions/2018/1/29/why-is-russia-helping-turkey-in-afrin.
52. Issaev, "Why is Russia helping Turkey in Afrin?"
53. "'Land Swaps': Russian-Turkish Territorial Exchanges in Northern Syria."
54. Angus McDowall and Tuvan Gumrukcu, "Turkey warns Syrian army against helping Kurdish YPG in Afrin," *Reuters*, February 19, 2018, https://www.reuters.com/article/us-mideast-crisis-syria-afrin/syrian-tv-pro-syrian-government-forces-to-enter-syrias-afrin-within-hours-idUSKCN1G30SB.
55. Reuters Staff, "Turkey-Backed Forces Pull Down Kurdish Statue in Afrin Town Center: Statement," *Reuters*, March 18, 2018, https://www.reuters.com/article/us-mideast-crisis-syria-afrin-statue-idUSKBN1GU0CU.
56. Hoffman and Makovsky, "Northern Syria Security Dynamics," 21.
57. Sirwan Kaggo, "Rights Groups: Abuses on the Rise in Syria's Afrin," *VOA*, June 1, 2019, https://www.voanews.com/a/rights-groups-abuses-on-the-rise-in-syria-s-afrin/4942242.html#:~:text=The%20Syrian%20Observatory%20for%20Human%20Rights%2C%20a%20group,taking%20control%20of%20the%20city%20in%20March%202018.
58. Bureau of Democracy, Human Rights, and Labor, "2020 Country Reports on HUman Rights Practices: Syria," *U.S. Department of State*, 2020, https://www.state.gov/reports/2020-country-reports-on-human-rights-practices/syria/.
59. Dan Wilkofsky, Amberin Zaman, and Mohammed Hardan, "Turkish-Backed Rebels Leave Trails of Abuse, Criminality in Syria's Afrin," *Al-Monitor*, July 22, 2021, https://www.al-monitor.com/originals/2021/07/turkish-backed-rebels-leave-trail-abuse-and-criminality-syrias-afrin#ixzz72qw87wlw.
60. Fehim Tastekin, "Turkey's 'Olive Branch' Takes Root in Syrian Olive Business,"

Al-Monitor, December 13, 2018, https://www.al-monitor.com/originals/2018/12/turkey-syria-making-money-from-afrin.html#ixzz72r0FxcBq.
61. Ibid.
62. Martin Chulov and Kareem Shaheen, "'Nothing is Ours Anymore': Kurds Forced Out of Afrin after Turkish assault," *The Guardian*, June 7, 2018, https://www.theguardian.com/world/2018/jun/07/too-many-strange-faces-kurds-fear-forced-demographic-shift-in-afrin.
63. "Oral Briefing by the Commission of Inquiry on Burundi, at 43rd Human Rights Council Session," *United Nations Human Rights Office of the High Commissioner*, March 9, 2020, https://www.ohchr.org/EN/HRBodies/HRC/Pages/NewsDetail.aspx?NewsID=26811&LangID=E.
64. Author's interview in Mersin, April 26, 2019.
65. İlnur Çevik, "Turkey Liberates Afrin, PKK Humiliated," *Daily Sabah*, March 19, 2018, https://www.dailysabah.com/columns/ilnur-cevik/2018/03/19/turkey-liberates-afrin-pkk-humiliated.
66. Rachel Hagan, "How Syria's Afrin Became Hell for Kurds," *Open Democracy*, November 11, 2020, https://www.opendemocracy.net/en/north-africa-west-asia/how-syrias-afrin-became-hell-for-kurds/.
67. Phone interview with a senior Turkish diplomat who was serving in a Middle Eastern country at the time of the interview, October 20, 2020.
68. Ibid.
69. Hoffman and Makovsky, "Northern Syria Security Dynamics," 39.
70. Khayrallah al-Hilu, "The Turkish Intervention in Northern Syria: One Strategy, Discrepant Policies," *European University Institute*, January 14, 2021, https://cadmus.eui.eu/bitstream/handle/1814/69657/Khayrallah%20al-Hilu%20-%20The%20Turkish%20Intervention%20in%20Northern%20Syria%20One%20Strategy%20Discrepant%20Policies.pdf?sequence=1, 6.
71. Lewis Sanders IV and Khaled Salameh, "Syrian Mercenaries Sustain Turkey's Foreign Policy," *DW Akademie*, September 30, 2020, https://www.dw.com/en/turkey-syrian-mercenaries-foreign-policy/a-55098604.
72. Interview with an FSA commander who fought in Aleppo in 2016.
73. Talk with Obama administration official who was involved in the decision-making on Syria, April 22, 2018.
74. McGurk, "Opinion: Baghdadi's Death Underscores What We've Lost."
75. Cansu Çamlıbel, "US: Relations with YPG Temporary, Transactional, Tactical," *Hürriyet Daily News*, May 19, 2017, https://www.hurriyetdailynews.com/us-relations-with-ypg-temporary-transactional-tactical-113277
76. "Ankara Bombing: Erdogan Seeks to Widen Terrorism Definition," *BBC*, March 14, 2016, https://www.bbc.com/news/world-europe-35807987.
77. Hilmi Hacaloğlu, "Erdoğan: 'ABD'nin YPG Desteği Sürerse Kendi Göbeğimizi Kendimiz Keseriz'," *Amerika'nın Sesi'nde Ayrıca*, April 30, 2017, https://www.amerikaninsesi.com/a/Erdoğan-abdnin-ypg-destegi-surerse-kendi-gobegimizi-kendimiz-keseriz/3831856.html.

78. "Erdoğan: Başkanlık sistemi gelirse terörle daha iyi mücadele edilir," *Yeniçağ*, Last updated March 8, 2017, https://www.yenicaggazetesi.com.tr/Erdoğan-baskanlik-sistemi-gelirse-terorle-daha-iyi-mucadele-edilir-158702h.htm.
79. Max Hoffman, Michael Werz, and John Halpin, "Turkey's 'New Nationalism' Amid Shifting Politics," *Center for American Progress*, February 11, 2018, https://www.americanprogress.org/issues/security/reports/2018/02/11/446164/turkeys-new-nationalism-amid-shifting-politics/.
80. Colin Kahl, "The United States and Turkey Are on a Collision Course in Syria."
81. Tom Perry and Orhan Coskun, "U.S.-led Coalition Helps to Build New Syrian Force, Angering Turkey," *Reuters*, January 14, 2018, https://www.reuters.com/article/us-mideast-crisis-syria-sdf/u-s-led-coalition-helps-to-build-new-syrian-force-angering-turkey-idUSKBN1F30OA.
82. Patrick Wintour, "Erdogan Accuses US of Planning to Form 'Terror Army' in Syria," *The Guardian*, Janaury 15, 2018, https://www.theguardian.com/world/2018/jan/15/turkey-condemns-us-plan-for-syrian-border-security-force.
83. Recep Tayyip Erdogan, "Erdogan: How Turkey Sees the Crisis With the U.S.," *New York Times*, August 10, 2018, https://www.nytimes.com/2018/08/10/opinion/turkey-erdogan-trump-crisis-sanctions.html.
84. Asli Aydintasbas, "Unhappy Anniversary: Turkey's Failed Coup and the S-400," *European Council on Foreign Relations*, July 17, 2019, https://ecfr.eu/article/commentary_unhappy_anniversary_turkeys_failed_coup_and_the_s_400/.
85. Gonul Tol, "Why is Turkey Silent on Russia's Cooperation with the Syrian Kurds?," *War on the Rocks*, December 19, 2017, https://warontherocks.com/2017/12/why-is-turkey-silent-on-russias-cooperation-with-the-syrian-kurds/.
86. Zoom interview with a Turkish diplomat, on October 6, 2020.
87. Alec Luhn and Ian Black, "Erdogan Has Apologised for Drowning of Russian Jet, Kremlin Says," *The Guardian*, June 27, 2016, https://www.theguardian.com/world/2016/jun/27/kremlin-says-erdogan-apologises-russian-jet-turkish.
88. Jim Townsend and Rachel Ellehuus, "The Tale of Turkey and the Patriots," *War on the Rocks*, July 22, 2019, https://warontherocks.com/2019/07/the-tale-of-turkey-and-the-patriots/.
89. Townsend and Ellehuus, "The Tale of Turkey and the Patriots."
90. Closed roundtable with a US military official serving in Ankara, February 26, 2021.
91. Roundtable at the Middle East Institute, August 17, 2017.
92. Gonul Tol and Omer Taspinar, "Turkey's Russian Roulette," in *The MENA Region: A Great Power Competition* (Washington, DC: The Atlantic Council, 2019), 107, https://www.atlanticcouncil.org/wp-content/uploads/2019/10/MENA-Chapter-seven.pdf/.
93. 2019 Public opinion poll by Kadir Has University in Istanbul, "2019 Turk Dis

6. ERDOĞAN'S NATIONALIST GAMBLE BACKFIRES

1. Kaya Genc, "Why Turkey's Election Results Test Erdogan's Grip on Power," *The New Yorker*, April 2, 2019, https://www.newyorker.com/news/newsdesk/why-turkeys-elections-results-test-erdogans-grip-on-power.
2. "New Zealand to 'Confront' Erdogan over Christchurch Mosque Shooting Remarks," *DW Akademie*, March 20, 2019, https://www.dw.com/en/new-zealand-to-confront-Erdoğan-over-christchurch-mosque-shooting-remarks/a-47984309.
3. Erkan Arikan, "Opinion: The Beginning of the End for the Erdogan Era," *DW Akademie*, April 1, 2019, https://www.dw.com/en/opinion-the-beginning-of-the-end-for-the-Erdoğan-era/a-48150157.
4. Jasper Mortimer, "AKP Vote Share Has Fallen More Than Election Results Show," *Al-Monitor*, June 12, 2019, https://www.al-monitor.com/originals/2019/06/akp-turkey-vote-share-election-instanbul.html.
5. Kareem Fahim, "As Turkey's Economy Struggles, Erdogan Goes It Alone," *The Washington Post*, January 21, 2022, https://www.washingtonpost.com/world/2022/01/21/erdogan-turkey-economy-inflation/.
6. Ayla Ganioglu, "Economic Woes Set to Seal Fate of Turkey's Local Polls," *Al-Monitor*, January 28, 2019, https://www.al-monitor.com/originals/2019/01/turkey-economic-woes-set-to-seal-fate-of-local-elections.html.
7. Gonul Tol, "Erdogan's Achilles Heel," *The Cairo Review*, Summer 2018, https://www.thecairoreview.com/essays/erdogans-achilles-heel/.
8. Tol, "Erdogan's Achilles Heel."
9. Ibid.
10. Selim Sazak, "Turkey Can't Host Syrian Refugees Forever," *Foreign Policy*, August 27, 2019, https://foreignpolicy.com/2019/08/27/turkey-cant-host-syrian-refugees-forever-Erdoğan-assad-idlib-hdp-chp-İmamoğlu/.
11. "KONDA: 'Suriyelilerle aynı şehirde yaşamam' diyenlerin oranı yüzde 28'den yüzde 60'a yükseldi," *Independent Türkçe*, July 29, 2019, https://www.indyturk.com/node/56091/haber/konda-suriyelilerle-aynı-şehirde-yaşamam-diyenlerin-oranı-yüzde-28den-yüzde-60a.
12. Alan Makovsky, "Turkey's Refugee Dilemma," *Center for American Progress*, March 13, 2019, https://www.americanprogress.org/issues/security/reports/2019/03/13/467183/turkeys-refugee-dilemma/#fn-467183–139.
13. Interview with the author, Mersin, July 20, 2019.
14. Selim Sazak, "Turkey's Refugee Problem is Reaching a Breaking Point," *Foreign Policy*, September 8, 2021, https://foreignpolicy.com/2021/09/08/turkey-refugee-Erdoğan-akp-crisis-chp-syria-afghanistan/.

15. Meeting with MHP supporters in Mersin, July 28, 2021.
16. "Turkey to Reduce Election Threshold from 10 to 7 Percent," *Bianet*, September 1, 2021, https://bianet.org/english/politics/249626-turkey-to-reduce-election-threshold-from-10-to-7-percent.
17. Baris Pehlivan, "Devlette yeni döneme hazırlık," *Cumhuriyet*, September 7, 2021, https://www.cumhuriyet.com.tr/yazarlar/baris-pehlivan/devlette-yeni-doneme-hazirlik-1866700.
18. "'Davutoğlu'nun manifestosu, ıslahat için referans bir metin'," *T24*, April 25, 2019, https://t24.com.tr/haber/Davutoğlu-nun-manifestosu-islahat-icin-referans-metin,818232.
19. Fatih Karagulle, "Yeni Şafak, Kemal Öztürk'ün yazısını yayımlamadı," *T24*, May 8, 2019, https://t24.com.tr/haber/yeni-safak-kemal-ozturk-un-yazisini-yayimlamadi,820283.
20. Phone interview with Cihangir Islam, October 27, 2020.
21. Phone interview with a member of parliament from the AKP, August 23, 2019.
22. Max Hoffman, "Turkey's President Erdogan Is Losing Ground at Home," *Center for American Progress*, August 24, 2020, https://www.americanprogress.org/issues/security/reports/2020/08/24/489727/turkeys-president-Erdoğan-losing-ground-home/.
23. Ibid.
24. "AKP'li eski vekil Ihsan Arslan: 15 Temmuz kimyamızı bozdu, FETÖ'nün taktiklerini kullandık," *Sözcü*, November 17, 2020, https://www.sozcu.com.tr/2020/gundem/akpli-eski-vekil-ihsan-arslan-15-temmuz-kimyamizi-bozdu-fetonun-taktiklerini-kullandik-6129518/,
25. Gonul Tol and Ayca Alemdaroglu, "Turkey's Generation Z Turns Against Erdogan," *Foreign Policy*, July 15, 2020, https://foreignpolicy.com/2020/07/15/turkey-youth-education-Erdoğan/.
26. Tol and Alemdaroglu, "Turkey's Generation Z Turns Against Erdogan."
27. Hakki Ozdal, "'Çatışma'nın alternatif bir yüzü: TÜSİAD ve MHP," *Gazete Duvar.*, June 27, 2021, https://www.gazeteduvar.com.tr/catismanin-alternatif-bir-yuzu-TÜSİAD ve mhp-makale-1526777.
28. Metin Gurcan, "Top Generals Step Down in Ominous Sign for Turkish Military in Syria," *Al-Monitor*, September 29, 2021, https://www.al-monitor.com/originals/2021/09/top-generals-step-down-ominous-sign-turkish-military-syria.
29. Fehim Tastekin, "Turkish Mobster's Revelations Extend to Arms Shipments to Syria," *Al-Monitor*, June 2, 2021, https://www.al-monitor.com/originals/2021/06/turkish-mobsters-revelations-extend-arms-shipments-syria#ixzz789tOKyre.
30. Orhan Coskun and Birsen Altayli, "With Poll Support Dropping, Erdogan's Party Looks to Change Turkish Election Law: Officials," *Reuters*, March 2, 2021, https://www.reuters.com/article/us-turkey-politics/with-poll-support-dropping-Erdoğans-party-looks-to-change-turkish-relection-law-officials-idUSKCN2AU1V4.

31. Interview with an AKP official in Brussels, October 9, 2019.
32. Interview with an AKP official in Brussels, October 9, 2019.
33. "Metropoll Araştırma: Başkanlık sistemine destek yüzde 34'e düştü," *Politikyol*, January 25, 2021, https://www.politikyol.com/metropoll-arastirma-baskanlik-sistemine-destek-yuzde-34e-dustu/.
34. Sazak, "Turkey's Refugee Problem Is Reaching a Breaking Point."

7. SYRIANS MUST GO

1. "Statement from the Press Secretary," *White House Archives*, October 6, 2019, https://trumpwhitehouse.archives.gov/briefings-statements/statement-press-secretary-85/.
2. Saphora Smith, "Turkey Launches Military Operation in Northeast Syria after U.S. Withdraws," *NBC News*, October 9, 2019, https://www.nbcnews.com/news/world/turkey-launches-operation-syria-3-days-after-trump-announces-u-n1063576.
3. "Syria: Damning Evidence of War Crimes and Other Violations by Turkish Forces and Their Allies," Amnesty International, October 18, 2019, https://www.amnesty.org/en/latest/press-release/2019/10/syria-damning-evidence-of-war-crimes-and-other-violations-by-turkish-forces-and-their-allies/.
4. Ibid.
5. "Read the Memo by a U.S. Diplomat Criticizing Trump Policy on Syria and Turkey," *New York Times*, November 7, 2019, https://www.nytimes.com/2019/11/07/us/politics/memo-syria-trump-turkey.html.
6. Ibid.
7. "Public support for Turkey's Syria offensive at 79 percent: Poll," *Duvar English*, November 18, 2019, https://www.duvarenglish.com/politics/2019/11/18/public-support-for-turkeys-syria-offensive-at-79-percent-poll.
8. Ali Kucukgocmen, Tuvan Gumrukcu, and Orhan Coskun, "Turkey's Syria Operation Reveals Cracks among Erdogan's Political Foes," *Reuters*, November 13, 2019, https://www.reuters.com/article/us-turkey-politics-syria/turkeys-syria-operation-reveals-cracks-among-Erdoğans-political-foes-idUSKBN1XN0E4.
9. Asli Aydintasbas, "A New Gaza: Turkey's Border Policy in Northern Syria," *European Council on Foreign Relations*, May 28, 2020, https://ecfr.eu/publication/a_new_gaza_turkeys_border_policy_in_northern_syria/.
10. UNHCR Operational Data Portal, https://data2.unhcr.org/en/situations/syria_durable_solutions.
11. "Turkey's Military Operation Has Displaced Thousands of Civilians, Worsened Syria's Dire Humanitarian Crisis, Top Official Warns Security Council," United Nations, https://www.un.org/press/en/2019/sc13994.doc.htm.
12. "2020 Country Reports on Human Rights Practices: Syria."
13. "Syria: Civilians Abused in 'Safe Zones'," *Human Rights Watch*, November 27,

2019, https://www.hrw.org/news/2019/11/27/syria-civilians-abused-safe-zones.

14. "Syria: Violations and Abuses Rife in Areas under Turkish-Affiliated Armed Groups—Bachelet," *UN Office of the High Commissioner for Human Rights*, September 18, 2020, https://www.ecoi.net/en/document/2037973.html.

15. "Lead Inspector General for Operation Inherent Resolve | Quarterly Report to the United States Congress | July 1, 2020—September 30, 2020," *Department of Defense Office of Inspector General*, Publicly released November 3, 2020, https://www.dodig.mil/reports.html/Article/2402679/lead-inspector-general-for-operation-inherent-resolve-i-quarterly-report-to-the/.

16. Zulfiqar Ali, "Syria: Who's in Control of Idlib?" *BBC*, February 18, 2020, https://www.bbc.com/news/world-45401474#:~:text=A%20major%20concern%20now%20is%20for%20the%20civilians,from%20other%20areas%20previously%20held%20by%20opposition%20forces.

17. "Erdoğan'dan İdlib mesajı: Gerekirse ölmeyi göze aldık, varsa aynı fedakarlığı göze alan hodri meydan diyoruz," *Independent Türkçe*, February 15, 2020, https://www.indyturk.com/node/132986/haber/erdoğandan-idlib-mesajı-gerekirse-ölmeyi-göze-aldık-varsa-aynı-fedakarlığı-göze.

18. Charles Lister, "Turkey's Idlib Incursion and the HTS Question: Understanding the Long Game in Syria," *War on the Rocks*, October 31, 2017, https://warontherocks.com/2017/10/turkeys-idlib-incursion-and-the-hts-question-understanding-the-long-game-in-syria/.

19. "İdlib'de büyük savaş artık kaçınılmaz mı?" *DW Akademie*, February 25, 2020, https://www.dw.com/tr/idlibde-büyük-savaş-artık-kaçınılmaz-mı/a-52531673.

20. Author's interview with a Turkish diplomat, Brussels, October 11, 2019.

21. "Silencing the Guns in Syria's Idlib," *International Crisis Group*, May 14, 2020, https://www.crisisgroup.org/middle-east-north-africa/eastern-mediterranean/syria/213-silencing-guns-syrias-idlib.

22. Kemal Kılıçdaroğlu, "CHP lideri Kılıçdaroğlu'ndan İdlib şehitleriyle ilgili açıklama," CNN Türk, February 29, 2020, YouTube video, 3:33, https://www.youtube.com/watch?v=PICiwxmzjh8.

23. Interview with Cemal Unlu, sixty-one-year-old hardware store owner in Hatay, August 1, 2021.

24. Levent Kemal, "Turkey Blamed syria for a Deadly Air Strike. Its Troops Blame Russia," *Middle East Eye*, Last updated December 2021, https://www.middleeasteye.net/big-story/turkey-syria-russia-troops-blamed-air-strike.

25. Lara Seligman and Nahal Toosi, "Pentagon, State Department Envoy Clash over Sending Patriot Missiles to Turkey," *Politico*, February 28, 2020, https://www.politico.com/news/2020/02/28/turkey-patriot-missiles-pentagon-118256.

26. Kemal, "Turkey Blamed Syria for a Deadly Air Strike."

27. Merve Aydogan, "Turkey Neutralizes 3,000+ Regime Elements in Idlib, Syria,"

NOTES

AA, March 4, 2020, https://www.aa.com.tr/en/middle-east/turkey-neutralizes-3-000-regime-elements-in-idlib-syria/1754130.

28. Andrew Roth, "Russia and Turkey Agree Ceasefire in Syria's Idlib Province," *The Guardian*, March 5, 2020, https://www.theguardian.com/world/2020/mar/05/russia-and-turkey-Agree-ceasefire-in-syrias-idlib-province.
29. "Kılıçdaroğlu'ndan Erdoğan'a: Komando marşı söyleyen TÜGVA'cıları gönder Suriye'ye, oradaki komutanı da Bilal Erdoğan olsun!," *T24*, October 26, 2021, https://t24.com.tr/haber/kilicdaroglu-herkes-turkiye-nereye-dogru-savruluyor-diye-endise-icinde,988519.
30. Max Hoffman, "Turkey's President Erdoğan Is Losing Ground at Home," *Center for American Progress*, August 24, 2020, https://www.americanprogress.org/article/turkeys-president-erdogan-losing-ground-home/.
31. Kerim Karakaya and Cagan Koc, "Erdogan's Poll Rating Hits All-Time Low as Economic Woes Grow," *Bloomberg*, May 24, 2021, https://www.bloomberg.com/news/articles/2021-05-25/erdogan-s-poll-rating-hits-all-time-low-as-economic-woes-grow.
32. Tuqa Khalid, "Turkish Opposition Parties Join Ranks to Push Out Erdogan: Report," *Al Arabiya English*, October 23, 2021, https://english.alarabiya.net/News/world/2021/10/23/Turkish-opposition-parties-join-ranks-to-push-out-Erdogan-Report.
33. "Only 31 Percent of Turks Approve of Turkish Military's Presence in Idlib," *Duvar English*, March 5, 2020, https://www.duvarenglish.com/politics/2020/03/05/31-percent-of-turks-approve-of-turkish-militarys-presence-in-idlib.
34. Interview with a Turkish colonel who served in Syria, Washington, DC, September 23, 2019.
35. Phone interview with the same Turkish colonel who served in Syria, October 18, 2021.
36. Gurcan, "Top Generals Step Down in Ominous Sign."
37. "Kılıçdaroğlu'ndan Erdoğan'a: Komando marşı söyleyen TÜGVA'cıları gönder Suriye'ye, oradaki komutanı da Bilal Erdoğan olsun!."
38. "Bilal Celik, "CHP 'hayır' demişti: İYİ Parti tezkereye 'Evet' oyu verecek," *Cumhuriyet*, October 26, 2021, https://www.cumhuriyet.com.tr/turkiye/chp-hayir-demisti-iyi-parti-tezkereye-evet-oyu-verecek-1879855.
39. Nazlan Ertan, "Turkey's Parliament Votes to Extend Mandate for Troops in Iraq, Syria," *Al-Monitor*, October 26, 2021, https://www.al-monitor.com/originals/2021/10/turkeys-parliament-votes-extend-mandate-troops-iraq-syria.
40. "Son dakika… CHP'den Irak-Suriye tezkeresine 'hayır' oyu!," *Milliyet*, Last updated October 26, 2021, https://www.milliyet.com.tr/siyaset/son-dakika-chpden-irak-suriye-tezkeresine-hayir-oyu-6627848.
41. Ibid.
42. Can Izbul, "Erdoğan: 'Suriye İç Meselemiz, Gereğini Yapmak Durumundayız',"

Amerika'nin Sesi'nde Ayrica, August 7, 2011, https://www.amerikaninsesi.com/a/Erdoğan-suriye-ic-meselemiz-geregini-yapmak-durumundayiz-127078293/898713.html.
43. Anand Gopal, "Syria's Last Bastion of Freedom," *The New Yorker*, December 3, 2018, https://www.newyorker.com/magazine/2018/12/10/syrias-last-bastion-of-freedom.
44. David Hearst, "EXCLUSIVE: Mohammed bin Zayed Pushed Assad to Break Idlib Ceasefire," *Middle East Eye*, Last updated April 2020, https://www.middleeasteye.net/news/abu-dhabi-crown-prince-mbz-assad-break-idlib-turkey-ceasefire.

CONCLUSION

1. Meeting with a group of Syrian refugees in Mersin. August 3, 2021.
2. Tima Kurdi, *The Boy on the Beach* (New York, London, Toronto, Sydney, New Delhi: Simon and Schuster, 2018), 50.
3. Ibid., 51.
4. Robert Worth, "Aleppo After the Fall."
5. Kurdi, *The Boy on the Beach*, 57.
6. Ibid., 72.
7. Ibid., 84.
8. "Boy on the Beach: How Alan Kurdi's Family Are Turning Their Grief into a Fight to Help Refugees," *CBC Radio*, Last updated August 16, 2018, https://www.cbc.ca/radio/thecurrent/the-current-for-april-17-201-1.4622103/boy-on-the-beach-how-alan-kurdi-s-family-are-turning-their-grief-into-a-fight-to-help-refugees-1.4622212.
9. CTV Staff, "'They Were All Dead': Abdullah Kurdi Describes Losing His Family at Sea," *CTVNews*, https://www.ctvnews.ca/world/they-were-all-dead-abdullah-kurdi-describes-losing-his-family-at-sea-1.2546299
10. Adnan R. Khan, "Alan Kurdi's father on his family Tragedy: 'I Should Have Died with Them'," *The Guardian*, December 22, 2015, https://www.theguardian.com/world/2015/dec/22/abdullah-kurdi-father-boy-on-beach-alan-refugee-tragedy.
11. Bryan Walsh and Time Photo, "Alan Kurdi's Story: Behind the Most Heartbreaking Photo of 2015," December 29, 2015, https://time.com/4162306/alan-kurdi-syria-drowned-boy-refugee-crisis/.[0]
12. Sebnem Arsu, "Turkish Premier Urges Assad to Quit in Syria," *New York Times*, November 22, 2011, https://www.nytimes.com/2011/11/23/world/middleeast/turkish-leader-says-syrian-president-should-quit.html.

INDEX

Note: Page numbers in italics refer to n denotes endnotes

Abbas, Mahmoud, 117
Abdulhamit II, 83–5
Abdullah, 291–3
Abu Ahmed, 209, 212
Abu Ahmet, 209, 212
Abu Dhabi, 284
Abu-Duhur airport, 222
academics, 36
activists, 182
Adana agreement (1998), 71
Adana, 142, 160–1
Afghanistan, 68, 162
Afghans, 250
Afrin operation, 220–1, 222
Afrin, 155, 206, 219–20, 223
Ahmadinejad, Mahmoud, 60
Ahrar al-Sham, 161–2, 215
Ahrar al-Sharqiya, 267
Akar, Hulusi, 193–4, 195–6, 199, 222, 232
Akdoğan, Yalçın, 22–3, 57–8, 178
Akman, Zahid, 43
AKP (Adalet ve Kalkınma Partisi), 1, 3–4, 42, 76–7, 241, 258–9
    fall of, 246
    ideology as "conservative democracy", 22–3
    relations with foreign actors, 99
    victory in presidential election, 35
    See also Erdoğan, Recep Tayyip
AKP convention, 76
Aksakallı, Zekai, 205–6
Akşener, Meral, 248
Al Udeid Air Base, 141
Al Wafd (newspaper), 116
Ala, Efkan, 160, 183
Alawis, 125, 126–7
"Alawite Shiite" oppression, 245
al-Bab, 212, 217
Albanians, 51
Albayrak, Berat, 44, 253–4
Albayrak, Bilal, 100
Albayrak, Esra, 100
Aleppo, 70, 71, 150, 208–9, 211–12
Alevi regime, 146
Alevis, 3, 82, 146

INDEX

Alexandretta. *See* Hatay
Al-Nusra fighters, 149
Alparslan, 93
al-Qaeda in Iraq (AQI), 150
al-Qaeda, 73, 282
Al-Rai, 206
Altima, 134
Ambrosetti Forum, 23
Anatolia, 69–70, 88
Anatolian Tigers, 69
Anderson, Becky, 190
"Angry Young Turks", 249–50
Ankara and the Research Centre for Islamic History, Art and Culture (IRCICA), 62
Ankara, 11, 15, 54, 57, 72, 129–30, 202
   Damascus vs., 271
   frustration with Washington, 237–8
   and Jabhat al-Nusra, 149
   joined anti-Assad camp, 127
   "land swap" deal between Damascus and, 209
   Libya Dawn coalition, 119
   protest against Erdoğan, 31
   suicide bombings in, 190
   support to Morsi, 117–18
   Washington and, 159
Annan plan, 61
Annan, Kofi, 25, 142
Ansar Al-Sharia, 119
Antakya, 71, 145
anti-American sentiment, 202, 235
anti-Americanism, 221
anti-Assad front, 154
anti-Kurdish nationalism, 239, 249
Anti-Kurdish policies, 249
anti-Kurdish sentiment, 230
"anti-Muslim Australians", 242
anti-Muslim sentiment, 293
anti-refugee sentiment, 246–7, 250–1
anti-terror law, 182
anti-Western foreign policy, 257
anti-Western Kemalists, 178
anti-Westernism, 198
Apaydin camp, 133
AQI. *See* al-Qaeda in Iraq (AQI)
"Arab belt", 154
Arab Christians, 144
Arab Islamists, 9
Arab League plan, 140
Arab League, 267
Arab nationalism, 67, 125, 154
Arab revolt (1916), 64
Arab socialism, 67, 125
Arab state, 52
Arab tribes, 132
Arab uprisings, 5, 9, 49, 111–12
Arab world, 1, 8, 52
   European colonialism in, 125
   "Islamic awakening", 121
Arabs, 51, 52, 239, 284
Arınç, Bülent, 22, 23, 30, 175–6, 252
Armenia, 227
al-Assad, Hafez, 67, 125, 154
Armenians, 144, 184
Assad regime, 11, 66, 126, 127, 146, 245
al-Assad, Bashar, 60, 71–2, 109, 124–6
Assad, Riad, 133, 138
Association of Independent Industrialists and Businessmen (MÜSİAD), 47, 69–70
Association of Turkish Industrialists and Businessmen (TÜSİAD), 47, 69, 97, 257
Astana peace talks, 214
Astana process, 216–17

INDEX

Astana, 213, 214, 227, 271
Atalay, Beşir, 107
Atatürk, Mustafa Kemal, 17, 193, 198
ATV (TV channel), 44
Austria, 29
authoritarianism, 173, 255, 288
Avcı, Hanefi, 37
Ayyubid dynasty, 148
Azad, 162, 211, 217
Azerbaijan, 227, 282

Baath Party, 67, 125, 140, 290
Baath regime, 125
Baathism, 125
Baathist secularism, 125
Baathists, 68
Babacan, Ali, 252
Babuşcu, Aziz, 77–8
Baghdad, 72
al-Baghdadi, Abu Bakr, 149, 163, 229
Bahçeli, Devlet, 48, 186, 187–8
Bahrain, 10, 136
Balkan Wars, 113
Balkans, 84, 98, 113
Bank Asya, 97
Barzani, Masoud, 76
Başbuğ, Ilker, 99, 107
al-Bashir, Omar Hassan, 62
BaskentGaz, 101
Battle of Manzigert (1071), 92
Battle of Stalingrad (1942–43), 212
Bayancuk, Halis, 191
Bayik, Cemil, 175
Baykal, Deniz, 108
Ben Ali, Zine El Abidine, 115, 127
Benghazi, 119
Berlin, 235
Beylikdüzü, 242

Biden, Joe, 163
bin Laden, Osama, 161
Black Turks, 18
blocking laws, 30
Bodrum, 290
Bosphorus, 146
Bouazizi, Mohamed, 115
British intelligence, 142
Brunson, Andrew, 233, 244
Bush administration, 72, 114
businessmen, 36, 37
Büyükanıt, Yaşar, 31, 32

Cairo, 114, 157
California, 232, 316n100
Çalık Holding, 44
Cameron, David, 136
Çandar, Cengiz, 57
Çavuşoğlu, Mevlüt, 223
Cem, Ismail, 57, 66
center-right Motherland Party (MP), 55
Central Asian republics, 98
Central Bank, 34
Ceylanpınar, 188–9
Chamber of Commerce and Industry, 225
Chambers of Commerce, 69–70
China, 140
Chinese defense missile system, 238
Chirac, Jacques, 29
CHP, 31, 41–2, 46, 89, 120, 197
Christchurch, 242
Christian Byzantine army, 93
Christian Byzantines, 79
Christian Crusaders, 105, 148
Christians, 127
CIA, 141–2, 201
Çiçek, Cemil, 32
Cihaner, I.lhan, 39

INDEX

Circassians, 51, 144
Clapper, Jim, 152
Clinton, Hillary, 144, 147
CNN (news channel), 152
"cocktail terrorism", 190
Cold War, 50, 228
columnists, 230
Commission of Inquiry for Syria (COI), 270
"compassionate Islamist", 245, 246
Confederation of Turkish Businessmen and Industrialists (TUSKON), 70, 97
"conservative democratic", 4
Constantinople, 136
Constitution (1982), 91
Constitutional Court, 21, 30, 39
   declared president election as invalid, 31–2
   restructuring of, 40–1
consumerism, 50, 288
Council of Higher Education (YÖK), 24, 41
Council of Ministers, 59
Covid 19 pandemic, 256
Covid lockdowns, 288
"Crusader West", 187
Cumhuriyet (newspaper), 44
Cypriots, 25
Cyprus question, 25–6, 61, 62
Cyprus, 25, 28, 273

Dabiq, 218
Damascus, 11, 64, 66, 136, 208
   Adana agreement with Turkey, 67
   Ankara vs., 271
   "land swap" deal between Ankara and, 209, 226
Daraa province, 216
Davos, 61

Davutoğlu, Ahmet, 49–51, 58, 68–9, 207, 252
   "four-phase strategy", 128–9, 136
   problems between Erdogan and, 192–3
   views on uprisings, 112–13
   visit to Damascus, 136
de facto buffer zone, 143
"de facto client state", 217, 228
Defense Intelligence Agency, 270
Demirel, Süleyman, 67
Demirtaş, Selahattin, 179, 184, 191
democracy, 22, 38
Democrat Party (DP), 53, 89, 259–60
"democratic autonomy", 180–1, 191
"democratic Islam", 117
Democratic Society Party (DTP), 106, 107–9
Democratic Union Party (PYD), 132, 155–6
"democratization package", 180
Dempsey, Marty, 152
Deniz Feneri, 43
Denktaş, Rauf, 25, 62–3
Deraa, 124, 136
Derik, 155
"*derin devlet*", 36
Dilipak, Abdurrahman, 253
Directorate for Religious Affairs, 194, 288
Disaster and Emergency Management Authority (AFAD), 218
Dişli, Mehmet, 193–4
divorce rates, 247
Diyala, 150

INDEX

Diyanet (Religious Affairs), 88, 92, 102–4
Diyarbakır, 30, 109, 179–80, 254, 260–1
Dogan Media Group, 28
Doğan, Aydın, 43, 44
Doha, 66, 147
Dolmabahçe, 182–3
"Down with Israel", 20
DP. *See* Democrat Party (DP)
Druzes, 125
DTP. *See* Democratic Society Party (DTP)

East Ghouta, 216
East Jerusalem, 20
eastern Syria, 151
Ebu Hanzala. *See* Bayancuk, Halis
ECHR (European Court of Human Rights), 24, 28
Edelman, Eric, 72
Egypt, 10, 76, 81, 116
Egyptian Brotherhood, 114
Eid Al-Fitr, 248
"e-memorandum", 32–3
Emergency Law system, 200
"enlightened Islam", 87
Ennahda (political party), 115–16
ensar, 245
environmentalists, 184
Erbakan, Necmettin, 18, 19, 23, 44, 49, 58, 68, 174
Erdoğan, Bilal, 83
Erdoğan, Emine, 26
Erdoğan, Recep Tayyip
  alliance with Gülenists, 98
  alliance with nationalists, 192
  Arab Spring tour, 116–17
  e-memorandum in election campaign, 33
  EU capitals tour, 24
  foreign policy strategy, 2, 45–6, 63
  general elections victory (2011), 75–6
  Islamist populist strategy, 203
  as leader of AKP, 16
  "Muslim nation" project, 111
  neoliberal populism, 244
  Osmanoğlu support to, 85
  "promoting Muslim domination", 91–2
  Qaddafi International Prize, 60
  recast AKP as pro-Western conservative democratic party, 6
  "the red apple is our goal" strategy, 186–8
  redefines Turkey as Sunni Muslim nation, 128
  regime change, reaction to, 148
  Syria policy, 69, 72, 257–8
  views on Kurdish nationalism, 166
  views on Kurds, 105–6
  visit to Syria, 71
  war against Kurds, 10–11
  See also Gezi protests; Istanbul; nationalism; Turkey
Erenköy community, 100
Ergenekon trials, 37–8
Ergenekon, 36, 43, 178
Erzincan, 39
Erzurum, 90, 97
ESZ. *See* Euphrates Shield zone (ESZ)
EU Helsinki Summit (1999), 25
EU. *See* European Union (EU)
Euphrates River, 66, 71, 206, 217

INDEX

Euphrates Shield zone (ESZ), 217–18, 225
Eurasianism, 202
Eurasianists, 202
Euro-Atlantic alliance, 236
European colonialism, 125
European constitution, 23
European Council, 25
European Parliament, 22, 201
European Union (EU), 6, 22, 42, 264
   Turkey's entry into, 23–4
   See also Turkey
Evren, Kenan, 90

F-35 fighter jets, 236, 238–9
F-35 program, 237
Facebook, 104, 174
#FakeCoup (#SahteDarbe), 196
Faylaq Ar-Rahman, 222
"February 28 process", 21, 23, 28
female YPG fighters, 156–7
feminists, 184
FETÖ (Gülenist Terror Organization), 178
Fidan, Hakan, 118, 130, 148, 195, 232
FJP. *See* Freedom and Justice Party (FJP)
Ford, Robert, 147
France, 77, 142, 267
Frankfurt, 43
Free Officers Movement, 135
Free Syrian Army (FSA), 133, 138, 140, 216, 290
Freedom and Justice Party (FJP), 117
Freedom House report, 82–3
French positivism, 87
Friends of Syria, 129, 131
Fuele, Stefan, 42

"fundamentalist groups", 21

Gallipoli campaign (1915), 242
Galyon, Burhan, 209
Gaza, 61, 117
Gaziantep, 70, 71, 149, 182, 210, 217
"Genç Parti" (the Young Party), 27–8
Gendarmerie Headquarters, 35
Germany, 29, 77, 234, 267
Gezi Park, 171–3
Gezi protests, 174–5, 176–7
Ghalib, 291–3
Ghannouchi, Rachid, 115
"gift from God", 196, 197
GNA. *See* Government of National Accord (GNA)
"God is great", 16
"Godless" regime, 169
Gönül, Vecdi, 31, 238
Government of National Accord (GNA), 227
Graham, Lindsey, 141, 265, 267
Great Union Party (*Büyük Birlik Partisi*), 42
Greece, 264, 277
Greek Cypriot government, 25
Greek Cypriots, 25, 28, 61
Greek island, 235, 290
Guardian, The (newspaper), 134
Gül, Abdullah, 23, 26, 30, 41–2, 106
   elected as presidency candidate, 31–2
Gülen community, 96–7
Gülen movement, 37, 39, 97–8, 177–8
Gülen schools, 98
Gülen, Fethullah, 42, 96–7, 178, 195, 202, 231
"Gülenist pawns", 199

INDEX

Gülenist schools, 101
Gülenists, 41, 98–9, 177–8, 196, 201
Güler, Yaşar, 164
Gulf countries, 101
Gulf crisis (1990–91), 55
Gulf War (1991), 54, 114
Güneş, Hurşit, 133

Habur gate, 108
Hagia Sophia, 260
Halabja, 165
Hama massacre (1982), 7, 123
Hamas, 20, 68, 114
haram, 96
Harazi, Kemal, 57
Hariri, Rafik, 72
al-Harmoush, Hussein, 135
Hatay, 65, 71, 133
Hayat Tahrir al-Sham (HTS), 258, 271–4
HDP. *See* Peoples' Democratic Party (HDP)
Hersh, Seymour, 141
Hezbollah militants, 146
Hezbollah, 20, 68
high-fashion magazines, 287
Holy lands, 146
Homs province, 216
Horn of Africa, 61
Hosni Mubarak regime, 81
HSYK. *See* Supreme Board of Judges and Prosecutors (HSYK)
Human Rights Watch (HRW), 148
human rights, 16, 22
Hussein, Sharif, 64

"identity red lines", 7
Idlib, 142, 222, 271–3, 278–9, 282–4

iftar, 124
IHH, 160
I.HO graduates, 26–7
İhsanoğlu, Ekmeleddin, 62
Imam Hatip graduates, 86, 93
Imam Hatip schools (I.HO), 21, 26–7, 86, 89, 93–4, 200
I.mamoğlu, Ekrem, 242, 243, 248
IMF, 33–4
immorality, 50
I.nce, Muharrem, 148
Incirlik Air Base, 190
individual freedom, 16
"infidel regime", 7, 123
Intellectual Hearth (*Aydınlar Ocağı*), 90–1
intellectuals, 37
Interim Transitional National Council (ITNC), 137
"internal colonizers", 9
"internal Orientalists", 83
Internal Service Act, 26
"international collaborators", 174
International Women's Day, 29, 242
Iran, 20, 54, 58, 137
Iranian Kurds, 165
Iranian military, 146
Iraq, 54, 59
  ISIS's capture of, 166–7
  US invasion of, 71
Iraqi Kurds, 165
ISI. *See* Islamic State in Iraq (ISI)
Iskenderpasa community, 100
Iskenderpasa, 95
Iskenderun, 149
Islam, 8–9, 22, 89, 288
"Islamic fundamentalism", 32
Islamic law, 27
Islamic revivalism, 54

INDEX

Islamic State in Iraq (ISI), 149, 150
Islamic State of Iraq and Syria (ISIS), 11, 95, 150–1, 162–3, 183, 292
   SDF captured Manbij from, 230–1
   siege of Kobani, 164, 208, 254
Islamic State, 163
Islamic unity (Pan-Islamism), 84
Islamism, 2–3, 7, 21, 86, 101, 288
Islamist Felicity Party, 42, 253, 259–60, 268
Islamist ideology, 2
Islamist insurrection, 137–8
"Islamist manifesto", 1, 143
Islamist National Salvation Party (NSP), 89
Islamist NGOs, 87
Islamist populism, 4
Islamist Welfare Party (WP), 15–16, 19–20, 114
Islamist, 1, 8–9, 21, 38
Islamization, 288
Ismailis, 127
Israel, 19, 66
Istanbul convention, 260
Istanbul university, 28, 256
I.stanbul, 15, 94, 118, 128, 162
   Erdoğan defeat in, 241, 243
   Friends of Syria meeting in, 142
Italy, 23
ITNC. *See* Interim Transitional National Council (ITNC)
I.YI. Party, 246, 248, 250–1, 280
Izmir, 246

Jabhat al-Nusra, 147
Jabhat Fateh al-Sham (JFS), 214–15
Jacobinism, 87
Jarablus, 206, 211, 218
Jarabulus, 206, 211, 218
Jasmine Revolution, 115
JCP. *See* Justice and Construction Party (JCP)
Jeffrey, James, 129
"Jerusalem nights", 19
Jerusalem, 83
JFS. *See* Jabhat Fateh al-Sham (JFS)
jihad, 19
jihadi groups, 135, 216
jihadis, 10, 147
jihadist groups, 147, 214
Jisr al-Shugur, 134, 135
Joint Economic Committee, 67
Jordan, 70
Jordanians, 141
journalists, 36, 37, 182
judiciary, 39–42
juristocracy, 40
Justice and Construction Party (JCP), 119
Justice and Development Party. *See* AKP (Adalet ve Kalkınma Partisi)

Kabataş, 176
Kahl, Colin, 163
Kalin, Ibrahim, 232
KanalTürk (tv channel), 44
Karayılan, Murat, 189
Karlov, Andrei, 213
Kars, 179
Kart, Atilla, 143
Kasab, 119
Kasımpaşa, 18
Kavala, Osman, 198
Kawa, 223

INDEX

Kazakhstan, 213
Kemal, Mustafa, 52, 79, 88
Kemalism, 3, 17, 173
Kemalist ideology, 40
Kemalist revolution, 95
Kemalists, 46–7, 52, 56, 60, 99
  Erdoğan views on, 201
  policy divergence between
    Erdoğan and, 61–2
Kerry, John, 165
Khaddam, Abdul Halim, 138
Khalaf, Hevrin, 267
Khaled, Ahmad, 225
Kılıç, Taner, 198
Kılıçdaroğlu, Kemal, 82, 120, 139, 160, 275
Kilis, 162, 217
Kırkıncı, Mehmet, 90
Kizilay, 101
Kobani, 154, 159, 164, 208, 292
Kos, 290
Kurdi, Alan, 289–90, 291–3
Kurdish fighters, 188, 255
Kurdish forces, 236
Kurdish language, 132, 181, 193
Kurdish militants, 10–11
Kurdish militia, 280
Kurdish nationalism, 54
"Kurdish opening", 106, 157
Kurdish peace process, 5
Kurdish Peshmerga forces, 166
Kurdish question, 281
Kurdish rights, 182
Kurdish separatism, 7, 26
Kurdistan Communities Union (KCK), 191
Kurdistan Democratic Party, 56
Kurds, 29, 51, 104–5, 187, 228, 266
  avoiding Gezi protests, 175
  captured government buildings, 166
  Russia's relationship with, 235–6
  symbolic gestures, 261
  tension between the Arabs and, 239
  war against, 280–1
  See also Erdoğan, Recep Tayyip
Kuwait, 136

laicism, 87
Latakia, 148, 216
Law on Settlement (1934), 251
lawyers, 36, 182
League of Arab States, 140
Lebanese Hezbollah, 95
Lebanese War (2006), 72
Lenin, Vladimir, 202
Levent, Hediye, 134
LGBT community, 184
liberalism, 23
liberals, 17
Libya, 20, 58, 118, 137, 282
Loğoğlu, Faruk, 138
London Review of Books (magazine), 141
Lufthansa, 174
Luxembourg Summit (1997), 22

M4 Aleppo-Latakia highway, 274
M4 highway, 277
M5 highway, 274
Maarif Foundation, 101
mafia leaders, 36
Mahabad Kurdish Republic, 165
Mahmur refugee camp, 108
Manbij, 206, 219
MANPADS, 141
Al Maree, Mohamed, 210
Marie Claire, 156–7
Marmaris, 194
Martyr's Bridge, 199

343

INDEX

Marxism, 89
Marxist-Leninism, 104
Mattis, Jim, 233
Mazlumder, 132
MBZ. *See* Mohammed bin Zayed (MBZ)
McCain, John, 141
McGurk, Brett, 163, 229
Mecca, 105, 245
Mechanical and Chemical Industry Cooperation, 134
Medina Covenant, 94
Medina, 105, 245
Mediterranean, 143, 293
Mehmet, 136
Menzil, 99–100
Merkel, Angela, 136
Mersin, 149, 247, 313n46
Meshaal, Khaled, 1, 76, 114, 143
Metiner, Mehmet, 22
MHO. *See* Nationalist Movement Party (MHP)
Middle East Defense Organization, 53
Middle East policy, 18, 52
Middle East, 7, 29, 48–9, 113, 235
migration crisis, 290
military (Turkish), 35–9, 51, 91, 207, 242, 257
Military Recruitment Office, 221
Milli Gazete (newspaper), 68–9
Millî Görüs movement, 260
Ministry of Defense, 277
Ministry of Education, 98, 100, 199
Ministry of Foreign Affairs, 59, 61, 98
Ministry of Health, 99
Ministry of Justice, 39
Ministry of National Education, 255
Ministry of the Interior, 59, 98
Ministry of Youth and Sports, 93
Mohammed bin Zayed (MBZ), 284
Mohammed, Salah, 224
monetary policy, 257
Morsi government, 117–18
Morsi, Mohammed, 1, 76, 116, 117–18
Moscow, 202, 207–8, 216, 235
Mosul, 150
Motherland Party (MP), 19–20
MP. *See* Motherland Party (MP)
Mubarak, Hosni, 1
"*Mücahit Erdoğan*", 143
Mukhabarat, 124
Murted Air Base, 238
MÜSI.AD. *See* Association of Independent Industrialists and Businessmen (MÜSI.AD)
Muslim Brotherhood, 7, 53, 62, 66, 68, 138
Muslim fashionistas, 287
Muslim world, 19
Muslim, Salih, 157–8, 207
Muslimness, 92
Muslims, 3, 86

Naqshbandi networks, 85
Naqshbandi order, 95
Naqshibandis, 96
Nasrallah, Hassan, 146
National Intelligence Service, 59
National Liberation Front, 224
National Order Party, 95
National Security Policy Document (NSPD), 59–60
National Vision movement, 114
"national will", 81
nationalism, 2–3, 192, 198, 248–52
Nationalist Movement Party

INDEX

(MHP), 29, 41–2, 48, 185, 246, 258–9
nationalists, 249
"national-patriotism", 188
NATO (North Atlantic Treaty Organization), 20, 53, 119, 202, 221, 233, 234–5
"neoliberal populist" strategy, 34
neo-Ottomanism, 57–8
Netherlands, 267
"new War of Independence", 272
New York Times (newspaper), 157, 210, 234
New York, 290
New Zealand, 242
Newruz (Kurdish New Year), 109–10
newspaper columnists, 36
NGO leaders, 36
"Night of Shame", 20
9/11 attack, 282
North Africa, 175
northeastern Syria, 264, 265
northern Iraq, 54, 55–6, 106
northern Syria, 11, 154, 185, 218, 263–4, 284
northwest Syria, 210
northwestern Syria, 274
NSC (National Security Council), 21, 24, 58
NSPD. *See* National Security Policy Document (NSPD)
Nurcu brotherhood, 90
Nurcu movement, 96–7
"Nusayri" regime, 130
Nusra Front, 210
Nusra Front. *See* Jabhat Fateh al-Sham (JFS)

Obama administration, 141, 152–3, 159–60, 162–3, 164–5, 231
supports YPG to fight ISIS, 167
Obama, Barack, 136, 141, 151–2, 167, 208–9
envoy to counter ISIS, 228–9
Öcalan, Abdullah, 56, 63, 65–6, 109–10, 158, 182
OIC, 62–3, 66
"OIC-EU Joint Forum: Civilization and Harmony", 63
Ombudsman, 40
Ömerli, 162
Önhon, Ömer, 134, 157
Operation Euphrates Shield, 205–6, 207–8, 217, 239
Operation Olive Branch, 219, 222, 226–7, 239
Operation Peace Spring, 265, 268, 270–1
Organization of the Islamic Conference, 59
Orontes River, 128
Oslo, 106
Osmanoğlu, Nilhan, 85
Ottoman Armenians, 48
Ottoman conquest (1453), 260
Ottoman Empire, 3, 17, 50
collapse of, 64
lost territories in Russo Turkish War, 84
Ottoman forces, 242
Ottoman state, 51
Ottomanism, 52
Ottomanist ideology, 52
#OyMoyYok, 256
Öz, Zekeriya, 36, 38
Özal, Turgut, 56, 57, 63, 106
Özel, Necdet, 206
Özkan, Tuncay, 44
Özkök, Hilmi, 26, 27, 32

INDEX

Öztürk, Kemal, 252–3

Pakistan, 43, 162
Palestine, 43
Palestinian Authority, 116
Palestinians, 59
pan-Arabism, 125
Panetta, Leon, 130, 140
Papandreou, Yorgos, 25
Patriot missiles, 234
Patriotic Party, 187
Patriotic Union of Kurdistan, 56
"Pax Ottomana", 83
Peace and Democracy Party, 42
Peker, Sedat, 257–8
penal code (2005), 29–30
penal law, 182
Pence, Mike, 266
Pentagon, 265
People's Alliance, 192
Peoples' Democratic Party (HDP), 179, 184–5, 268
Peres, Shimon, 61
Perinçek, Doğu, 186–8
personnel appointments, 30
Peshmerga forces, 165
Phillips, Christopher, 126
PKK, 29, 44, 54, 106, 155–6
  armed insurgency against Turkey, 66
  ceasefire between Turkey and, 200
  conflict between Turkey and, 89
  members' Habur gate arrival, 108–9
  military support from Syria, 63–4
  withdrawal from Turkey, 110, 179–80
plastic bullets, 173
pluralism, 23

political Islam, 40
polygamy, 247
populist, 2–4
post-Assad Syria, 132, 148, 155
"post-Islamists", 22
"post-modern coup", 21, 174
post-war Syria, 10
Powell, Colin, 62
"privileged partnership", 29
pro-Kurdish party, 175, 184
pro-EU agenda, 18
pro-Kurdish protesters, 190
Prophet Muhammed, 90, 94, 105, 245
pro-WP protests, 21
Putin, Vladimir, 213–14, 222, 272, 278
PYD. *See* Democratic Union Party (PYD)

Qaddafi regime, 137
el-Qaddafi, Muammar, 20, 118–19, 144
Qatar, 141, 142, 147
Quilliam Foundation, 147
Quneitra province, 216
Quran, 90, 105, 143, 183–4

Rabaa massacre, 118
"radical terrorist groups", 272
Radio and Television Supreme Council (RTÜK), 24
"raising pious generations", 100
Raqqa, 149, 151, 212, 219, 232–3
Ras al-Ain, 266, 268–9
Raytheon, 237
"real people", 3
"reconciliation agreement", 227
Red Apple coalition", 187, 188
Red Apple, 186, 220
refugee crisis, 5

INDEX

Rehanna, 291–3
Religious Affairs Directorate, 218
religious communities (*cemaat*), 95
religious foundations, 95
"religious manner", 21
religious orders (*tarikat*), 95
Republican Party, 265
"Respect for the National Will", 174
retired military officers, 37
Reyhanlı, 134, 145, 245
Roebuck, William V., 267
Rojava, 156, 219
Rukn al-Din, 291
rule of law, 23, 38
Russia, 136–7, 140, 202, 207, 215–16
    militarily intervened in Syria, 217
    tension between Turkey and, 234
    Turkey's Afrin operation approval, 222
    See also Syria
Russian forces, 236
Russian media, 277
Russian Special Forces, 235
Russo-Turkish War (1877–78), 84

S-400 surface-to-air defense system, 236–7
Sabah (newspaper), 20, 44
Sabah group, 44
SADAT, 258
Sahin, Fatma, 218
Şahin, Leyla, 28
Salafi networks, 284
Salafism, 101
Salafist groups, 160–1
Salafists, 145, 215

Salih, Muhammad, 155
Salma, 119
Samanyolu TV, 178
Saraqeb, 274
Sarkozy, Nicholas, 72, 136
Saudi Arabia, 100, 136, 142, 284
Saudis, 141
Savings Deposit Insurance Fund (TMSF), 27, 43, 44
SDF. *See* Syrian Democratic Forces (SDF)
secularism, 16, 22, 87
secularists, 38
secularization, 95
SEEs. *See* state economic enterprises (SEEs)
Selim I, 146
Seljuk Turks, 79, 93
Seventh EU Harmonization package, 24
Sever, Ahmet, 38–9
Sezer, Ahmet Necdet, 26, 27, 30, 67
"shadow government", 24
#ShamCoup (#ÇakmaDarbe), 196
sharia law, 95
"shariah state", 16
Sheikh ul-Islam, 102
Shiite Iran, 105
"silent revolution", 18
Sincan, 19, 20
Sinirlioğlu, Feridun, 157, 164
Sledgehammer (*Balyoz*), 37–8
Sledgehammer trials, 178
Sloat, Amanda, 167
small and medium sized enterprises (SMEs), 256–7
Smurfs, 193
SNA. *See* Syrian National Army (SNA)

347

INDEX

SNC. *See* Syrian National Council (SNC)
Sochi agreement (2018), 271, 272–3, 278
social Islam, 95
socialists, 184
sohbet, 97
Southeast Anatolia Development Project (GAP), 65
southern Turkey, 142
Soviet expansionism, 228
Soviet Union, 55, 89, 235
Soylu, Süleyman, 253
SpongeBob, 193
St Petersburg, 236
Standing Committee for Economic and Commercial Cooperation (COMCEC), 62
Star newspaper, 28
Star TV, 28
state economic enterprises (SEEs), 34
state intelligence agency (MI.T), 135
State Security Courts, 24
Statistical, Economic and Social Training Centre for Islamic Countries (SESRIC), 62
Strategic Cooperation Council, 70
Sudan, 20, 61–2
Sufi orders, 95
Süleyman Şah tomb, 164, 207
Sultan Murad brigade, 211–12
Sunni Arabs, 125, 144, 269
Sunni freedom fighters, 146
Sunni Islam classes, 91
Sunni Islam, 78, 79, 87, 89
Sunni Islamic orders (*cemaat*), 89
Sunni Muslimhood, 8
Sunni Muslims, 125

Supreme Board of Higher Education, 21
Supreme Board of Judges and Prosecutors (HSYK), 38, 39–40, 41
"SuriyelilerDefoluyor", 248
Suruç, 188
sycophants, 244
Syria, 4, 10, 11, 54
  anti-regime protests in, 134
  free trade agreement with Turkey, 71
  hardships faced by, 124–5
  ISIS's capture of, 166–7
  Kurdish-Arab ethnic tension, 225
  military support to PKK, 63–4
  Russia militarily intervened in, 217, 275
  Sarkozy visit to, 72
  Turkish troops stationed in, 280
  See also Turkey
Syrian Arab Republic, 155
Syrian Armed Forces, 130
Syrian Army, 130, 217
Syrian Baathist regime, 66
Syrian Democratic Forces (SDF), 206, 225, 230–1, 270
Syrian Interim Government, 217
Syrian Kurdish forces, 267
Syrian Kurds, 11, 153, 154, 209, 213, 230
  Russian help to, 236
Syrian Muslim Brotherhood, 132
Syrian National Army (SNA), 220
Syrian National Coalition, 147, 209
Syrian National Council (SNC), 137–8, 147

INDEX

Syrian refugees, 148, 243–5, 247–8, 250, 269
   laws for, 251–2
   as problem for Erdoğan 11–12
Syrian Turkmens, 258
Syrian uprising, 12, 124
Syrian war (2015), 12
Syrians, 64, 135, 144, 247, 269, 289

Taksim Square, 171–3
Tel Abyad, 168, 266, 269
Tanzimat era, 84
Taraf (newspaper), 38
tear gas, 173
Terzi, Semih, 206–7
#TheaterNotCoup (#Darbe DegilTiyatro), 196
"They're Partners, We're the Market", 47
Tigris (river), 66
Tikrit, 150
Tillerson, Rex, 232–3
Tima, 292, 293
TIS. *See* Turkish-Islamic Synthesis (TIS)
Torumtay, Necip, 55
TPP. *See* True Path Party (TPP)
Transitional National Council, 119
Treaty of Lausanne (1923), 52
Tripoli, 119, 284
TRT, 110–11
"true democracy", 12
"true Muslims", 9
True Path Party (TPP"), 19
Trump administration, 265, 267
Trump, Donald, 231–2, 233–4, 265–6, 267–8
TÜGVA (The Service for Youth and Education Foundation of Turkey), 100–1

Tunisia, 10, 115, 128–9
TÜRGEV (Turkish Foundation to Serve the Youth and Education), 100–1
Turk, Ahmet, 107
Turkey, 158, 276
   authoritarian turn, 5–6
   become logistical hub for ISIS's finances, 162–3
   Chirac views on, 29
   conflict between PKK and, 89
   "de-escalation zones" establishment (Syria), 216
   EU membership process, 46–8
   initiated GAP scheme, 65
   joined anti-Assad camp, 109
   Operation Euphrates Shield, 211
   Middle East policy, 7
   PKK armed insurgency against, 66
   pro-Muslim Brotherhood policy, 283
   relationship with Russia, 207
   resettled Arab families, 224
   struggles faced by, 16–17
   support for anti-Assad opposition, 127–8
   Syria signed free trade agreement with, 71
   views on Syria, 64
Turkish Armed Forces, 134
Turkish Armed Forces' (TSK) website, 77
Turkish citizens, 247, 261
Turkish Cooperation and Coordination Agency (TI.KA), 219
Turkish courts, 24
Turkish Cypriots, 61
Turkish Hezbollah, 95

INDEX

Turkish Islam, 284
Turkish Islamists, 7, 49, 68
Turkish law, 27
"Turkish model", 120–1
Turkish National Movement, 272
Turkish nationalism, 248
Turkish Orthodox Patriarchate, 36
Turkish Parliament, 101, 143, 251–2
Turkish police, 258
Turkish secularism, 87, 88
Turkish soldiers, 279
"Turkish spring", 175
Turkish troops, 272, 273–4, 275–6, 279, 283
Turkish Twitter, 256
Turkish warplanes, 191
Turkish-Islamic Synthesis (TIS), 79, 90–1
Türkkan, Levent, 193–4
Turkmens, 160, 161
Turks, 51, 105, 186–7, 199
TÜSİ.AD. *See* Association of Turkish Industrialists and Businessmen (TÜSİ.AD)
Twitter, 103, 174, 196, 201

U.S. military, 163, 167–8
UK. *See* United Kingdom (UK)
ultranationalists, 17, 37
Umayyad Mosque, 148
ummah (Muslim community), 4, 49, 50, 68, 80
UN peace plan, 25, 28
UN Security Council (UNSC), 80, 118, 131, 142
UN *See* United Nations (UN)
UN-Arab League Joint Special Envoy, 142
unemployment, 243–4, 255–6

UNHCR (United Nations High Commissioner for Refugees), 269
Union of Kurdistan Communities (KCK), 155
United Arab Emirates, 258, 284
United Kingdom (UK), 80
United Nations (UN), 80, 117, 213, 264
United Nations General Assembly (2019), 263
United States Armed Forces, 265
United States. *See* US (United States)
UNSC. *See* UN Security Council (UNSC)
Urfa, 269
US (United States), 42, 71, 141–2, 213, 266
 administration, 152
 military support to SDF, 167–8
 refusal to extradite Gülen, 231
 slammed by Erdoğan, 221
US-YPG cooperation, 230
Uzan, Cem, 27–8, 43–4

Van Hollen, Chris, 267
Venice Commission, 41
Verheugen, Gunter, 27
Virtue Party (VP), 21, 23
Votel, Joseph, 164, 233
VP. *See* Virtue Party (VP)

War of Liberation, 198
Washington Consensus, 69
Washington, 137, 140, 165, 233, 237–8
water cannon, 173
Western alliance, 55
Western civilization, 50

INDEX

Western hegemony, 50
Western Libya, 137
Western metropolises, 247
Western missile defense system, 238
western Syria, 216, 236
"Western working group", 21
Westernization, 95
Westerwelle, Guido, 42
White House, 147, 231, 265
White Turks, 18
women
    headscarf ban for, 16
    violence against, 260
World Bank, 34
World Economic Forum, 61
World War I, 48, 64, 113, 186
World War II, 65
Worth, Robert, 210
WP. *See* Islamist Welfare Party (WP)

Yazidis, 156, 184
Yeni Şafak (newspaper), 252
Yıldırım, Binali, 199
Young Turk Movement (1889), 51
Young Turks, 51, 52, 87
Youtube, 104, 256, 287
YouTube, 104, 256, 287
YPG, 155, 167, 206, 214, 225
Yüksekdağ, Figen, 184, 198
Yunus Emre Alagöz, 190

Zaman Group, 178
al Zarqawi, Abu Musab, 150
al-Zawahiri, Ayman, 161
al-Zayat, Ibrahim, 114
"zero problems with neighbors" policy, 7, 46, 49, 73
    helped to control military, 17–18, 50–1
Zionists, 85–6